CAMBRIDGE GREEK

GENERAL

E. J. K
Emeritus Kennedy Professor of . ..., of Cambridge

AND

P. E. EASTERLING
Regius Professor of Greek, University of Cambridge

HORACE
EPISTLES
BOOK I

EDITED BY

ROLAND MAYER

*Senior Lecturer in the Department of Classics,
King's College London*

CAMBRIDGE
UNIVERSITY PRESS

Published by the Press Syndicate of the University of Cambridge
The Pitt Building, Trumpington Street, Cambridge CB2 1RP
40 West 20th Street, New York, NY 10011-4211, USA
10 Stamford Road, Oakleigh, Melbourne 3166, Australia

First published 1994

Printed in Great Britain at the University Press, Cambridge

A catalogue record for this book is available from the British Library

Library of Congress cataloguing in publication data

Horace.
[Epistulae]
Epistles/Horace; edited by Roland Mayer.
v. cm. – (Cambridge Greek and Latin Classics)
Latin text, commentary in English.
Includes indexes.
ISBN 0-521-25898-7. – ISBN 0-521-27754-X (pbk.)
1. Rome – Politics and government – Poetry.   2. Epistolary poetry,
Latin.   3. Political poetry, Latin.   I. Mayer, R. (Roland)
II. Title.   III. Series.
PA6393.E8H67 1994 871'.01 – dc20 93-42188 CIP

ISBN 0 521 25898 7 hardback
ISBN 0 521 27754 X paperback

CONTENTS

PREFACE

A commentary on a standard classical author is a dialogue with the dead. The commentator engages not just with the ancient text but also with the long exegetical tradition that has accumulated around it. One starts by asking the author what he meant, or why he said it one way rather than another, but soon one's predecessors are asked why they understood a passage thus, and not thus, why they annotated this, and not that; a note may turn out to be less concerned with the author than with how he has, in the latest commentator's view, been misunderstood (lest he be misunderstood again). Thus the learned sixteenth-century bishop of Antwerp, Laevinus Torrentius, must often set straight (as he believes) the misapprehensions of Dionysius Lambinus; later, André Dacier is much occupied with the errors of Torrentius. Most nineteenth-century German commentators felt called upon to grapple with the subtle explanations of the poems offered by C. M. Wieland, whose long-influential translation with notes has deservedly been reprinted (to it is devoted Dr J. V. Curran's doctoral dissertation for the University of Newcastle upon Tyne (1991): *Horace's* Epistles, *Wieland and the reader: a three-way translation*). An intricate dialogue of the living took place between Schmid and Obbar, who published comment in several formats in the first half of that century. (Obbar's, indeed, is the last comprehensive treatment of the poems – he offers eight interpretations of *adrasum* at 7.50!) Later, Adolf Kiessling in the earliest editions of his commentary had his eye on the recent work (admirable it is, too) of Schütz. By accident or design, however, Kiessling's work achieved its own classic status, thanks to frequent revisions by Heinze, and so the original response of Kiessling to Schütz became fainter, even as Kiessling's own voice was often silenced by Heinze after two re-editions. The latecomer overhears these discourses and willy-nilly joins in the debate.

The reader of any one commentary, however, may not be aware of the existence of a subtext (or rather subtexts) and may fail to detect the submerged voices. Commentators on a large scale, say Brink or Nisbet and Hubbard, try fairly to air alternative views. The format of the present work, however, precludes such evenhandedness. This is the more to be regretted since the first book of *Epistles*, for all its excellence, has yet to find its Lejay, to whom constant reference for the balancing of opinions might be made. Instead, a brisker approach: explication from the editor's point of view alone, with only infrequent reference to alternative interpretations. But the reader should be aware that there lies just beneath the surface a silenced majority, some nodding agreement, others crying for equal time to state their case.

Predecessors apart, advice from a number of friends and colleagues is recorded in the notes, where appropriate, and gratefully acknowledged here. It is a particular pleasure to record that most of the introduction was written at the Fondation Hardt in Vandoeuvres; the British Academy and the Fonds National Suisse de la Recherche Scientifique made the visit possible. My greatest debt, now as always, is to the series editor, Professor E. J. Kenney.

R.G.M.

INTRODUCTION

1. THE *EPISTLE* AS A LITERARY FORM

In his earlier works Horace honoured the Roman literary tradition and trod the highway of imitation. For each form he chose an exemplary model to follow. In his *Sermones* he took Lucilius for a guide (*S.* 2.1.34 *sequor hunc*), in his *Epodes* Archilochus (19.23–4n.[1]); the lyric *Odes* were modelled on various Greek masters, especially Alcaeus (19.32–3n.). The one element common to all these poetic kinds is the expression of a personal point of view (unlike epic and drama); in formal terms, there is usually a direct address to someone imagined as being present (even in the second book of *Sermones*, which is made up of dialogues, the poet is one of the interlocutors, except in the fifth satire). This restless exploitation of the inherited genres of personal poetry did not content Horace. At the height of his creative powers he himself became the 'discoverer' of a new verse form, the epistle. The novelty is to be seen in the synthesis of the conversational hexameter of his *Sermones* and of the more personal addresses found in the lyric odes.[2] Like all letters, the poetic epistle presents one half of a dialogue, since the addressee is by definition absent; the themes are chosen as being of interest to both correspondents, usually avoiding the generalized topics of the *Sermones*. Original as the *Epistles* are, they nevertheless had an ancestor in the personal letter. Its uses influenced Horace in his choice of topics and presentation.[3]

Personal letters duplicate many of the face-to-face verbal exchanges of daily life but also, thanks to the formality of writing, may perform them in somewhat elevated tones. Horace uses the letter to invite people to visit him or to come to a party (IV and V), to recommend one friend to the notice of another (XII), and to provide a character reference for one seeking a post (IX), all the sort of thing we still find ourselves writing. (On the other hand, there are here no love letters or

---

[1] References given in this form refer the reader to the Commentary *ad loc.* References to whole poems within the first book are in Roman numerals.

[2] So Campbell 257.

[3] See W. Allen Jr *et al.*, *C.J.* 68 (1978) 119–33.

consolations.) But the personal letter in prose had also been developed as a vehicle of instruction, above all by philosophers.[4] Epicurus, for instance, had used the letter to clarify his doctrine and exhort his followers; so enduring is the appeal of the personal note that these are now all that survive of his original writings. Even a philosopher's letter will be tailored to some particular and pressing need of the recipient that gives an urgency to the presentation. This comes across still in the letters of St Paul.[5]

There were even verse letters before Horace's.[6] His model for satire, Lucilius, had composed a letter to a friend who had failed to pay him a visit during an illness; it was a longish piece and occupied the fifth book of his collection. Catullus too jotted down a note to a friend (35; cf. 8.2n.) and perhaps a dinner invitation too (13); some of his poems look like dedicatory letters (65, 68A). The existence of these pieces establishes the verse epistle as a literary form distinct from those letters of every day that are actually delivered to their addressees. But Horace might still claim the distinction of having invented a new poetic genre, in that he first put together a whole collection of verse letters. It is however crucial to the understanding of his moral position at the time of writing that he regards his letters as a branch of *satura*, and so not true poems. They are rather compositions of a poetically indetermi- nate character, like the earlier *Sermones*.[7] The novelty of his undertak- ing has produced a special issue for academic debate, the fictionality of the letters.

It used sometimes to be held that Horace intended his letters in the first place as personal communications between himself and his ad-

[4] For general discussions and illustrations see K. Dziatzko, *RE* III 836–43, esp. 842; Sykutris, *RE Suppl.* IV 185–220; F. Susemihl, *Geschichte der griechischen Litteratur in der Alexandrinerzeit* (Leipzig 1892) II 579–601 (forgeries); J. Schnei- der, *RAC* II 564–85, esp. 571 'Lehrbriefe'; H. Peter, *Der Brief in der römischen Literatur* (Leipzig 1901) esp. 181–2. For Horace in particular see W. Y. Sellar, *The Roman poets of the Augustan age: Horace and the elegiac poets* (Oxford 1891) 87–8; O. A. W. Dilke, 'Horace and the verse letter' in C. D. N. Costa (ed.), *Horace* (London and Boston 1973) 94–112.

[5] See J. Schneider, *RAC* II 574–6; E. Norden, *Die antike Kunstprosa* (Leipzig and Berlin 1909) II 492–510.

[6] See E. H. Haight, *S.Ph.* 45 (1948) 525–40.

[7] See *Ep.* 2.1.111 *ipse ego, qui nullos me adfirmo scribere uersus, AP* 306 *nil scribens ipse.*

dressees.[8] Eduard Fraenkel, following Edmond Courbaud, stuck to this
belief through thick and thin, and even XIV was in his view 'a genuine
letter, spontaneously written' (311). The general weaknesses in this
position were ably exposed by Gordon Williams,[9] though the fictional
character of a number of pieces had long been accepted by some. That
the whole collection was made up of 'pretend' letters was argued in a
fine essay by E. P. Morris,[10] who put his finger on the crucial point that
the *Epistles* are in essence no different from the *Odes*, or indeed from
any poem which imitates reality. If Horace's verse letters were genuine
and spontaneous they would cease to be imitations and, in ancient
eyes, lose their status as literature. As in the *Odes* the addressee is not
necessarily a convention, for the chosen theme may reflect his personal
interests and preoccupations, but none of the letters is merely occasional. Even an invitation to a party (V) blossoms into larger issues
that leave the guest, Torquatus, momentarily in the background.[11]
Apart from the challenge of a new form, the letter offered Horace the
chance to signalize a change of direction both in his life and in his art.
Since this point is sometimes blunted, it deserves special notice here.

In the first epistle he says that he renounces 'et uersus et cetera
ludicra' (10) because of advancing years and a change of heart ('non
eadem est aetas, non mens' 4). The repetition *et ... et* binds *uersus*
closely to *ludicra* so that Horace may once again exploit an ambiguity
of contemporary literary theory, as he had done when ascribing to his
Sermones a doubtfully poetic status.[12] (Comedy too seemed to some
theorists insufficiently poetic, and Horace had already made it clear
that he saw comedy as the remote ancestor of Lucilian satire.)[13] The
epistles are deemed to continue the 'unpoetic' tradition of the *Sermones*,
and so to mark a break with the genuine poetry of the *Odes*, celebrations of the life of pleasure which the poet now relinquishes. The fiction
that the letters are not poems is sustained at *AP* 306 'nil scribens ipse'

[8] K. Dziatzko, *RE* III 842.54–9, with special reference to XIII and 20.5 *non
ita nutritus.* He seems to have ignored the implications of 20.4 *paucis ostendi gemis.*

[9] *Tradition and originality in Roman poetry* (Oxford 1968) 7–24.

[10] *Y.C.S.* 2 (1931) 81–114.

[11] See Williams (n. 9) 9–10.

[12] See *S.* 1.4.39–40.

[13] See *S.* 1.4.45–6, then 1–6 and cf. Cic. *Or.* 67.

(by contrast, when Statius imitates Horace and writes a poetic epistle, *Siluae* 4.4, he draws attention to the fact that it is in verse: 'inclusa modis haec ... uerba' (11)). Indeed this fiction decides the issue in XIII of what Vinnius is delivering to Augustus: *carmina* (17) can only refer to what men call poems and must exclude the present 'unpoetic' collection; M. L. Clarke believed that there could be no difficulty about the use of *carmina* to describe the *Epistles*.[14] Every difficulty, in fact.

Thus the letter, a document but conversational in tone, offers fresh strategies for dealing with old issues. The central issue remains Horace himself. This is of course appropriate to a letter; our friends want to know what we are up to. But more to the point is the Roman tradition of seeing oneself as setting an example.[15] One of the qualities Horace had admired in Lucilius was the exposure of a whole life in poetry (*S.* 2.1.30–4), whole in the sense that we learn from him both good and bad, we see him 'warts and all'. Clearly, Horace did not feel that he had yet done with himself as a theme and the letter offered a fresh form in which to pursue a programme of self-revelation.[16] The traditional situations found in lyric had not allowed him the fullest exploitation of this ever fascinating matter, but he could not simply produce a third book of satires to round out the picture of himself. Mocking vice, even in his own person, was played out; a more positive note was wanted. Moreover, his own position in Roman society was more conspicuous than ever; he was a public figure and his friendship had been sought by the greatest in the land.[17] He had moved high up the social ladder and of course had attracted criticism, which he sought to answer in *S.* 1.6. His approach there had been defensive, but now, endorsing his view that the poet should instruct as well as entertain, he adopts a more positive and self-confident tone. What is more surprising, indeed

[14] See *C.R.* 22 (1972) 157–9, esp. 158. His point that there is an apparent delay between the publication of the Odes in 23 B.C. and their (fictive) delivery to Augustus rests on the unnecessary assumption that no epistle can have a fictive date earlier than the late 20s; see §3 below.

[15] See R. G. Mayer, 'Roman historical *exempla* in Seneca' in P. Grimal (ed.), *Sénèque et la prose latine*, Entretiens sur l'antiquité classique 36 (Vandoeuvres – Genève 1989) 168–9.

[16] As Quintus said to Marcus Cicero, 'te totum in litteris uidi' (*Fam.* 16.16.2).

[17] Cf. *C.* 2.18.10–11 *pauperemque diues | me petit*; 4.3.22 *quod monstror digito praetereuntium*; *S.* 2.1.75–7 *me | cum magnis uixisse inuita fatebitur usque | inuidia*; 6.52 *deos* (i.e. the chief men of Rome) *quoniam propius contingas*.

so surprising that many decline to focus upon it, is that in addition
to the sort of moral improvement he had encouraged in the satires
Horace now defends and advises upon the life of the dependant in
Roman society. The *Epistles* thus become his most essentially Roman
production (just as the letter was to prove a most fertile genre in
Roman hands generally). They prosecute a dual programme centred
on spiritual and social self-improvement. A glance at the poet's own
social rise will help to account for this unusual feature.

2. HORACE'S CAREER[18]

Horace's father was a *libertus*, a former slave who had obtained his
freedom perhaps through a combination of talent and hard work. His
son was born *ingenuus*, a gentleman, but of indeterminate grade. When
he was of an age for serious schooling, it was clear that the local education in Venusia was inadequate, so Horace was taken to Rome for the
sort of instruction a senator's son might receive despite his father's
poverty (*S.* 1.6.71–82, esp. 71 *macro pauper agello*; 20.20). After Rome,
Athens, where, among the sons of the nobility, for instance Cicero's
own Marcus, he studied philosophy and rhetoric. From all this it is
clear that Horace's father had ambitions for his son's improvement,
which was not to be purely intellectual, but social as well. In fact, the
two were hard to keep apart. In a city like Rome, with no institutions
of higher learning and no consistent state patronage for the arts, a life
dedicated to poetry and study was only possible within the ranks of the
highest society. Wealth alone facilitated scholarly leisure for a Varro or
an Atticus; others needed patronage. Horace, whatever his father's
intended provision for his financial security, would only be able to
make his way in such a society thanks to his personal address. And it is
clear that his father was fitting him to take some place in that society
at its higher levels. Such an ambition was honourable, in the eyes of his
son and of Rome generally.

The son did not throw away his chances, though he came close to
doing so through miscalculation. In 43 B.C. he joined the military staff

---

[18] For a fuller discussion of the issues raised in this section see R. Mayer,
'Horace's *moyen de parvenir*' in S. J. Harrison (ed.), *Aere perennius: celebrations of
Horace* (Oxford 1995).

of M. Brutus, who was recruiting for his campaigns against Antony, as a *tribunus militum*. Since Horace had no military training and the post was often something of a staff appointment, Brutus may have chosen Horace for his character. However that may be, this proved an essential step in his social rise, for it guaranteed his equestrian status and unimpeachable respectability.[19] Horace unfortunately picked the loser and after Brutus' defeat at Philippi in 42 B.C. his chances, like his fortune, took a nose-dive. Not that he was destitute; some property he lost (*Ep.* 2.2.50–1 *inopemque paterni | et laris et fundi*), but he had enough money (and presumably influential support) to buy a treasury secretaryship. This post, which there is no reason to suppose he ever relinquished, provided a fair income.[20] His social relations at this time are altogether obscure but he clearly moved amid the *vie mondaine* of Rome (indeed, if the *Epodes* are to be believed, he was something of a toy-boy (*Epod.* 12.2, 21–2)); it was presumably in such a milieu that he met two rising poets, Varius and Virgil. They liked him (as Brutus, perhaps, had liked him) and introduced him to Maecenas, who also came to like him very much. So much so in fact that at the very end of his life in 8 B.C. when he was hastily making a will in which to leave all of his estate to Augustus, he did not forget his poet: 'Horati Flacci ut mei esto memor'.[21] Through Maecenas he came to the notice of Octavian, an association not at first close, but developing to a point where the *princeps* wanted the poet for his personal secretary (a post he knew was not for him, and so declined on grounds of health[22]). So even the most powerful man in the world came to like the freedman's son. Something about him appealed to all of these very different men and not unreasonably he was impressed by his social rise: 'non ego, pauperum |

[19] See L. R. Taylor, *A.J.P.* 46 (1925) 161–70 and Rostagni's note on the Suetonian *uita* 6.

[20] Fraenkel 15–16 and see A. H. M. Jones, *Studies in Roman government and law* (Oxford 1960) 154 and 156 for discussion of the equestrian status of *scribae* and the purchase of the office. Both Suetonius and Porphyrio assumed that this was the implication of the scene in *S.* 2.6.36; their sense of the meaning is preferable to that of C. Ampolo, *P.P.* 39 (1984) 193–6, who believes it refers to the *collegium poetarum*.

[21] Suet. *uita Hor.* 17 Rostagni.

[22] Suet. *uita Hor.* 29 Rostagni.

sanguis parentum, non ego, quem uocas, | dilecte Maecenas, obibo'
(C. 2.20.5–7). More than that, he reflected upon how he had achieved
it and identified its key element in the power of pleasing: 'me primis
Vrbis belli *placuisse* domique'.[23] This was also the very element that
made for his success in poetry too: 'quod spiro et *placeo, si placeo*, tuum
est'.[24]

So once again poetry and life came into close contact for Horace,
and the world of his imagination is founded upon his experience (indeed their relationship is the underlying issue in XIX). To succeed in
both poetry and in society, giving pleasure counts. In the case of poetry
we agree that this is so, but the social aspects of pleasing are trickier
and need justification. Success owed to wealth or power or inherited
social connections is easy to understand and approve (these were Roman values). But a social success owed entirely to agreeable character
was perhaps a difficult concept for a Roman; it smacked of the pliancy
of the Greek, suggesting a want of firmness in the character. It is
therefore to just this issue that Horace addresses himself in a number
of the *Epistles*. How does a man make his way in Rome by arts purely
social, without (or in spite of) the adventitious attractions of money or
family name? How does he keep his self-respect and confirm his independence in a society founded upon patronage? How, amid other aspirants, does he honourably distinguish himself? How, after all, does he
learn when to call a halt? These issues Horace had reflected upon and
the *Epistles* represent the literary mould in which his views were cast.
No other poetry is so intimately bound up with the workings of Roman
social life. For that reason alone Horace needed a new literary form,
since the available ones, even satire, could not be used as vehicles for
reflection upon the use to be made of society as it is (satire *must* criticize). Horace, an outsider whose talents and personality brought him
to the very *solium Iouis* (17.34), charted the social adventure in an
original poetic form. To give his inventions due plausibility he chose
his addressees carefully; they are almost invariably young men of
good, but not especially remarkable, family on the way up in Rome's
meritocracy.

[23] 20.23; cf. 17.35 and *S.* 1.6.63 *placui tibi* (Maecenas).
[24] *C.* 4.3.24; cf. 19.2 and *AP* 365 *haec placuit semel, haec deciens repetita placebit.*

3. THE ADDRESSEES AND THE DATE OF COMPOSITION

Apart from Maecenas, to whom three letters are addressed, Horace's correspondents all appear to be young with their careers in full flood.[25] It is worth noting that there are only two aristocrats of ancient name in the whole collection, Torquatus (V) and Tiberius Claudius Nero (IX). The bulk of the rest are presumably equestrians pursuing upward mobility by attaching themselves to the eminent. Thus III abounds in the names of a budding élite, the *cohors amicorum* of Tiberius. (Even the unidentifiable Titius (3.9; some think he was a friend of Ovid's (*Pont.* 4.16.28)) and Munatius (3.31) have names suggestive of the new aristocracy.)[26] Septimius in IX would like to join their company. Iccius in XII has also found a good billet (not that he fully appreciates this) in the service of Agrippa, the emperor's son-in-law.

We cannot say anything certain about Albius (IV), Numicius (VI), Bullatius (XI), Vala (XV) or Scaeva (XVII). Quinctius (XVI), it has been speculated, may come from a newly prominent family.[27] Of course the name of Horace's bailiff (XIV) cannot be known, but even he fits the general pattern of upward mobility. He started life as a drudge in his master's town house (*mediastinus* 14.14); his aspirations to greater responsibilities and rewards were realized.[28] Of Julius Florus (III), to whom *Ep.* 2.2 is also written, we know only what Porphyrio tells us, namely that he was a *scriba* (8.2n.) and wrote satires.

Perhaps the most tantalizing figure is Lollius, because he receives two letters, II and XVIII, both prominently placed in the collection. It used to be assumed that he was a son of M. Lollius, consul in 21 B.C., a *nouus homo*, and the addressee of *C.* 4.9. But the arguments of E. Groag against this, founded upon no more than the tone of address in XVIII and a belief that a rich young man needs no advice on dealing

---

[25] See in general W. Allen Jr *et al.*, *S.Ph.* 67 (1970) 253–66 and F. M. A. Jones, *L.C.M.* 18 (1993) 7–11.

[26] L. Munatius Plancus, *cos.* 42 B.C., the addressee of *C.* 1.7, was the uncle of M. Titius, *cos.* 31 B.C.; Munatius certainly and Titius possibly had a son.

[27] See N–H on *C.* 2.11, p. 168 and Syme, *AA* 386.

[28] It would be a mistake to agree with P. Guthrie, *C.P.* 46 (1951) 116–17, that Horace blundered in promoting the man; the letter nowhere suggests that the bailiff failed to give satisfaction in his new post.

with the rich, have somewhat surprisingly obtained a measure of assent;[29] we must, however, always be wary when the character, pursuits and social status of a recipient are to be inferred from the language.[30] It might have been thought that a young man of a very recently 'ennobled' family might well stand in need of guidance in negotiating the treacherous waters of high society, indeed of court life. The Lollii were rich and famous, but had no smoky busts in their entrance hall to validate their pretensions (if any). Horace's advice nowhere suggests a mercenary motive in the young man's attachment to an unnamed great person (though he prudently hints at the acceptance of worthwhile gifts (75), it hardly seems fair of Nisbet–Hubbard to call Lollius a social-climber (*Odes* 2, p. 67)). Lollius served under Augustus in Spain and is preparing himself for public life. There is no evidence that compels a belief that he is not a son or other close relation of the consul of 21 B.C. Speculation about the identity of his important friend is also tempting. Tiberius figures considerably in the collection. It may not be wholly accidental that Lollius is urged in II to learn lessons from the *Odyssey*, a poem which provided Tiberius himself with sculptural motifs for his grotto dining-room at Sperlonga.[31] Horace is certainly aware that the most significant patronage now flows from but one household, that of Augustus, and that Rome has in effect a monarchical court. This sense would give a special edge to his advice to Lollius, since there is a greater need than ever to preserve the old Roman virtue of independence of manner. The risks of toadying are greater where the social hierarchy rises to a point; for everyone will feel a sense of inferiority to those at the apex. This would also have a bearing on the juxtaposition of XVIII and XIX, which are related in theme. These, like many other letters, are designed to help young men negotiate the pitfalls of Roman high society.

Maecenas too deserves a word here, not that any of the three letters to him (I, VII, XIX) concentrate upon his current activities. For in 22 B.C. his friendship with Augustus was dented by the ugly and confusing

---

[29] See *RE* XIII 1387.30–42; R. Syme, *J.R.S.* 56 (1966) 59, *History in Ovid* (Oxford 1978) 185 n. 4 and *AA* 396.

[30] So Syme himself, *AA* 390.

[31] See A. F. Stewart, *J.R.S.* 67 (1977) 76–90.

conspiracy of Varro Murena.[32] The opening line of the whole collection is therefore the very balm of friendship to one cast down. Horace leaves no doubt about his devotion and Maecenas is alone the object of his warmest feelings (*dulcis amice*, 7.12). His interest in the rising young is keen, but his old friend, albeit now perhaps in a conceded retirement,[33] still has his fullest attention. There may even be a specially personal note attaching to the expression *uates tuus* (7.11). For Augustus had, as mentioned above, tried to secure Horace's service as personal secretary;[34] he failed, because Horace, who knew when to call a halt to ambition, declined. Thus he remained Maecenas' own poet and did not hesitate to advertise the strength of his continued attachment to the former favourite.

Since the *Epistles* imitate personal correspondence Horace naturally conformed what he says or how he says it to the interests (so far as they may be known) of his recipients. Thus, for example, the wine offered Torquatus at the party in his honour would be redolent of his family's history (5.5n.); likewise, the language in which the letter is composed parodies the legalisms he was used to as a barrister (5.14, 15, 21nn.). There may be a glance at Fuscus' profession (10.45n.) and there is certainly some pun implied in the reference to Vinnius' name (13.8–9n.).

The composition of the *Epistles* is generally reckoned to have begun shortly after the publication of the *Odes* in late 23 B.C. Epistle XIII cannot have been written very long after that. Few other letters can be dated. At the close of XX Horace refers to his age in the year 21 B.C. A number of others relate or refer to the embassy of Tiberius in the East and the recovery of the Roman standards (III, VIII, XII, XVIII); XII also refers to the success of Agrippa in Spain. These all fall in 20 B.C. No letter contains a clear reference to a later date. Thus

[32] See Syme, *AA* 387–9; the rift, however, may not have been so complete as Syme believed: see G. Williams, 'Did Maecenas "fall from favour"? Augustan literary patronage' in K. A. Raaflaub and M. Toher (edd.), *Between Republic and Empire: interpretations of Augustus and his principate* (Berkeley and Los Angeles 1990) 258–75, and P. White, *C.P.* 86 (1991) 130–8.

[33] Cf. Tac. *Ann.* 14.53.2.

[34] Suet. *uita Hor.* 18–23 Rostagni; this is usually dated to the mid- to late 20s, but the precise date is not known.

the book is generally believed to have been published in either 20 or
19 B.C.

4. POETIC STYLE

In returning to the dactylic hexameter Horace resumed what may be
called the plain style, as distinct from the more elaborated manner of
the lyric poems. The difference between them can be illustrated by
comparing the treatment of similar themes in the two genres (as is
done briefly for instance by Nisbet–Hubbard in their note to *C.*
2.7.28). Two brief examples and one more extended must suffice.
Horace illustrates the inevitability of death by an appeal to historical
exempla in a late ode thus: 'nos ubi decidimus | quo pius Aeneas, quo
Tullus diues et Ancus, | puluis et umbra sumus' (*C.* 4.7.14–16), and in
an epistle thus: 'cum bene notum | porticus Agrippae, uia te con-
spexerit Appi, | ire tamen restat Numa quo deuenit et Ancus' (6.25–7).
The ode employs the pathetic anaphora of *quo* and the ornamental
(but hardly superfluous) epithets, chiastically ordered; these are absent
from the epistolary style, as too is the tragic note of *puluis et umbra*.[35] In
the epistle, on the other hand, the references to everyday localities,
Agrippa's portico and the Appian way, drive home the ordinary truth
of the poet's claim. Similarly at 2.47–9 he says simply and without
ornament that neither *domus* nor *fundus* nor *aeris aceruus et auri* will cure
a sick man; in an ode he more elaborately says that Phrygian stone, the
wearing of star-bright purple, Falernian wine and Assyrian nard will
not alleviate pain (3.1.41–4). The thought is the same but the manner
of its presentation could not be more different in the two genres, as the
third example will show.

The praise of wine's beneficial power is common to *Ep.* 1.5.16–20
and *C.* 3.21.14–20:

> tu lene tormentum ingenio admoues
> plerumque duro; tu sapientium
>   curas et arcanum iocoso
>   consilium retegis Lyaeo;

---

[35] Cf. Soph. *El.* 1159, Eur. *Mel.* 536 N.

> tu spem reducis mentibus anxiis
> uirisque et addis cornua pauperi
>> post te neque iratos trementi
>> regum apices neque militum arma.

Again, ornamental epithets distinguish the ode (the anaphora of *tu* should perhaps be disregarded, since it is characteristic of the hymn form into which the ode is cast, rather than of the lyric style in general). One clause is embraced by epithets of opposite sense (*lene*)(*duro*), and there is an oxymoron in *iene tormentum*. Another epithet, *iratos*, is transferred from *regum* to *apices*, itself remarkably concrete. The transitive use of *trementi* is confined at this date still to poetry. The image of the horns of courage is perhaps proverbial, but no less striking for that. In the epistle five cola in asyndeton make up the sentence.[36] The first four limbs increase in length; the two words of the last recall the shape of the first. The language is brisk and businesslike with little concrete imagery and no ornament, unlike the ode, but contrasting words, *contracta* and *solutum*, as in the ode, enclose a line. The anaphora of *quem non* (19–20) emphasizes wine's universal efficacy; 19 refers to a new skill, 20 to the loss of a burden, both thus tied in to what has preceded.

The lyric style of course would hardly do for a letter, which is generally a plain-style document, but Horace had also to decide whether to recast his hexameter verse style after a pause of some ten years in its use. If we are to believe Porphyrio, a second- or third-century commentator, the *Epistles* differ from the *Sermones* in nothing but title; the metre, subject matter and language remain the same in his opinion.[37] It is useful for purposes of the following analysis to keep to his identification of topics. We do not have to hold with his opinion.[38] Let us begin with the hexameter itself.

---

[36] Cf. the asyndeton in the similar praise of wine at Aristoph. *Equit.* 92–4.

[37] The text at this point of his note seems garbled, but he clearly isolates these three points.

[38] The first to make an attempt to distinguish between Horace's satiric and epistolary mode was C. Morgenstern in an agreeable pamphlet, *De satirae atque epistolae Horatianae discrimine* (Leipzig 1801); he rightly drew attention to metrical differences (28–30), and to the change of tone, especially the greater involvement of the addressee in the epistle.

(i) *The hexameter*

The epistolary hexameter recalls its satiric predecessor, but with some
significant differences. In the *Satires* Horace claimed to reproduce the
rhythms of speech: 'sermoni propiora' (*S.* 1.4.42). To achieve this he
dismantled the formal patterns that were being imposed upon the hexameter by Lucretius, Catullus and the young Virgil and recomposed
the verse so as to reflect better the lively turns of phrase in spoken
Latin. His model for this was Lucilius, whose hexameters are clearly
suppler than those of Ennius, except when he tries to be serious and
impressive. But the influence of the comedies of Terence ought to have
been considerable too, for his iambic dialogue shows far greater fluidity from line to line than that of Plautus. Whatever Horace learned
from his models was transformed and elaborated to a degree well beyond earlier experiments. This is most evident in his handling of a
crucial part of the verse, the last two feet.

The formal hexameter of heroic and didactic epos restricted the
normal pattern at the end of a line to little more than two sorts of word
length. The last foot might be a word of two syllables (*includere ludo*,
1.3) or consist of two monosyllables (*omnis in hoc sum*, 1.11); it might
also be the end of a three-syllable word (*dicende Camena*, 1.1). It is
sometimes assumed that these patterns grew in favour because they
secured exact coincidence of word accent and verse ictus and so asserted the metrical shape of the line at the close. What is more, there
was a tendency either to keep units of sense enclosed within the con-
fines of a single line or, if enjambment was employed, to terminate the
clause just after the beginning of the next line (e.g., 1.54–5 *haec Ianus
summus ab imo* | *prodocet*).[39] These were the established patterns which
Horace deconstructed in his *Sermones*. The word shapes he admitted
into the last two feet were very various.[40] More audaciously still, he
employed unusual sense pauses before the end of the line in the fifth
and sixth feet. Above all, he favoured beginning new clauses in the

---

[39] Winbolt §8.
[40] He allows five-syllable words to occupy the whole of the last two feet, as at
5.8 and 26; he specially favours the pattern found at 1.13 *quo lare tuter*, where the
first word of the fifth foot is a monosyllable (cf. 32, 106, 2.51, 62, 3.6, 21, 30, 31,
4.6, 14.26, 18.88). More rarely, he ends a word in the *longum* of the fifth foot,
e.g. 2.40, 56, 14.22, 16.10. See Waltz 225.

sixth foot itself, sometimes even with a final monosyllable starting the clause. These practices he continues into the *Epistles*.[41] Their effect is to create a deliberate inconcinnity between verse period and the run of the sentence which is bound to weaken the reader's (and above all the hearer's) sense of the traditional metrical shape of the heroic line.[42] This, as Horace says, keeps his satiric verses creeping along the ground, rather than soaring away.[43]

In addition to the unusual patterns of word-length and sense pause at the end of the line, the main caesura too undergoes some alteration from the heroic norm to produce a sense of informality. The favoured rhythm had from the first been a strong caesura in the third foot. Next in preference was a strong caesura in the fourth foot following a weak (or trochaic) caesura in the third. Now these are the normal patterns in Horace too, but he was prepared to abandon them quite often to give an impression of nonchalance.[44] But there is a difference between the earlier and later hexameters. The *Epistles* are more strict;[45] the reason for this ought to be that letters, as written documents, are always more formal in presentation than speech, especially among the educated. The pen in the hand produces verbal patterns different from the loose rhythms of speech, however choice. This formality Horace aims at reproducing in his own verse letters, without the regularity of heroic epos. Thus he shows a special fondness for the weak caesura in the third foot, which he does not always support with a strong one in the fourth. This sometimes produces a rhythm avoided by Virgil, a false line end within the verse.[46] Horace strews just enough deviations from the norm into his letters to create a distance between the very irregular patterns found in his conversational poems on the one hand and the strictly regulated scansion of the contemporary heroic epos on the other.[47] Yet even the irregularities follow certain patterns. For instance, in the case of the false line ends just mentioned it is noteworthy that Horace has a clever way of evoking the norm by creating the weak caesura with *-que* or some other enclitic that might at a pinch be

[41] See 1.8 *ne*, 23 *quae spem*, 24 *id quod*, 36 *quae te*, 80 *uerum*, 2.33 *atqui*, 3.25 *quodsi*. There is a discussion by Brink on *Ep.* 2.1.241.

[42] Nilsson 151.   [43] *Ep.* 2.1.251.   [44] Waltz 219.   [45] Waltz 239.

[46] E.g. 1.24, 2.25, 3.3, 4.12, 5.11, 7.89, 14.30, 16.42, 18.88, 19.47.

[47] The hexameter in Horace's lyrics is pretty carefully restricted, as is the hexameter of contemporary elegy.

regarded as separable for metrical purposes.[48] Horace bows in the direction of the established norm, but the epistolary hexameter goes its own way and with a kind of *sprezzatura* creates its own standard of refinement.

The move away from freedom is also found in the use of elision and of prosodical licences generally. The major differences between *Sermones* and *Epistulae* are listed by the standard authorities.[49] For example, short final syllables are no longer lengthened before a double consonant beginning with *s* (called sigmatism). In the *Sermones* they are also lengthened *in arsi*, an artificial practice found in the *Odes* as well, but now dropped.[50] In the *Epistles* there are no instances of prosodic hiatus,[51] of hypermetric lines, or of the correption ('shortening') of final *o* in words either of cretic or of iambic value.[52] Elision in general is less common and more strictly handled; for instance, elisions of a long syllable by a following short vowel are rare.[53] Monosyllables are less frequently elided, and this elision is confined to pronouns.[54] An indication of the nice refinement of the epistolary hexameter is to be found at 6.26 (quoted above, p. 11), where *Agripp(ae) et*, if correctly transmitted, would be the only instance in the collection of the elision of the diphthong *ae*; for this reason and since *et* is omitted from some MSS, the elision is felt to be inauthentic. Horace can thus be detected following the growing fashion for avoiding elision of long syllables, especially *ae*.[55] The trend of all these details is plain: the freedoms of the spoken word and some artificial metrical practices give way to the more strictly measured rhythms of the written language.

[48] E.g., 3.3, 4.12, 5.15 (not a false ending; but the prefix of the word in the fourth foot *in-* might also be felt to be metrically separable), 7.89, 16.42; Waltz 202. This particular phenomenon is also discussed by W. Meyer, *Sitzungsb. der bayer. Akad. der Wissen.* (1884) 1045–6.

[49] Waltz 160–80; Bo *Index*; Klingner *Index*.

[50] Klingner *Index* 325; Bo *Index* 88; L. on *S.* 1.4.82; N–H on *C.* 2.13.16.

[51] Hence Shackleton Bailey (100) was rightly hesitant in proposing to read *nam* at 15.13.

[52] This is not uncommon in the *Sermones*; see Klingner *Index* 325 (*nescĭŏ quod Ep.* 2.2.35 is the sole exception).

[53] So at 7.24 and 18.104 (pronouns), 1.11 and 39.

[54] See L. on *S.* 1.1.52 and the table in E. Norden's edition of Virg. *A.* 6, p. 457.

[55] See Leo (1912) 357–8.

(ii) *Diction and word order*

The choice of language too is chastened in the *Epistles*. They naturally welcome *colloquial* or *conversational* idiom,[56] yet some words or phrases found in the *Sermones* are absent, perhaps by design. Before describing the diction of the letters in detail, it will help to explain why the term 'prosaic' is here repudiated. There are two reasons. First, prosaic now suggests not so much language specially suited to the formal style of oratory or history, but rather a use of language flat, tame or pedestrian. Secondly, the ancient terms for prosaic (πεζός, *pedestris*) chiefly referred to the absence of music and metre, not to an undistinguished level of diction. In fact, the bulk of all Latin poetry was composed with words that were on the lips of men, at any rate of men who cared to choose how they spoke or wrote (cf. *AP* 95 *et tragicus plerumque dolet sermone pedestri*).[57] It is fairer then to notice that some words are absent from the work of certain poets who felt them insufficiently appropriate to the matter in hand. Let the case of the adverb *eo*, meaning 'for this reason', illustrate the point.

The *Sermones* and *Epistulae* admit the word readily enough and the commentators call it prosaic (so L. on *S.* 1.1.56 and B. on *AP* 222). That description is partly justified by the word's absence from the lyrics. But on the other hand *eo* appears in the cultivated dialogue of Terence; it is what Romans actually said, and therefore appropriate to a conversational and epistolary style. The reason it is not used in the lyrics (or by Virgil and the elegists) is perhaps rather that its logical function was too precise, insufficiently suggestive; some poets scout words that give a rigorous connection to their thoughts and it is for that reason, not for any 'prosaic' quality that *eo* and words of similar sense are avoided. By the same token, some words in everyday use may have been felt to lack distinction without being flat, for instance *pecunia* (which anyway is inappropriate to the heroic societies of epos and tragedy). In the discussion that follows and in the commentary, there-

---

[56] Cicero said that the language of every day was the most appropriate to a letter (*Fam.* 9.21.1 *epistolas ... quotidianis uerbis texere solemus*). Italicized English words henceforth direct the reader to the Index for specific examples.

[57] Williams (n. 9) 745 reckons that there was no lexicographical boundary in Latin between prose and poetry; for further doubts about the validity of the distinction modern scholars employ between prosaic and poetic diction see also D. T. Benediktson, *Phoenix* 31 (1977) 345–7.

fore, words and phrases will be described as colloquial rather than as prosaic.

First, then, words that do not reappear from the *Sermones*. The colloquial use of *ac* or *atque* after a comparative and *hoc* in the sense of *ideo* are not to be found in the letters.[58] Others which fail to reappear are *ast*, *nequeo*,[59] *nihilum*, *num/numquid* (introducing direct questions), *quin* and *sicut* (taken as one word). Moreover, the forms of the words allowed admission are now more restricted than in the *Sermones*. Some forms found there are either abandoned altogether or much reduced in use in the *Epistles*. Their archaic or colloquial tone may have rendered them less fit to Horace's ear for inclusion in a documentary style.[60] Forms that fall out of use are adjectives or adverbs compounded with *per* ('very'),[61] *quis* (the dative and ablative plural of the relative pronoun), the old (and literary) passive infinitive ending in *-ier*,[62] the syncopated forms of the perfect system, the suffixes *-n*, *-met*, and *-ne* (joined to an interrogative word), the dative *mi*. Forms of the pronoun *is* are reduced in frequency.[63] On the other hand, the by now more literary ending of the third person plural of the perfect indicative active in *-ere* becomes commoner in the *Epistles*.[64]

In most of his poetry Horace dealt with everday matters. The lyric poems exploited a certain elevation of diction as appropriate to the genre, but in the hexameter poems something more in keeping with the subject matter was wanted. The challenge therefore was to distinguish his style from that of even the best conversation without sound-

[58] See L. on *S.* 1.1.46.   [59] See 12.10n. on *nescit*.

[60] A useful test of the tone of a word or construction is to see if it is used in a speech rather than in the narrative of the *Aeneid* or *Metamorphoses*, for both Virgil and Ovid admit usages to their speeches that are absent from the more formal narrative. For example, Virgil uses *queo* twice, but only in speeches (*A.* 6.463, 10.19).

[61] See B. on *AP* 349; in fact they are unusual as early as the second book of *Sermones*, where only *perraro* is found at 5.50.

[62] The passive infinitives in *-ier*, however, reappear in the second book of Epistles, a warning against confident claims about the tone of the different collections; see Roby 1 §614 for the form.

[63] L. provides references on *S.* 1.4.80.

[64] Jocelyn on Enn. *scen.* 71 reckons the stylistic level of the termination in *-ere* is obscure (in the time of Ennius); it is, however, rare in late Republican prose (Roby 1 §578).

ing far-fetched. One of his most subtle devices for achieving this was
the invention of new words or phrases which evoke from a slight distance a common expression of daily life (the practice was as old as
Ennius[65]). When, for example, a Roman wanted to say 'in(to) the
open' he might use the phrases *in apertum* or *in aperto*; but when Horace
wants this idea at 6.24 he invents the unusual and more suggestive
expression, *in aprico*. Or again, the common Latin for 'at last' is *ad
extremum*; we find it at 1.9. But at 18.35 we meet instead the phrase *ad
imum*; commentators assume that this means basically the same thing
as *ad extremum* though in the context it also suggests a moral nadir.[66]
Such novelties give distinction to their sentences by moving a step
away from the everyday expressions which they recall.

Somewhat similarly at 15.29 where Horace refers to a man distinguishing between friend and foe he could easily have written the common verb *discerneret*, but instead he prefered a *coinage, dinosceret*. The
first readers had no trouble, but were surely aware that this was not
the run-of-the-mill word. In an opposite direction to coinage, Horace
will take already available verbs, say *elimino* at 5.25 or *limo* at 14.38,
and endow them with a sense different from what they had in ordinary usage, but still reasonable, given the etymology of the words; the
reader recognizes the verb well enough but has to think about its etymology and the context for the meaning to become clear. At 20.26 he uses
percontor for the first time in Latin with a common noun (instead of a
pronoun) as direct object; a prose writer would presumably have used
de aeuo where Horace more crisply writes *aeuum*. There is no ambiguity,
but a clear little break with standard practice. A similar sort of break
with usage is seen at 8.4, where a rejected reason is introduced with the
phrase *haud quia*. Cicero had developed the formulae for contrasting a
rejected with a true reason, and it seems that he rarely used *quia* for the
rejected one and never introduced it with *haud*; he preferred *non quo*,
which, it should be noted, is the exact metrical equivalent of *haud quia*
(at least at the beginning of a line). Horace's reformulation is in fact
unique and perhaps therefore would have struck his first readers as

---

[65] See Jocelyn on Ennius, p. 39 n. 7.
[66] So Kiessling, followed in *TLL* vii 1.1403.47–50: 'fere i. q. *imo gradu*'. For
ad extremum see *TLL* v 2.2008.28–44.

unusual, but yet perfectly clear.[67] Similarly at 19.43 *ait* is used instead
of *inquit* when no definite speaker is in mind; it may seem an insignificant enough change, but the fact is that we encounter it nowhere else
in Latin, not even in poetry.

Sometimes we find him endowing common words with new mean-
ings, for instance, *fluito* (18.110n.); or he will venture an unusual form,
such as *imperor* (5.21n.). Many more such small points of usage are
clear divergences from the prose (and, it is assumed, the spoken) norm;
in this way Horace, without using an obviously poetic diction, creates
his own idiom, a language that moves alongside that of the prose-
speakers, evoking their idiom but not reproducing it.

A similar feature of Horace's poetic style (one not confined to his
hexameters) is the avoidance of *technical terminology*.[68] It might have
been expected that in poems which refer to daily life it would be possible to refer bluntly to, say, the magistrate's seat, but that becomes in
his urbane idiom 'the curule ivory' (6.54n.). Horace seems to anticipate the objection of Dr Johnson to the graceless pedantry of Milton,
who did not hesitate to obtrude technical jargon into his epos.[69] On the
other hand, Horace is ready enough to employ *legal* or *medical* terminology where it makes its point.[70]

Other strategies for distinguishing his diction from everyday usage
are his *coinages* and *lexical Grecisms*. It is important to appreciate that he
intended the procedure to benefit speakers of Latin generally; Horace
did not want to create a merely poetic diction. As usual, he has his eye
on serving the Roman people as a whole. He sees coinages particularly
as enriching Latium, not just her poets.[71] So his new words are not
meant to sound highfalutin; his first readers were being implicitly
invited to make use of the novelties in their own daily lives. Once

---

[67] For Cicero's practice see H–S 588, for *haud quia TLL* VI 3.2564.1–2 and for
Horace's use of *haud* generally L. on *S.* 1.1.35.

[68] Cf. Jocelyn on Enn. *scen.* 2, 39, 127, 232.

[69] See S. Johnson, *Life of Milton* 110 (Everyman edn).

[70] Dr D. R. Langslow drew my attention to Horace's medical vocabulary.
Legalisms came naturally to Romans; cf. Jocelyn on Ennius, Index s.v. legal
language.

[71] *Ep.* 2.2.119–21 *adsciscet noua, quae genitor produxerit usus ... Latiumque beabit
diuite lingua.*

again, it is part of Horace's belief that the poet has his use in the community. The Muse is not a specimen in a zoological garden but a valued member of society.

The two practices of coining and of borrowing usages from Greek are combined at times to produce the Latin equivalent of Greek words, calques. Horace himself gives advice on the principle to follow at *AP* 52–3:

> et noua fictaque nuper habebunt uerba fidem, si
> Graeco fonte cadent parce detorta.

A considerable number of words are formed in this way.[72] The practice goes back to Cicero and confirms the Roman receptivity to foreign influences that improve and enrich. Horace's other coinages tend to follow certain traditional lines, such as the use of the prefix *in* with adjectives (2.22n.) or of new prefixes on common verbs (e.g., *adcredo, addoceo, prodoceo*). Waltz (64) reckoned that Horace ventured more new words in his later poetry, once he was sure of his audience's willingness to countenance the innovations and of his own tact. But coinages were not the only or even chief way of enriching the language from abroad. Horace also regularly employed loan-shifts, the translated imitation of a meaning.[73] At need he will even go so far as to give an entirely Greek word like *hydropicus* the freedom of Latin verse (2.34n.). In that case his reason may be guessed. Latin could only express the idea 'dropsical' by means of a periphrasis, which conflicted with Horace's love of brevity. Better one loan-word than a clause, however Latin!

The word order of the *Epistles* is in general far more straightforward than that of the *Sermones*. We no longer disentangle remarkable sentences such as that found at *S.* 1.5.71–2 *sedulus hospes | paene, macros, arsit, dum turdos uersat in igni.*[74] Two other more or less relinquished oddities deserve a word here. One was the fashion, borrowed first by Catullus and his contemporaries from Greek poetry, of postponing a co-ordinating conjunction or particle. Though nothing could be further from normal speech patterns (Plautus, Terence and Lucretius

---

[72] See Index s.v. *coinages modelled on Greek*, and Waltz 84–5.

[73] See Index s.v. *Grecism, lexical*.

[74] Others in the *Sermones* are found at 2.1.60, 3.133, 211; there is a convenient list from many poets in Housman I 140–1; *Ep.* 2.2.21–2 should be noted.

know nothing of the practice), Horace nevertheless adopted the artificiality into his verse conversations and employed it often with a variety of words.[75] He ventures on some highly artificial patterns, e.g. *captiuus ut* (*S.* 1.3.89 – a borrowing from Greek poetry?) or *aulaea ruant si* (*S.* 2.8.71). These all but disappear later (this is especially true of the use of the ἀπὸ κοινοῦ construction discussed below). In the first book of *Epistles* there are but two instances: 15.35 *et* and 18.37 *neque*. Licence has been curbed. A further reinstatement of the norm is seen in the placing of the preposition. In the *Sermones* there were some remarkable dislocations thanks to inversion or separation,[76] but in the letters we encounter only three, all of which conform to a common enough use of disyllabic prepositions.[77] In his earlier conversation pieces we see a tiro eager to put his technique through its paces; the late master has nothing to prove on that score. In his epistolary hexameters Horace dispensed with purely literary refinements of word order and recovered the more natural word order of spoken and written Latin.

Still, appearances can be deceiving and the poet himself ironically tries to mislead us. Of his own and Lucilius' style he had said that, if you alter its artificial word order, you get a different effect from a normalized passage of Ennius.[78] This self-disparagement has a grain, but perhaps no more, of truth in it. What really strikes the attentive reader is that Horace's syntax favours constructions found in his own day only in the poets. To that matter we may now turn.

(iii) *Poetic syntax*

Horace works with available syntax much as we find him exploiting the everyday words of his language. As with the words, so with their syntactical relations he has a way of extending their range without departing far from the norm. It was, for instance, common to omit a preposition with the word *rus*, in the singular, when one wanted to speak of going 'to the country'; but at 7.76 we find the wholly unusual

---

[75] For *nam* see L. on *S.* 2.3.20, for *atque S.* 1.5.4n., for *et S.* 1.5.86n. (a most remarkable case) and 1.6.31n. See also Klingner's index, pp. 337–8; to his examples add *namque* at *S.* 1.6.57 (cf. Norden on Virg. *A.* 6, p. 403).

[76] See L. on *S.* 1.2.40, 3.68, 70, 6.58; 2.4.84 'et *Tyrias* dare *circum* illuta toralia *uestes*'.   [77] 2.6, 3.4, 4.4.   [78] *S.* 1.4.57–63, quoted below, 30.

use of the plural *rura* in the same construction. The norm lies behind this, but the novelty should probably be regarded as a poeticism, something not available to the speaker or prose writer. We find the same principle of economy at 17.52 *Surrentum amoenum*; prose would use an appositional expression, *Surrentum, oppidum amoenum*. The attribute attached directly to the town name is unusual, thrifty of words, perhaps poetic.

Poets usually prefer to pare down their language and so dispense with prepositions and conjunctions. To compensate, they work the simple cases hard, often with an eye on Greek usage.[79] Horace puts all the oblique cases into harness. The *genitive*, especially with adjectives, is an area of innovation in Augustan verse generally, which he is not slow to exploit.[80] Many of his uses of the *dative* case on its own are borrowed from Greek, for instance its government by words suggesting difference or conflict. The *ablative* he likes to use after a comparative because it is more economical than the prose construction with *quam*. It must be stressed that such constructions cannot be normalized by a mere change of word order, as Horace himself implied. Complete rewriting would be needed if they were really to reflect 'sermo merus'; the Roman reader will have felt the divergence from the spoken or prose norm at every turn, for he was in fact regularly confronted by a discreetly poetic syntax, a fresh concretion of language.

The late Republic saw the gradual establishment of grammatical norms for prose style, above all in the subordination of ideas. From the poet's point of view, the difficulty with this periodic style, as we call it, was that clarity was purchased at the price of a certain wordiness. One has but to think of Lucretius' use of correlatives like *propterea ... quia* to see that such means of articulating the thought take up a lot of space in a verse. So too do the variety of subordinate clauses introduced by *ut*. Horace like other poets of his generation tries to evade these constructions and to introduce greater flexibility into his syntax. One of his commonest devices for achieving this is the use of the *complementary infinitive*.[81] At bottom this kind of infinitive is native to Latin, but its

---

[79] See R. Coleman, *Trans. Philol. Soc. 1975* (1977) 101–56 for an up-to-date account of many of the syntactical usages discussed here and in the commentary.   [80] See C. Wagener, *N. Ph. R.* 22 (1902) 1–3.

[81] See also Waltz 115, 125-32; N–H on *C.* 1.1.8 *tollere*.

early use had been considerably restricted. Lucretius was the first to attach it to adjectives and Horace greatly extends the range of possibilities; for this they had a warrant in the Greek poets, and are in effect naturalizing an exotic.[82] The success of such experiments is seen by contrast when we compare the Latinisms of our own Milton; they remained intrusive and have never been domesticated, a ground for censure.[83] Horace, however, showed greater tact in borrowing unusual syntax by keeping to lines either already laid down or being actively pursued by Virgil (though it should be remembered that he too was faulted for subtly deforming Latin usage[84]). Horace's success is endorsed by the praises of his style found in later writers; Suetonius observed that he is never obscure and Petronius admired his painstaking aptness.[85]

The art lay in choosing such features of Greek as seemed to have already some footing in Latin, for instance the *dative of the agent*. What animated these novelties was not a desire to be different. It will be noticed that in general the poetic syntax is crisper than its prose equivalent. The agent dative dispenses with the preposition *ab*. By the same token, the infinitive is but a single word (often of handy metrical shape as well) and may replace a cumbersome construction with *ut*. It is surely something of a tease on Horace's part that his most poeticized syntax is occasionally to be found in snatches of direct speech (where Virgil on the other hand admitted colloquialisms) or where something as mundane as, say, a haircut is being described.[86]

(iv) *Compositio*

When we turn to consider how Horace puts his thoughts together, what the Romans called *compositio*, it again proves useful to contrast

[82] See C. Wagener, *N. Ph. R.* 22 (1902) 4–9; he collects sixty-five instances and notes the metrical advantages of the practice, perhaps underestimating the Greek influence.

[83] See again Johnson (n. 69).

[84] One Vipsanius criticized Virgil for being a 'nouae *kakozeliae* repertor, non tumidae nec exilis, sed ex communibus uerbis atque ideo latentis'; Suet. *uita Verg.* 205–7 Rostagni.

[85] Suet. *uita Hor.* 69–70 Rostagni, Petr. *Sat.* 118.5 *Horatii curiosa felicitas.*

[86] See 1.94, 16.61, 17.47nn. and cf. N–H on *C.* 2.7.25.

the practice of the *Sermones*. We have already looked at some of the simpler units of word order (e.g., the prepositional phrase) and seen that the *Epistles* re-establish the norm. On a larger scale too the letters abandon some of the freedoms of the conversations. This is specially seen in the use of enjambment.

Enjambment has already been glanced at in the discussion of the rhythms used at the end of the hexameter line. Now it will be considered in its most important role, as the means of continuing the thought between lines. As noted above, whilst the norm was to run the sense over only as far as the beginning of the following line, Horace preferred to start a new sense-unit near the end of a line, often by means of two monosyllables, pronouns, conjunctions and even the preposition *inter*.[87] Sometimes there is a particularly strong break produced by placing an adversative or the logical particle *ergo* in the last foot.[88] In the *Sermones* he showed considerable freedom, and a variety of words or phrases used to introduce new ideas is found in the sixth foot, but they disappear from the *Epistles*. We no longer find *adde, an, aut, cur non, ecce, eheu, nam, non, num si, si, sicut, unde, utque* at the end of the line or as last word. Nor in the *Epistles* does Horace allow a demonstrative word to begin a new thought in the last foot. The only monosyllabic co-ordinating conjunctions he sets there now are *et* (which he uses as last word of the line more frequently now than in the *Sermones*) and *nec*;[89] once at that position he begins an indirect question (1.70 *cur*), once a negative purpose clause (1.8 *ne*), once a new thought (7.60 *dic*), once a main clause (12.5 *nil*). Monosyllabic relative pronouns occupy the last position only at 16.67 and 18.81. Most remarkable is a newly imposed restraint in the use of *atque* as last word in the line. Clearly in that position the unemphatic conjunction overrides the verse and achieves conversational fluidity; it is no surprise that Terence introduced the practice.[90] Horace liked it well enough in the *Sermones* but reduced the

[87] See Brink on *Ep.* 2.1.84 *et quae*; cf. 1.23, 36, 2.24, 3.32, 4.9, 5.21, 7.63, 11.12, 12.8, 17.3; for *inter* see 14.18 and cf. *S.* 1.3.82, 7.11; 2.2.92, B. on *Ep.* 2.1.36.

[88] So at 1.80 *uerum*, 2.33 *atqui*, 3.25 *quodsi*, 7.2, 9.11, 17.38, 19.17; 6.46, 7.70, 16.31 *nempe*, 18.78.

[89] For *et*: 2.30, 6.31, 34, 7.27, 14.2, 16.76, 17.19, 18.15, 50 (in the *Sermones*: 1.3.13, 9.62; 2.2.58 and 8.92); for *nec* 7.35.

[90] See *TLL* II 1049.56–69; Virgil comes to use it towards the end of the *Aeneid*.

usage in the *Epistles*.[91] The overall effect, compared to the *Sermones*, is one of measured pace. The lively changes of direction in the conversations give way to a more deliberate ordering of the sentences. Horace is chastening his style to approximate it to the more formal tone of a written document. A passage like 2.33–9, where five clauses begin in the sixth foot with conjunctions or particles of transition, is exceptional in the collection.[92]

One of the most characteristic features of Horace's poetic composition of sentences is his fondness for *parataxis*, the co-ordination of the elements of a complex thought.[93] Prose writers, following Greek models, had elaborated a system of logical subordination, called hypotaxis; of course, the hypotactic style is found in poetry too, especially where the poet wishes to emphasize cool and rational analysis (e.g., at 8.4–8). Subordinate conditional, temporal and concessive clauses are not abandoned. But for all that the hypotactic style is essentially logical and associated with formal prose; its very regularity differentiates it from speech and the more casual kind of document. So Horace tries to copy the looser connection of thought found in daily life by co-ordinating rather than subordinating his ideas.[94] If we pay close attention to the implicit logic of his verse sentences we often find that one of two co-ordinated clauses may be regarded as being in a logically subordinate relationship to its partner of cause (2.55, 56nn.) or comparison (2.33–7n.) or concession (1.57n.) or condition (1.33n.). It may seem at first wearisome to be invited to analyse the thought in this way. But it is only after dogged observation of such phenomena that one comes to appreciate a style whose subtleties and flexibility were created out of such patterns of thought. To ignore these technicalities is to miss the essentially poetic character of the style, which is designed not to sound like formal prose. The paratactic style is nevertheless sufficiently lively to be felt by any reader, and that effect is what Horace intended. Analysis is always possible at later readings of this inexhaustible text.

One compositional feature that removes Horace's verse style some way from even the written norm may be generally called ellipse, the

---

[91] In *S.* I it is found twelve times, in *S.* II thirteen times, but in *Ep.* I only six times: 7.83, 10.40, 11.7, 28, 18.3, 41.

[92] For similar sentences in *S.* see 1.1.46–51; 2.2.40–2; 5.103–9.

[93] L. on *S.* 1.3.57.   [94] Ruckdeschel 132–3.

omission of verbal elements that are deemed unnecessary for full com-prehension.[95] To be sure, nothing is commoner in everyday speech than ellipse, but context always provides helpful clues. Ellipse in writ-ten documents has to be more carefully controlled if a reader is to grasp the point. Horace therefore favours certain traditional patterns of ellipse which the Roman reader might be expected to be acquainted with. The most pregnant of these devices is the distributional figure, recognized by commentators in antiquity, that still goes under the name of ἀπὸ κοινοῦ ('in common');[96] by means of this figure single words or phrases are attached to more than one point of reference in the sentence. The chief benefit of this construction is, once again, econ-omy: it says once what may be understood twice or even more times. But it can also bind the clauses of a complex sentence more tightly together, since the reader understands the whole idea only once the sentence is finished; then alone can all the elements be recombined in their correct relation.

The patterns taken by the ἀπὸ κοινοῦ construction are very various. Some are simple, requiring nothing more than that one adverb or epithet or verb be understood 'in common' with other parts of the sentence. What makes the figure hard for us to grasp is that the com-mon word does not always come early in its sentence, but may be, indeed usually is, reserved to a later position. For example, in their translations of 1.17 *custos rigidusque satelles* Wickham and Fairclough (but not Villeneuve) agreed with Gesner that *rigidus* belongs to both nouns.[97] In the same spirit Dillenburger and Lejay applied *uetus* at 6.17

[95] A peculiar form of ellipsis has been recently analysed and named by E. A. Schmidt, 'Σχῆμα Horatianum', *W.S.* 103 (1990) 57–98; see notes, to 4.8–11, 7.35, 36, 83. It is worth pointing out that Lambinus long ago observed the principle, but his choice of example, 1.39, was rightly impugned by Torrentius.

[96] See Index s.v.

[97] Dillenburger has a handy collection of examples from the *Odes* of this most straightforward kind of ἀπὸ κοινοῦ on *C.* 1.2.1–2 *niuis atque dirae | grandinis.* Wickham discusses the figure on *C.* 4.9.29. See G. Zündel, *Historia structurae quae dicitur* ἀπὸ κοινοῦ *eiusque figurae usus Horatianus* (Diss. Vienna 1914) (a copy of this useful essay was procured for me by Miss A. Huber of the Institut für klassische Philologie der Universität Wien and is now deposited in the Uni-versity Library, Cambridge); J. C. M. Grimm, *The construction* ἀπὸ κοινοῦ *in the works of Horace* (Diss. University of Pennsylvania 1928). Ribbeck catego-rizes some examples in his edn of *Epp.*, pp. 225–6.

to all the nouns in the vicinity. What encourages this common practice (perhaps more common in poetry) is the general mode of connected expression in Latin, whether prose or verse; this was neatly described by J. P. Postgate as arrangement within a circle.[98] Whereas English syntactical order must be linear, the Roman wrote sentences in which the thought and structure were often coterminous. This was achieved notoriously in formal prose by delaying the main verb until the end of the sentence, so that the thought and the sentence are completed in the same moment. In verse particularly the ἀπὸ κοινοῦ construction achieves a similarly circular arrangement. Postgate pointed out that at Ter. *Hec.* 160 the word order of 'maligna multo et magis procax' is not, as had been claimed in Ashmore's commentary, capricious. The English reader is doubtless happier with 'multo magis maligna et procax', but, as Lejay said on *S.* 1.3.63, Latin by synthesis creates a unit where our modern logical analysis distinguishes two propositions. The Roman knew to take the phrase or sentence as a whole and to wait until the end before recombining the elements to supplement the expression.

Apart from the multiple reapplication of a single word, the figure appears in altogether more elaborate guises, for instance at 1.77–9:

> sunt qui
> crustis et pomis uiduas uenentur auaras
> excipiantque senes quos in uiuaria mittant.

This would construe in prose as follows: 'sunt qui crustis et pomis uiduas auaras et senes ⟨auaros⟩ uenentur excipiantque quos [includes the feminine] in uiuaria mittant', for it is plain that the cakes and apples are meant for the equally greedy old men and women who are alike to go into the game preserves. This complex idea is analysed into more manageable elements with the figure ἀπὸ κοινοῦ. Another instance of this analytic usage of the figure is found at 16.50–1:

> cautus enim metuit foueam lupus accipiterque
> suspectos laqueos et opertum miluus hamum.

---

[98] *P.B.A.* 3 (1908) 6–7, a stimulating discussion.

cautus, suspectos, and *opertum* should all be taken ἀπὸ κοινοῦ throughout
the sentence since all the animals are cautious and all the snares,
though hidden, are suspect. The figure illustrates Horace's ability to
express in clear and simple syntax a complex idea.[99]

Before leaving discussion of this figure of thought, it is worth observ-
ing that Horace now restricts its former complexity and variety. We
will no longer find prepositions, subordinating conjunctions or interrogative pronouns deployed ἀπὸ κοινοῦ, as for instance at *S.* 1.2.62–3
'quid inter | est *in* matrona, ancilla peccesne togata?', 1.9.50–1 'nil mi
officit, inquam, | ditior hic aut est *quia* doctior', 1.4.17–18 'di bene
fecerunt, inopis me *quodque* pusilli | finxerunt animi' and 1.4.115
'uitatu *quidque* petitu'. Moreover, one of his most characteristic
earlier uses of the construction takes the pattern of the last two examples, especially if the word connected by *-que* is the main verb, as found,
for instance, at *C.* 1.30.5–6 'feruidus tecum puer et solutis Gratiae
zonis | *properentque* Nymphae'. This pattern too appears nowhere in
Epistles I.[100] The stylistic point is the more remarkable since it is found
in the earlier *Sermones* (there are striking examples at 1.6.43–4 *con-
currantque ... uincatque*). Perhaps he now regards this particular form of
the device as mannered (and it is striking that most of the experiments
are found in the first book of *Sermones*), and so inappropriate to the
'depoeticized' style of his epistolary hexameters, in which ἀπὸ κοινοῦ
is pretty much confined to nouns, adjectives and verbs without compli-
cations of word order (an observation in keeping with what was noted
above, p. 15).

One of his most favoured forms of compressed thought and expression occurs in his similes, which abandon the usually clear demarca-
tion found in epic poems. Horace tends so to blur his similes into
metaphors that the subject is both compared to and becomes identified
with the object of comparison. The form of implicit comparison thus
stands somewhere between a fully articulated simile and a pure metaphor. (To be sure, the phenomenon is found in earlier writers, espe-

[99] See also 1.25–6, 5.7, 25–6, 6.25–6, 19.16nn. *S.* 1.5.49 *namque pila lippis
inimicum et ludere crudis* is the same.

[100] The pattern is illustrated by Orelli *ad loc.* and noted by F. Leo, *Ausge-
wählte kleine Schriften* (Rome 1960) I 104–5.

cially Greek.)[101] The practice was noted and approved by his ancient commentators, who often paraphrase the pure metaphors with the addition of the comparative word, *ut.* So Acro on *S.* 1.7.29–31 says 'bene perseuerauit in metaphora ... modo illum duro comparat uindemiatori', on *Ep.* 1.2.41–2 'rustico similis est ...', 7.74 'quasi piscis. metaphora est', 10.10–11 'allegoricos: urbem fastidio'; so too Porphyrio on *Ep.* 1.7.74 says 'allegoricos' and on 10.10–11 he offers a very full paraphrase glossing the slave's *liba* as *ciuitatem* and saying that the whole is to be taken *allegorice.* Modern commentators too have not failed to note the practice. Thus Kiessling says on *S.* 1.7.29: 'the two halves of what was originally intended as a comparison (*uelut uindemiator*) are, in Horace's way, condensed into a single image' and he refers to 2.5.83 as an 'abbreviated comparison'. (He gives still fuller descriptions of the phenomenon in his notes to 2.42 and *AP* 348.) Lejay says of the same passage in the *Sermones*: 'Horace emmêle la comparaison et la réalité ... La comparaison devient métaphore' (but he finds this particular instance awkward). Most recently the practice has been fully discussed by Brink, who notes the complete identification rather than comparison at *AP* 357 *fit Choerilus*; on *AP* 476 he observes that Horace has moved from comparison (*uelut ursus*, 472) to apposition. On *Ep.* 2.1.100 he says that 'the grammatical subject is *Graecia* not *puella*. But ... this verse is not wholly distinct in thought from the one immediately preceding. Thus ... the two are run together into one composite notion. When an explicit comparison is wanting, this device obtrudes, as at *AP* 475–6, *Ep.* 1.7.74, but it also occurs with *uelut* or *ut*, as in this passage and *Ep.* 1.10.42–3.' We might compare the shift from

---

[101] See A. S. F. Gow on Theocr. 3.54: 'the simile is of that type in which there is used of the object compared language appropriate only to that with which it is compared' (he cites Theogn. 458 and some examples drawn from J. Vahlen, *Opuscula Academica* (Leipzig 1907) 301; he has similar observations on 12.8 and 25.201). Further discussions by A. E. Housman on Manil. 1.704–6 and on Lucan 7.125; M. Davies on Soph. *Trach.* 31ff.: 'two constituent parts of a simile, *illustrans* and *illustrandum*, become fused or interwoven' (129, 147, [537–8], 770–1, 1261–2nn.; see also L. Campbell, *Essay on the language of Sophocles* §§35, 42: 'the thing compared is expressed in terms suggested by the comparison'); E. Fraenkel on Aesch. *Agam.* 966: 'the image assimilates elements characteristic of the thing compared' (also nn. on 732ff., 1005ff., 1011, 1182) and *Elementi Plautini in Plauto* (Florence 1960) 161–9.

simile to metaphor in Shakespeare's *Sonnet* 29.10–12: 'Haply I think on thee, and then my state | (Like to the lark at break of day arising | From sullen earth) sings hymns at heaven's gate.'[102]

(v) *The verse period and verse paragraph*

We come now to the larger structures, where, as before, a contrast with the *Sermones* is instructive, since in them we find sentence structures unknown to the *Epistles*. In *S.* 1.4 for instance we encounter this at 56–62:

> his, ego quae nunc,
> olim quae scripsit Lucilius, eripias si
> tempora certa modosque et quod prius ordine uerbum est
> posterius facias, praeponens ultima primis,
> non, ut si soluas ... inuenias etiam disiecti membra poetae.

Perhaps the word order parodies the point at issue. But the modern reader has to refashion the sentence to make it comprehensible. *scribo* needs to be supplied for *ego quae nunc* from the following *scripsit*; *eripias si* has to be reversed. A similar inversion is found later in the same poem at 107–8:

> cum me hortaretur parce frugaliter atque
> uiuerem uti contentus eo quod mi ipse parasset

where again the subordinating conjunction (*uti*) follows its verb, but on top of that the noun clause *uiuerem uti* is considerably separated from *hortaretur* which governs it. In fact, even the ancient reader seemed to need help with this sort of structure, as the scholiasts felt when they paraphrased the lines in clearer prose. Such potentially baffling sentences are avoided in the *Epistles*. It may be suggested that, as representations of the often wayward-seeming structures of the spoken language, the complex arrangements found in the *Sermones* are a success (they can, after all, be analysed). But a letter, unless dashed off, is

---

[102] The chief passages of note, additional to any mentioned above, are 1.2 (where Obbar notices the *mira ars* of the practice); 2.28; 3.19; 6.63; 15.37; 19.37.

the product of reflection, and the thought can be more carefully organized; there is not the same justification for intricacy.

The different tone of the two collections is set by the opening sentences of their first poems. These justify a comparative scrutiny, since
they are both questions three lines long and addressed to the same
dedicatee.

> qui fit, Maecenas, ut nemo quam sibi sortem,
> seu ratio dederit seu fors obiecerit, illa
> contentus uiuat, laudet diuersa sequentis?

> prima dicte mihi, summa dicende Camena
> spectatum satis et donatum iam rude quaeris,
> Maecenas, iterum antiquo me includere ludo?[103]

The first satire opens abruptly, without ceremony, without ornament.
Maecenas is no more than named, for he has no obvious interest in the
point at issue. The theme is promptly brought to our attention, *sortem*,
'way of life, vocation', but the syntax has been inverted to effect this
prominence and the antecedent has been set into the relative clause.
This may be in imitation of conversational style, which often brings a
leading idea into focus as soon as possible. Within this relative clause
there is a carefully signposted alternative, *seu . . . seu. illa* is needed to
pick up the antecedent as the sentence proceeds, and it forms an enjambment by its close connection with *contentus*. The verbs of the *ut*
clause are juxtaposed to enhance the contrast of ideas (an instance of
adversative asyndeton), but to come at the subject of *laudet* the reader
has to extract from *nemo* a positive word, *quisque* (a feat the Roman
reader took in his stride). So the theme is enunciated and all Horace
goes on to do for the next ten lines is illustrate it with examples.

The first letter on the other hand opens with careful formality. A
balanced eulogistic formula, like that in the first ode of the first book,
is distinct from the rest of the thought; it identifies the as yet unnamed
addressee intimately with Horace's poetic production. (The opening of
the first epode stresses friendship pure and simple, that of the first ode
emphasizes the addressee's genealogy and the support he gives the

---

[103] Some editors print this as a statement; a question, however, would be
more urgent and bewildered (K–S II 501).

poet.) Their relationship spans past and future (*dicende* is in effect
a future passive participle). The second and third line, as Müller
thought, might for the sake of clarity be transposed; that would bring
Maecenas' name closer to the opening address. But the transmitted
order of the lines is subtler and forms a smoother transition of ideas. In
the second line the poet himself is introduced in a metaphor, that of
the gladiator (though we do not know that it applies to him until we
reach *me* in the third line); the participles focus on his past to date
(*iam*). The single main verb *quaeris* shows that Maecenas is very much
interested in the theme of the letter, indeed he has occasioned it, as the
withholding until this moment of his name, which is spoken with a hint
of surprise ('you, of all people!'), makes clear. When the crucial pronoun *me* appears it is artfully sandwiched within the *antiquo . . . ludo* (an
instance of 'concrete' poetry) and elided almost out of existence. In
fact, each line contains some reference to the speaker or to his addressee; their relationship and its foundation – Horace's poetry – is the
focus of attention throughout. And yet, unlike the opening of the satire, the point at issue is not completely stated; the gladiatorial metaphor conceals its secret. The reader is drawn on by the desire to have
the indeterminacy clarified. In the satire the argument does not at
once advance; in the epistle it does with every sentence, so that we
have a sense of genuine conclusion at the *itaque* of line 10. We see
Horace here exploiting the potential of the verse paragraph by not
laying all his cards on the table at once. He plays them out carefully
because each subtly announces a theme to be developed later in the
collection. The first letter is thus programmatic, unlike the first satire.
But this care and foresight is appropriate to the new literary form. A
letter may be the fruit of reflection, and its style deliberate; its reader
can be drawn by easier stages to the points at issue. This brings us to a
consideration of the disposition or layout of the poems.

(vi) *The layout of the poems*

The *Epistles* are neither treatises controlled by the logic of an argument
based upon first principles (like Lucretius' *De rerum natura*) nor narra-
tives driven by the chain of causality; the progression of their thoughts
has to be excogitated by the poet. The reason for this is that the moral
topics out of which the poem is made all exist at the same time and in

no particular or necessary relation with one another. It is the poet's job to create and impose a design upon scattered and loosely interconnected themes which he wants his readers to reflect upon with him. His design will be for the most part urbanely concealed, since a letter is an informal communication between friends in which hints suffice. Help towards an understanding of Horace's manner of proceeding is offered by Geoffrey Tillotson in a study of the designing of the sense in some English poems, especially Pope's, which were indeed modelled upon Horace's.[104] Tillotson stresses that carefully composed non-narrative poems should be read slowly with a sharp eye to the quality of their sense of order, which defies reduction to argument (a point some logically minded editors of the last century, Ribbeck for instance, failed to appreciate). There exists a pull in one direction towards continuity and in another towards design. To achieve continuity the *gliding transition* between paragraphs may be so carefully managed as to be quite unobtrusive; on the other hand, to produce a conviction in the reader of design there may be abrupt changes of direction (the only letter somewhat mechanically organized is VI). Some modern editions of Horace eschew paragraphing altogether and print the poems as continuous; this is meant to be complimentary, but it obscures the fact that there are focal points in the argument that can be isolated by paragraphing.[105]

Horace proceeds above all by indirection. Typically he begins somewhat off the point and sidles up to it. This is best seen in XIX, where it seems at the start that we are to be treated to a discourse upon the true nature of artistic inspiration. It turns out, however, that Horace is more interested in the poet's independence within a literary tradition. It seems at one point as if he may give way to anger (*bilem*, 20) but by the end he cannot be bothered with the plagiarist's objections. Themes move to the front and then slip into the background to rhythms other

[104] 'The manner of proceeding in certain eighteenth- and early nineteenth-century poems' in *Augustan studies* (London 1961) 111–46, esp. 130–6. This essay also has valuable observations on word order in verse.

[105] Fraenkel desiderated a return to the use of paragraphs in the longer poems (139n., 384). The compilation by R. E. Watkins, *A history of paragraph divisions in Horace's Epistles* (Iowa studies in classical philology x 1940) is useful; his own suggested divisions are offered on p. 123.

than logical or narrative. It is equally instructive to compare the argumentative and narrative sections of the seventh letter. It will be found
that the narrative of the friendship of Philippus and Mena is plain
sailing; the causal chain of events has its own easy inevitability. On the
other hand, the five lines from 20 to 24 place extraordinary demands
upon the reader and have occasioned much scholarly debate (the same
may be said of 19.23–34). The reader is in this way induced to reflect
upon the meaning, which is tied to the context more by implication
and the use of balanced phraseology than by logical or causal signposts. We wonder how we got to this point and so try to absorb the full
force of the idea.

Horace's characteristic manner was well understood by A. Y.
Campbell, who offered a crisp analysis of the opening section of the
seventh epistle.[106] He found it to be the best example of the poet's
mature hexameter style: terse, elliptical, not easy reading, yet worth
the trouble of thinking out; it is marked by abrupt transitions where
the connection with what has preceded can only be made out by reading on for some distance. The abruptness of the transitions, however, is
more apparent than real, for what Horace leaves out, as we have seen
in discussing his sentence structure, are the blatantly logical signposts.
The argument works as the clauses and sentences work, by co-ordination rather than by subordination. The alert and reflective reader may
detect the subtler logical connection, but the poet prefers to submerge
it at a level of implication. Still, the poems are not easy reading and
this makes Horace one with the poets of the eighteenth century who
believed that verse had the dignity to be a vehicle of expository
thought or of rational discourse about serious concerns.

Tillotson also pointed out that men used to believe that every
thought that was worth thinking (those were the only thoughts man
needed to concern himself with) had already been thought;[107] Horace
is of their tribe, for he never offers a moral idea that is not part of the
great tradition of ancient thinking about how a free man should behave in the world. His special duty as poet is to present these received

[106] 265–6; in n. 1 he draws attention to 17.39–42.
[107] Tillotson (n. 104) 131. Professor Kenney draws attention to the opinion
of Walter Headlam, to the effect that the motto of Greek lyric would have been
τὰ κοινὰ καινῶς (*Walter Headlam: his letters and poems* (London 1910) 53).

notions in new and attractive forms; his appeal is as much to the mind as to the emotions or imagination, but it is an appeal of a specially poetic kind in the design of the argument. Rhetoric and the more obvious musical qualities of verse are subordinated to this design (it is instructive to see how Juvenal reverses the balance). The reader, who feels complimented by the expectation that he will prove equal to the 'violent labour of excogitation', collaborates with the poet far more in this sort of writing than in narrative (which can be gulped down) or in philosophical exposition (where the clear steps of the argument lead us gently on). In moral discourse the poet has far greater control of the pattern of the argument and he guides our thoughts. He becomes quintessentially the 'maker' in giving shape to the ideas which in turn shape our lives.

To conclude, it is only appropriate to notice how Horace ends his letters.[108] Conclusions characteristic of the epistolary kind are necessarily few (he must not overdo it). He twice bids farewell (6.67, 13.19); he refers to the place from which the letter is sent at 10.49–50.[109] Two end with requests for reply: 3.30, 5.30; similar is 6.67–8 in offering the recipient the chance to give his own opinion. He ends his letter of recommendation with the actual request (9.13), that to Albius with a teasing invitation (4.15–16), and that to Celsus with a line of advice (8.17). The usual closural techniques are similar to ones found in his earlier poetry (though he could of course cleverly refer to the end of the sheet of paper only once at *S.* 1.5.104). A general reflection sums up the argument at 7.96–8, 14.44, 16.79 (where the reference to death is in line with a number of similar endings in the *Odes*[110]) and 19.48–9. In the first epistle the end is announced with *ad summam* (106) and reinforced with the emphatic *praecipue* (108), but a jest concludes the letter, a pattern Horace specially favours;[111] there is also a joke to conclude at 13.19. Sometimes a more purely personal reflection is

---

[108] Schütz is helpful in this matter. For the devices which conclude the *Odes* see P. H. Schrijvers, *Mnem.* 26 (1973) 140–59, and for more general reflections upon this issue see D. P. Fowler, *M.D.* 22 (1989) 75–122.

[109] The two-line closure of this letter is also characteristic, cf. 2.70–1, 4.15–16, 5.30–1, 6.67–8, 18.111–12, 19.48–9.

[110] See Heinze on *C.* 3.4.80.

[111] See Schütz on 1.108 where he refers to the conclusion of several satires.

found, as at 2.70–1 and 15.42–6 (in self-mockery); personal too is the
ending of XVIII, and its hint of prayer form enhances the sense of
conclusion.

(vii) *Poetic tone*

The most difficult element to describe and yet the most rewarding for
the reader is the tone of Horace's poetic discourse. Needless to say, it is
various and his technique as described above is equal to any demands
he chooses to make upon it to convey a particular feeling. We have
already noted the coolly analytical tone of 8.3–12, where the dissec-
tion of discontent is neat. There is a similar list at 7.25–8, where
Horace reels off the sorts of things Maecenas must provide him with if
he is to resume comradeship in the life of pleasure. Yet there the local
texture of rhythm, epithet and repetition convey a tone of considerable
pathos. The most helpful approach to an appreciation of the changes
in tone may be to offer a brief analysis of one letter, XVI, to chart the
shifts and to suggest the reasons for them.

Horace offers Quinctius a description of his farm. The tone is to be
chatty (*loquaciter* 4), a hint at the writer's pride of possession, but it
has already been somewhat poeticized by the description of the elm
'cloaked with vines' (Ovid did not hesitate to reuse the phrase at
Met. 10.100 *amictae uitibus ulmi*). The tone becomes more pronouncedly
epic at 6 where Horace perhaps borrows phraseology from Virgil, *A.*
7.218 *ueniens sol aspiciebat*. The use of *uenio* rather than the commoner
orior for the appearance of heavenly bodies is largely poetic[112] and
the sun as viewer is a notion grand enough to appear in the *Carmen
Saeculare* (12). The rhythm of the line closing with the monosyllable
evokes the tone of epos, for example, Enn. *Annales* 87 Sk. *exoritur sol*,
Lucr. 3.1044 *aetherius sol*, Cic. *Arat.* 510 M. *curriculum sol*.[113] Of course
the fleeing chariot of the setting Sun could hardly be more in the
manner of grand epos, and it again finds a natural place in the *Carmen
Saeculare* (9).[114] The glamour of epos is thus diffused over Horace's

[112] See *OLD uenio* 6.

[113] See Norden on Virg. *A.* vi, p. 439 and cf. Ov. *Met.* 7.663, 15.30; for other
examples of this rhythm in *Ep.* I see 5.6n.

[114] See *TLL* iv 1522.24–35.

rural landscape and shed too upon the local stream, which reminds
him of the mythical Hebrus in remote Thrace (sites epically evoked
earlier in the collection at 3.3). But the poet still has his feet on the
Italian soil, which is fruitful. It is health that the water and shade
secure for him after all the poetical suggestiveness of the language.
For Horace his farm may be beautiful (*amoenae* 15) but its beauty is
founded upon its use (*utilis* 14). The description closes with a picture of
himself in good trim despite the unhealthy season.

He moves somewhat abruptly to his addressee but we soon find that
health, albeit of a different sort, is still his concern. There is a pointed
opposition established between living well (*recte*) and being fortunate
(*beatum*). A weight of public sentiment, which Horace shares (*iactamus*),
is introduced in all Rome's sense of Quinctius' felicity (18); the notion
of unanimity (*omnis*) will be important in the subsequent argument.
To be sure, as to reputation, public opinion has a validity. But the
poet conversationally introduces a personal reservation (*uereor* 19), expressed in a grand tricolon crescendo (19–22), in which he limits that
validity by redefining felicity in terms of private morality. As usual he
regards the verdict of the people (now not endorsed by him nor, he
hopes, by Quinctius) as suspect when it oversteps certain bounds. A
sharp line sums up the issue so far (24).

Horace proceeds to look into Quinctius' case and starts from a position that his addressee must repudiate. The praises due to an Augustus
he knows do not apply to him. The argument will proceed henceforth
by reference to extremes of this sort. The tone is once again grand and
public. But when the application to his friend's case is made and we are
concerned not with wars but with the moral life, the language becomes
conversational (*dic sodes* 31). In correcting a false notion of the value of
public opinion about virtue Horace again appeals to political life, to
show that mistakes are made by the sovereign people, both at the
elections and in courts, where a reputation is maintained or lost. So he
arrives at the central question (40, almost centrally placed in the letter): how is the good man to be defined?

The answer from the people's point of view has the dignified tone of
civic utterance. Their definition, couched in terms of the legal life of
Rome, is carefully articulated by relative pronouns in weighty end-
stopped lines (41–3). Popular opinion is subverted, however, by an ap-

peal beyond the Forum to the private household and neighbourhood; their united and unanimous (*omnis, tota* 44) opinion challenges the inadequacy of the purely civic point of view. The simple language now recalls *fable*, which carries the validation of traditional wisdom. (Horace is specially fond of using fables to answer attacks and to set out a positive programme.)[115] Abandoning the free citizen, Horace turns in a snatch of lively dialogue to a slave whom he is interviewing about his moral character (46–9). The lack of a criminal record is granted, but not the claim to good conduct. An illustration from the country-side with its hunt and chase makes the point that avoidance of danger is no virtue (50–1). So our definition is still to be sought.

In returning to the free citizen of fair repute Horace again sounds the note of unanimity (*omne* twice in 57) that was established at the outset (*omnis Roma* 18) only to undermine its authority with a further scene of hypocrisy (58–62). Once the public figure thinks he is in private he reveals his base side. Again the language becomes elevated; it was suggested by Orelli that the prayer to the god to shroud his bad deeds (62) recalls the divine interventions in epic when a god puts a cloud round a favourite. The argument moves forward by demoting the free citizen to the moral level of the slave. True freedom to the moralist is not to be seen just in the exercise of the civic virtues; the private sphere and the inner life are also to be taken into account.

So at 73 we once again confront the need for a definition; it comes not from popular wisdom or from philosophy but from literature,[116] which Horace as usual reads for its moral lessons. A scene from Euripides' *Bacchae* is taken to represent the good man's indifference to his material possessions, for he is neither *bonus* by virtue of his *bona* nor *liber* only when free to go where he wants. In the play Pentheus threatened to cut the Stranger's hair and rob him of his thyrsus (*Ba.* 493, 495). Horace adapts this to the context and tone of the moral epistle by concentrating the two original threats into a curt phrase, *adimam bona*,

[115] G. Warmuth, *Autobiographische Tierbilder bei Horaz* (Altertumswissenscha-ftliche Texte und Studien 22, Hildesheim–Zurich–New York 1992).

[116] As Wilkins noted, this passage was quoted by J. H. Newman in 1845 when, *dead* to the Anglican Church, he was confronted by the Vice-Chancellor of Oxford University (= Pentheus) with the Thirty-nine Articles (= *manicis et compedibus*); see *Apologia pro vita sua*, Note A 'Liberalism'.

referring vaguely to the confiscation of goods, and he has the Stranger specify them with a list of four nouns (75–6) that is at once highly characteristic of his moral verse, yet remote from tragic elevation.[117] In this way he evokes tragedy without compromising the style appropriate to a moral letter. With the conversational *opinor* (79) he introduces his personal interpretation of the tragic scene, which was unexpectedly grave with its suggestion of suicide. The single word *moriar* dispels the gloom and generalizes the notion. Though the dignified tone of epos at the opening is counterbalanced by the evocation of a tragic scene at the close, we have insensibly moved a long way from the sun warming the Sabine hills.

5. THEMES

Horace's subject matter in the *Epistles*, what Porphyrio called their *res*, is substantially different from what we find in the *Sermones*. The difference lies in the change of tone from criticism to analysis and exhortation. The voice of the satires was essentially public, that of the letters is private. Thus, for example, in the satires Horace referred to the state of religion in Rome, but in the letters a religious note is never sounded.[118] He draws his themes from his own world, and if we want a comprehensive description of the central issue of the collection it could be summed up in the phrase *recte uiuere*.[119] How does a Roman 'live aright' in the world as he finds it? Many guides were ready to offer their services, above all the philosophers, and the view took root in antiquity that Horace himself had turned decisively to philosophy for answers to his questions about right living. Thus even quite unspecific passages, such as 4.4 where Albius is described as sauntering through the woods, or 7.12 where Horace refers to his reading, or 8.9 where he speaks of his annoyance with his doctors, have all been interpreted (the first passage by the ancient scholiasts) as referring to philosophical

[117] For lists in the hexameter poems see B. on *Ep.* 2.2.180–1 and cf. Juv. 2.169, 7.11 and 10.64.

[118] J. F. D'Alton, *Horace and his age* (London 1917) 129, referring to *S.* 2.2.103–4.

[119] See 2.41n.

interests, despite the absence of clear pointers in the context. This common opinion can only be endorsed with reservations.[120]

The modern use of the word philosophy to mean a serious approach to ethical (and other) issues was not unknown in Horace's day. Cicero, for example, can say that a passage from Terence's *Phormio* is drawn from philosophy, even though it appears to be little more than practical wisdom.[121] On a stricter understanding, philosophy (like Christianity still) was parcelled out among fiercely rival schools which eagerly sought converts. Horace expressly holds aloof from them (1.14) nor does he ever encourage a correspondent to betake himself to a philosophical teacher, though in XII he advises Iccius, a committed student of philosophy, to redirect his researches from physics to ethics. At most, he recommends unspecified reading, consultation with the informed and an awareness of the sorts of questions philosophers ask (18.96–103). It is just here that philosophy takes its due place in the life of a mature and cultivated man. It is not the truth of any answer provided by this or that school which counts, but philosophy's implicit assumption that to discuss among friends important issues about life is appropriate. It is not always to be a question of how best to succeed in society; other matters deserve our attention. Such questions, rightly posed, bear upon the way we conceive and execute our lives; they waken us to our capacity to reflect about what matters most to us and to construct our lives in accordance with what we think is best for us as individuals.[122] We are not members of a tribe whose views we are

---

[120] Obbar spoke the truth long ago: 'At poetae non includendi sunt arte factis philosophorum cancellis' (ed., p. 25). For a fuller account of what follows see R. G. Mayer, *A.J.P.* 107 (1986) 55–73; the position set out there is broadly endorsed and very fully reviewed by Niall Rudd, 'Horace as a moralist' in N. Rudd (ed.), *Horace 2000: a celebration (Essays for the bimillennium)* (London 1993) 64–88, esp. 85 n. 2. A level-headed approach is still to be found in W. S. Maguinness, *Hermathena* 52 (1938) 27–46. There is, however, a much stronger belief in the philosophical character of the collection to be found in the work of C. Becker, *Das Spätwerk des Horaz* (Heidelberg 1963), G. Maurach, *A.C.D.* 11 (1968) 73–124, McGann, C. Macleod, *J.R.S.* 69 (1979) 16–27 = *Collected essays* (Oxford 1983) 280–91, J. Moles, *P.L.L.S.* 5 (1985–6) 33–60, F. della Corte, *Maia* 43 (1991) 67–81 and F. M. A. Jones, *L.C.M.* 18 (1993) 7–11.

[121] *Tusc.* 3.31.

[122] See the excellent essay on Horace by R. A. Brower in *Alexander Pope: the poetry of allusion* (Oxford 1959) 163–87, esp. 173.

bound to share. Philosophy is always inviting us to ask questions, to
make up our own minds, and to build our lives afresh.

None the less, so far as explicit reference to philosophers goes,
Horace belittles them in preference to Homer at a suggestively early
point in the collection (2.4). On balance, then, his position is hardly
likely to have struck his contemporaries as philosophical, for they expected commitment to one of the well-known sects, usually either the
Stoic or the Epicurean. To Roman eyes philosophy was an import, and
might be regarded with suspicion for many reasons; Cicero, for one,
was well aware that a good number of Romans did not like it.[123] If
Horace had been convinced of the practical value of philosophy he
might have spent more time removing objections to its pursuit. Yet we
find him neither defending nor enjoining a life lived in accordance
with any philosophical principles. But principles of behaviour there
must be and for these he turned to poetry as a guide. Homer is singled
out prominently in II and the practical moral guidance to be extracted
from his text is found also at 7.40–4. The collection as a whole exploits
the work of a number of other poets. A scene from Euripides' *Bacchae*,
as we have seen, provides a picture of the *uir bonus* who is the object of
investigation in XVI, and there are reminiscences of Ennius, Hesiod,
Pindar, Mimnermus and Sophocles to remind us that poetry offers
sufficiently varied lights to guide us through life.

The contemporary presentation of philosophy nevertheless offered
Horace a number of lively strategies that could be employed in woo-
ing the unregenerate from the paths of vice and in encouraging the
thoughtful to take stock.[124] His use of *fable* and *anecdote*, the analogy
between physical and moral health,[125] even the moral interpretation of
literary texts may all be a reflection of the popular moralizing of the
day. It is also clear that Horace was ready to plunder Rome's own
philosophical literature, recently created by such masters as Lucretius
and Cicero,[126] for use in his own *satura*. Going back further still, Plato

---

[123] See *Luc.* 5 *sunt enim multi qui omnino Graecas non ament litteras, plures qui
philosophiam*; H. D. Jocelyn, *B.R.L.* 59 (1977) 323–66.

[124] This is demonstrated in A. Oltramare, *Les origines de la diatribe romaine*
(Lausanne 1926).   [125] See 1.28–32n.

[126] See T. Zielinski, *Cicero im Wandel der Jahrhunderte* (Leipzig and Berlin
1908) 107.

and, somewhat unexpectedly, Aristotle he regards as classics of literature, whose work will be known to his readers; they too make a significant contribution to the moral texture of his poems and validate with
their intellectual authority notions like that of the mean or of being a
friend to oneself,[127] which his own experience had brought him to
endorse.

Philosophy is not therefore ignored, but its partisan and exclusive
claims are much reduced, so as to give the collection a wider appeal
than it would have had if its moral horizons were confined to school
dogmatics. Horace's object is, after all, the young man of general culture in good society: his addressees write poetry and serve the state
abroad, they play games, administer the property of others and interest themselves in the mysteries of natural science. Horace assumes that,
in addition to all this, they want to understand how to live (*sapere,
sapientia*).[128] Rome certainly provided her male citizens with guidance
on this point in the traditional *mos maiorum*, which Horace's own father
encouraged his son to follow (or so he says at *S.* 1.4.117). He sees,
however, that this really only deals with men as public figures (XVI).
A change had come over Roman society and there were now legitimate attractions in retirement and self-appraisal to which Horace
draws his readers' attention at the beginning of XVII and the end of
XVIII. But this must be balanced against the claims of society. So
Horace may remind his young friends that achievement takes various
forms, not all of them public; there is no disgrace in taking a back seat.
But however much you want to succeed, it is still necessary to keep an
eye on how to live aright. This involves a man in making choices; it is
above all the power to make choices which interests the Horace of the
Epistles.[129]

Choice, the privilege of independence, can only be exercised by free
men. Choice may appear in the guise of making the most of the opportunities life offers (IV, V) or as independence and self-reliance (XIX).
These themes are perhaps the most prominent in the collection and
can be used to show how ethics is subsumed in the poet's own experi-

[127] See 18.9, 101nn.

[128] See U. Klima, *Untersuchungen zu dem Begriff* Sapientia (Diss. Bonn 1971)
145–59, M. Massaro, *S.I.F.C.* 46 (1974) 85–128.

[129] 'The themes of personal ethos and choice reach their culmination in the
first book of *Epistles*', says Brink in *Horace on poetry* (Cambridge 1982) III 539.

ence. One of the basic tenets of the ancient moralist was that the popular view of correct behaviour was a distortion from which the man who would live well must free himself in order to arrive at a correct opinion.[130] Horace embraces this notion not because he is now a student of philosophy but because he has always been a poet. In order to realize the law of his being – *poeta nascitur, non fit* – he had had to set himself apart: 'me gelidum nemus | Nympharumque leues cum Satyris chori | secernunt populo' (*C.* 1.1.30–2); 'odi profanum uulgus et arceo' (*C.* 3.1.1).[131] He had only to apply his experience of being a poet to that of being a moral agent in society; that he agrees with the philosophers is helpful, for their position authenticates his own. This is true too of his insistence upon the need for self-reliance. The philosophers agreed upon the need for autarkeia, but the poet who wants to make his mark within a tradition that is essentially imitative arrives by his own road at the same assurance; thus Horace combines his experience as a poet with his moral outlook to endorse the need for self-reliance in III, XVI and XIX. The neatest instance of the harmony between poet and moralist is seen in his use of the phrase *ultra quam satis est*; at 6.16 it is applied morally to the pursuit of goodness and at 7.82–3 it serves to make the aesthetic point that brevity is best when telling a story. That his own point of view can be, should be, more widely applied only goes to demonstrate the value of the poet's experience to his fellow men.

The beauty of the freedom to choose for oneself also explains Horace's emancipation from the philosophical schools, for once committed to one of them you automatically restricted the exercise of choice, your answers were provided for you and the chief issue became their implementation. But in the second letter to Lollius (XVIII) we find Horace inviting the young man to construct and execute his own way of life, while the closing scene shows the poet still at work building his own peace of mind. The invitation poems may also be seen as reminding their recipients and us of the availability of choices. Albius need not wander alone in the woods, Torquatus does not have to work himself to death; they have but to exercise the independence their means and social position have conferred. Of course, we can make bad choices, as Mena and the bailiff do in mistakenly taking up the coun-

---

[130] See 1.70n.   [131] See N–H's note on *C.* 1.1.30–2.

try life. Still, Mena, a free man, had the choice and exercised it; the former town slave had his silent prayer realized. Or, like Iccius', our choice may prove a mixture of good and less good. Then it is a matter of turning circumstances to our own advantage. For this we need adaptability (1.20) and a philosopher at last emerges as our model, Aristippus.

The engaging figure of Aristippus appealed to Horace first and foremost because, of all the philosophers of Greece, he advertised his willingness to associate with the rich and powerful, and so could best serve as a role model for the young careerists of the *Epistles*.[132] If he left a doctrine and a school they had ceased to be a force in Horace's day. His friendship on independent terms with the leaders of society validated Horace's own way of life and that of those among his correspondents (Septimius, Celsus, Florus, Scaeva, even Lollius) who associated or aspired to associate with men like Tiberius. Aristippus had embodied his teaching in his life, another attraction for Horace, who regularly uses himself as an example. His chief and enduring doctrine was the value of adaptability. Aristippus' adaptability was not undignified; 'he was capable of adapting himself to situation and occasion and role, *appropriately* performing his part in every circumstance'.[133] Adaptability, so long as it was becoming, had long been encouraged in the popular morality found in early poetry,[134] and was accorded philosophical respectability by Aristo of Chios and Marcus Aurelius.[135] Its embodiment in Aristippus' way of life was central to Horace's programme in the *Epistles*, so he is the one philosopher whose practice is held up for approval.

The issues that Horace focusses upon help in the construction of a

[132] This point is stressed in the admirable essay by A. Traina, *R.d.F.* 119 (1991) 285–305, esp. 302; for Aristippus generally see R. Goulet (ed.), *Dictionnaire des philosophes antiques* (Paris 1989) I 370–5. His appeal was long-lived; the second-century philosopher Demonax is said to have revered Socrates, marvelled at Diogenes and loved Aristippus (Luc. *Demon.* 62).

[133] Diog. Laert. 2.66.

[134] See Theognis 213–8 (a famous comparison to the polypus, which changes colour, see Campbell's note *ad loc.* for the later tradition) and Eur. *Hipp.* 1115–19 (the chorus deplore intransigence).

[135] See Diog. Laert. 7.160 for Aristo's view that one should be ready to play either Thersites or Agamemnon; for Marcus' approval of περιτροπή see 4.1, 5.20.

life at a particular level of Roman society (about which he is not inclined to generalize). He begins with the need for sound education, and the imagery of the school is prominent. The literary text that forms the basis of this education is an inexhaustible resource, Homer. The aim of this education is the acquisition of *uirtus* and *sapientia*, moral excellence and practical wisdom, both of which can only be exercised by an independent man. Independence is a theme to be approached by a variety of avenues: the relationship to a patron (VII, XVIII) or to a literary tradition (III, XIX). One's independence is never absolute; as social creatures we need one another by definition. Friendship becomes the dominant relationship,[136] but its aspects are various and hard to define. The letter offers Horace the chance, not to theorize, but to show friendship in characteristic activities, mediating between the estranged (III), soliciting a place for a deserving junior (IX), effecting introductions (XII), or inviting the hard-worked to take an agreeable and well-earned rest (V). Above all, Horace advises upon behaviour, especially upon the bearing of inferiors towards the great ones of the land (VIII, XIII, XVII, XVIII).[137]

One theme largely ignored in the collection is that of love. It is remarkable that though his addressees are in the main young men Horace has little advice for them on their sexual appetencies, beyond a curt reference to the passion at 1.38 *amator*, a general warning at 2.37 that lovesickness may keep you awake, and at 18.72–5 a prudent observation that falling for your patron's slave will give him a chance to gratify you at little cost to himself. This gap in his coverage of the troubles to which his addressees may be prone is the more striking when the strictures of Cicero and Lucretius are borne in mind.[138] It is almost as if he were trying to marginalize the contemporary poetic fashion for *grands amours*. On the other hand, Horace himself never married,[139] and it should be borne in mind that his call to retirement and self-determination only works for the solitary.

Horace's addressees are, so far as we can tell, men on the way up. He for his part has arrived at the goal they aspire to, financial indepen-

---

[136] R. S. Kilpatrick, *The poetry of friendship: Horace, Epistles 1* (Edmonton 1986).
[137] This is discussed at more length in R. Mayer, *P.C.P.S.* n.s. 31 (1985) 33–46. [138] *Tusc.* 4.68–76; *DRN* 4.1058–1191. [139] See 5.13n.

dence and public esteem. What is the view like from up there? The
reader is in for a surprise. Our poet is not content and, like many
successful men in middle life, he shows himself the prey of boredom
and malaise.[140] The first avowal of this is found in the attack of Davus
upon his master's inconstancy at *S.* 2.7.111–15; it is perhaps significant
that malaise does not appear in the first book, in which we see Horace
still bustling forward; by the second book, however, his position is
more secure and so he falls victim to indifference. In the *Epistles* this
comes out most clearly in VIII, where he diagnoses his malady as a
deadly lethargy, the sort of thing that drives some men to pointless
travel (XI). Indeed, Horace too, whose physical well-being causes him
some concern (VII), journeys for the sake of health (XV); it is in this
letter that he fleetingly voices a poet's worst nightmare, a failure of the
springs of language.[141] There is after all no specific against this boredom, though retirement to the countryside is certainly an alleviation
(X, XIV, XVI). But he knows that the only cure lies in the achievement of *aequanimitas*, a notion emphasized in the last lines of XI and
XVIII (where he does not claim to have succeeded).

The countryside forms an important element in all of Horace's poetry. It usually provides a retreat from the fray, a notion found in the
opening lines of the first poem (1.5 'latet abditus agro'). Horace frequently makes it plain that he is writing from the country (2.1, 7.1,
10.2, XIII) or finds himself reluctantly in the city (XIV). He lovingly
describes the setting of his estate in the Sabine country (XVI), and
does not miss details of natural beauty, like the sheen and fragrance of
grass (10.19; an observation worthy of Virgil in the *Georgics*). Yet for
all his devotion to his life in the country it is hard to imagine him
expressing Virgil's wish at *Georgic* 2.485–6 'rura mihi et rigui placeant
in uallibus amnes, | flumina amem siluasque inglorius'. Such ardour is
not to be sought in Horace, for the countryside did not feed his imagination as it did Virgil's. On the other hand, his feeling for it is genuine
enough and perhaps closer to what many of his readers felt, namely
that it provided a 'not-quite-absolute retreat'[142] from the cares of busi-

---

[140] See L.'s edition of *Sermones* p. 555 and A. La Penna, *Orazio e la morale
mondana europea* (Florence 1968) 135–42.   [141] See 15.20n.

[142] The phrase is Brower's; his discussion of Horace's feel for the countryside
is ably balanced (176, n. 122 above).

ness and so gave a man the chance, if he would but take it, to be more truly himself, a concept neatly expressed at 14.1 'mihi me reddentis agelli'.

It may also be noticed that the ethos of the countryside is markedly different from that found in the *Odes* and even in the *Sermones*. In the *Odes* above all the countryside provided a retreat for Horace the poet and he placed himself in a landscape pre-eminently poetic.[143] This is even to an extent true of the second book of *Sermones* in which he describes himself as a writer (or a would-be writer) when he is in the country.[144] In the first epistle, as we have seen, he claims to have put poetry aside; in line with this new direction, the countryside no longer serves to promote poetic composition. Almost as if to draw attention to the change, the only writer and poet set in the countryside is Albius. It seems therefore a misjudgement when Schütz, for instance, says that the praise of a *nemus* at 10.7 has regard to Horace's poetic calling; that is true of *C.* 1.1.30 and 4.2.30, but he nowhere refers to his 'former' vocation in the letter to Fuscus. By the same token, R. F. Thomas overstates his case when he finds the epistolary landscape in XVI an 'ideal poetic setting'.[145] Rather Horace, his true poetry now behind him, finds in the countryside advantages exclusively moral, above all that independence which is given its most resonant statement at 10.8 'uiuo et regno', where each verb is a distillation of themes developed more fully elsewhere. The solitude of the country proves more generally beneficial. There we may read morally improving literature (7.12), Homer say; there we may learn independence and balance of mind so as to live to ourselves: 'mihi uiuam' (18.107). This aspect of the countryside has the merit of being more widely available to his readers, who, after all, are not all poets. But we all want to run our own lives in our own way, and Horace, by reshaping his landscape so as to remove a purely personal and poetic advantage, opens it to all of us.

---

[143] See I. Troxler-Keller, *Die Dichterlandschaft des Horaz* (Heidelberg 1964).

[144] So, e.g., at *S.* 2.3.4–12 and 6.16–17 *ergo ubi me in montis et in arcem ex urbe remoui | quid prius illustrem satiris musaque pedestri?*

[145] R. F. Thomas, *Lands and peoples in Roman poetry: the ethnographical tradition* (Cambridge Philological Society Supplement 7, Cambridge 1982) 17; he also detects suggestions of the secluded world of the poet in the word *latebrae* (16.15). The need however to observe generic distinction is rightly stressed by E. W. Leach in *A.J.P.* 114 (1993) 275.

6. THE ORGANIZATION OF THE BOOK

Poets in Rome first 'published' their poems by distributing them among friends for their amusement, but also for comment and criticism; Horace, for instance, gave his to Quintilius for his advice (*AP* 438–9). It is clear from this practice that each poem had to make sense purely in terms of itself. Once the individual pieces were collected into a book, however, it was possible to make cross-references to earlier, extant poems. Catullus, for instance, replies to critics of his 'kissing' poems (5 and 7) in a later piece (16); his practice in the latter poem is instructive, for even if the earlier ones were lost we should still know what the point at issue was. Virgil works similarly when, at the end of his fifth *Eclogue*, he quotes part of the opening lines of the second and third. Horace follows this tradition in the first book of *Sermones*. He criticized Lucilius in what is now the fourth poem of the collection. That piece must have circulated independently for a while since it attracted adverse comment which Horace tries to mollify with a fuller account of his attitude to his model in what is now the tenth and last piece in the collection. The relationship between poet and audience was a lively part of the literary life of the day that the book could reflect.

The practice of publishing one's own poems in book form suggested a new artistic strategy, the arrangement of the individual pieces in a satisfying order. It is a pity that we cannot be sure of having the first poetry book in Rome, Catullus' *Carmina*, in the exact form which he intended. Virgil's *Eclogues* by default offer the starting-place for the reliable study of the poet's interest in the design of his collection.[146] What strikes all students of late Republican literature is the poets' fondness for collections founded upon a multiple of five:[147] the *Eclogues*, the first book of *Sermones*, the first book of Tibullus all have ten poems; the second and third books of *Odes* have twenty and thirty respectively, the fourth fifteen. The twenty epistles thus maintain an established tradition.

[146] Various theories are discussed by N. Rudd in *Lines of enquiry* (Cambridge 1976) 119–44.
[147] Indeed, not just poets, for Livy used pentads and decades of books to organize his history.

Numbers apart, the format of the book offered the poet a chance to fix the order of his pieces and at least invite the reader to adhere to it (browsers will always subvert design). Moreover, it is clear that the ability to fix the format encouraged the composition of some poems to occupy a particular place, usually at the beginning or end, poems of dedication and epilogues. These poems often came to serve a function of general introduction or conclusion, standing as they do in the privileged position of doorkeepers. They advertise the poet's wares, his themes and literary principles. Last poems may offer a summing up, with some biographical information as in the last epigram in Propertius' first book.[148]

By the time he came to collect together his verse letters, Horace had had considerable experience in the arranging of his books and it is not unreasonable to detect his artistry in this as in every other aspect of his work.[149] The first letter is clearly an advertisement of the poet's new spiritual direction, an account of its origin and the effect it has upon his writing. The addressee is Maecenas, who is also therefore the dedicatee of the book. But there is a difference from other such dedications. Usually the poet says that the dedicatee has prompted or encouraged the poems now offered to the public. Here, however, Horace explains why he cannot produce the sort of poems his old friend would like to have. This novel undedication prepares us for the novelty of the collection of verse epistles itself.

At the other end of the book stands the one outsider. The scholiasts were right to see that the address to the slave/book is not epistolary because the reprobate is pretty clearly in his master's presence. This has implications for the supposed pattern of arrangement of the rest of the collection. The twentieth poem is designed to be last, like Virgil's tenth *Eclogue*. Horace takes advantage of the tradition of offering personal details at the close and he even gives his age. If this piece is rightly set apart from its fellows, some design for the rest leaps to the eye.

---

[148] For Horace's lyric epilogues see Fraenkel 297–307 and for the tradition of personal statement at the end of a long poem or collection see N–H on *C.* 2.20 p. 335, where the whimsicality of the last epistle is noted.

[149] See G. Kettner, *Die Episteln des Horaz* (Berlin 1900) 33–8; Fraenkel 314–15; La Penna (n. 140) 155; Maurach (n. 120); L. Herrmann, *Lat.* 28 (1969) 372–7; O. A. W. Dilke, *A.N.R.W.* II 31.3.1839–42.

The nineteenth letter is, like the first, addressed to Maecenas and again its theme is literature, especially that lyric poetry of which he wanted more. But that is merged in the central idea of true independence of spirit, here set against the traditions of poetic imitation. Thus Horace blends together his themes to produce a credo both artistic and moral: 'qui sibi fidet, dux reget examen'. Maecenas is an appropriate recipient of such reflections, for, as *docte* in the opening line hints, he symbolizes Horace's ideal audience, the only one who really knows and understands, the true connoisseur. The placement of this poem gives prominence to the poet's personal ideals.

The nineteenth letter, moreover, is so placed before the epilogue as to repeat the thematic arrangement of the last two poems of the second book of *Odes*. There too the penultimate poem focussed on Horace as poet, but it stressed, appropriately to the lyric genre, his inspiration; the more mundane letter treats of his place in the literary tradition and the right use of imitation. The last poem of each book dwells upon fame and success, but the ode still deals with Horace the poet and his success as a writer, whereas the epistle, conformably to the character of the whole collection, emphasizes the position he has achieved in Roman society. Moreover, if the penultimate epistle is taken together with the epilogue, an odd detail will be noticed. In his biographical sketch (20.20–8), there is no reference to his poetic achievement, as there had been in the last ode of the second book. This would be strange had not the preceding epistle focussed upon that very issue; the point does not need to be made again. In a sense then, the epilogue takes its predecessor as read.

Moving inwards from beginning and end, we find that the second and eighteenth poems are both dedicated to the same man, Lollius; he is only a little less privileged than Maecenas. The placement just within the frame of these pieces strikes no one as accidental, for once again the themes seem to have a particular prominence, moral education in II and the best choices in the conduct of one's life in XVIII. Moreover the second letter seems to take up a line of thought only adumbrated in the first.[150] At the other end of the collection XVIII is obviously similar in theme to its predecessor; now some might have expected

---

[150] See the end note to II.

poems on related topics to be kept apart on the principle of *uariatio*, but the juxtaposition, which must be deliberate, encourages the reader to take the poems as complementary (indeed Porphyrio ran the two together in his commentary). *Epistle* XVII offers the fundamental justification for the role of the client which XVIII pursues into the grey area where tensions arise between friends of roughly equal social status. Horace binds these two poems even more closely together by reminding Scaeva at the beginning of his letter and Lollius at the end of his of the attractions of a retired life.

So far so good. A measure of agreement will be found supporting the account of the placement of the poems just discussed. Further pursuit of patterns commands less assent, not least because it always seems to exact a terrible cost in reducing poems to their paraphrasable content; the *Odes* have suffered a good deal from this sort of treatment.[151]

Another approach to the organization of the collection has sought rather for a linear progression of the thought.[152] It is undeniable that the closing lines of XVIII enunciate a moral programme, an undertaking to pursue *aequanimitas*. What precedes can be regarded as the stages, not without backslidings, by which Horace makes his way to this now clarified goal. So long as no scheme is applied too rigidly, it is not impossible to entertain a variety of patterns and interpretations at the same time. Thus X seems to some to be given special prominence in that it closes the first half, and so Horace dedicates it to a favoured theme, the importance to him of the life in the country. On the other hand, as E. J. Kenney has argued, *Epistles* X to XIV form a group in which the chief emphasis lies on the issue of whether or not place contributes to happiness; the seeming consistency of Horace's view in these letters is then demolished in XV.[153] As in the assessment of the shape of individual poems, so in the search for the arrangement of the collection, it is perhaps safest to look not only for continuity but for design as well. The logic of a predetermined argument would be profoundly unHoratian.

[151] See A. Minarini, *Lucidus ordo* (Bologna 1989) reviewed in *C.R.* 42 (1992) 44-5.
[152] So Maurach (n. 120), McGann.
[153] *I.C.S.* 2 (1977) 237-9.

7. THE TRANSMISSION OF THE TEXT[154]

Horace's rise to the status of a classic author appears to have been gradual. The first-century A.D. scholar M. Valerius Probus worked on the text, but it goes beyond the evidence – all trace of his Horatian scholarship has vanished – to say that he produced an edition for general consumption. Commentaries were written to elucidate the poet's text, which in Juvenal's time is a school book (7.227; cf. 20.17 for Horace's dread of this fate).[155] In spite of this, there is no MS of his poems earlier than the ninth century and by then numerous errors had entered the tradition. From that time on the number of copies of his works increased and new commentaries for a new readership were produced.[156] Scribal errors were shared and transmitted both vertically and horizontally. Attempts used to be made to try to group the large number of MS witnesses into classes, but such endeavours now find little support among textual critics, who prefer to base their texts upon a number of MSS deemed to offer variant readings worthy of consideration (Brink believes that it is the variants, not the MSS that fall into classes[157]). The text of the present edition reproduces none of the currently available texts in all details, but is founded upon the Oxford edition of Wickham–Garrod and the Teubner edition of D. R. Shackleton Bailey. The latter has the additional merit of reinstating paragraphs in the hexameter poems.

[154] See R. J. Tarrant's account in L. D. Reynolds (ed.), *Texts and transmission* (Oxford 1983) 182–6.

[155] The tradition of ancient comment is preserved in the dilapidated remains of Porphyrio and pseudo-Acro.

[156] There are a number of mediaeval commentaries only now in the process of being edited and published.

[157] See his edition of *AP*, p. 20.

Q. HORATI FLACCI EPISTVLARVM
LIBER PRIMVS

Q. HORATI FLACCI EPISTVLARVM
LIBER PRIMVS

I

Prima dicte mihi, summa dicende Camena,
spectatum satis et donatum iam rude quaeris,
Maecenas, iterum antiquo me includere ludo?
non eadem est aetas, non mens. Veianius armis
Herculis ad postem fixis latet abditus agro,　　　　　　5
ne populum extrema totiens exoret harena.
est mihi purgatam crebro qui personet aurem:
'solue senescentem mature sanus equum, ne
peccet ad extremum ridendus et ilia ducat.'
nunc itaque et uersus et cetera ludicra pono:　　　　　　10
quid uerum atque decens, curo et rogo et omnis in hoc
　　　　　　　　　　　　　　　　　　　　　　　　sum:
condo et compono quae mox depromere possim.
ac ne forte roges, quo me duce, quo lare tuter:
nullius addictus iurare in uerba magistri,
quo me cumque rapit tempestas, deferor hospes.　　　　15
nunc agilis fio et mersor ciuilibus undis
uirtutis uerae custos rigidusque satelles,
nunc in Aristippi furtim praecepta relabor
et mihi res, non me rebus, subiungere conor.
　　Vt nox longa quibus mentitur amica diesque　　　　20
lenta uidetur opus debentibus, ut piger annus
pupillis quos dura premit custodia matrum,
sic mihi tarda fluunt ingrataque tempora quae spem
consiliumque morantur agendi nauiter id quod
aeque pauperibus prodest, locupletibus aeque,　　　　　25
aeque neglectum pueris senibusque nocebit.
restat ut his ego me ipse regam solerque elementis.

    Non possis oculo quantum contendere Lynceus:
non tamen idcirco contemnas lippus inungi;
nec, quia desperes inuicti membra Glyconis,   30
nodosa corpus nolis prohibere cheragra.
est quadam prodire tenus, si non datur ultra.
    Feruet auaritia miseroque cupidine pectus:
sunt uerba et uoces, quibus hunc lenire dolorem
possis et magnam morbi deponere partem.   35
laudis amore tumes: sunt certa piacula, quae te
ter pure lecto poterunt recreare libello.
inuidus, iracundus, iners, uinosus, amator,
nemo adeo ferus est, ut non mitescere possit,
si modo culturae patientem commodet aurem.   40
    Virtus est uitium fugere et sapientia prima
stultitia caruisse. uides, quae maxima credis
esse mala, exiguum censum turpemque repulsam,
quanto deuites animi capitisque labore:
impiger extremos curris mercator ad Indos,   45
per mare pauperiem fugiens, per saxa, per ignes:
ne cures ea quae stulte miraris et optas,
discere et audire et meliori credere non uis?
quis circum pagos et circum compita pugnax
magna coronari contemnat Olympia, cui spes,   50
cui sit condicio dulcis sine puluere palmae?
uilius argentum est auro, uirtutibus aurum.
    'O ciues, ciues, quaerenda pecunia primum est;
uirtus post nummos': haec Ianus summus ab imo
prodocet, haec recinunt iuuenes dictata senesque.   55
[laeuo suspensi loculos tabulamque lacerto]
est animus tibi, sunt mores, est lingua fidesque,
sed quadringentis sex septem milia desunt:
plebs eris. at pueri ludentes 'rex eris' aiunt
'si recte facies'. hic murus aeneus esto: 60
nil conscire sibi, nulla pallescere culpa.
Roscia, dic sodes, melior lex an puerorum est

nenia, quae regnum recte facientibus offert,
et maribus Curiis et decantata Camillis?
isne tibi melius suadet, qui, rem facias, rem,   65
si possis, recte, si non, quocumque modo, rem,
ut propius spectes lacrimosa poemata Pupi,
an qui Fortunae te responsare superbae
liberum et erectum praesens hortatur et aptat?

    Quodsi me populus Romanus forte roget, cur   70
non ut porticibus sic iudiciis fruar isdem
nec sequar aut fugiam quae diligit ipse uel odit:
olim quod uolpes aegroto cauta leoni
respondit, referam: 'quia me uestigia terrent,
omnia te aduersum spectantia, nulla retrorsum.'   75
belua multorum est capitum. nam quid sequar aut quem?
pars hominum gestit conducere publica; sunt qui
crustis et pomis uiduas uenentur auaras
excipiantque senes, quos in uiuaria mittant;
multis occulto crescit res fenore. uerum   80
esto aliis alios rebus studiisque teneri:
idem eadem possunt horam durare probantes?
'nullus in orbe sinus Bais praelucet amoenis'
si dixit diues, lacus et mare sentit amorem
festinantis eri; cui si uitiosa libido   85
fecerit auspicium, cras ferramenta Teanum
tolletis, fabri. lectus genialis in aula est:
nil ait esse prius, melius nil caelibe uita;
si non est, iurat bene solis esse maritis.
quo teneam uoltus mutantem Protea nodo?   90
quid pauper? ride: mutat cenacula, lectos,
balnea, tonsores, conducto nauigio aeque
nauseat ac locuples, quem ducit priua triremis.

    Si curatus inaequali tonsore capillos
occurri, rides; si forte subucula pexae   95
trita subest tunicae uel si toga dissidet impar,
rides: quid? mea cum pugnat sententia secum,

quod petiit spernit, repetit quod nuper omisit,
aestuat et uitae disconuenit ordine toto,
diruit, aedificat, mutat quadrata rotundis?   100
insanire putas sollemnia me neque rides
nec medici credis nec curatoris egere
a praetore dati, rerum tutela mearum
cum sis et praue sectum stomacheris ob unguem
de te pendentis, te respicientis amici.   105
    Ad summam: sapiens uno minor est Ioue, diues,
liber, honoratus, pulcher, rex denique regum,
praecipue sanus, nisi cum pituita molesta est.

II

Troiani belli scriptorem, Maxime Lolli,
dum tu declamas Romae, Praeneste relegi;
qui, quid sit pulchrum, quid turpe, quid utile, quid non,
planius ac melius Chrysippo et Crantore dicit.
cur ita crediderim, nisi quid te detinet, audi.   5
    Fabula qua Paridis propter narratur amorem
Graecia barbariae lento collisa duello,
stultorum regum et populorum continet aestus.
Antenor censet belli praecidere causam:
quid Paris? ut saluus regnet uiuatque beatus,   10
cogi posse negat. Nestor componere lites
inter Peliden festinat et inter Atriden:
hunc amor, ira quidem communiter urit utrumque.
quidquid delirant reges, plectuntur Achiui.
seditione, dolis, scelere atque libidine et ira   15
Iliacos intra muros peccatur et extra.
    Rursus, quid uirtus et quid sapientia possit,
utile proposuit nobis exemplar Vlixem,
qui domitor Troiae multorum prouidus urbes
et mores hominum inspexit latumque per aequor,   20

dum sibi, dum sociis reditum parat, aspera multa
pertulit, aduersis rerum immersabilis undis.
Sirenum uoces et Circae pocula nosti;
quae si cum sociis stultus cupidusque bibisset,
sub domina meretrice fuisset turpis et excors; 25
uixisset canis immundus uel amica luto sus.
nos numerus sumus et fruges consumere nati,
sponsi Penelopae nebulones Alcinoique
in cute curanda plus aequo operata iuuentus,
cui pulchrum fuit in medios dormire dies et 30
ad strepitum citharae cessantem ducere somnum.
    Vt iugulent hominem, surgunt de nocte latrones:
ut te ipsum serues, non expergisceris? atqui
si noles sanus, curres hydropicus; et ni
posces ante diem librum cum lumine, si non 35
intendes animum studiis et rebus honestis,
inuidia uel amore uigil torquebere. nam cur
quae laedunt oculum, festinas demere, siquid
est animum, differs curandi tempus in annum?
dimidium facti, qui coepit, habet: sapere aude, 40
incipe. uiuendi qui recte prorogat horam,
rusticus exspectat, dum defluat amnis; at ille
labitur et labetur in omne uolubilis aeuum.
    Quaeritur argentum puerisque beata creandis
uxor et incultae pacantur uomere siluae: 45
quod satis est cui contingit, nihil amplius optet.
non domus et fundus, non aeris aceruus et auri
aegroto domini deduxit corpore febres,
non animo curas; ualeat possessor oportet,
si comportatis rebus bene cogitat uti. 50
qui cupit aut metuit, iuuat illum sic domus et res
ut lippum pictae tabulae, fomenta podagram,
auriculas citharae collecta sorde dolentis.
sincerum est nisi uas, quodcumque infundis acescit.

    Sperne uoluptates: nocet empta dolore uoluptas.   55
semper auarus eget: certum uoto pete finem.
inuidus alterius macrescit rebus opimis;
inuidia Siculi non inuenere tyranni
maius tormentum. qui non moderabitur irae,
infectum uolet esse, dolor quod suaserit et mens,   60
dum poenas odio per uim festinat inulto.
ira furor breuis est: animum rege; qui nisi paret,
imperat; hunc frenis, hunc tu compesce catena.
    Fingit equum tenera docilem ceruice magister
ire uiam, qua monstret eques; uenaticus, ex quo   65
tempore ceruinam pellem latrauit in aula,
militat in siluis catulus. nunc adbibe puro
pectore uera puer, nunc te melioribus offer.
quo semel est imbuta recens seruabit odorem
testa diu. quodsi cessas aut strenuus anteis,   70
nec tardum opperior nec praecedentibus insto.

III

Iuli Flore, quibus terrarum militet oris
Claudius Augusti priuignus, scire laboro.
Thracane uos Hebrusque niuali compede uinctus
an freta uicinas inter currentia turres
an pingues Asiae campi collesque morantur?   5
    Quid studiosa cohors operum struit? hoc quoque curo.
quis sibi res gestas Augusti scribere sumit,
bella quis et paces longum diffundit in aeuum?
quid Titius, Romana breui uenturus in ora,
Pindarici fontis qui non expalluit haustus,   10
fastidire lacus et riuos ausus apertos?
ut ualet? ut meminit nostri? fidibusne Latinis
Thebanos aptare modos studet auspice Musa,
an tragica desaeuit et ampullatur in arte?
quid mihi Celsus agit, monitus multumque monendus,   15

priuatas ut quaerat opes et tangere uitet
scripta, Palatinus quaecumque recepit Apollo,
ne, si forte suas repetitum uenerit olim
grex auium plumas, moueat cornicula risum
furtiuis nudata coloribus? ipse quid audes?   20
quae circumuolitas agilis thyma? non tibi paruum
ingenium, non incultum est et turpiter hirtum:
seu linguam causis acuis seu ciuica iura
respondere paras seu condis amabile carmen,
prima feres hederae uictricis praemia. quodsi   25
frigida curarum fomenta relinquere posses,
quo te caelestis sapientia duceret, ires.
hoc opus, hoc studium parui properemus et ampli,
si patriae uolumus, si nobis uiuere cari.

   Debes hoc etiam rescribere, sit tibi curae   30
quantae conueniat Munatius. an male sarta
gratia nequiquam coit et rescinditur ac uos
seu calidus sanguis seu rerum inscitia uexat
indomita ceruice feros? ubicumque locorum
uiuitis, indigni fraternum rumpere foedus,   35
pascitur in uestrum reditum uotiua iuuenca.

IV

Albi, nostrorum sermonum candide iudex,
quid nunc te dicam facere in regione Pedana?
scribere quod Cassi Parmensis opuscula uincat
an tacitum siluas inter reptare salubres
curantem quidquid dignum sapiente bonoque est?   5
   Non tu corpus eras sine pectore: di tibi formam,
di tibi diuitias dederunt artemque fruendi.
quid uoueat dulci nutricula maius alumno,
qui sapere et fari possit quae sentiat et cui
gratia fama ualetudo contingat abunde   10
et mundus uictus non deficiente crumina?

inter spem curamque, timores inter et iras
omnem crede diem tibi diluxisse supremum:
grata superueniet quae non sperabitur hora.
    Me pinguem et nitidum bene curata cute uises,					15
cum ridere uoles Epicuri de grege porcum.

V

Si potes Archiacis conuiua recumbere lectis
nec modica cenare times holus omne patella,
supremo te sole domi, Torquate, manebo.
uina bibes iterum Tauro diffusa palustres
inter Minturnas Sinuessanumque Petrinum.					5
si melius quid habes, arcesse, uel imperium fer.
iamdudum splendet focus et tibi munda supellex:
mitte leuis spes et certamina diuitiarum
et Moschi causam: cras nato Caesare festus
dat ueniam somnumque dies; impune licebit					10
aestiuam sermone benigno tendere noctem.
    Quo mihi fortunam, si non conceditur uti?
parcus ob heredis curam nimiumque seuerus
adsidet insano: potare et spargere flores
incipiam patiarque uel inconsultus haberi.					15
quid non ebrietas dissignat? operta recludit,
spes iubet esse ratas, ad proelia trudit inertem,
sollicitis animis onus eximit, addocet artes.
fecundi calices quem non fecere disertum,
contracta quem non in paupertate solutum?					20
    Haec ego procurare et idoneus imperor et non
inuitus, ne turpe toral, ne sordida mappa
corruget nares, ne non et cantharus et lanx
ostendat tibi te, ne fidos inter amicos
sit qui dicta foras eliminet, ut coeat par					25
iungaturque pari: Butram tibi Septiciumque
et nisi cena prior potiorque puella Sabinum

detinet adsumam; locus est et pluribus umbris;
sed nimis arta premunt olidae conuiuia caprae.
    Tu quotus esse uelis rescribe et rebus omissis   30
atria seruantem postico falle clientem.

VI

Nil admirari prope res est una, Numici,
solaque, quae possit facere et seruare beatum.
hunc solem et stellas et decedentia certis
tempora momentis sunt qui formidine nulla
imbuti spectent: quid censes munera terrae,   5
quid maris extremos Arabas ditantis et Indos,
ludicra quid, plausus et amici dona Quiritis,
quo spectanda modo, quo sensu credis et ore?
qui timet his aduersa, fere miratur eodem
quo cupiens pacto; pauor est utrubique molestus,   10
improuisa simul species exterret utrumque.
gaudeat an doleat, cupiat metuatne, quid ad rem,
si, quidquid uidit melius peiusue sua spe,
defixis oculis animoque et corpore torpet?
insani sapiens nomen ferat, aequus iniqui,   15
ultra quam satis est uirtutem si petat ipsam.
    I nunc, argentum et marmor uetus aeraque et artes
suspice, cum gemmis Tyrios mirare colores;
gaude quod spectant oculi te mille loquentem;
nauus mane Forum et uespertinus pete tectum,   20
ne plus frumenti dotalibus emetat agris
Mutus et – indignum, quod sit peioribus ortus –
hic tibi sit potius quam tu mirabilis illi.
quidquid sub terra est, in apricum proferet aetas,
defodiet condetque nitentia. cum bene notum   25
porticus Agrippae, uia te conspexerit Appi,
ire tamen restat, Numa quo deuenit et Ancus.
    Si latus aut renes morbo temptantur acuto,

quaere fugam morbi. uis recte uiuere – quis non?:
si uirtus hoc una potest dare, fortis omissis   30
hoc age deliciis.
            Virtutem uerba putas et
lucum ligna: caue ne portus occupet alter,
ne Cibyratica, ne Bithyna negotia perdas;
mille talenta rotundentur, totidem altera porro et
tertia succedant et quae pars quadret aceruum.   35
scilicet uxorem cum dote fidemque et amicos
et genus et formam regina Pecunia donat
ac bene nummatum decorat Suadela Venusque.
mancupiis locuples eget aeris Cappadocum rex:
ne fueris hic tu. chlamydes Lucullus, ut aiunt,   40
si posset centum scaenae praebere rogatus,
'qui possum tot?' ait; 'tamen et quaeram et quot habebo
mittam'; post paulo scribit sibi milia quinque
esse domi chlamydum; partem uel tolleret omnes.
exilis domus est, ubi non et multa supersunt   45
et dominum fallunt et prosunt furibus. ergo
si res sola potest facere et seruare beatum,
hoc primus repetas opus, hoc postremus omittas.
  Si fortunatum species et gratia praestat,
mercemur seruum, qui dictet nomina, laeuum   50
qui fodicet latus et cogat trans pondera dextram
porrigere: 'hic multum in Fabia ualet, ille Velina;
cui libet hic fasces dabit eripietque curule
cui uolet importunus ebur.' 'frater' 'pater' adde;
ut cuique est aetas, ita quemque facetus adopta.   55
  Si bene qui cenat bene uiuit, lucet, eamus
quo ducit gula, piscemur, uenemur, ut olim
Gargilius, qui mane plagas, uenabula, seruos
differtum transire Forum Campumque iubebat,
unus ut e multis populo spectante referret   60
emptum mulus aprum. crudi tumidique lauemur,
quid deceat, quid non, obliti, Caerite cera

digni, remigium uitiosum Ithacensis Vlixei,
cui potior patria fuit interdicta uoluptas.
    Si, Mimnermus uti censet, sine amore iocisque   65
nil est iucundum, uiuas in amore iocisque.
    Viue, uale. siquid nouisti rectius istis,
candidus imperti; si nil, his utere mecum.

VII

Quinque dies tibi pollicitus me rure futurum
Sextilem totum mendax desideror. atqui
si me uiuere uis sanum recteque ualentem,
quam mihi das aegro, dabis aegrotare timenti,
Maecenas, ueniam, dum ficus prima calorque   5
dissignatorem decorat lictoribus atris,
dum pueris omnis pater et matercula pallet
officiosaque sedulitas et opella forensis
adducit febres et testamenta resignat.
quodsi bruma niues Albanis illinet agris,   10
ad mare descendet uates tuus et sibi parcet
contractusque leget: te, dulcis amice, reuiset
cum Zephyris, si concedes, et hirundine prima.
    Non quo more piris uesci Calaber iubet hospes
tu me fecisti locupletem: 'uescere sodes.'   15
'iam satis est.' 'at tu, quantum uis, tolle.' 'benigne.'
'non inuisa feres pueris munuscula paruis.'
'tam teneor dono, quam si dimittar onustus.'
'ut libet: haec porcis hodie comedenda relinques.'
prodigus et stultus donat quae spernit et odit: 20
haec seges ingratos tulit et feret omnibus annis.
uir bonus et sapiens dignis ait esse paratus,
nec tamen ignorat, quid distent aera lupinis:
dignum praestabo me etiam pro laude merentis.
quodsi me noles usquam discedere, reddes   25
forte latus, nigros angusta fronte capillos,

reddes dulce loqui, reddes ridere decorum et
inter uina fugam Cinarae maerere proteruae.
  Forte per angustam tenuis uulpecula rimam
repserat in cumeram frumenti, pastaque rursus   30
ire foras pleno tendebat corpore frustra.
cui mustela procul 'si uis' ait 'effugere istinc,
macra cauum repetes artum, quem macra subisti.'
hac ego si compellor imagine, cuncta resigno:
nec somnum plebis laudo satur altilium nec   35
otia diuitiis Arabum liberrima muto.
saepe uerecundum laudasti, rexque paterque
audisti coram, nec uerbo parcius absens:
inspice, si possum donata reponere laetus.
  Haud male Telemachus, proles sapientis Vlixei: 40
'non est aptus equis Ithace locus, ut neque planis
porrectus spatiis nec multae prodigus herbae:
Atride, magis apta tibi tua dona relinquam.'
paruum parua decent: mihi iam non regia Roma,
sed uacuum Tibur placet aut imbelle Tarentum.   45
  Strenuus et fortis causisque Philippus agendis
clarus ab officiis octauam circiter horam
dum redit atque Foro nimium distare Carinas
iam grandis natu queritur, conspexit, ut aiunt,
adrasum quendam uacua tonsoris in umbra   50
cultello proprios purgantem leniter ungues.
'Demetri' – puer hic non laeue iussa Philippi
accipiebat – 'abi, quaere et refer, unde domo, quis,
cuius fortunae, quo sit patre quoque patrono.'
it, redit et narrat, Volteium nomine Menam,   55
praeconem, tenui censu, sine crimine, notum
et properare loco et cessare et quaerere et uti,
gaudentem paruisque sodalibus et lare certo
et ludis et post decisa negotia Campo.
'scitari libet ex ipso quodcumque refers: dic   60
ad cenam ueniat.' non sane credere Mena,

mirari secum tacitus. quid multa? 'benigne'
respondet. 'neget ille mihi?' 'negat improbus et te
neglegit aut horret.' Volteium mane Philippus
uilia uendentem tunicato scruta popello   65
occupat et saluere iubet prior; ille Philippo
excusare laborem et mercennaria uincla,
quod non mane domum uenisset, denique quod non
prouidisset eum. 'sic ignouisse putato
me tibi, si cenas hodie mecum.' 'ut libet.' 'ergo   70
post nonam uenies; nunc i, rem strenuus auge.'
ut uentum ad cenam est, dicenda tacenda locutus
tandem dormitum dimittitur. hic ubi saepe
occultum uisus decurrere piscis ad hamum,
mane cliens et iam certus conuiua, iubetur   75
rura suburbana indictis comes ire Latinis.
impositus mannis aruum caelumque Sabinum
non cessat laudare. uidet ridetque Philippus,
et sibi dum requiem, dum risus undique quaerit,
dum septem donat sestertia, mutua septem   80
promittit, persuadet uti mercetur agellum.
mercatur. ne te longis ambagibus ultra
quam satis est morer: ex nitido fit rusticus atque
sulcos et uineta crepat mera, praeparat ulmos,
immoritur studiis et amore senescit habendi.   85
uerum ubi oues furto, morbo periere capellae,
spem mentita seges, bos est enectus arando:
offensus damnis media de nocte caballum
arripit iratusque Philippi tendit ad aedes.
quem simul adspexit scabrum intonsumque Philippus,   90
'durus' ait, 'Voltei, nimis attentusque uideris
esse mihi.' 'pol me miserum, patrone, uocares,
si uelles' inquit 'uerum mihi ponere nomen.
quod te per Genium dextramque deosque Penates
obsecro et obtestor, uitae me redde priori.'   95
    Qui semel agnouit, quantum dimissa petitis

praestent, mature redeat repetatque relicta.
metiri se quemque suo modulo ac pede uerum est.

VIII

Celso gaudere et bene rem gerere Albinouano
Musa rogata refer, comiti scribaeque Neronis.
   Si quaeret quid agam, dic multa et pulchra minantem
uiuere nec recte nec suauiter, haud quia grando
contuderit uites oleamue momorderit aestus,   5
nec quia longinquis armentum aegrotet in agris;
sed quia mente minus ualidus quam corpore toto
nil audire uelim, nil discere quod leuet aegrum,
fidis offendar medicis, irascar amicis
cur me funesto properent arcere ueterno;   10
quae nocuere sequar, fugiam quae profore credam,
Romae Tibur amem, uentosus Tibure Romam.
   Post haec, ut ualeat, quo pacto rem gerat et se,
ut placeat iuueni percontare utque cohorti.
si dicet 'recte', primum gaudere, subinde   15
praeceptum auriculis hoc instillare memento:
ut tu fortunam, sic nos te, Celse, feremus.

IX

Septimius, Claudi, nimirum intellegit unus,
quanti me facias; nam cum rogat et prece cogit
scilicet ut tibi se laudare et tradere coner
dignum mente domoque legentis honesta Neronis,
munere cum fungi propioris censet amici,   5
quid possim uidet ac nouit me ualdius ipso.
multa quidem dixi, cur excusatus abirem,
sed timui, mea ne finxisse minora putarer,
dissimulator opis propriae, mihi commodus uni.

sic ego maioris fugiens opprobria culpae   10
frontis ad urbanae descendi praemia. quodsi
depositum laudas ob amici iussa pudorem,
scribe tui gregis hunc et fortem crede bonumque.

X

Vrbis amatorem Fuscum saluere iubemus
ruris amatores. hac in re scilicet una
multum dissimiles, at cetera paene gemelli
fraternis animis, quidquid negat alter, et alter,
adnuimus pariter. uetuli notique columbi   5
tu nidum seruas, ego laudo ruris amoeni
riuos et musco circumlita saxa nemusque.
quid quaeris? uiuo et regno, simul ista reliqui
quae uos ad caelum effertis rumore secundo,
utque sacerdotis fugitiuus liba recuso;   10
pane egeo iam mellitis potiore placentis.
   Viuere naturae si conuenienter oportet
ponendaeque domo quaerenda est area primum:
nouistine locum potiorem rure beato?
est ubi plus tepeant hiemes, ubi gratior aura   15
leniat et rabiem Canis et momenta Leonis,
cum semel accepit solem furibundus acutum?
est ubi diuellat somnos minus inuida cura?
deterius Libycis olet aut nitet herba lapillis?
purior in uicis aqua tendit rumpere plumbum   20
quam quae per pronum trepidat cum murmure riuum?
nempe inter uarias nutritur silua columnas
laudaturque domus longos quae prospicit agros:
naturam expellas furca, tamen usque recurret
et mala perrumpet furtim fastidia uictrix.   25
   Non qui Sidonio contendere callidus ostro
nescit Aquinatem potantia uellera fucum
certius accipiet damnum propiusue medullis

quam qui non poterit uero distinguere falsum.
quem res plus nimio delectauere secundae,   30
mutatae quatient. siquid mirabere, pones
inuitus. fuge magna: licet sub paupere tecto
reges et regum uita praecurrere amicos.

    Ceruus equum pugna melior communibus herbis
pellebat, donec minor in certamine longo   35
implorauit opes hominis frenumque recepit.
sed postquam uictor uiolens discessit ab hoste,
non equitem dorso, non frenum depulit ore.
sic, qui pauperiem ueritus potiore metallis
libertate caret, dominum uehit improbus atque   40
seruiet aeternum, quia paruo nesciet uti.
cui non conueniet sua res, ut calceus olim,
si pede maior erit, subuertet, si minor, uret.

    Laetus sorte tua uiues sapienter, Aristi,
nec me dimittes incastigatum, ubi plura   45
cogere quam satis est ac non cessare uidebor.
imperat aut seruit collecta pecunia cuique,
tortum digna sequi potius quam ducere funem.

    Haec tibi dictabam post fanum putre Vacunae,
excepto quod non simul esses, cetera laetus.   50

XI

Quid tibi uisa Chios, Bullati, notaque Lesbos,
quid concinna Samos, quid Croesi regia Sardes,
Zmyrna quid et Colophon, maiora minorane fama?
cunctane prae Campo et Tiberino flumine sordent?
an uenit in uotum Attalicis ex urbibus una?   5
an Lebedum laudas odio maris atque uiarum?
scis, Lebedus quid sit: Gabiis desertior atque
Fidenis uicus; tamen illic uiuere uellem
oblitusque meorum, obliuiscendus et illis,
Neptunum procul e terra spectare furentem.   10

1. 1. 13

Ac ne forte roges, quo me duce,
                          quo lare tuter:
nullius addictus iurare in verba
                          magistri,
quo me cumque rapit tempestas,
                          deferor hospes.

. 19 :–

et mihi res, non me rebus, ~~conor~~
                          subiungere conor.

1. XI. #12

vivere naturae si convenienter
                          oportet
ponendaeque domo quaerenda est
                          area primum:
noristine locum potiorem ~~vag~~ rure ?
                          beato ?

24

naturam expellas furca, tamen
                          usque recurret
et mala perrumpet ~~furtim~~
                  furtim fastidia victrix

39

sic, qui pauperiem veritus potiore metallis
libertate caret, dominum vehit improbus
                                        atque
serviet aeternum, quia parvo nesciit uti.

Sed neque qui Capua Romam petit, imbre lutoque
adspersus uolet in caupona uiuere; nec qui
frigus collegit, furnos et balnea laudat
ut fortunatam plene praestantia uitam;
nec si te ualidus iactauerit Auster in alto,   15
idcirco nauem trans Aegaeum mare uendas.
incolumi Rhodos et Mytilene pulchra facit quod
paenula solstitio, campestre niualibus auris,
per brumam Tiberis, Sextili mense caminus.
dum licet ac uoltum seruat Fortuna benignum,   20
Romae laudetur Samos et Chios et Rhodos absens.
    Tu quamcumque deus tibi fortunauerit horam
grata sume manu neu dulcia differ in annum,
ut, quocumque loco fueris, uixisse libenter
te dicas; nam si ratio et prudentia curas,   25
non locus effusi late maris arbiter aufert,
caelum, non animum mutant, qui trans mare currunt.
strenua nos exercet inertia; nauibus atque
quadrigis petimus bene uiuere. quod petis, hic est,
est Vlubris, animus si te non deficit aequus.   30

XII

Fructibus Agrippae Siculis quos colligis, Icci,
si recte frueris, non est ut copia maior
ab Ioue donari possit tibi. tolle querelas;
pauper enim non est, cui rerum suppetit usus.
si uentri bene, si lateri est pedibusque tuis, nil   5
diuitiae poterunt regales addere maius.
si forte in medio positorum abstemius herbis
uiuis et urtica, sic uiues protinus, ut te
confestim liquidus Fortunae riuus inauret,
uel quia naturam mutare pecunia nescit,   10
uel quia cuncta putas una uirtute minora.
    Miramur, si Democriti pecus edit agellos

cultaque, dum peregre est animus sine corpore uelox,
cum tu inter scabiem tantam et contagia lucri
nil paruum sapias et adhuc sublimia cures: 15
quae mare compescant causae, quid temperet annum,
stellae sponte sua iussaene uagentur et errent,
quid premat obscurum lunae, quid proferat orbem,
quid uelit et possit rerum concordia discors,
Empedocles an Stertinium deliret acumen.   20

Verum seu pisces seu porrum et caepe trucidas,
utere Pompeio Grospho et, siquid petet, ultro
defer: nil Grosphus nisi uerum orabit et aequum.
uilis amicorum est annona, bonis ubi quid deest.

Ne tamen ignores quo sit Romana loco res: 25
Cantaber Agrippae, Claudi uirtute Neronis
Armenius cecidit; ius imperiumque Prahates
Caesaris accepit genibus minor; aurea fruges
Italiae pleno defudit Copia cornu.

XIII

Vt proficiscentem docui te saepe diuque,
Augusto reddes signata uolumina, Vinni,
si ualidus, si laetus erit, si denique poscet;
ne studio nostri pecces odiumque libellis
sedulus importes opera uehemente minister.   5
si te forte meae grauis uret sarcina chartae,
abicito potius quam quo perferre iuberis
clitellas ferus impingas Asinaeque paternum
cognomen uertas in risum et fabula fias.

Viribus uteris per cliuos flumina lamas.   10
uictor propositi simul ac perueneris illuc,
sic positum seruabis onus, ne forte sub ala
fasciculum portes librorum, ut rusticus agnum,
ut uinosa glomus furtiuae †Pirria† lanae,
ut cum pilleolo soleas conuiua tribulis.   15

neu uulgo narres te sudauisse ferendo
carmina quae possint oculos auresque morari
Caesaris. oratus multa prece nitere porro.
uade, uale, caue ne titubes mandataque frangas.

XIV

Vilice siluarum et mihi me reddentis agelli,
quem tu fastidis, habitatum quinque focis et
quinque bonos solitum Variam dimittere patres,
certemus, spinas animone ego fortius an tu
euellas agro, et melior sit Horatius an rus.   5

Me quamuis Lamiae pietas et cura moratur
fratrem maerentis, rapto de fratre dolentis
insolabiliter, tamen istuc mens animusque
fert et auet spatiis obstantia rumpere claustra.

Rure ego uiuentem, tu dicis in urbe beatum: 10
cui placet alterius, sua nimirum est odio sors.
stultus uterque locum immeritum causatur inique:
in culpa est animus, qui se non effugit umquam.
tu mediastinus tacita prece rura petebas,
nunc urbem et ludos et balnea uilicus optas: 15
me constare mihi scis et discedere tristem,
quandocumque trahunt inuisa negotia Romam.

Non eadem miramur; eo disconuenit inter
meque et te; nam quae deserta et inhospita tesqua
credis, amoena uocat mecum qui sentit, et odit   20
quae tu pulchra putas. fornix tibi et uncta popina
incutiunt urbis desiderium, uideo, et quod
angulus iste feret piper et tus ocius uua
nec uicina subest uinum praebere taberna
quae possit tibi, nec meretrix tibicina, cuius   25
ad strepitum salias terrae grauis; et tamen urges
iampridem non tacta ligonibus arua bouemque
disiunctum curas et strictis frondibus exples;

addit opus pigro riuus, si decidit imber,
multa mole docendus aprico parcere prato.   30
   Nunc age, quid nostrum concentum diuidat audi.
quem tenues decuere togae nitidique capilli,
quem scis immunem Cinarae placuisse rapaci,
quem bibulum liquidi media de luce Falerni,
cena breuis iuuat et prope riuum somnus in herba.   35
nec lusisse pudet, sed non incidere ludum.
non istic obliquo oculo mea commoda quisquam
limat, non odio obscuro morsuque uenenat:
rident uicini glaebas et saxa mouentem.
cum seruis urbana diaria rodere mauis,   40
horum tu in numerum uoto ruis: inuidet usum
lignorum et pecoris tibi calo argutus et horti.
optat ephippia bos piger optat arare caballus:
quam scit uterque, libens, censebo, exerceat artem.

X V

Quae sit hiems Veliae, quod caelum, Vala, Salerni,
quorum hominum regio et qualis uia – nam mihi Baias
Musa superuacuas Antonius, et tamen illis
me facit inuisum, gelida cum perluor unda
per medium frigus. sane murteta relinqui   5
dictaque cessantem neruis elidere morbum
sulpura contemni uicus gemit, inuidus aegris
qui caput et stomachum supponere fontibus audent
Clusinis Gabiosque petunt et frigida rura.
mutandus locus est et deuersoria nota   10
praeteragendus equus. 'quo tendis? non mihi Cumas
est iter aut Baias' laeua stomachosus habena
dicet eques; sed equis frenato est auris in ore – ;
maior utrum populum frumenti copia pascat,
collectosne bibant imbres puteosne perennes   15
iugis aquae – nam uina nihil moror illius orae.

rure meo possum quiduis perferre patique:
ad mare cum ueni, generosum et lene requiro,
quod curas abigat, quod cum spe diuite manet
in uenas animumque meum, quod uerba ministret,   20
quod me Lucanae iuuenem commendet amicae – ;
tractus uter pluris lepores, uter educet apros;
utra magis pisces et echinos aequora celent,
pinguis ut inde domum possim Phaeaxque reuerti,
scribere te nobis, tibi nos accredere par est.   25
   Maenius, ut rebus maternis atque paternis
fortiter absumptis urbanus coepit haberi,
scurra uagus, non qui certum praesepe teneret,
impransus non qui ciuem dinosceret hoste,
quaelibet in quemuis opprobria fingere saeuus,   30
pernicies et tempestas barathrumque macelli,
quidquid quaesierat uentri donabat auaro.
hic ubi nequitiae fautoribus et timidis nil
aut paulum abstulerat, patinas cenabat omasi
uilis et agninae, tribus ursis quod satis esset,   35
scilicet ut uentres lamna candente nepotum
diceret urendos, correctus Bestius. idem,
quidquid erat nactus praedae maioris, ubi omne
uerterat in fumum et cinerem, 'non hercule miror'
aiebat 'siqui comedunt bona, cum sit obeso   40
nil melius turdo, nil uolua pulchrius ampla.'
nimirum hic ego sum; nam tuta et paruula laudo,
cum res deficiunt, satis inter uilia fortis;
uerum ubi quid melius contingit et unctius, idem
uos sapere et solos aio bene uiuere, quorum   45
conspicitur nitidis fundata pecunia uillis.

XVI

Ne perconteris, fundus meus, optime Quincti,
aruo pascat erum an bacis opulentet oliuae,

pomisne an pratis an amicta uitibus ulmo,
scribetur tibi forma loquaciter et situs agri.

Continui montes, ni dissocientur opaca 5
ualle, sed ut ueniens dextrum latus adspiciat Sol,
laeuum discedens curru fugiente uaporet.
temperiem laudes. quid si rubicunda benigni
corna uepres et pruna ferant, si quercus et ilex
multa fruge pecus, multa dominum iuuet umbra? 10
dicas adductum propius frondere Tarentum.
fons etiam riuo dare nomen idoneus, ut nec
frigidior Thracam nec purior ambiat Hebrus,
infirmo capiti fluit utilis, utilis aluo.
hae latebrae dulces et, iam si credis, amoenae 15
incolumem tibi me praestant Septembribus horis.

Tu recte uiuis, si curas esse quod audis.
iactamus iam pridem omnis te Roma beatum;
sed uereor ne cui de te plus quam tibi credas
neue putes alium sapiente bonoque beatum 20
neu, si te populus sanum recteque ualentem
dictitet, occultam febrem sub tempus edendi
dissimules, donec manibus tremor incidat unctis.
stultorum incurata pudor malus ulcera celat.

Siquis bella tibi terra pugnata marique 25
dicat et his uerbis uacuas permulceat aures:
'tene magis saluum populus uelit an populum tu,
seruet in ambiguo qui consulit et tibi et urbi
Iuppiter', Augusti laudes agnoscere possis:
cum pateris sapiens emendatusque uocari, 30
respondesne tuo, dic sodes, nomine? nempe
uir bonus et prudens dici delector ego ac tu.
qui dedit hoc hodie, cras, si uolet, auferet, ut, si
detulerit fasces indigno, detrahet idem.
'pone, meum est' inquit: pono tristisque recedo. 35
idem si clamet furem, neget esse pudicum,
contendat laqueo collum pressisse paternum,
mordear opprobriis falsis mutemque colores?

falsus honor iuuat et mendax infamia terret
quem nisi mendosum et medicandum? 40
                              Vir bonus est quis?
'qui consulta patrum, qui leges iuraque seruat,
quo multae magnaeque secantur iudice lites,
quo res sponsore et quo causae teste tenentur.'
sed uidet hunc omnis domus et uicinia tota
introrsum turpem, speciosum pelle decora. 45
'nec furtum feci nec fugi' si mihi dicat
seruus, 'habes pretium, loris non ureris' aio.
'non hominem occidi.' 'non pasces in cruce coruos.'
'sum bonus et frugi.' renuit negitatque Sabellus.
cautus enim metuit foueam lupus accipiterque 50
suspectos laqueos et opertum miluus hamum:
oderunt peccare boni uirtutis amore.
tu nihil admittes in te formidine poenae:
sit spes fallendi, miscebis sacra profanis.
nam de mille fabae modiis cum surripis unum, 55
damnum est, non facinus, mihi pacto lenius isto.
uir bonus, omne forum quem spectat et omne tribunal,
quandocumque deos uel porco uel boue placat,
'Iane pater' clare, clare cum dixit 'Apollo',
labra mouet metuens audiri: 'pulchra Lauerna, 60
da mihi fallere, da iusto sanctoque uideri,
noctem peccatis et fraudibus obice nubem.'
   Qui melior seruo, qui liberior sit auarus,
in triuiis fixum cum se demittit ob assem,
non uideo. nam qui cupiet, metuet quoque; porro 65
qui metuens uiuet, liber mihi non erit umquam.
perdidit arma, locum uirtutis deseruit, qui
semper in augenda festinat et obruitur re.
uendere cum possis captiuum, occidere noli:
seruiet utiliter; sine pascat durus aretque, 70
nauiget ac mediis hiemet mercator in undis,
annonae prosit, portet frumenta penusque.
   Vir bonus et sapiens audebit dicere 'Pentheu,

rector Thebarum, quid me perferre patique
indignum coges?' 'adimam bona.' 'nempe pecus, rem,   75
lectos, argentum: tollas licet.' 'in manicis et
compedibus saeuo te sub custode tenebo.'
'ipse deus, simulatque uolam, me soluet.' opinor,
hoc sentit 'moriar'. mors ultima linea rerum est.

XVII

Quamuis, Scaeua, satis per te tibi consulis et scis
quo tandem pacto deceat maioribus uti,
disce, docendus adhuc quae censet amiculus, ut si
caecus iter monstrare uelit; tamen adspice, siquid
et nos quod cures proprium fecisse loquamur.   5
    Si te grata quies et primam somnus in horam
delectat, si te puluis strepitusque rotarum,
si laedit caupona, Ferentinum ire iubebo;
nam neque diuitibus contingunt gaudia solis
nec uixit male, qui natus moriensque fefellit.   10
si prodesse tuis pauloque benignius ipsum
te tractare uoles, accedes siccus ad unctum.
'si pranderet holus patienter, regibus uti
nollet Aristippus.' 'si sciret regibus uti,
fastidiret holus, qui me notat.' utrius horum   15
uerba probes et facta, doce, uel iunior audi,
cur sit Aristippi potior sententia. namque
mordacem Cynicum sic eludebat, ut aiunt:
'scurror ego ipse mihi, populo tu: rectius hoc et
splendidius multo est. equus ut me portet, alat rex,   20
officium facio: tu poscis uilia rerum,
dante minor, quamuis fers te nullius egentem.'
omnis Aristippum decuit color et status et res,
temptantem maiora, fere praesentibus aequum.
contra, quem duplici panno patientia uelat,   25

mirabor, uitae uia si conuersa decebit.
alter purpureum non exspectabit amictum,
quidlibet indutus celeberrima per loca uadet
personamque feret non inconcinnus utramque;
alter Mileti textam cane peius et angui   30
uitabit chlanidem, morietur frigore, si non
rettuleris pannum. refer et sine uiuat ineptus.

   Res gerere et captos ostendere ciuibus hostes
attingit solium Iouis et caelestia temptat:
principibus placuisse uiris non ultima laus est.   35
non cuiuis homini contingit adire Corinthum.
sedit qui timuit, ne non succederet. esto.
quid? qui peruenit, fecitne uiriliter? atqui
hic est aut nusquam, quod quaerimus. hic onus horret
ut paruis animis et paruo corpore maius,   40
hic subit et perfert. aut uirtus nomen inane est,
aut decus et pretium recte petit experiens uir.

   Coram rege sua de paupertate tacentes
plus poscente ferent. distat, sumasne pudenter
an rapias; atqui rerum caput hoc erat, hic fons.   45
'indotata mihi soror est, paupercula mater
et fundus nec uendibilis nec pascere firmus'
qui dicit, clamat: 'uictum date.' succinit alter:
'et mihi.' diuiduo findetur munere quadra.
sed tacitus pasci si posset coruus, haberet   50
plus dapis et rixae multo minus inuidiaeque.

   Brundisium comes aut Surrentum ductus amoenum
qui queritur salebras et acerbum frigus et imbres
aut cistam effractam et subducta uiatica plorat,
nota refert meretricis acumina, saepe catellam,   55
saepe periscelidem raptam sibi flentis, uti mox
nulla fides damnis uerisque doloribus adsit.
nec semel irrisus triuiis attollere curat
fracto crure planum. licet illi plurima manet
lacrima, per sanctum iuratus dicat Osirim   60

'credite, non ludo; crudeles, tollite claudum',
'quaere peregrinum' uicinia rauca reclamat.

XVIII

Si bene te noui, metues, liberrime Lolli,
scurrantis speciem praebere, professus amicum.
ut matrona meretrici dispar erit atque
discolor, infido scurrae distabit amicus.
est huic diuersum uitio uitium prope maius,   5
asperitas agrestis et inconcinna grauisque,
quae se commendat tonsa cute, dentibus atris,
dum uolt libertas dici mera ueraque uirtus.
uirtus est medium uitiorum et utrimque reductum.
alter in obsequium plus aequo pronus et imi   10
derisor lecti sic nutum diuitis horret,
sic iterat uoces et uerba cadentia tollit,
ut puerum saeuo credas dictata magistro
reddere uel partes mimum tractare secundas;
alter rixatur de lana saepe caprina et   15
propugnat nugis armatus: 'scilicet ut non
sit mihi prima fides?' et 'uere quod placet ut non
acriter elatrem? pretium aetas altera sordet.'
ambigitur quid enim? Castor sciat an Dolichus plus;
Brundisium Minuci melius uia ducat an Appi.   20
    Quem damnosa uenus, quem praeceps alea nudat,
gloria quem supra uires et uestit et unguit,
quem tenet argenti sitis importuna famesque,
quem paupertatis pudor et fuga, diues amicus,
saepe decem uitiis instructior, odit et horret,   25
aut, si non odit, regit ac ueluti pia mater
plus quam se sapere et uirtutibus esse priorem
uolt et ait prope uera: 'meae – contendere noli –
stultitiam patiuntur opes, tibi paruula res est:

arta decet sanum comitem toga: desine mecum   30
certare.' Eutrapelus cuicumque nocere uolebat
uestimenta dabat pretiosa: beatus enim iam
cum pulchris tunicis sumet noua consilia et spes,
dormiet in lucem, scorto postponet honestum
officium, nummos alienos pascet, ad imum   35
Thraex erit aut holitoris aget mercede caballum.
   Arcanum neque tu scrutaberis illius umquam,
commissumque teges et uino tortus et ira.
   Nec tua laudabis studia aut aliena reprendes,
nec, cum uenari uolet ille, poemata panges.   40
gratia sic fratrum geminorum Amphionis atque
Zethi dissiluit, donec suspecta seuero
conticuit lyra. fraternis cessisse putatur
moribus Amphion: tu cede potentis amici
lenibus imperiis, quotiensque educet in agros   45
Aeoliis onerata plagis iumenta canesque,
surge et inhumanae senium depone Camenae,
cenes ut pariter pulmenta laboribus empta:
Romanis sollemne uiris opus, utile famae
uitaeque et membris, praesertim cum ualeas et   50
uel cursu superare canem uel uiribus aprum
possis. adde, uirilia quod speciosius arma
non est qui tractet: scis, quo clamore coronae
proelia sustineas campestria. denique saeuam
militiam puer et Cantabrica bella tulisti   55
sub duce, qui templis Parthorum signa refigit
nunc et, siquid abest, Italis adiudicat armis.
ac ne te retrahas et inexcusabilis absis:
quamuis nil extra numerum fecisse modumque
curas, interdum nugaris rure paterno.   60
partitur lintres exercitus, Actia pugna
te duce per pueros hostili more refertur;
aduersarius est frater, lacus Hadria, donec

alterutrum uelox Victoria fronde coronet.
consentire suis studiis qui crediderit te,   65
fautor utroque tuum laudabit pollice ludum.

   Protinus ut moneam, siquid monitoris eges tu,
quid de quoque uiro et cui dicas, saepe uideto.
percontatorem fugito; nam garrulus idem est
nec retinent patulae commissa fideliter aures   70
et semel emissum uolat irreuocabile uerbum.

   Non ancilla tuum iecur ulceret ulla puerue
intra marmoreum uenerandi limen amici,
ne dominus pueri pulchri caraeue puellae
munere te paruo beet aut incommodus angat.   75

   Qualem commendes, etiam atque etiam aspice, ne mox
incutiant aliena tibi peccata pudorem.
fallimur et quondam non dignum tradimus; ergo
quem sua culpa premet, deceptus omitte tueri,
ut penitus notum, si temptent crimina, serues   80
tuterisque tuo fidentem praesidio: qui
dente Theonino cum circumroditur, ecquid
ad te post paulo uentura pericula sentis?
nam tua res agitur, paries cum proximus ardet,
et neglecta solent incendia sumere uires.   85

   Dulcis inexpertis cultura potentis amici:
expertus metuet. tu, dum tua nauis in alto est,
hoc age, ne mutata retrorsum te ferat aura.
oderunt hilarem tristes tristemque iocosi,
sedatum celeres, agilem nauumque remissi,   90
potores [bibuli media de nocte Falerni
oderunt] porrecta negantem pocula, quamuis
nocturnos iures te formidare tepores.
deme supercilio nubem: plerumque modestus
occupat obscuri speciem, taciturnus acerbi.   95

   Inter cuncta leges et percontabere doctos,
qua ratione queas traducere leniter aeuum,

num te semper inops agitet uexetque cupido,
num pauor et rerum mediocriter utilium spes,
uirtutem doctrina paret naturane donet,   100
quid minuat curas, quid te tibi reddat amicum,
quid pure tranquillet, honos an dulce lucellum
an secretum iter et fallentis semita uitae.

Me quotiens reficit gelidus Digentia riuus,
quem Mandela bibit, rugosus frigore pagus,   105
quid sentire putas, quid credis, amice, precari?
'sit mihi quod nunc est, etiam minus, et mihi uiuam
quod superest aeui, siquid superesse uolunt di;
sit bona librorum et prouisae frugis in annum
copia neu fluitem dubiae spe pendulus horae.'   110
sed satis est orare Iouem quae ponit et aufert:
det uitam, det opes: aequum mi animum ipse parabo.

XIX

Prisco si credis, Maecenas docte, Cratino,
nulla placere diu nec uiuere carmina possunt,
quae scribuntur aquae potoribus. ut male sanos
adscripsit Liber Satyris Faunisque poetas,
uina fere dulces oluerunt mane Camenae.   5
laudibus arguitur uini uinosus Homerus;
Ennius ipse pater numquam nisi potus ad arma
prosiluit dicenda. 'Forum putealque Libonis
mandabo siccis, adimam cantare seueris';
hoc simul edixi, non cessauere poetae   10
nocturno certare mero, putere diurno.
quid? siquis uoltu toruo ferus et pede nudo
exiguaeque togae simulet textore Catonem,
uirtutemne repraesentet moresque Catonis?
rupit Iarbitam Timagenis aemula lingua,   15

dum studet urbanus tenditque disertus haberi.
decipit exemplar uitiis imitabile: quodsi
pallerem casu, biberent exsangue cuminum.
o imitatores, seruum pecus, ut mihi saepe
bilem, saepe iocum uestri mouere tumultus!   20
   Libera per uacuum posui uestigia princeps,
non aliena meo pressi pede. qui sibi fidet,
dux reget examen. Parios ego primus iambos
ostendi Latio, numeros animosque secutus
Archilochi, non res et agentia uerba Lycamben.   25
ac ne me foliis ideo breuioribus ornes,
quod timui mutare modos et carminis artem:
temperat Archilochi musam pede mascula Sappho,
temperat Alcaeus, sed rebus et ordine dispar,
nec socerum quaerit, quem uersibus oblinat atris,   30
nec sponsae laqueum famoso carmine nectit.
hunc ego, non alio dictum prius ore, Latinus
uulgaui fidicen. iuuat immemorata ferentem
ingenuis oculisque legi manibusque teneri.
   Scire uelis, mea cur ingratus opuscula lector   35
laudet ametque domi, premat extra limen iniquus:
non ego uentosae plebis suffragia uenor
impensis cenarum et tritae munere uestis;
non ego, nobilium scriptorum auditor et ultor,
grammaticas ambire tribus et pulpita dignor.   40
hinc illae lacrimae. 'spissis indigna theatris
scripta pudet recitare et nugis addere pondus'
si dixi, 'rides' ait 'et Iouis auribus ista
seruas; fidis enim manare poetica mella
te solum, tibi pulcher.' ad haec ego naribus uti   45
formido et, luctantis acuto ne secer ungui,
'displicet iste locus' clamo et diludia posco.
ludus enim genuit trepidum certamen et iram,
ira truces inimicitias et funebre bellum.

XX

Vortumnum Ianumque, liber, spectare uideris,
scilicet ut prostes Sosiorum pumice mundus;
odisti claues et grata sigilla pudico,
paucis ostendi gemis et communia laudas,
non ita nutritus: fuge quo descendere gestis.   5
non erit emisso reditus tibi. 'quid miser egi?
quid uolui?' dices, ubi quid te laeserit; et scis
in breue te cogi, cum plenus languet amator.

    Quodsi non odio peccantis desipit augur,
carus eris Romae, donec te deserat aetas: 10
contrectatus ubi manibus sordescere uulgi
coeperis, aut tineas pasces taciturnus inertes
aut fugies Vticam aut uinctus mitteris Ilerdam.
ridebit monitor non exauditus, ut ille
qui male parentem in rupis protrusit asellum   15
iratus; quis enim inuitum seruare laboret?
hoc quoque te manet, ut pueros elementa docentem
occupet extremis in uicis balba senectus.

    Cum tibi sol tepidus plures admouerit aures,
me libertino natum patre et in tenui re   20
maiores pennas nido extendisse loqueris,
ut, quantum generi demas, uirtutibus addas;
me primis Vrbis belli placuisse domique,
corporis exigui, praecanum, solibus aptum,
irasci celerem, tamen ut placabilis essem.   25
forte meum siquis te percontabitur aeuum,
me quater undenos sciat impleuisse Decembres,
collegam Lepidum quo dixit Lollius anno.

ed some lyric slight (*nugis* 19.42; *C.* 1.32.1 *lusimus*) because its
s are transient (*C.* 1.6.17 *conuiuia; proelia uirginum*). In giving up
ful pleasure H. also puts away the poetry celebrating it; cf. *Ep.*
–7 [*anni*] *eripuere iocos, Venerem, conuiuia, ludum;* | *tendunt extorquere*
a; 141–4 *sapere est abiectis utile nugis* | *et tempestiuum pueris concedere*
ac non uerba sequi fidibus modulanda Latinis, | *sed uerae numerosque*
e ediscere uitae.

o = *depono* (*OLD* 10); poets prefer the crisper uncompounded
Bo 387–9).

id: supply *sit*, indirect qu. *uerum* 'right' (*OLD* 9); *decens*
riate', a concept central to H.'s code of behaviour (cf. 6.62;
he neuter sing. of adjectives (usually of the second declension)
only turned into a noun to provide philosophical technical
ut the only present part. so used before H. is *consequens* (K–S
may be that he devised the present usage to avoid the already
decorum, which had a pronounced Stoic colour.

mplies moral reflection (4.5), *rogo* advice to be sought, the
y theme (18.96). *omnis . . . sum* ≈ *S.* 1.9.2 *totus in illis* of absorb-
hts.

o . . . compono: metaphors for poetic composition (3.24; *Ep.*
mina compono) elegantly revert to more basic senses, which
new metaphor, 'psychic stewardship'; for the language of
conomy applied to morals cf. Sen. *Ep.* 94.53 *possimus felici-*
promere. H. admired the prudent ant (*S.* 1.1.32–8) and the
ouse (*S.* 2.6.79–83). For *compono* 'organize' cf. *C.* 3.29.32–3
emento | *componere aequus.*

and by', cf. Sen. *Ep.* 108.35 *captemus . . . profutura praecepta*
in rem transferantur.

final subjunc. in a relative clause (G–L §630, *NLS* §147).
icipate the presupposition that the search for a moral code
o an established system. The new theme of self-reliance is
H. depends on himself.

roges 'to prevent your asking . . .' (*OLD* 13, G–L §545
. of *tuter.*

uce, quo lare: instrumental abl. *dux* has military over-
epare for the oath of 14; *lar* suggests the household in
es of a sect met (*C.* 1.29.14 *Socraticam . . . domum; OLD*

COMMENTARY

Epistle I

1–19 Maecenas is supposed to have invited H. to resume lyric poetry
(1–3). In declining (4–9), H. explains what now occupies him (10–
19). The imaginary request is cast in a metaphor (Introduction pp.
28–30) that hints at some leading themes. A gladiator, if not already a
slave or condemned criminal, virtually enslaved himself to the trainer
by oath (*S.* 2.7.58–9 *uri uirgis ferroque necari* | *auctoratus;* and cf. 14).
Success might lead to retirement and even manumission; the theme of
release from obligation is to be developed in VII. So the metaphor
suggests re-enslavement and the loss of independence, at the same time
introducing the major theme of training and learning. Müller noted
that 1–15 consist of five thoughts, each three lines long.

1 Prima ... summa: an encomiastic formula (Gow on Theocr.
17.1f.), though the first book of *Sermones, Epodes* and *Odes* had all borne
Maecenas' name. The respectful opening admits a gratitude unfail-
ingly acknowledged; its warmth is recalled at the end. With *prima*
understand *Camena* ἀπὸ κοινοῦ.

dicte 'sung of' (*OLD* 7b; N–H on *C.* 1.21.1). The polyptoton (see
81n.) of *dicte . . . dicende* has sacral overtones, cf. *CS* 2–3 *o colendi* | *semper*
et culti.

mihi: the agent dat. of personal pronouns is common with the past
part. pass. and the gerundive (with which *mihi* should here be taken
ἀπὸ κοινοῦ); with the finite verb or of noun agents it is poetic syntax
(G–L §§354 N1, 355).

Camena: perhaps originally a water-spirit, but early identified with
the Greek Muse.

2 spectatum satis 'sufficiently proven' (*OLD spectatus*) is often
found in Terence (McGlynn s.v. *specto* III). *satis* strikes a keynote (*Epod.*
1.31–2 *satis superque me benignitas tua* | *ditauit, C.* 2.18.14 *satis beatus* (of
himself), 3.1.25 *desiderantem quod satis est;* 3.16.44 (quoted at 89n.)).

rude: a wooden baton was presented to gladiators on their retirement (hence *rudiarius*); the metaphor became popular among later
poets (Ovid, *Tr.* 4.8.24 (he had also just used the image of the aged
racehorse, 19–20), Martial, Juvenal; Otto §1557).

2–3 quaeris ... includere: poetic syntax (L. on *S.* 1.9.8); the infin., metrically handy and syntactically crisp, is attached to verbs, past participles (14n.), and adjectives (2.64n.) which do not usually have it in prose. Grammarians call this infin. complementary, epexegetic or prolative (*NLS* §§22–3, 26; Wickham's edn 3 of the *Odes* (Oxford 1896) 406–9).

3 includere ... ludo: assonance emphasizes *ludo*, echoed by *ludicra* 10. The invitation is unintentionally the reverse of kind, for the compassionate redeemed gladiators (Sen. *Clem.* 2.6.2 *ludo eximet*).

4 non ... non: anaphora drives home the reply, which is a variant of the device nowadays called *recusatio*, in that the poet declines to tackle a proposed theme or genre. The theme of change of attitude (*OLD mens* 8) is elsewhere linked by H. to that of behaviour appropriate to a particular age, cf. 7.25–8, 14.32–6 and *C.* 3.15, 4.13.

4–6 The example of Veianius, a contemporary gladiator, now retired, prolongs the metaphor and introduces the theme of retreat to the countryside (X; XIV); it also hints at the dangers of trying to maintain pre-eminence.

4–5 armis ... fixis: tools of a trade were dedicated on retirement to an appropriate god; cf. *C.* 3.26.3–6 *nunc arma defunctumque bello | barbiton hic paries habebit, | laevum marinae qui Veneris latus | custodit*.

5 latet: cf. 16.15 *latebrae*, used of H.'s farm. *abditus agro* < Virg. *G.* 3.95–6 *hunc* [an aged stallion] ... *abde domo*, also referring to retirement.

6 extrema ... harena 'at the end of the match' (so Torrentius, cf. *OLD harena* 3b); but pseudo-Acro took it to mean 'at the edge of the sand', i.e. near the platform on which the patron of the match sat.

exoret: pseudo-Acro rightly assumed that the gladiator begs for discharge. This alone gives point to *totiens*: the fans are loath to part with a favourite, who must then repeatedly appeal for permission to retire. Cicero supports such an interpretation when he asks how Antonius, so good a gladiator, was retired so soon (*Phil.* 2.74). Many believe, however, that the gladiator seeks *missio* 'a reprieve'. If the combatants were so wounded or wearied that they could not fight on, reprieve had to be requested; such a gladiator was styled *stans missus* or, if defeated, *missus*. Inscriptions record both victories and numerous reprieves of both sorts (*RE Suppl.* III 782). Müller argued for an interpretation still less suited to the context: the successful gladiator begs the audience for applause, money etc. At any

rate, like the gladiator, the poet too needs to cou[2.2.103 *supplex populi suffragia capto*).

7 The first allusion in the collection to a philos[common consent the father of all ethical though[Like Socrates (Plat. *Ap.* 31D2–4), H. heeds a[with cleansed ears, i.e. attentively (a colloquial[*perpurgatis ... auribus* and *The academic papers*[Greek comedy, Hellenistic literature, Greek religion[1990) 169 on the phrase καθαροῖς οὔασιν). T[of receptivity to advice (40, 48; contrast 2.53[

personet 'to make ring' (*OLD* 2); the pot[but not invariable in sentences of this kind[K–S II 303–5; B. on *Ep.* 2.2.182).

8 sanus '*if you* are reasonable' (*OLD* 3; L.[idea should be understood.

equum: Ibycus, a sixth-century Greek[himself to a superannuated racehorse dri[the boy-rider, Love (*PMG* 287); his poem[(*Parm.* 137A) and exploited by Ennius (A[Catull. 4.26). H. recalls it at *C.* 4.1.1 (for[8). Again there is a latent sense of cor[habit. Age is emphasized (*senescentem*) [emplified the contrast between brilliar[(Smith on Tibull. 1.4.31–2). The p[(*mature*). Failure provokes mockery (*r*[young men on the veteran *meretrix* L[ment effected by *ne* see Introduction[

9 peccet 'stumble' may be the se[imaginative, if H. believed the verb[animal' (L. R. Palmer, *The Latin la*[*ilia ducat* 'wheeze' (*OLD duco* 22b).

10–12 In obedience to this voic[introduces his new interests.

10 itaque admits the force of th[to gladiator and horse; logical ac[tional poems (29 and 19.26nn.; [second word is poetic word ord[130).

ludicra 'trifles' colours the[

pon[verbs [

11 q['appro[7.44). [is comr[terms. [I 228); [availabl[

curo[receptiv[ing thou[

12 con[2.2.91 *ca*[suggest a[domestic [*tatem domo*[country m[*quod adest r*[

mox 'b[... *quae mo*[

possim[

13–15 an[must lead [announced;[

13 ne ...[R3); *me* is ob[

quo ... o[tones that p[which devot[*domus* 6b).

14 nullius ... magistri: emphatic enclosing word order; the negative is prominent. (The motto of the Royal Society of London, *nullius in uerba*, derives from this line.) *addictus* 'bound' keeps up the metaphor of the gladiator, who enslaved himself by oath to his *magister*; cf. Petr. 117.5 *legitimi gladiatores domino corpora animasque religiosissime addicimus.* For the infin. *iurare* see 2–3n.

in uerba: cf. *Epod.* 15.4 *in uerba iurabas mea* (*OLD in* 18b). Soldiers swore oaths of loyalty (Livy 28.29.12) and, among philosophical sects, the Epicureans appear to have exacted an oath (Philodemus, *Lib.* 45.9–11). Hence Seneca's disdain, *Ep.* 12.11 *in uerba iurant, nec quid dicatur aestimant, sed a quo*, and Quintilian's disparagement, *IO* 12.2.6 *uelut sacramento rogati uel etiam superstitione constricti nefas ducunt a suscepta semel persuasione discedere*; cf. his earlier assertion of independence, 3.1.22 *neque enim me cuiusquam sectae uelut quadam superstitione imbutus addixi.*

15 quo ... cumque: a common instance of tmesis, the separation for metrical convenience of (here) the universal relative from its suffix (Winbolt §181).

tempestas 'the weather' (*OLD* 2) may change travel plans, but the *hospes* proceeds when he can; the metaphor was used of philosophical choice by Cicero, *Acad.* 2.8 *ad quamcumque sunt disciplinam quasi tempestate delati* (a book he tried to suppress, so perhaps not known to H.) and *Fam.* 7.30.2 *philosophiae portus*, but here it suggests inconstancy (16–19), the themes of VIII and XV.

hospes may hint at the saying of Aristippus that he was everywhere a guest: ξένος πανταχοῦ εἰμί (Xen. *Mem.* 2.2.13).

16 nunc ... 18 nunc: a poetic alternative for *alias ... alias* or *modo ... modo* (K–S II 70).

agilis 'active' in public life (*OLD* 3). Since one can only become what one is not already, *fio* suggests that H. must give up his preferred *otium*. The Stoics, hinted at in 16–17, approved of participation in civic life (L–S I 423 §66B; I 433 §67W); XVI takes up the theme.

ciuilibus undis: metaphorical for the hectic life of the citizen, cf. *Ep.* 2.2.84–5 *rerum | fluctibus in mediis et tempestatibus urbis.*

17 uirtutis uerae: 'the alliterative phrase was a cliché of Roman public moralising': Jocelyn on Enn. *scen.* 254, a passage from the *Phoenix* also in H.'s mind at 2.67–8 (cf. 18.8; *C.* 3.5.29–30). Here as at 17.41 *uirtus* is less philosophical than Roman in sense, and refers to a man's physical power in public life.

rigidus 'unwavering' goes ἀπὸ κοινοῦ with *custos*, which has a Stoic flavour (Sen. *Dial*. 12.12.4). *uirtus* is seen as a monarch attended by bodyguards (at 16.67 in charge of an army; cf. 6.37 *regina Pecunia*); at *Ep*. 2.1.229–31 she is a goddess with attendants (*aeditui*).

18–19 An unexpected alternative, for reference to the arch-rivals of Stoicism, the Epicureans, might have been made (4.15–16). Aristippus of Cyrene, Epicurus' forerunner in making pleasure the goal of life (J. C. B. Gosling and C. C. W. Taylor, *The Greeks on pleasure* (Oxford 1982) 40–3), is not here cited as a hedonist, but for his attitude to circumstances (*res*), a pre-echo of XVII.

18   furtim 'unconsciously' (*OLD* 2). The prefix *re-* hints that this is the more congenial alternative; cf. Cic. *Acad*. 2.139 *uideo quam suauiter uoluptas sensibus nostris blandiatur: labor eo ut adsentiar Epicuro aut Aristippo*, a passage that demonstrates how far H. himself is from hedonism here.

19   res 'circumstances' (*OLD* 17b).

subiungere 'place under control'; the yoking metaphor contrasts with 8–9; cf. 10.42–3. Aristippus controlled circumstances by willingly using whatever came to hand, not by insisting on one and only one course of action as right (an attitude H. adopts in VI and XV).

conor suggests that the process is as yet incomplete, cf. 18.112n.

20–7 H. has hardly started his personal reformation and is eager to proceed. Three illustrations, 20–2 (as at 2.52–3, 11.11–16 and 13.13–15), emphasize impatience with his slow progress. Still, he has laid some secure foundations of principle. The main sentence, four lines long, 23–6, preserves the theme of time's slow passage, with the hint of dependence: the cheated lover, the labourer and the under-aged boy are all subject to others.

20   nox longa: supply *uidetur* ἀπὸ κοινοῦ from 21.

21   lenta 'protracted', a sense commoner in poetry than in prose (*OLD* 5); the reading, found in inferior MSS, is preferred to *longa* of the main tradition, a rhetorically pointless repetition from 20 (16.14 and 17.40 show how H. repeats epithets for emphasis).

opus debentibus: e.g. hired farm workers, cf. *S*. 2.2.115 *mercede colonum*, 2.6.11 *mercennarius*.

22   custodia 'oversight' generally; not legal *tutela*, which only a man could exercise (*OCD* s.v. Guardianship; *custodia* has a different sense 'safekeeping' in legal contexts, *RE* IV 1896–7). The implication is that the father is dead and so the boy is legally independent (*sui iuris*) though restricted in some respects.

23   tarda ... ingrata: predicative. *mihi* is dat. of disadvantage (*NLS* §64). H. is still to some extent caught up in the affairs and duties of life in Rome.

23–4   spem consiliumque: *spes* looks to the heart, *consilium* to the mind, cf. 18.33, Ter. *Eun.* 1025, Cic. *Inu.* 2.45; the intention is stated at 11–12 and the need to have done with delay is stressed at 2.32–43.

24   The caesura after a trochee in both the second and the third feet is unusual (Nilsson 75) and perhaps expressive of a certain agitation; cf. Introduction pp. 14–15.

25–6   aeque: anaphora stresses the universal application of H.'s plan, and binds together the three polar expressions, the first of which is disposed chiastically: rich/poor (3.28), young/old, help/harm. A single idea is presented analytically by ἀπὸ κοινοῦ in two clauses, for of course young and old as well as rich and poor will be helped and harmed (Introduction p. 28).

prodest ... nocebit: the help is immediate, the harm may be delayed (the verbs reappear together at 8.11); the fut. might also be taken as 'gnomic' (18.3–4n.).

26   neglectum '*but, if* neglected'; antithetical ideas are juxtaposed without a connective, what grammarians call adversative asyndeton (K–S I 156–7). The protasis of a condition may be contained in a participle (G–L §593.2).

27   his ... elementis 'these simple lessons' refer to H.'s moral reflections to date (11–12), which he is eager to put into practice (24); the metaphor of training and learning is resumed. To philosophers *elementa* were fundamental principles, but H. here has something more straightforward and generally appealing in mind.

ego me ipse: the answer to the anticipated question of 13; H. will rely on himself alone for guidance – *regam*)(*duce* 13 – in prosperity and for consolation in adversity. Nor does he impose his view on anyone else. The emphatic grouping of pronouns forges a subtle link with H.'s own role model, Aristippus at 17.19.

soler: the simple form of the verb is 'elevated, archaic, poetic' (B. on *Ep.* 2.1.131).

28–32   Improvement, not perfection, is the goal; this, the leading thought of the *sententia* in 32, is characteristically postponed until after two illustrations of it are given. The same argument and one of the illustrations are found in the first-century A.D. Stoic Epictetus: 'I shall not be Milo, either, and yet I do not neglect my body ... there is no field in which we give up the appropriate discipline merely from despair of attaining the highest' (Arr. *Epict*. 1.2.37). An analogy between physical and moral well-being, commonly employed by Cynics and Stoics, is introduced (Cic. *Tusc*. 3.1; L. on *S*. 1.6.30 *morbo*; N–H on *C*. 2.2.13).

28–9 form a paratactic concessive sentence, i.e. what is logically the subordinate clause is not introduced with an adv. meaning 'although'; cf. *Ep*. 2.2.201–2 *non ... non tamen* (Bo 295).

28 possis: in moral discourse the second pers., either subjunc. (28, 30, 35) or indic. (36, 42, 44, 45, 59), addresses the world at large (H–S §222(c), N–H on *C*. 2.2.9 and on 2.18, p. 290, B. on *Ep*. 2.2.145); Maecenas comes to the fore again at 91. The verb is pointedly emphasized in this section (35, 37, 39).

oculo ... contendere 'strive with the eye' (*OLD* 4); take both ἀπὸ κοινοῦ: *non* ⟨*tantum*⟩ *possis* ⟨*contendere*⟩ *oculo quantum contendere* ⟨*oculo*⟩ *Lynceus* ⟨*potuit*⟩. Lynceus was the watchman of the Argo, proverbial for far-sightedness (Otto §1003, *RE* XIII 39–46).

29 idcirco: the logical adv. conveys a matter-of-fact tone (B. on *AP* 265).

lippus '*if* blear-eyed'; H. suffered from the complaint (*S*. 1.5.30–1). Marcus Aurelius compared philosophy to eye-salve (5.9), because what the eye is to the body the mind is to the personality. *inungi* is complementary infin. with *contemnas*.

30–1 desperes: subjunc. of assumed reason (Roby §1744). H., unlike Epictetus, prefers a contemporary illustration – Glycon was a pancratiast from Pergamum (*AP* 7.692 = *GP* 675–80) – to one drawn from the remote past (though *Milonis* was read in some texts in antiquity; the more usual name replaced the less familiar).

31 corpus ... prohibere cheragra: the syntax is also found in prose, *OLD prohibeo* 3 (cf. 8.10n.). Since gout or arthritis seemed to be the penalties of over-indulgence (*S*. 2.7.15 *iusta cheragra*), they could be avoided by self-discipline.

32 restates H.'s position at 27, and links his medical remedies to their moral analogues. *est* 'it is possible' (*OLD sum* 9), a syntactical Grecism (K–S I 669, L. on *S*. 1.2.79), emphatically affirms the hinted point of the previous neg. sentences.

quadam: take with the prep. *tenus* as another instance of tmesis (15n.; Williams on Virg. *A*. 5.603 *hac ... tenus*); the abl. fem. sing. is analogous to the use of *ea, hac, qua*, with all of which *uia* is in ellipse. *si* 'even if' (*OLD* 9); with *datur* understand *prodire*.

33–40   This process of moral care will be furthered by receptivity to the words we hear or the books we read in order to mitigate a variety of spiritual disorders (cf. 7).

33–5, 36–7   The first clauses (33, 36a) are asserted as suppositions ('Let's say your heart . . .'), the second (34–5, 36b–7) as consequences ('then there are . . .'), thus producing paratactic conditional sentences (G–L §598, Roby §1553, K–S II 164; cf. 28–9n.).

33   Feruet: greed, the chief of the vices (Kenney on Lucr. 3.59 *auarities et honorum caeca cupido*), produces a metaphorical fever, cf. Cic. *Quinct.* 38 [*Naeuius*] *feruet ferturque auaritia*.

misero goes ἀπὸ κοινοῦ with *auaritia*, notwithstanding the difference of gender.

34   uerba et uoces form a traditional alliterative pair (Wölfflin 280). The sentiment echoes Eur. *Hipp.* 478 'there are spells and soothing utterances'. H. has in mind Plato's *Charmides* 157A–B (a passage famous in antiquity, as Dr M. B. Trapp observes), where the Thracian Zalmoxis teaches the holistic medical doctrine that bodily ills derive from the soul's distemper; spells or 'good words' could produce a healing moderation.

34–5   lenire . . . magnam . . . partem: alleviation is all we can hope for (cf. 32); the younger H. spoke more confidently of eradication at *S.* 1.2.110 *e pectore pelli. possis* is still indefinite, but the subjunc. is final.

36   tumes: the next vice, ambition, causes a metaphorical swelling like that of the dropsical (2.34) or the proud (*S.* 2.3.213 *purum est uitio tibi, cum tumidum est, cor?*).

37   ter: the magic number as at *S.* 2.1.7–8 *ter . . . transnanto Tiberim, C.* 1.28.36 *iniecto ter puluere* and 3.22.2 *ter uocata* (*RAC* IV 286 s.v. Drei 'Lustrale Kulthandlungen').

recreare: complete recovery of health (= *sanare*) is not promised; cf. *S.* 2.2.84 *recreare . . . tenuatum corpus.*

libello 'booklet' of the spells used in propitiatory rites (*piacula*). But H. has other books in mind, such as Homer (11); he never expressly recommends philosophical texts, but may be hinting at the Epicureans' reliance on 'tracts' (Cic. *Pis.* 59).

38   The five vices listed here asyndetically (K–S II 154), added to the preceding two, produce the seven deadly sins of later Christianity.

(For the popularity of lists of moral traits see B. on *AP* 121 and Introduction p. 39 n. 117.) *amator* has a pejorative sense (*C.* 3.4.79–80 *amatorem ... Pirithoum*); Cicero distinguished it from *amans* (*Tusc.* 4.27).

39–40 Cf. Accius *trag.* 683–4R *nullum est ingenium tantum neque cor tam ferum | quod non ... mitiscat malo*, Sen. *Dial.* 4 (= *Ira* 2).12.3 *nullique sunt tam feri et sui iuris affectus ut non disciplina perdomentur*. The metaphor derives from the cultivation of wild trees and plants to produce edible crops; cf. Lucr. 5.1368–9 *fructusque feros mansuescere terra | cernebant ... colendo*, and Virgil's imitation at *G.* 2.36 *fructusque feros mollite colendo*. (H. had used Lucretius' argument for material progress at *S.* 1.3.99–106.)

39 adeo ... ut: only found before in H. at *S.* 1.7.7; the fact that they are only used in a speech by Virgil at *A.* 11.436–7 suggests that the tone is colloquial.

40 culturae, gen. with *patientem*, continues the metaphor of 'psychic husbandry' (a phrase owed to Dr M. B. Trapp), cf. 14.5n., Cic. *Tusc.* 2.13 (a text noticed by pseudo-Acro) *ut ager quamuis fertilis sine cultura fructuosus esse non potest, sic sine doctrina animus ... cultura autem animi philosophia est; haec extrahit uitia radicitus*.

patientem ... aurem introduces the receptivity theme, for books were usually read aloud in antiquity (B. M. W. Knox, 'Books and readers in antiquity', in P. E. Easterling and B. M. W. Knox (edd.), *The Cambridge history of classical literature* I: *Greek literature* (Cambridge 1985) 7); cf. 48.

commodet: the potential subjunc. is poetic syntax with *si modo* (K–S II 429).

41–52 A definition of *uirtus* further clarifies H.'s present moral position. He is reassuringly negative, since excessive demands might discourage; we are told what we can avoid or do without. We pursue less worthy goals at greater personal cost. An implied comparison is set up between moral striving and a provincial athlete offered an easy victory (49–51). We are encouraged to seek the highest goal, since it is after all easier to secure than our perverted ambitions.

41 prima goes with *uirtus* ἀπὸ κοινοῦ; cf. Quint. *IO* 8.3.41 *prima uirtus est uitio carere*; it is stressed in order to encourage us to get that far at least, if no further (cf. 32). *uirtus* combined with *sapientia* will be found in Ulysses (2.17).

uitium fugere recalls a Platonic doctrine (*Theaet.* 176B), variously taken up by later writers (e.g., Cic. *Off.* 1.114 *nec tam est enitendum, ut bona, quae nobis data non sint, sequamur quam ut uitia fugiamus*; see Fortescue on Boethius, *Consol.* 1.4.26, p. 18). Quintilian praised this *sententia* for its vigorous expression; he reckoned that the prose formulation would have been either *uirtus est fuga uitiorum* or *uirtutis est uitium fugere* (*IO* 9.3.10).

42 stultitia)(*sanus* 8; it is ignorance of moral behaviour (Dodds on Plat. *Gorg.* 477b7 ἀμαθία).

caruisse 'to have got free of' (*OLD* 3). The perf. infin. may indicate that all have a measure of *stultitia* that has to be eradicated; it might, however, be regarded as a metrical convenience (17.5n.).

credis: the Stoics claimed that all of our passions are founded upon what we only imagine to be good or bad. Cicero called this *opinio* to translate their δόξα (*Tusc.* 3.24).

43 censum ... repulsam: in apposition to *mala. censum* picks up *auaritia* (33), *repulsam* 'election defeat' *laudis amor* (36); cf. 18.102. For *turpem* cf. *C.* 3.2.17 *repulsae ... sordidae.*

44 quanto ...: indir. qu. dependent on *uides* 42.

labore)(*sine puluere* 51 means 'effort' with *animi* and 'risk' with *capitis* 'life' (*OLD* 4), as Schütz argued.

45–6 The trader was a traditional emblem of the drive to secure wealth against all odds; cf. 6.32–3 (N–H on *C.* 1.1.16 *mercator*). Porphyrio traced the sentiment to some often-quoted lines of the sixth-century Greek elegiac poet, Theognis, fr. 175–6 W. 'The man who dreads poverty ... must launch into the deep-yawning sea and over steep crags.'

45 The words are disposed in the so-called 'golden' pattern, two epithets separated by a verb from their nouns.

46 per in anaphora enhances the urgency of the pursuit; *mare, saxa, ignes* are proverbial of dangers to be run (L. on *S.* 1.1.39–40 *hiems ignis mare ferrum,* | *nil obstet tibi*).

47 continues the thought of the preceding lines by adversative asyndeton. *ne* is final, not a prohibition; *stulte* recalls *stultitia* 42: obtuse admiration (*AP* 272 *stulte mirati*) leads astray, the theme of VI.

48 discere ... audire: key words (cf. 8.8), referring to education, cf. Cic. *Parad.* 42 *egone me audisse aliquid et didicisse non gaudeam* (derived, as Lee noted, from the Greek orator Aeschines, 1.141). For *meliori* cf. 2.68.

non uis: like a preacher, H. rounds upon the addressee (N–H on

C. 2.18.17) and asks if it is not a question of will, rather than capacity, the concern of the previous section.

49–51   A clinching illustration (J. L. Heller, *A.J.P.* 85 (1964) 297–301). A backstreet brawler (not *pugil* 'boxer') would happily win the most prestigious prize, despite its low monetary value, if he had no rivals for it; just so, it is easier for us to pursue *uirtus* (there will be no competition, cf. N–H on *C.* 2.2.22 *deferens*) than harmful and fleeting goals.

   quis ... contemnat ... cui sit 'can he be imagined as refusing if he had ...'; a conditional sentence in which the protasis is a relative clause (cf. 4.9; Roby §1558) and the apodosis a repudiating question with its verb in the subjunc. (Repudiating questions are a lively way of dismissing a suggestion as somehow unreasonable; *LS* §95.) For the infin. *coronari* see 2–3n.

49   **circum ... circum** 'from one ... to another' (*OLD* 4); repetition enhances the sense of the wearisome round at local festivals like the Paganalia and Compitalia (cf. Virg. *G.* 2.382).

50   **magna** specifies the oldest and most renowned games at Elis, for in H.'s time there were several festivals in the Greek world held in honour of Olympian Zeus (*RE* xviii 1.45–6).

   coronari ... Olympia 'to crown himself with an Olympic wreath'; the acc. is internal, expressing the verbal idea more concretely (K–S i 277); here it is a syntactical Grecism, cf. Enn. *Ann.* 523 Sk. *uincere Olympia* 'to win an Olympic victory'. The athlete and his crown were traditional symbols of moral triumph (Sen. *Ep.* 78.16; Paul, 1 Corinth. 9.25; N–H on *C.* 2.2.21 *diadema*; G–H s.v. Wettkampf).

51   **sine puluere** = ἀκονιτί, i.e. unchallenged; for the palm as an award for victory in addition to the older crown see N–H on *C.* 1.1.5. A first-rate athlete might find no rival in the field and so be awarded the prize without a contest; the pursuer of *uirtus* need only master his will.

52   forms an epiphonema, i.e. a pithy concluding statement; it makes here a generalized observation, which is only connected by implication with what precedes (cf. 28–32n.). *uirtutibus* echoes *uirtus* 41 (ring-composition, for which cf. N–H on *C.* 2.6.21); for the sentiment cf. 10.39–40 and Plat. *Resp.* 1.336E 'justice, the goal of our discussion, is more valuable than gold'. It was remarkable that athletes at the 'crown' festivals did not compete for cash prizes (as did those at lesser festivals) but, notionally, for renown alone (H. A. Harris, *Greek athletes and athlet-*

ics (London 1964) 36–7, 42); *uirtus* is like that crown, more precious than money. The reference to metals forms a gliding transition to the next section on the average Roman's goal, wealth.

53–69 The school reappears from 3, with Janus as master and the citizens of Rome his pupils. They do not learn to value *uirtus*, but to pursue material gains; *uirtus post nummos* is hardly even a sop to morality. H. offers a counter-lesson, antique and Roman (59–69).

53 **O** is emotional, as is the repetition of *ciues. primum*)(*prima* 41. Janus' lesson derives from Phocylides, a sixth-century gnomic poet from Miletus (cf. Plat. *Resp.* 3.407A: 'Haven't you heard the saying of Phocylides that whenever a man has got his livelihood he should practise virtue?' (Otto §1910)).

54 **nummos** 'cash' (*OLD* 5).

Ianus summus ab imo 'Janus from end to end' with reference to the passageways (*iani*) along the *cloaca maxima*, which ran through Rome's business district (Richardson 206). (But the exact meaning of the expression, presumably clear to H.'s first audience, eluded even the later scholiasts, who guess in contradictory ways at the topography. The present interpretation is therefore only tentative.) Since Janus was credited with the invention of stamped bronze coinage (Athenaeus 15.692E) and his faces appeared on the Roman penny, his interest in money is not accidental.

55 **prodocet:** found only here, a lexical Grecism = προδιδάσκει. The force of *pro* is not clear (Dodds on Plat. *Gorg.* 489D); it does not restrict the lesson to preliminaries or to the master's dictation (so *OLD*), but indicates that teaching precedes the practice of what is taught (Dover on Aristoph. *Nub.* 476). *iuuenes ... senesque* recalls *pueris senibusque* 26.

haec ... dictata: anaphora stresses the parroting of the unreflecting students, cf. 18.13.

56 Editors delete this line as an inept repetition from *S.* 1.6.74 (Jachmann 395–6); old men have no use for satchels and writing-tablets which were anyway not carried in the classroom and not employed during recitation; nor did boys in Rome tote their own equipment, which was the job of the *capsarius*, cf. Juv. 10.117.

57–9 Janus' lesson is reflected in the state's assessment of social standing, which puts a lower value on character than on wealth. See 33–5, 36–7nn. for the syntax.

57 **est ... sunt ... est:** anaphora emphasizes the fact of possession of *all* these qualities. *animus* and *mores* form an Horatian doublet: *C*. 4.2.22–3 *animumque moresque | aureos educit in astra* and *Ep*. 2.1.249–50 *per uatis opus mores animique uirorum | clarorum adparent*.

lingua 'eloquence' (*OLD* 2d), a specific instance of *animus*, was a requirement in Roman public life, cf. 2.2, 5.1–11n., *C*. 4.1.14 *pro sollicitis non tacitus reis*.

fides both 'creditworthiness' (*OLD* 5) and 'loyalty' (*OLD* 8), a specific instance of sound *mores*.

58 quadringentis: dat., sc. *milibus sestertium*, the 400,000 sesterces needed for equestrian status.

sex septem 'a few'. The expression, unnoticed in *OLD*, is colloquial, as is the asyndeton (K–S II 151 collects examples).

desunt: emphatic, a negative echo of the preceding verbs.

59 plebs eris 'you will prove to be a nobody'; the fut. is often used in conclusions (G–L §242 R3; cf. *C*. 2.14.12 *inopes erimus coloni*). The two words come as a jolt after the line-filling sentence that precedes. *plebs* for *plebeius* is unusual, but may be a calque upon Homer's equally unusual use of δῆμος at *Il*. 12.213 δῆμον ἐόντα 'being a commoner', the self-description by the worthy and sensible Polydamas as he gives unwelcome advice to the headstrong Hector.

59–60 Now out of the schoolroom, but still among children, who assist H., though he has done with games (*ludicra* 10), to find a counter-lesson to Janus'. For the unstudied wisdom of children at play cf. Callim. *Epig*. 1 = *HE* 1277–92: Pittacus sent a man who had asked him about his marriage prospects to listen to boys spinning tops; from their cry 'drive your own line' (τὴν κατὰ σαυτὸν ἔλα) he learned not to aspire above his station. Epictetus urged that we be like children who refuse to play any more (Arr. *Epict*. 1.24.20); Jesus compared 'this generation' to children at play (Matt. 11.16–19, cited by Dacier). Augustine, sitting in an agony of spiritual doubt beneath a fig tree in his Milanese garden, heard amidst his tears a child at play singing '*tolle, lege*'; so God directed him to consult scripture for guidance (*Conf*. 8.12.28–9). There was also a Greek proverb, recorded by Photius, that wine and children tell the truth (οἶνος καὶ παῖδες ἀληθεῖς).

rex eris ... si recte facies: a proverbial expression (Otto §1537) deriving from the children's award of the title of 'king' to whoever plays a game 'according to the rules' (*OLD recte* 5). The criterion of right action opposes popular goals. The chime *rex/recte* draws attention to an etymological link; cf. Cic. *Fin*. 3.75 *rectius* [*sapiens*] ... *appellabitur rex quam Tarquinius qui nec se nec suos regere potuit*, Isidore (a seventh-century bishop of Seville), *Orig*. 1.29.3 *reges a recte agendo* and 9.3.4 *reges a regendo uocati ... non autem regit qui non corrigit. recte igitur faciendo regis nomen tenetur, peccando amittitur* (he then quotes H.'s jingle in a fuller form). The king is not only the polar opposite of the *plebs*, he is also the type of absolute freedom and happiness; cf. 107n. and *OLD rex* 4.

60 hic points forward to the infinitives of 61, which redefine *recte facere* in moral terms (still negative, as at 41–2); it owes its gender to the predicate, *murus* (cf. *AP* 396–7 *fuit haec sapientia quondam,* | *publica priuatis secernere*; G–L §211 R5, Roby §1068). The metaphor of the wall had been used by the founder of the Cynic sect, Antisthenes: 'intelligence is the securest wall' (Diog. Laert. 6.13).

61 nil conscire sibi 'to know nothing against oneself'; *conscire*, a unique back-formation from *conscius*, is a lexical Grecism = αὐτῶι συνειδέναι. The expression implies knowledge of evil (C. S. Lewis, *Studies in words* (Cambridge 1960) 187–8). The third pers. reflexive is usual where the second pers. (*eris, dic*) is indefinite (B. Axelson, *Neue Senecastudien* (Lund 1939) 196–7, cf. Roby §2270).

62–4 Janus' lesson is also embodied in a *lex*, the expression of the popular will, but the children's jingle still offers a corrective. Rejection of popular opinion prepares for 70–5.

62 Roscia ... lex: see 12.20n. In 67 b.c. the tribune L. Roscius Otho legally instituted or perhaps reinstituted the assignment of the first fourteen rows in the *cauea* of the theatre to the *equites*, a privilege, at first unpopular, for the monied; for his law see E. D. Rawson, *Roman culture and society* (Oxford 1991) 530 n. 110.

sodes 'if you please', contracted from *si audes* (Cic. *Orat*. 154), a deprecating colloquialism (B. on *AP* 438).

63 nenia 'jingle', cf. the salutary *uerba et uoces* 34.

64 Construe: *decantata et maribus Curiis et Camillis*; the past part. in the second member should be understood ἀπὸ κοινοῦ, as should *maribus*, for both sets of men are 'manly'; cf. *AP* 402 *mares animos*. The masculinity of the early Roman heroes validates the jingle: as the boy, so the man. H. may also be hinting at his deeply held belief that verse, however simple, should improve us morally (cf. *Ep*. 2.1.128 [*poeta*] *pectus praeceptis format amicis*).

Curiis ... Camillis 'by men like ...', the plur. generalizes (K–S 1

72; Bo 310), the dat. is of the agent; the two figures, also coupled at *C*. 1.12.41–3, were proverbial (Otto §§311, 485). M' Curius Dentatus, a plebeian and four times consul in the third century, was a hero of the Samnite and Pyrrhic wars. M. Furius Camillus conquered Veii *c.* 396 B.C. and refounded Rome after the Gallic capture of 390 B.C. Their singing of the jingle tips the balance in its favour (*decantata*) (*recinunt* 55); it is also more venerable than the Roscian law, 'new-fangled ill'.

65–9 Alternatives are again presented (*melius* echoes *melior* 62).

65   qui: understand *suadet*, which governs the jussive subjunc. *facias* without *ut* (*OLD* 1d, G–L §546 R2, Roby §1606).

   rem 'wealth' (*OLD* 1, cf. Ter. *Adel.* 220 *numquam rem facies*) thrice emphatically repeated and placed twice as last word in adjacent lines (cf. 16.68); the monosyllable at line-end is a traditional poetic device (Norden on Virg. *A.* VI, p. 439, Nilsson 119). Commercial interests informed Roman education; cf. *AP* 325–30 for the *aerugo et cura peculi* behind arithmetic lessons. *rem facere* parodies the *nenia* (*recte* 66) (60, 63).

67   propius refers to the provisions of the Roscian law (62n.); the advantage of equestrian status is ironically trivialized when it is seen at another sort of *ludus*, the *ludi scaenici*. The irony is enhanced by alliteration and by the ambiguous reference to the object of the spectators' attention. The poems of Pupius (now lost) were presumably tragedies and so 'tearful' in content; but *lacrimosa* also suggests 'lamentable' quality (cf. N–H on *C.* 2.9.9).

68   Fortunae … responsare: defiance of capricious Fortune, who takes back her gifts (but *uirtus* was not one of them), was a goal of all the philosophical sects. For the Stoic *sapiens* cf. Cic. *Fin.* 4.17 *magnitudo … animi existebat, qua facile posset repugnari obsistique fortunae, quod maximae res essent in potestate sapientis* and Sen. *Dial.* 9.11.1 *tanta enim fiducia sui est, ut obuiam fortunae ire non dubitet nec umquam loco illi cessurus sit* (G. Busch, *A.&A.* 10 (1961) 131–54); for the Epicurean see Diog. Laert. 10.121. The infin. is found with *hortor* in prose as well as poetry, where it is common (K–S 1 682).

69   liberum et erectum: also paired at Sen. *Dial.* 7.4.3 and Plin. *Ep.* 3.5.5, the predicates restate the theme of self-reliance. The elision of -*um* in *liberum*, a quasi-cretic, is unusual but conforms to a pattern in Augustan poetry where the next word is a monosyllable (Austin on Virg. *A.* 4.684).

praesens 'helpful', often used of gods (*OLD* 3 and 5, N–H on *C.* 1.35.2), goes ἀπὸ κοινοῦ with *aptat*.

70–93 H., having characterized popular materialism, turns to a defence of his nonconformity. (There may be an allusion to Socrates' not honouring the same gods as the city; cf. Plat. *Apol.* 24c1.) It is practically forced on him when he observes both the diversity (76–82) and inconstancy (82–93) of men's pursuits. Their failure to agree on a pattern of behaviour provides no reliable standard.

70 Quodsi, avoided by some writers, is common in the *Epistles* (Axelson 47–8).

populus Romanus: in the background till now (6, 53), H.'s fellow citizens now engage him in brief debate. *populus Romanus* has an official ring, though its authority is to be undermined. It was a common ethical strategy, at least as old as Heraclitus (fr. 104 D–K), to denigrate the people as bad teachers and so encourage the independence needed for moral improvement; cf. Cic. *Tusc.* 3.3 *quasi maximus quidam magister populus atque omnis undique ad uitia consentiens multitudo*, *Parad.* 1.8 *plus apud me uera ratio ualebit quam uulgi opinio*, Sen. *Ep.* 99.17 *populo nullius rei bono auctori* (see *Index rerum memorabilium* s.v. *populus* in Haase's edn of Sen., and A. Oltramare, *Les origines de la diatribe romaine* (Geneva 1926) Index s.v. 'Opinion de la foule'). H. shares this view, cf. *C.* 2.2.17–24, where *Virtus* is described as *dissidens plebi*, and *S.* 1.6.15–17 *iudice ... populo, qui stultus honores | saepe dat indignis et famae seruit ineptus, | qui stupet in titulis et imaginibus*. For the enjambment see Introduction p. 24.

71 porticibus: places of public resort, of which a good number had recently been built in Rome (Richardson 310–11); a man could be alone with his thoughts in them (*S.* 1.4.134).

72 Take *quae diligit* with *sequar* and [*quae*] *odit* with *fugiam*; there seems no appreciable difference between *aut* and *uel*.

73 olim 'once upon a time' introduces H.'s defensive answer in the form of a fable found in Babrius 103, Lucilius 980–1 M., and perhaps alluded to by Seneca, *Dial.* 8.1.3. Fables were popular forms of political persuasion (Arist. *Rhet.* 2.20.7), hence one is appropriate here. Its implicit moral is that following the herd irreversibly compromises independence of judgement.

75 te aduersum: anastrophe of this preposition with a pronoun is common in comedy, and perhaps therefore colloquial (*TLL* 1 851.10–14). *spectantia* 'facing' (*OLD* 10a).

76   belua keeps up the image of the fable, but a new topic, diversity of opinion, is prepared for by the genitive phrase.

multorum ... capitum: descriptive gen.; chiefly poetic when used for external characteristics (*NLS* §85 III, p. 68). The phrase = πολυκέφαλος (Plat. *Resp.* 9.588c); Latin poets preferred paraphrase to the compound epithets peculiar to Greek verse (for exx. in the *Odes* see E. Norden, *Agnostos Theos* (Berlin 1923) 161 n. 4).

est, a reading found in some inferior MSS, is preferred to *es* of the tradition, since 74–5 concluded H.'s exchange with the people. He now asks questions of himself, not directed at the *populus Romanus*.

nam quid = *quidnam*, a lively form of question, answered from 80 to 90; *nam* is placed before the interrogative word in comedy and later poetry (*OLD nam* 7; K–S II 117). *sequar* is subjunc. in a deliberative question (*NLS* §172, *LS* §72). The answer to the question posed by *quem* (with which *nam* belongs ἀπὸ κοινοῦ) comes first, 77–80.

77–80   All popular occupations aim at wealth, as Janus had taught (but agriculture, tacitly omitted, was a respectable source of profit, cf. 7.85n.). Some, while not illegal, are discreditable, all verge on the unscrupulous (cf. 66). The list is elegantly varied in presentation: *pars, sunt qui, multis*; cf. *C.* 1.1.19 *est qui*, 23 *multos* (the whole ode is structured on variations of this theme).

77   conducere publica 'to take state contracts' (*OLD conduco* 5) refers to the *publicani* (*OCD* s.v.), still chiefly associated with tax-farming, though they undertook other public works, e.g. construction of roads and harbours.

77–9   describe *captatores*, who ingratiated themselves with the old and childless to secure an inheritance (cf. *S.* 2.5). The form of the sentence is discussed in the Introduction p. 27.

78   crustis 'cakes', the reading of an inferior MS, is better than *frustis* 'scraps' (an unenticing gift, as Cruquius noted) of the tradition. Tiresias urged Ulysses to send *dulcia poma* to a rich old man at *S.* 2.5.12; for the subjunc. see *personet* 7n.

uiduas 'unmarried', 'widowed' or 'divorced' (*OLD* 1, 2).

79   uiuaria 'preserves' (*S.* 2.5.44 *cetaria* 'fish ponds'). For *mittant* see *possim* 12n.

80   multis: dat. of advantage (*NLS* §64). *occulto* 'imperceptible', both because interest mounts gradually and with a hint that some of Rome's first citizens lent money at interest through intermediaries to avoid social stigma; cf. Cic. *Off*. 1.150 (P. A. Brunt, *The fall of the Roman republic* (Oxford 1988) 174).

80–93 A transition to inconstancy (cf. 16–19), as exemplified by both rich (83–90) and poor (91–3), who are again linked (*aeque* 92, cf. 25). From 94 H. reintroduces himself as sharing in this inconsistent behaviour.

81 teneri is the subj. of *esto* (K–S 1 691); the sentence is equivalent to a concessive clause paratactically linked to what follows (28–9n.).

aliis alios: polyptoton, i.e. the use of the same word in different cases, is a rhetorical figure favoured by H. (Bo 400). The diversity of human pursuits was proverbial, cf. *S*. 2.1.27–8 *quot capitum uiuunt, totidem studiorum | milia* (Otto §826).

82 idem: nom. plur.; *eadem* is obj. of *probantes*.

durare probantes 'persevere in approving', a syntactical Grecism (unnoticed by *TLL*) = καρτερέω + part.; *horam*, acc. of extent of time, goes closely with it (*S*. 1.6.128 *diem durare*, Prop. 1.6.11 *non horam possum durare*). To the moralist inconstancy was a vice, cf. 85 and Sen. *Ep*. 20.3–6, esp. *unam semel ad quam uiuas regulam prende et ad hanc omnem uitam tuam exaequa ... uitium est haec diuersitas.*

83 sinus 'retreat' (so Ascensius, *OLD* 3); the rich man is looking for a hideaway, not necessarily by the sea, though his first choice, Baiae, happens to be on the bay of Naples.

Bais '*that of* Baiae', an abbreviated comparison (N–H on *C*. 2.6.14 *Hymetto*). This was a popular resort of the rich on the northern shore of the bay of Naples (J. H. D'Arms, *Romans on the bay of Naples* (Ann Arbor 1970); *praelucet* 'outshines' suggests its clear atmosphere, cf. *C*. 3.4.24 *seu liquidae placuere Baiae*.

84 lacus: the Lucrine lake was separated from the bay by a causeway; it was fringed with villas and famed for its oysters (N–H on *C*. 2.15.3).

sentit 'feels to its cost', a common sinister sense (*OLD* 4; N–H on *C*. 2.7.9); the singular with several non-personal subjects is usual, especially in H. (K–S 1 44, Bo 391). The rich man means to build out into the water (N–H on *C*. 2.18.19–21 *struis domos | marisque Bais obstrepentis urges | submouere litora*).

85 festinantis 'hasty', i.e. unreflecting, but there may be overtones of inconsiderate haste towards sexual climax (W. D. Lebek, *Z̧.P.E.* 45 (1982) 53–7).

cui si uitiosa libido '*but* if his morbid whim'; *cui* = *at ei*, since an adversative idea is often to be understood with a relative pronoun (2.46, 16.33; L. on *S*. 1.1.36). For the thought cf. 41 and Cic. *Tusc*. 4.29 *uitiositas est habitus ... in tota uita inconstans et a se ipsa dissentiens*. The epithet corrects the common indifference to the fault. The sense 'lust' may also be felt and that lends colour to the interpretation of *festinantis* offered above.

86 auspicium 'authorization' (*OLD* 6b). The *diues* follows his caprice as if it were a sign from heaven. The theme of restlessness is here introduced (cf. VIII and XI). *Teanum* was an important town in the mountains of northern Campania, *T. Sidicinum* (Paget 219), so the whim takes an opposite turn.

87 tolletis: apostrophe imparts a brisk liveliness.

87–90 For the form of the sentences see 33–5, 36–7n. and esp. Munro on Lucr. 3.935.

87 lectus genialis: a symbolic marriage bed placed in the *atrium* to honour the *genius* of the head of the family (*OCD* s.v. Genius). For the indecisive bachelor as a type of inconsistency cf. Sen. *Ep*. 120.21 *nemo non cotidie et consilium mutat et uotum: modo uxorem uult habere, modo amicam* (H. was in his mind, for he had just quoted *S*. 1.3.11–17).

aula = *atrio*; the Greek loan word is used, perhaps for the first time in this specific sense, because the only dactylic forms of *atrium* are the nom. or acc. pl. (cf. 5.31); the diction is therefore poetic (cf. 2.66).

88 nil ... nil: anaphora and chiasmus emphasize eagerness (B. on *Ep*. 2.1.17; cf. 15.41). *prius* 'superior' (*OLD prior* 7b). *caelibe uita* was recalled by Seneca (*Phaed*. 231) and Tacitus (*Ann*. 12.1); the epithet is transferred from the person to his way of life (*OLD* 1b), a figure characteristic of poetry called enallage.

89 bene ... esse 'are comfortable' (*OLD* 9b), cf. *C*. 3.16.43–4 *bene est cui deus obtulit | parca quod satis est manu*.

90 teneam: see *sequar* 76n.

Protea: a Greek acc. form; Proteus was the old man of the sea proverbial for his ability to change his shape rapidly (Otto §1478).

91 quid 'what of' (*OLD quis*¹ 12). *ride* is addressed to Maecenas, whose laughter links the sections (95, 97). The poor man's mimicry of the rich is funny, as was H.'s own attempt to vie with Maecenas (*S*. 2.3.311 *ridiculus*).

92–3 A traditional illustration, cf. *Ep*. 2.2.199–200 *ego, utrum | naue ferar magna an parua, ferar unus et idem*, and Plut. *Moral*. 466B–C.

93   ducit 'transports', a rare sense (*OLD* 19c). *priua*)(*conducto* (92) was archaic and largely poetic by H.'s day (Ruckdeschel 52). His yacht is as big as a battleship, cf. *C.* 3.1.39 *aerata triremi* (N–H on *C.* 2.16.21).

94–105   In closing H. reintroduces himself in his friendship with Maecenas. Both have their inconsistencies. Maecenas laughs at some of H.'s external discordances (cf. *S.* 1.3.30–1 *rideri possit eo quod | rusticius tonso toga defluit*); others, however, annoy him (Maecenas himself was a byword for his foppish appearance, cf. Vell. Pat. 2.88.2). Yet after all he is not troubled by H.'s spiritual disharmony (97–101).

94   In Rome then as now a haircut was not a matter of indifference (except to Augustus, cf. Suet. *Aug.* 79). Humdrum as the theme is, its syntactical expression is highly artificial (Introduction p. 23).

curatus: used of barbering only here in literature (*TLL* IV 1504.81–2); the perf. part. passive governs the acc. of words referring to parts of the body (*capillos*) commonly in poetry (*NLS* §19(ii), Bo 118).

inaequali: enallage again (88n., Bo 134 does not include this example), here best treated adverbially.

tonsore: probably abl. of agent without *ab*; the usage, chiefly poetic, is variously explained: the agent may be seen as a quasi-instrument (Courtney on Juv. 1.13 *assiduo lectore*) or as standing for an abstract idea, here 'haircut' (so Torrentius; *NLS* §96(i)).

95   pexae 'brushed', i.e. new)(*trita* 'worn' (96). The better garment is on the outside, a hint at the theme of hypocrisy; cf. 16.45. The imagery of appropriate dress is abundant: 3.20 (stolen feathers), 10.42–3 (ill-fitting shoes), 11.18 (seasonal clothing), 14.32 (H.'s youthful party attire), 16.45 (the hypocrite's pelt), 17.25–32 (Aristippus and Diogenes), 18.30 (the toga of the inferior) and 31–6 (Eutrapelus' cruel gift), 19.13 (Cato's skimpy toga). Here *toga* suggests the formality of the morning visit to the patron (*salutatio*), at which care would be expected (statues of Romans show how elaborately the toga could be hitched round the body). On such occasions dress is a matter of etiquette; cf. G. della Casa, *Galateo* (trans. R. S. Pine-Coffin, Harmondsworth 1958) 34: 'people who wear their garments untidily show either that they are indifferent whether they please other people or not, or that they lack taste'. Maecenas, however, does not take offence in this matter at any rate.

96   dissidet 'sits awry' (*OLD* 2); *impar* 'uneven' (*OLD* 6) is predicative.

97   quid ... cum 'how do you react when' (*OLD quis*[1] 13b).

98   The line clarifies the nature of H.'s inconsistency; its pattern is an elegant chiasmus. Take *nuper* also with *petiit* ἀπὸ κοινοῦ.

99   aestuat 'is unsettled' (*OLD* 6). *disconuenit* 'is in disarray', not found earlier (cf. 14.18), is used by late technical writers, so may not be a coinage. *ordine toto* is a local abl. (*NLS* §51 (iii)). Maecenas should now understand why H. is searching for order (*compono* 12).

100   diruit, aedificat, mutat '*makes them* destroy, build, change'; by a common idiom someone is said to do what he causes others to do (G–L §219; Courtney on Juv. 16.12 *punire*. Cf. 3.14n.). The change of building plans recalls 84–7.

mutat quadrata rotundis: the allusion is not clear, though it might refer to a change in the design of some architectural feature, e.g., a tower.

101   insanire)(*sanus* (8, 108) in both its senses, 'reasonable' and 'healthy'; cf. *S*. 2.3.301–2 *qua me stultitia ... insanire putas?*

sollemnia 'in the usual way'; the acc. *plur*. used adverbially is poetic (K–S I 281, L. on *S*. 2.3.62).

neque 'and yet ... not' 'without' (*OLD* 5, Mayor on Plin. *Ep*. 3.1.9).

102   credis ... egere: take both ἀπὸ κοινοῦ. The management of the property of a *furiosus* or of a *prodigus* could be assigned to a guardian, *curator* (*OLD* 3, *RE* IV 1771–3).

103   rerum tutela mearum < *C*. 2.17.3–4 *Maecenas, mearum | grande decus columenque rerum*; the use of the abstract *tutela* for the concrete *tutor*, as at *C*. 4.14.43, is chiefly poetic diction (*OLD* 2). The compliment expresses H.'s debt to his friend for his material well-being (cf. 105), a theme of VII.

104   cum sis 'though you are', emphasized by its position. Maecenas' annoyance with the ill-pared fingernail is inconsistent with his amusement at the poor haircut or sloppy dress; yet he is unconcerned for his dependant's moral well-being.

105   de te ... te: anaphora and the assonance of the participles enhance the warmth of H.'s sentiment (> Ov. *Tr*. 2.217).

respicientis 'centred on' (*OLD* 3b). *amici*, the emphatic final word, reasserts the relationship in spite of H.'s refusal of Maecenas' imagined invitation. There is an equal emotional power at *C*. 2.6.24 *uatis amici* and 2.7.28 *recepto ... amico*.

106–8 The concluding sentence summarizes the attributes of a perfect *sapiens* in a list which picks up points already touched upon; its tone is Stoic, and recalls Lucilius, 1226 M. *formosus diues liber rex solus* (L. on *S.* 1.3.124–5). But the perfection of the *sapiens* is ironically guyed in the final line as an unattainable ideal.

106 Ad summam: a conversational expression, common in Petronius (Ruckdeschel 54).

uno 'alone' (*OLD* 7) **... Ioue:** the abl. of comparison in an ordinary comparison is infrequent at all times, yet specially favoured by H. (Löfstedt 316–7, B. on *Ep.* 2.1.197; cf. 2.4n.); it is poetic syntax.

diues: cf. Cic. *Parad.* 6 *quod solus sapiens diues.* The list of vices began with *auaritia* (33, cf. *exiguus census* 43). But since *uirtus* is worth more than precious metal (52), its possessor is truly rich (*S.* 1.3.124 *diues qui sapiens est*).

107 liber: cf. Cic. *Parad.* 5 *omnes sapientes liberos esse et stultos omnes seruos.* The theme of independence had opened the epistle (cf. 69); it is one of the leading topics in the book, esp. in regard to Rome's hierarchical society.

honoratus: cf. *laudis amor* (36) and *repulsa* (43). In XIX H. will refer to his own special distinctions (cf. too 17.35 and 20.23).

pulcher: the Stoic *sapiens* claimed beauty (*S.* 1.3.125 *solus formosus*), viz. the superior beauty of consistency of spirit, the theme of the closing section; cf. Cic. *Off.* 3.75 [*sapiens*] *recte etiam pulcher appellabitur; animi enim lineamenta sunt pulchriora quam corporis.*

rex ... regum: the parody of an oriental title (*OLD* 2f, Pelling on Plut. *Ant.* 54.7) overstates the Stoic's claim to sole kingship (N–H on *C.* 2.2.21 *regnum*). But H. has redefined the true king in the light of a children's jingle (59–60, 62–4); cf. also *regno* 10.8n.

108 sanus: cf. Cic. *Parad.* 4 *omnes stultos insanire.* The sense is above all moral (8, 101), referring to the reasonableness of the *uir bonus et sapiens* (7.22; 16.20, 73), but the hint of physical health (28–31) paves the way to the concluding joke.

pituīta: even the *sapiens* catches cold (*S.* 2.2.76; cf. Hippocrates, *Aër.* 3.10–13, a reference owed to Dr D. Langslow); but H. also directs a jibe at tiresome Stoic disquisitions about indifference to illness, in which a runny nose commonly figured (Arr. *Epict.* 1.6.30). To fit *pītuīta* into dactylic verse, *u* is hardened into a consonant, a type of synizesis (Winbolt §164, Williams on Virg. *A.* 5.432).

molesta: common of troublesome complaints and used of *pituita* by Columella (7.5.18; *TLL* VIII 1353.57–64).

The first epistle is a programme poem, i.e. one specially designed to offer the reader a foretaste of the whole collection. Yet the opening is paradoxical, since H. pretends to have given up writing poetry; he explains why he has done so and what he is doing instead. It was usual to dedicate a collection of poems to a friend, often by suggesting that he 'commissioned' their publication. Again H. surprises the reader in refusing Maecenas' invitation to compose further lyrics. So he begins with an 'un-dedication' that also serves to introduce the major theme of the book, independence. But declining the request of a patron needs tact, and the theme of 'managing one's superiors' is thereby also hinted at.

Other themes are introduced as well: retirement to the country, receptivity to moral advice, illness of body and of spirit, hypocrisy, the delusions of popular opinion, inconsistency and inconstancy of purpose, the attractions of philosophers like Aristippus.

Imagery too is brought into play: the schoolroom and its lessons (to be developed in II), competitive games, gladiatorial combat, clothing. Rome herself has a significant part to play as the arena in which the contest between the social world and the individual is to be fought out. But H. is one of those who aim to be at home in the world, and Rome, with her attractions and snares, is the world with which he and his addressees had to come to terms.

One persuasive device, the beast fable, also puts in its first appearance here; there will be more to come.

Lastly, H. hints at some literary debts: Ibycus, Theognis, Homer in the reference to Proteus, Euripides at 36, Phocylides, Cicero, Ennius, Lucilius and above all Plato. When at *AP* 310 he advises the poet to study *Socraticae chartae*, the moral dimension is not his only interest, for Plato's classic dialogues still presented the good life as a quest to be pursued through discourse, not an orthodoxy to be adhered to. Plato was H.'s vacation reading (*S*. 2.3.11).

For all its preparatory role the poem is complete in itself. H. politely renounces lyric composition and the life of pleasure it celebrates because the years have wrought a change of heart and prompted a search for order in life. The nature and scope of this quest are set out in the poem. But one point is left tantalizingly vague. The self-reliant still want guidance, which can be found in words (34) and books (37). But what books, whose words? H.'s surprising answer is reserved for the next epistle.

Further reading: D. Gagliardi, *Civ. class. e crist.* 6 (1985) 199–215, S. Jäkel, *Eirene* 26 (1989) 5–22.

Epistle II

1–31   H. has been rereading Homer for the moral lessons to be derived from the *Iliad* (6–16) and the *Odyssey* (17–26); the latter he finds specially relevant to us (27–31).

1–4   Hinted contrasts fill the sentence. The addressee is in the busy capital, H. in retreat; Lollius is practising to speak publicly in court, H.'s reading serves a private purpose.

1   Troiani belli scriptorem: an unusual phrase, as Heinze noted, based upon the commoner *rerum scriptor*; Homer is seen as a sort of historian. But *scriptor* is often used for 'poet' (B. on *AP* 38, *OLD* 3b, c).

Maxime Lolli: for names artificially reversed see N–H on *C*. 2.2.3 *Crispe Sallusti*. The identity of Lollius, the recipient of XVIII also, is unclear (Introduction pp. 8–9). It is possible that *Maximus* is not a *cognomen* and rather indicates that the addressee is the eldest son (*TLL* VIII 126.13–16).

2   dum 'during the time that' denotes a longer period in the course of which the action of the main sentence takes place; the pres. indic. is usual, whatever the tense of the main verb (*NLS* §221). For emphatic *tu* without an answering *ego*, cf. 17.21. Lollius has moved into tertiary education and is studying rhetoric, esp. in the fashionable exercise of *declamatio* (extemporaneous speaking on a set theme, see *OCD* s.v.). This should prepare him to take an active part in public life.

Romae, Praeneste (locatives) are juxtaposed both to enhance the contrast between the metropolis and the holiday retreat (*C*. 3.4.22–3 *frigidum P*., mod. Palestrina, whence the name of the pleasure garden at Rousham in Oxfordshire) and to establish the need for a letter. The *docti* might have recalled that Praeneste was reckoned by some to have been founded by Telegonus, son of Ulysses, or by his grandson Praenestes.

relegi: H. by paradoxical contrast has gone back to secondary schooling where Homer was a basic text whose usefulness cannot be exhausted, even by those whose pursuits have moved on. This picks up the theme of education from I.

3–4 A poet challenges the philosophers; cf. J. Milton, *Areopagitica*: 'our sage and serious poet Spenser, whom I dare be known to think a better teacher than Scotus or Aquinas'. Homer's role as a moralist was undiminished; he had been endorsed early by Antisthenes, among others (Plut. *Aud. Poet.*); the orator Lycurgus reckoned Homer better than the laws at persuading men by reason and demonstration to act well (*Leocr.* 101).

3 pulchrum 'morally beautiful' (*OLD* 3); *turpe* 'morally shameful' (cf. 25; *OLD* 3) has a specially Roman ring; such behaviour led to *infamia* (16.39n.). For the philosophical terms see 1.11n.

4 planius ac melius: the nub of the issue. Homer's unambiguous examples are preferable to the puzzling precepts and paradoxical arguments of the philosophers. Chrysippus (280–207 B.C.), a most eminent Stoic, is cited just because he often used poetry to illustrate his doctrine (Diog. Laert. 7.180). Crantor (340–275 B.C.), an Academic, also admired Homer and Euripides, and even composed poems himself (Diog. Laert. 4.25–6). For the abl. of comparison see 1.106n. and for its use with comparative adverbs L. on *S.* 1.1.97.

dicit: the tense stresses that his words are still effective; the professional moralists (*docet* would suit them better) have not replaced him and cannot.

5 crediderim 'have formed and hold this opinion', a pres. perf. as at *C.* 3.5.1 (H–S 318). *nisi quid te detinet* is a formula of politeness (cf. 5.28); *quid* 'anything' (*OLD quis²*). For *audi* cf. 14.31.

6–16 The examples of the *Iliad* are deterrent.

6 Paridis propter ... amorem: the separation of the prep. from its noun is usual in poetry (K–S 1 588).

7 Graecia ... collisa 'the conflict of Greece'; a part. or gerundive with a pronoun or noun forms an abstract noun phrase, a common idiom (cf. *ab urbe condita*, *NLS* §95, G–L §664 R2; N–H on *C.* 1.37.13). The sense of *collido* appears first here in Latin, a loan-shift from συγκρούειν (*TLL* III 1604.1).

barbariae: the Trojans are first called barbarians by Herodotus; cf. *C.* 2.4.9. The dat. with a verb implying conflict is a syntactical Grecism

(K–S I 319). *lento* (1.21n.) alludes to the ten-year duration of the war, a grim result of a poor cause; the solemn tone is enhanced by the artificially trisyllabic *duellum*, owed to Ennius (Skutsch on *Ann.* 573 Sk.).

8   stultorum)(*sapientia* 17, a key word (24; 1.42). 'Kings and peoples' forms a polar expression admitting of no exception, common in historians, cf. Sall. *Cat.* 51.4, Livy 21.43.11, 24.49.2, 37.45.8 and see Mayer on Luc. 8.140.

aestus 'mental disturbances' (*OLD* 9b).

9–13   The Trojan Antenor (*Il.* 7.347–53) and the Greek Nestor (*Il.* 1.254) used their eloquence (a glance, perhaps, at Lollius' current pursuits) in an attempt to resolve strife (as H. will do in III); they are commonly linked, cf. Eur. fr. 899 N. and Plat. *Symp.* 221C.

9   censet 'recommends' (*OLD* 3a).

10   quid Paris?: 1.91n.

ut ... beatus: take with *cogi* 11; Antenor's advice was, of course, to return Helen and the goods he had stolen from Menelaus; here, instead, its result is ironically presented.

saluus ... beatus: understand adverbially (G–L §325 R6, Roby §1069, H–S 172, Bo 134) and take ἀπὸ κοινοῦ with both verbs. Poets preferred adjectives to adverbs; but for some words an adverb was unavailable (see 3.21 and 13.8nn.), its form was unmanageable in verse (see 6.68, 7.71 and 10.26nn.), or, as here, the sense (of *salue*, at any rate) was inappropriate.

regnet uiuatque: echoed at 10.8, but here *uiuo* is an emphatic colloquial equivalent of *sum* (cf. 26; Fordyce on Catull. 10.33; *OLD* 2).

11   posse negat: sc. *se*; omission of the reflexive subj. acc. of the infin. with *nego* is poetic syntax, but it conforms to colloquial practice (Austin on Virg. *A.* 4.428; K–S I 701).

componere 'bring to an end' (*Ep.* 2.1.7–8 *bella | componant*).

12   inter: not uncommonly repeated thus, even in prose (*TLL* VII 1.2147.75–2148.1).

Peliden ... Atriden: Greek acc. forms of patronymics; Achilles was the son of Peleus, Agamemnon of Atreus.

13   hunc 'the first one', i.e. Achilles (*TLL* VI 2.2713.74–6); his love for Briseis is thwarted when she is taken from him by Agamemnon in *Il.* 1; cf. *C.* 2.4.2–4 *prius insolentem | serua Briseis niueo colore | mouit Achillem* (N. Rudd, *C.P.* 75 (1980) 68–9).

ira ... utrumque: the wrath of Achilles motivates the *Iliad*, but Agamemnon is no less angry, cf. Hom. *Il.* 1.247 Ἀτρεΐδης δ' ἑτέρωθεν ἐμήνιε.

14 A summary, perhaps relying on a proverb found as early as Hesiod (Otto §1536), cf. Phaedr. 1.30.1 *humiles laborant ubi potentes dissi-dent. quidquid* is internal acc. with *delirant* (G–L §333, Roby §1094).

plectuntur, often of undeserved punishment (Palmer on Ov. *Ep.* 11.110), refers both to the plague sent by Apollo in *Il.* 1 to pay back the Achaeans for the theft of Chryseis as well as to the unnecessarily protracted fighting.

15 For the list cf. 1.38n. The ablatives are causal.

16 peccatur 'wrong is done'; intransitive verbs form an impersonal passive (*NLS* §60, G–L §208.2).

extra: the prep., with which *muros* goes ἀπὸ κοινοῦ; the expression is Ennian in colour, cf. *Ann.* 390 Sk. *aut intra muros aut extra.*

17–31 On the other hand the *Odyssey* is a positive spur to virtue, and its lesson is applicable to ourselves (27–31). Its moral tone early re-commended itself in Rome; one of the first pieces of Latin literature was the third-century adaptation by Livius Andronicus. H.'s use of scenes from the poem in moral education was part of a long tradition (E. Kaiser, *M.H.* 21 (1964) 109–36, 197–224).

17 uirtus ... sapientia: key words, forging a link with 1.41. *possit* 'avails' (*OLD* 8; B. on *AP* 410) points to practical use, not a theoretical definition of terms. The indir. qu. explains *exemplar*; the pres. subjunc. is normal sequence after a pres. perf. (*proposuit*, 18).

18 utile ... exemplar picks up 3; one of poetry's duties was to supply the young with *nota exempla* (*Ep.* 2.1.130–1) on which to frame the conduct of their lives. The subj. of *proposuit* is Homer; *nobis*, suggest-ing that we apply the lessons to ourselves, is picked up by *nos* 27.

Vlixem, in apposition to *exemplar*, is the correct form of the acc. (Housman II 834–5). Ulysses was held up as a model of the *contemptor uoluptatis*, esp. by the Stoics (Cic. *Off.* 3.97, Sen. *Dial.* 2.2.1; F. Buffière, *Les mythes d'Homère* (Paris 1956) 365–91, W. B. Stanford, *The Ulysses theme*[2] (Oxford 1963) 121–7); but he was also open to criticism, esp. on the stage (Stanford 102–17).

19–22 adapt *Odyssey* 1.1–5. *domitor* is justified, since Ulysses, as Cicero noted (*Fam.* 10.13.2), is called 'city-sacker' for devising the ruse of the Horse (*Od.* 8.492–5, 9.504), a demonstration of his combining bravery and practical wisdom. *prouidus* 'exercising forethought' replaces Homer's πολύτροπος 'versatile'. *multorum* and *hominum* go together ἀπὸ κοινοῦ (= Homer's πολλῶν ἀνθρώπων; cf. *AP* 141–2 *dic mihi, Musa, uirum, captae post tempora Troiae | qui mores hominum multorum uidit et urbes*).

20 homin(um) inspexit: the main caesura of the verse is called a 'quasi-caesura', produced by elision of the first *longum*, here *um*, before the monosyllabic prefix, here *in*, which was reckoned for prosodical purposes to be etymologically separable from its compound; there are strong caesuras in the second and fourth feet as well (Kenney on Lucr. 3.174). *inspexit* = Homer's ἔγνω; both suggest critical scrutiny, not mere observation; cf. the parody of Pl. *Pers.* 550 *urbis speciem uidi, hominum mores perspexi parum*.

latum ... per aequor 'far and wide over the sea'; the epithet is predicative and the phrase = Hom. *Il.* 2.159 ἐπ' εὐρέα νῶτα θαλάσσης.

21 dum 'all the while' (*OLD* 4), giving the motive for or logical concomitant of the activity described.

22 aduersis goes in sense with *rerum* (enallage: 1.94n.).

immersabilis: a coinage = ἀβάπτιστος; for H.'s compounds with *in* see B. on *Ep.* 2.1.223. The metaphor perhaps recalls 1.16.

23 The Sirens notoriously lured sailors to their death by inducing them with song to sail too close to their rock (*Od.* 12.39). Circe offered visitors a drink which turned them into beasts (*Od.* 10.135). These were two sorts of pleasure that ruined the imprudent; Ulysses used his wits (*prouidus*) to enable him to enjoy the pleasures unscathed; against Circe's drugs he used the antidote moly (*Od.* 10.305, in fact it was a gift from Mercury) and to listen to the Sirens he lashed himself to the ship's mast and blocked the crew's ears with wax.

24 sociis: cf. 6.63–4 for further application of the myth to our own behaviour. *stultus*, recalling 8, and *cupidus* should be understood adverbially (10n.; cf. 1.47).

25 domina meretrice: the lover's loss of independence is implied; it was part of the tradition to regard Circe as a sort of courtesan (Kaiser (17–31n.) 201–2). For the rhythm of the line see Introduction p. 14.

turpis 'ugly' literally for having lost their humanity, but with the moral note of 3. *excors* 'brute' is untrue to Homer (*Od.* 10.240 'but the human mind was in them just as before'), but again it became a part of the traditional moral exegesis (Kaiser (17–31n.) 203–4).

26   uixisset: see *uiuat* 10n. Dogs (*canis*) do not appear in Circe's Homeric zoo, but their filthy habits suit H.'s purpose.

   amica luto = φιλοβόρβορος or φιλοκονίμων (1.76n.). The final monosyllable *sus* parodies epic style (B. on *AP* 139).

27   nos emphatically brings the message home.

   numerus 'cipher' is a calque on ἀριθμός (but *OLD* 8b translates 'mob'). *fruges consumere* recalls an Homeric phrase (*Il.* 6.142 'mortals, who eat the fruit of the earth'), here given a pejorative sense; the infin. is complementary with *nati* (*OLD nascor* 14).

28   sponsi = *proci*, who hoped to become her betrothed (Fordyce on Catull. 65.19). The suitors notoriously spent their time eating up Ulysses' substance and debauching the maidservants. Likewise the sons of Alcinous, king of the Phaeacians, were reckoned corrupt sensualists by the moralizing critics of antiquity (however agreeable they now appear), cf. 15.24 and Plat. *Resp.* 10.614; the scholia to the *Odyssey* take a similar line, e.g., on 8.100 and 248 (Kaiser (17–31n.) 217–20). From this point, the application of the terms is metaphorical (Introduction pp. 28–30).

29   in cute curanda ... operata 'occupied with looking after (*OLD curo* 1c) their physical well-being'. *corpus curare* is a common phrase (*TLL* IV 1012.55–60), so H. subtly lowers the tone by substituting the more vivid *cutis* (*TLL* IV 1501.70–3). *operatus*, on the other hand, is poetic (until Livy, *TLL* IX 2.689.74), and frequently refers to ritual activities. The whole forms a sort of oxymoron. *operata iuuentus* might be owed to Virg. *A.* 3.136.

   plus aequo: essential qualification (L. on *S.* 1.3.57); the *iuuentus* lack moderation in what is, after all, a necessary activity.

30   cui 'in whose opinion', dat. of person judging, as usual, a pronoun (*NLS* §65); *pulchrum* 'glorious' (*OLD* 2b) recalls 3. *in* 'until' (*OLD* 13b). For the enjambment with *et* see Introduction p. 24.

31 The Phaeacians 'woo tardy sleep' to the sound of the lyre (*C.* 3.1.20–1 *non auium citharaeque cantus | somnum reducent*), as did Maecenas when love-sick (Sen. *Dial.* 1.3.10); sleep is slow to come to those who are not tired out by any exertions. Unresolved textual difficulties bedevil the line. *cessantem*, an early conjecture, is here preferred to the reading of the MSS, *cessatum*; *ducere* = 'induce' (*OLD* 15b, *Epod.* 14.3 *pocula ... ducentia somnos*); *somnum*, which forms a gliding transition to the next section, introduced by the notion of waking up, is clearly superior to *curam*, an alternative reading of the tradition.

32–43 The picture of self-indulgence prompts a call to attend to the need for moral education; as usual, the second pers. becomes general, but the advice still concerns young men, if not necessarily Lollius in particular (Fraenkel 315).

32–3 form a rhetorical inference *e contrario*, called enthymeme (cf. K–S II 141). Two sentences, each complete in itself, are juxtaposed. The first, usually introduced by Cicero with *ergo*, states an admitted fact; the second asks a question.

32   **de** 'whilst it is ...' (*OLD* 4).

33   **expergisceris** 'will you not wake up?', of course, metaphorically; the pres. is used in anticipation of the fut., esp. in questions (G–L §228, Roby §1461, K–S I 120).

33–7   **atqui ... et ni ... si non:** the sentence forms a paratactic comparison (Kiessling); the illustration from physical health is not introduced by *ut* but co-ordinated by *et* with the main thought (cf. 47–9, 6.31–2n., Fraenkel 220); for the prominent enjambments see Introduction p. 25. Since dropsy was reckoned the penalty of overindulgence (1.31n.) it often appears in moral advice as a dreadful warning against avarice (N–H on *C.* 2.2.13–16; *Ep.* 2.2.146–8).

34   **noles:** sc. *expergisci* (others supply *currere*, which fails to complete the antitheses of the argument); the fut. is usual in a subordinate clause if the main verb is fut. (G–L §242 R1, Roby §1464(a)).

   hydropicus: a Greek loan-word, first found here in literature, though its earlier use as a technical term seems likely (Waltz 80–1); H. was also the first to bring *hydrops* into literary Latin at *C.* 2.2.13, and in both cases the reason seems to have been that the Latin term, *aqua intercus*, was too wordy (it appears in Lucilius, 764 M.). The analogy between physical and spiritual health is again employed (1.28–40n.); running was recommended to the dropsical (Celsus 3.21).

35   **posces ante diem ... cum lumine:** a slave (cf. *Ep.* 2.1.112 or *S.* 2.3.2) brings the oil lamp and book so that the student may read before the business of the day begins at dawn.

   librum: Homer is in H.'s mind, not a philosophical text; cf. the booklet at 1.37, and 18.96 *leges*.

36 intendes animum 'will direct your attention', followed by the simple dat., is poetic syntax first used here, perhaps a calque upon προσέχω τὸν νοῦν (*TLL* VII 1.2113.63). *honestis* goes with *studiis* ἀπὸ κοινοῦ.

37 inuidia: Agamemnon envied Achilles (so the scholiast on *Il.* 2.225); *amore* looks to Achilles' love-lorn weeping in *Il.* 9.342.

uigil: untimely moral sleep leads to real insomnia (33).

nam cur = *curnam* (1.76n.) introduces contrasted questions, of which the first deploys once again the analogy of physical health; the second (*siquid . . .*) is joined to it by adversative asyndeton.

39 ēst: third pers. sing. pres. indic. of *ědo*.

in annum 'for a year', with a verb of postponing (*OLD in* 13b).

40 dimidium ... habet: a proverb (Otto §557). The diminishing length of the phrases emphasizes urgency, Heinze observed.

sapere 'to be a *sapiens*' (B. on *AP* 309); *aude* 'have the determination' (*TLL* II 1252.72–3). It all depends on us.

41 incipe: the strong pause after the first dactyl is specially vigorous (Winbolt §8).

recte 'in accordance with principles correctly determined' (B. on *Ep.* 2.2.213 *uiuere si recte nescis, decede peritis,* but see 6.29n. and cf. 8.4, 15; 16.17; *C.* 2.10.1 *rectius uiues*); its postponement and slight separation from *uiuendi* lend emphasis.

42 rusticus: for the condensed comparison see Introduction p. 29. The countryman has seen spring torrents which soon dwindle rather than proper rivers (Heinze). *expecto* normally takes *dum* 'until' + final subjunc., suggesting suspense or design (G–L §572, Roby §1664, *NLS* §224).

43 The coincidence of accent and ictus throughout the line (9.4n.), alliteration, and caesurae after the trochee in both third and fourth foot (Winbolt §70) enhance the image.

labitur et labetur: a favoured polyptoton, cf. Virg. *A.* 6.617 *sedet aeternumque sedebit* (Bo 400(d)). *uolubilis* goes with both verbs ἀπὸ κοινοῦ.

44–54 Spiritual health is essential; without it the achievement of even more or less legitimate aspirations will sour.

44 argentum 'money' (*OLD* 4), ousted by *pecunia* from most prose, has an archaic/poetic tone which dignifies the notion. These aims are not base (land-clearance could prove a public benefit) but we need to know when to call a halt to acquisition (46).

pueris ... creandis: dat. of purpose with the gerundive (G–L §429, *NLS* §207(4c), Bo 231–3); cf. Pl. *Aul*. 148 *liberis procreandis*. H. likes to evade the pedantic precision of technical formulae (Wickham on *C*. 3.5.42, N–H on *C*. 1.7.27), here the traditional *liberorum (pro)-creandorum causa (vel sim.)*. Romans saw the begetting of children as a social duty, the proper end of marriage (which H. shirked; Treggiari 8 n. 37). The interposition of *beata* (cf. 6.36, *C*. 3.24.19–20 *dotata ... coniunx*) is ironical, for it exposes another, but less socially necessary, motive for marriage.

45 incultae ... siluae: woodland not previously farmed was deemed fertile (Mynors on Virg. *G*. 2.203–11), cf. *Ep*. 2.2.186 *siluestrem flammis et ferro mitiget agrum*.

46 Construe: ⟨*sed is*⟩, *cui quod satis est contingit, nihil amplius optet* (jussive); a pre-eminently Horatian sentiment (*satis* 1.2n., *S*. 2.6.4 *bene est. nil amplius oro*); for *cui* see *cui* 1.85n.

47–9 The vigorous triple anaphora of *non* co-ordinates paratactically what is logically a comparison (33–7n.): '*just as* wealth cannot cure fevers, *so* it cannot heal the spirit either'. The objects of aspiration listed in 44–5 are crisply resumed with a fresh qualification, the need for spiritual health; cf. *C*. 3.1.41–4 (referred to at Introduction p. 11).

47 aceruus: the 'heap' of useless wealth or possessions is a moral commonplace (N–H on *C*. 2.3.19, B. on *Ep*. 2.2.190).

48 < Lucr. 2.34 *nec calidae citius decedunt corpore febres*, in a similar context. *aegroto domini* go ἀπὸ κοινοῦ with *animo* in 49.

deduxit, a medical term (*TLL* v 1.279.27–40), must also be taken ἀπὸ κοινοῦ as the predicate of 49a. The perf. indic. is called gnomic when it states a fact that has held good in the past and so into the present (G–L §236N, Roby §1479, K–S 1 132–3); it is poetic syntax, a Grecism of which H. is specially fond (Bo 261–2).

49 ualeat: asyndeton and the position of the verb at the head of its clause mark the contrast. The thought is a commonplace, cf. 12.4, *S*. 2.3.167 *an numquam utare paratis?*, *C*. 1.31.17–18 *frui paratis ... ualido mihi ... | dones. possessor* qualifies *domini* 48. Moralists stressed that no one really owns anything; but in Roman law *possessio* carried an entitlement to use (*uti* 50, 12.4n.; *OCD* s.v.).

oportet, colloquial and confined to H.'s hexameters, is unusual, but not altogether avoided, in poetry (*TLL* IX 2.737.5–12).

50   comportatis: the four heavy syllables suggest the trouble taken to amass the *aceruus. bene* goes with *uti* (cf. N–H on *C.* 2.12.15); *cogitat* 'intends' (*OLD* 6).

51   Possessions either fire our hope for more or frighten us at the prospect of their loss, so that our pleasure in them is short-lived; for the two passions cf. 4.12, 6.9–10, 16.65, 18.98–9, *Ep.* 2.2.155–6 *si diuitiae ... reddere possent | ... cupidum timidumque minus te* and N–H on *C.* 2.16.15–16 *nec leuis somnos timor aut cupido | sordidus aufert. domus* picks up 47, *res* 50.

52–3   The analogy of physical ailment concludes the illustration; the symptoms of certain disabilities can be pleasurably relieved, but the illness remains. The comparison is of the same implied negative type as that at 11.17–19. The list of three (1.20–3n.) shows a noteworthy *uariatio*: *lippus*, *podagra* and *auriculae* (Ovid too combined the first and last at *Am.* 3.7.61–2).

52   ut: sc. *iuuant* from 51. *fomenta* 'foot-warmers' were used to alleviate gout (Celsus 4.2.4).

53   The blocked ears contrast with 1.7; cf. 8.16.

54   Cf. 1.52n. *uas*: i.e. the mind; the image, a commonplace (Otto §1849), is resumed at 69–70. It makes a transition to the next section which offers precepts against various spiritual ills.

55–63   Advice concludes the preceding development; it may not be of particular relevance to Lollius, though some of it is undeniably appropriate to a young man. One detail deserves special notice, parody of the so-called *praecepta Delphica*. These two-word warnings, e.g. ἡδονῆc κράτει, θυμοῦ κράτει (cf. *sperne uoluptates, animum rege* 62), originated in Greece, where they were inscribed in gymnasia to instil traditional wisdom in the young (W. Dittenberger, *Sylloge Inscriptionum Graecarum*[3] (Leipzig 1920) III 392–7, §1268; L. Robert, *C.R.A.I.* (1968) 421–57; A. N. Oikonomides, *Z.P.E.* 37 (1980) 179–83; E. Schwertheim (ed.), *Die Inschriften von Kyzikos und Umgebung. Teil II, Miletupolis: Inschriften und Denkmäler*, no. 2 (Bonn 1983)). Though they first appear late in Latin, as the *breues sententiae* attached to the *Disticha Catonis* (e.g. *iracundiam rege*; J. Wight Duff and A. M. Duff, *Minor Latin poets* (Loeb edn 1935) 592–7), there seems to be an earlier parody of the format in

Plautus at *Men.* 249 *dictum facessas, datum edis, caueas malo.* H. evokes an educational device common to the two cultures.

55-6 Imperatives, arranged chiastically, deliver the advice, the reasons for which are appended paratactically (Bo 295).

55 Sperne uoluptates: cf. Cic. *Parad.* 33 *spernat uoluptates.*

empta dolore uoluptas < *S.* 1.2.39 *corrupta dolore uoluptas. empta dolore* 'when the price is pain' (Rudd) qualifies the advice; only harmful pleasure is to be shunned; cf. Sen. *Ep.* 90.34 *damnauit [sapiens] mixtas paenitentia uoluptates.* Ulysses had mastered pleasure (23-6).

56 semper: the insatiability of avarice is proverbial (Otto §227, N-H on *C.* 2.2.13).

uoto 'in your heart' (*OLD* 3d); *finem* 'limit', cf. *S.* 1.1.92 *sit finis quaerendi* (*OLD* 6). The limit is, of course, *quod satis est* (46); cf. Sen. *Ep.* 119.6 *qui satis habet consecutus est quod numquam diuiti contigit, finem.*

57-9 The advice becomes fuller and culminates in the warning against anger (59-63). Envy, singled out at 37, and anger are also linked at *Ep.* 2.1.129 *inuidiae corrector* [i.e. the poet] *et irae* and began the list of vices at 1.38.

57 inuidus: the envious man fuels his own discontent, a proverbial notion (Otto §59, cf. 14.11, *S.* 1.1.110-12). *alterius* goes in sense with *rebus* (causal abl.) and aligns H. with those who followed the Stoic Zeno (Diog. Laert. 7.111) in the belief that anyone could be the object of envy (so Cic. *Tusc.* 4.17 *inuidentiam esse dicunt aegritudinem susceptam propter alterius res secundas*). Socrates had held that we only envy our friends (Xen. *Memor.* 3.9.8), Aristotle that envy is confined to those like us in some respects (*Rhet.* 2.10.1-2, 1037B21-7, but cf. *EN* 2.7, 1108B4-5 'the envious man ... is pained at all good fortune').

macrescit)(*opimis*; perhaps a coinage (cf. *tabescat S.* 1.1.111).

58 inuidia: comparative abl. Sicilian tyrants were bywords for cruelty; Phalaris of Agrigentum, for example, roasted people in a brazen bull (Cic. *Verr.* 5.145).

59 tormentum picks up *torquebere* 37. The view that envy is the most lacerating of the vices was not uncommon, cf. Menander, *Sent.* 59 'Envy, the worst of all misfortunes'.

59-63 The fullest warning resumes the motive of the *Iliad* (13); cf. *C.* 4.15.19-20 *ira, quae procudit ensis | et miseras inimicat urbis.* The vice of anger is illustrated in III; ancient moralists devoted considerable time

to it (e.g., Seneca's three books *De ira*), and it was reckoned a failing to
which the hot-headed young were specially prone. Indeed, H. faults
himself on this score at 20.25.

59   moderabitur 'will check' (*OLD* 3), since the fault cannot be
extirpated (*S.* 1.3.76); for the tense see 34n.

60   infectum: sc. *id* as antecedent. *dolor* and *mens* 'mood' (N–H on *C.*
1.16.22) form a hendiadys: 'aggrieved attitude' (G–L §698).

61   poenas ... festinat 'he is quick to seek retribution'; the trans.
use is a syntactical Grecism = σπεύδειν (*OLD* 6).

    odio ... inulto 'from the unpunished object of his hatred'; *odium* is
concrete by metonymy (*OLD* 4). The phrase may, however, mean
'unappeased hatred' (*OLD inultus* 2b), and the case may be either dat.
or causal abl. Seneca discusses anger's pursuit of retribution, and its
link to hatred (*Dial.* 5.5.6).

62   For the parataxis see 55–6n. The thought is proverbial, cf. Sen.
Dial. 3.1.2 *quidam itaque e sapientibus uiris iram dixerunt breuem insaniam*
(Otto §874). *animum* is the seat not just of anger (*TLL* II 98–9) but of
all the passions.

62–3   For the sentiment cf. 10.47.

63   hunc ... hunc: anaphora drives home the warning. *frenis* (cf.
Sen. *Dial.* 5.1.1 *iram refrenare*) and *catena*, the means of curbing horses
and dogs, form a gliding transition to the opening images of the next
section, but the object compared shifts from the passion to the young
man.

    tu strengthens the exhortation (Page on *C.* 1.9.16 (quoted 11.22–
3n.); G–L §267N), cf. *S.* 1.4.85 *hunc tu, Romane, caueto, C.* 1.7.17–18 *sic
tu sapiens finire memento | tristitiam. compesce* goes ἀπὸ κοινοῦ with *hunc
frenis*.

64–71   The closing section, introduced asyndetically, reverts to the
theme hinted at the outset, early training, pointed up by *puer* 68.

64   'The trainer guides (*OLD fingo* 5) the horse of pliant neck, which
readily learns to go its way as its rider may direct.' *tenera* goes with
ceruice (poetic sing.), a descriptive abl. phrase (*NLS* §83).

    docilem governs *ire* (*TLL* V 1.1768.57–8); for the complementary
infin. with adjectives in H. see Introduction p. 23 n. 82.

65   uiam: internal acc. (G–L §333.2R, *OLD eo* 1e), not the antecedent of *qua* 'in whatever manner that ...' (*OLD* 6), i.e. fast or slow.

monstret (potential subjunc.) shows that the horse's obedience is now a characteristic; it does whatever it is bidden (Schütz).

65–7   uenaticus ... catulus: the sentence is enclosed by the subject words. The example may be chosen to appeal to a young man keen on the chase (18.40–52).

65–6   ex quo tempore: similar enjambment at Lucr. 1.550 and Virg. *A.* 1.623.

66   ceruinam pellem: a stuffed stag.

   aula 'yard', poetic diction, a loan word from Greek first found here in the sense *cohors*, which H. perhaps felt too humble (cf. 1.87); it is answered by *in siluis* 67. The point is that the puppy is the father to the hound (1.64n.).

67–8   nunc ... nunc: insistent anaphora and the alliteration of *puro pectore* and *puer* are reinforced by an etymological pun: Varro derived *puer* from *purus*, i.e. prepubescent, not yet corrupted (*apud* Censorinus, *De die natali* 14.2, R. Maltby, *A lexicon of ancient Latin etymologies* (Leeds 1990) s.v.). Lucilius has a similar formulation: *quod gracila est, pernix, quod pectore puro,* | *quod puero similis* (296–7M.). For the phrase cf. *S.* 1.6.64, Jocelyn on Enn. *scen.* 256 *pectus purum*; this passage in the *Phoenix* may also have been in H.'s mind at 1.17.

68   uera, independently proposed by Linker, Löwner and Birt, is more precise than the paradosis, *uerba*, which is either thought to refer to the words of 'the better' or to H.'s own advice, though the omission of *mea* is hard, since the notion is not latent in the context. (*uerba* could be kept if we read *pura* for *puro* in 67, but the formula should probably not be tampered with.)

   puer 'in your youth', predicative apposition to the subj. of the imperatives as at *C.* 1.9.15–6 (quoted 11.22–3n.; G–L §325 R3). *melioribus*, which may be neuter, (cf. *S.* 1.2.73 *meliora monet*) or masc., looks back to 1.48.

69–70 The image of 54 is redeployed in yet another proverbial analogy (Otto §1770).

69   quo: *odorem* is antecedent. *semel est imbuta* < Enn. *Ann.* 476 Sk. *quom illud quo iam semel est imbuta ueneno.*

70   diu: emphatic as last word of its sentence.

70–1 The pace of our moral advance depends on us, it is not a competition (H. Dörrie, *RAC* v 493 s.v. Entwicklung). The addition of the final sentence removes the impression of overbearing admonition by reminding us that H. too is on the road to self-improvement, as he hinted at the outset and at 27–31.

anteis: the last two syllables are fused into one by synizesis (Winbolt §163).

71   H. is obstinately moderate (cf. 6.16).

The first programmatic epistle made unspecific allusions to moral guides; in it, moreover, the city of Rome was dominant, where the bad moral training of Janus was endorsed by the populace. The second epistle, carefully placed in the collection as Wickham noted, pursues the issue of moral training in marked contrast. The writer has retreated from Rome to the country and he declares for the sound lessons of a specific text: Homer. But in specifying H. also takes a stand in the old battle between philosophy and poetry. Without altogether repudiating the study of philosophical texts he belittles them and reestablishes the poet as the superior moral guide by reason of his unmistakable lessons and useful illustrations. It is also noteworthy that H.'s moral interpretation of the Homeric texts is not allegorical nor does he attempt to accommodate them to a sect; it remains at a broad, uncontroversial level. The epistle is a sort of protreptic, but not towards philosophy. Just as H. himself in his later years has gone back to Homer, so he implicitly encourages Lollius, who is still a young man in training, not to leave behind the poems that will shape aright his moral outlook. The epistle is a protreptic to poetry (G. Kennedy, *The art of rhetoric in the Roman world* (Princeton 1972) 398 n. 27).

To be sure, one approach to the old enmity, much favoured in the Greek world, was to regard the study of poetry as a preparation or propaedeutic for philosophy. There is, however, no hint in this epistle that H. endorses this progression. Indeed, the fact that he returns to Homer (whose text he certainly knew already) strongly suggests that for him Homer suffices absolutely. Nowhere in the epistles does H. press a philosophical text upon his addressees, though like all cultivated men he saw that an acquaintance with philosophical figures and issues was a part of one's intellectual furniture. So by a paradox the middle-aged H. finds himself back in the schoolroom attending to the moral lessons to be found in the first of poets. The image of lessons dominated the previous epistle and holds no less sway in this.

Epistle III

1–5 establish the epistolary fiction. Julius Florus (Introduction p. 8) is in the East, but where exactly?

1 quibus terrarum ... oris 'in what region of the world', a poetic expression, cf. Virg. *A.* 1.331 *quibus orbis in oris*; the simple local abl. without *in* (cf. 2.67) and the attachment to it of the partitive gen., which is usually found with local adverbs (cf. 34, *OLD terra* 9d), contribute to the mannered effect.

militet need not entail fighting, cf. *militiae* 'abroad'.

2 priuignus: Tiberius Claudius Nero, the son of Livia, was not adopted by Augustus until A.D. 4; the word flatters both men. In late 21 B.C. he set off to place Tigranes on the throne of Armenia in place of the assassinated Artaxias (cf. 12.26–8; Tac. *Ann.* 2.3.4; *CAH* x 262 n. 3; *RE* x 481). He was attended by a suite, *cohors*, whose literary interests reflected his own, hence the presence of Florus (6n.; Suet. *Tib.* 70 *artes liberales ... studiosissime coluit*). *scire* is complementary infin. with *laboro*, found in Catull. 67.17.

3–5 ne ... an ... an: cf. 11.4–6. The language and expression are poetic, as befits a letter from one literary man to another. The list of places follows the journey overland from West to East.

3 Thraca: largely poetic for *Thracia*; sc. *moratur* from 5.

Hebrusque niuali: the unusual rhythm (2.25n.) teases Florus' cultivated ear. The Hebrus, now the Maritza or Meriç, flows through Bulgaria to form the border between Greece and Turkey.

niuali compede uinctus: high-flown, esp. the poetic sing. *compede* (N–H on *C.* 1.33.14) here, unusually, metaphorical.

4 Another learned tease for the well-read Florus. The common view held that there was a single tower, Hero's, on the European shore of the Hellespont at Sestos; that her lover, Leander, had a tower too on the Asian shore at Abydus is only mentioned, and casually at that, by Strabo 13.591; cf. Virg. *G.* 3.258–63 (Professor Kenney points out that the form of the line also recalls *G.* 2.157 *fluminaque antiquos subter labentia muros*). For the separation of *inter* from its acc. see 2.6n.

5 pingues: the fertility of Asia Minor was legendary, cf. N–H on *C.* 2.12.22 *pinguis Phrygiae.* Its beautiful cities drew Roman tourists, as their ruins draw us (cf. XI and Catull. 46).

6–29 H. asks about the activities of the company; he is at first con-

cerned with their literary pursuits, which he runs through in the traditional order determined by the importance of the genre (6–21); but in
dwelling upon Florus' accomplishments (21–5) he moves to moral
issues (25–9).

6 The *cohors* of a magistrate abroad might well include literary men
(*OLD studiosus* 2) who wished to travel in safety. They did not necessarily have an administrative role, though personal profit was not ruled
out; so, for example, Catullus and Cinna went with Memmius to
Bithynia.

Quid ... operum 'what by way of literary work'; the defining gen.
with *quid* is perhaps that of the rubric (*NLS* §72(5ii)) since *operum* is a
general term applied to a particular thing; the sense of some partitives
is similar (*NLS* §77(ii)).

struit 'compose' (*OLD* 3); *curo* 'am interested in' (*OLD* 8).

7–8 Epic, which held first place in the traditional hierarchy of poetic
kinds, is enquired about in two lines. Moreover the *laudes Augusti*
(16.38), to which H. flatteringly alludes, introduce a note of literary
patriotism.

7 res gestas 'exploits', esp. as a theme of poetry (*OLD gero* 9b, B. on
AP 73). *scribere* is complementary infin. with *sumit*.

8 bella ... et paces: *sc. Augusti*; *paces* seems to mean 'periods of
peace', though the plur. is unusual, as pseudo-Acro noted (B. on *Ep*.
2.1.102). *aeuum* is poetic (cf. *C*. 4.14.3 *in aeuum*, B. on *Ep*. 2.1.159).

diffundit 'is extending the reputation of (by writing about)', a subtle development of the verb's usage (*TLL* v 1.1111.70–1).

9–11 Titius and the choral lyric are given three lines, a steady increase. H. himself had chiefly imitated the monodic poet Alcaeus
(19.32), though some odes suggest Pindar (*C*. 1.12) or Bacchylides
(*C*.1.15). Others were venturing more widely into this territory.

9 quid: 1.91n. *breui uenturus in ora* 'soon (*OLD breuis* 6) sure to become
famous' (*OLD os*[1] 3c). *Romana* sounds again the patriotic note; Titius
will be the first to win fame for Latin choral lyric in imitation of
Pindar. H.'s confident prediction and reference to the Muse's protec-
tion (13) preclude the notion of irony at Titius' expense.

10 Pindarici fontis: springs were part of the metaphor of poetic
inspiration (N–H on *C*. 1.26.6), and a classic poet might be thought of
as a fount of inspiration for imitators, cf. Prop. 3.3.52 *Philitea ... aqua*;

Homer esp. was likened to a fount from which his successors drank (Housman on Manil. 2.9 with *addenda*, Russell on Longin. *Subl.* 13.3).

expalluit: trans. perhaps only here (poetic syntax). Imitation (an important theme) entails dangers; the grander the model, the greater the risk of failure. This was true esp. of Pindar, as H. later avows, cf. *C.* 4.2.1–4.

11 Construe *ausus fastidire lacus et riuos* with *apertos* 'public' (*OLD* 9d) ἀπὸ κοινοῦ. H. recalls Callimachus' disdain of the public well, *Epig.* 28.3–4 = *HE* 1043–4. He may also have in mind an image drawn from Pindar himself, found now only in an adaptation by Quintilian, *IO* 10.1.109: *non enim pluuias, ut ait Pindarus, aquas colligit, sed uiuo gurgite exundat* [*Cicero*].

ausus: cf. *audes* 20; in literary contexts this hints at the daring of the imitator, who should also aspire to rival and surpass his model (*TLL* II 1256.22–30; B. on *AP* 10 and 287).

12   ut ualet 'how's his health?', a colloquial question, cf. Pl. *Aul.* 117 *rogitant me ut ualeam*. The personal note is engagingly sounded between the literary enquiries.

fidibus ... Latinis: cf. 19.32–3 and *Ep.* 2.2.143; the patriotic note of 7–8 and 9 is echoed and amplified by the juxtaposition of *Latinis* and *Thebanos*; Titius works for the honour of Rome.

13   Thebanos: Thebes in Boeotia was the birthplace of Pindar; the *doctus poeta* expected his readers to be able to identify an author from such an allusion (cf. 19.23 Archilochus of Paros; *C.* 1.32.5 *Lesbio ... ciui* (Alcaeus), 2.1.38 *Ceae ... neniae* (Simonides of Ceos), 4.2.25 *Dircaeum ... cycnum* (Pindar)). On the other hand, H. believes that the birthplace gains renown from its distinguished poetic scions.

aptare 'accommodate to' (*OLD* 5), since Latin makes its own demands (cf. N–H on *C.* 2.12.4 *aptari*). *auspice Musa* goes ἀπὸ κοινοῦ with 14 (so Müller).

14   tragica ... in arte: the third great genre, tragedy, was to be of special interest to H. in *AP*. His tone here is lightly ironical, not so much at Titius' expense as because he believed that the Romans still fell short of the stylistic standards of the Greek model.

desaeuit 'exhausts his rage' (B. on *AP* 94). By a common figure the poet is said to do what he describes (N–H on *C.* 2.1.18 *perstringis auris*, L. on *S.* 1.10.36; cf. 1.100n.).

ampullatur = ληκυθίζει, a lexical Grecism. The *ampulla* was a jar, but the origin of the metaphor, which seems to point to highfalutin style, is unclear (Rudd on *AP* 97).

15 quid mihi Celsus agit? 'tell me, what's Celsus up to?' (*OLD ago* 22); *mihi* is ethic dat., expressing someone's interest in another's condition or behaviour (*OLD ego* c; *NLS* §66). Celsus is the addressee of VIII.

monitus ... monendus: polyptoton enhances H.'s warning against plagiarism (cf. *furtiuis* 20n.). Too great a reliance upon the model reduces independence and personal achievement (a theme of XIX). The adverbial *multum*, a colloquial usage found in Plautus but not Terence (L. on *S.* 1.3.57; B. on *AP* 357), goes also with *monitus* ἀπὸ κοινοῦ.

16 priuatas: emphatic by position; for the notion cf. *AP* 131 *publica materies priuati iuris erit. tangere*, complementary infin. with *uitet*, suggests profanation of sacred objects (and the newly founded libraries were, as usual, attached to a temple); see *OLD* 5b.

17 recepit: 'reception' (*OLD* 8) into the list of approved authors acknowledged the classic status of a literary work. On 9 Oct. 28 B.C. in fulfilment of a vow Octavian dedicated a temple to Apollo on the Palatine hill which also housed libraries of Greek and of Latin literature (*C.* 1.31, *Ep.* 2.1.216–7; Richardson 14, 58–9). Since the libraries were to be public, there is an implied contrast with *priuatas* 16.

18–20 An adaptation of the fable of the proud jackdaw and the peacock (Phaedrus 1.3, cf. Babr. 72), which may also have been used by the contemporary Epicurean philosopher and epigrammatist Philodemus to criticize meretricious rhetorical ornament, cf. *Rh.* II 68.25 (a supplement); H. knew his work (14.36n., *S.* 1.2.120–2). There is a concealed comparison between Celsus and the crow (Introduction pp. 28–30).

18 repetitum 'to recover', a legal term (*OLD* 9); the supine of purpose with a verb of motion is characteristic of colloquial speech and so found only once in the lyrics (*C.* 1.2.15, often reckoned an early poem) but fourteen times in the hexameters (*NLS* §152, Austin on Virg. *A.* 2.786). *olim* 'one day' (*OLD* 3).

20 furtiuis suggests *furtum* 'literary theft' (*TLL* VI 1.1646.1–12; *OLD* is inadequate on this sense). The colourful feathers, *coloribus*, are merely a superficial dressing-up (1.95–6n.); the bad imitator misses the essential character of the plundered work.

20–9 H. lastly enquires about Florus' own literary and other pursuits, with a hint at life's true goal.

21 quae ... thyma: poetic plur. The flitting bee suggests variety of interests, above all poetry (*C*. 4.2.27–9).

agilis: adverbial; *agiliter* does not scan in hexameter verse.

21–2 non ... non: emphatic anaphora and litotes (G–L §700) reveal Florus' talent as considerable. The division of the sentence points to the common distinction between *ingenium* and *ars*; *incultum* and *hirtum* show that training has refined his gift.

22 hirtum: in a figurative sense only here; more common is *hirsutus* 'shaggy' (e.g. Ov. *Tr*. 2.259).

23–4 Florus' pursuits are specified. The first two define some legal duties of a *patronus*, to defend his clients in court (1.57n.) or to advise them on questions of law (see *OCD* s.v. Jurisprudence, L. on *S*. 1.1.9 *iuris legumque peritus*).

23 linguam ... acuis: for the metaphor cf. Cic. *De orat*. 3.121 *non enim solum acuenda nobis neque procudenda lingua est* (also found in Greek, cf. LSJ s.v. ἀκονάω).

causis = *in causas dicendas*; dat. of the end aimed at (*NLS* §67), but the simple case is poetic syntax, cf. *C*. 3.27.61–2 *acuta leto* | *saxa*.

23–4 ciuica iura respondere = *ius ciuile r.* (*OLD respondeo* 4c); the acc. is an internal obj. (K–S 1 278). *ciuica*, a poetic word, sidesteps a technical expression (N–H on *C*. 2.1.1).

24 amabile carmen < Pindar, *Pyth*. 5.107 μέλος χαρίεν, suggests light verse, perhaps elegy, or love songs.

25 hederae: gen. of material or definition (*NLS* §72(5)). Since ivy crowns the poet (*C*. 1.1.29), its award for the civic achievements is purely metaphorical (N–H on *C*. 2.11.2 and cf. their n. on *C*. 1.35.13); moreover, in long disjunctive sentences the main clause tends to refer to the last item specifically (L. on *S*. 2.2.11–13 and cf. 17.55n., N–H on *C*. 2.8.23). For *uictricis* see 4.3n.

25–9 H. detects a dissatisfaction with these accomplishments and proposes a remedy of general application (28–9).

25 quodsi: 1.70n.; for the enjambment see Introduction p. 24.

26 frigida curarum fomenta 'the chilling compresses your cares apply'; *curarum* is gen. of definition (*hederae* 25n.; J. Foster, *Mnem*. 25 (1972) 303–6). Cold compresses would have suggested to H.'s readers the fashionable treatment of Antonius Musa, the most noted physician of the day; his curative, prescribed in season and out, saved Augustus but not Marcellus (*RE* 1 2633–4, cf. 15.3n.; Suet. *Aug*. 59.1, 81.1; Dio 53.30.3–4). Florus' cares – public business, perhaps love (24) and the pursuit of gain (*cohors* 6n.) – chill his *ingenium* (Crinagoras *AP* 9.234.2 = *GP* 2055). But the scholiasts and many commentators take the phrase to mean 'the ineffectual (*OLD* 8b) consolations of your cares' (obj. gen.), with particular reference to the last item, poetry (for poetry as supposed relief from care see N–H on *C*. 1.32.15). In that case too H. is found to be advising Florus to reassess his interests by moral standards.

27   quo ... caelestis sapientia duceret, ires: a parody, appropriately addressed to a young man 'on campaign', of a soldier's loyalty oath (cf. Headlam on Herodas 6.43, N–H on *C*. 2.17.11). *sapientia* is a sort of general, to be followed anywhere.

caelestis: the gods provide true understanding because reason, their viceroy in us, is divine (Cic. *ND* 2.147, Sen. *Ep*. 66.12; the phrase is found in Greek in Heracl. *All*. 33f.). *sapientia* here is neither 'wisdom' nor 'philosophy', which cannot be expected of young men; 'understanding', however, he does need, to succeed as a man and as a poet (so Müller; cf. *AP* 309 *scribendi recte sapere est et principium et fons*).

duceret: subjunc. by attraction to the mood of the apodosis, *ires* (*LS* §161).

28   hoc ... hoc: anaphora drives home the exhortation; the nouns realign the activities suggested at 6: *opus* implies action, *studium* reflection. The transitive use of *propero* (*OLD* 5) is archaic and poetic.

parui 'unimportant' (*OLD* 5b) forms with *ampli* a polar expression, emphasizing the universal need to drop our cares so as to be able to follow where *sapientia* leads (cf. 1.25–6).

**29   Take *uiuere cari* (2.10n.) and *uolumus* together ἀπὸ κοινοῦ. As in 21–2, the division by *si ... si* points up a contrast between public and private life; the *ampli* will attend to the state, we *parui* must look after ourselves. *patriae* strikes again the patriotic note; Florus and his friends are after all in the company of Tiberius as he performs state business. H. therefore stresses the need for *sapientia* in public life.

nobis ... cari: we naturally love ourselves, cf. Cic. *Amic*. 80 *ipse enim*

se quisque diligit ... quod per se quisque sibi carus est, 18.101n. Still, we do
not always correctly identify what is in our own best interest and for
that we need *sapientia*. Having stated the practical goals of *sapientia* in
the widest terms H. passes on to a particular application, prompted by
the notion *carus*.

30–6 Just as friends effect introductions, as in IX and XII, so they
act as go-betweens for estranged companions (*S.* 1.5.29 *auersos soliti
componere amicos*). The connection with the previous section lies in 33–4;
sapientia mitigates passion and error.

30 hoc prepares for the following indir. qu. (L. on *S.* 2.3.89), which
exceptionally has no introductory interrogative particle (K–S II 502).
Some editors propose to read *si tibi curae ⟨est⟩* (added by Chabot and
Bentley independently); but the indic. followed by the subjunc. *conueniat* is hard to stomach.

curae 'a subject for concern' 'dear to', predicative dat. (*OLD* 5b,
Roby II xliv–xlv, *NLS* §68 n. (i)).

31 conueniat 'is befitting', impersonal (*OLD* 6b); with it understand *esse*. For Munatius see Introduction p. 8 n. 26. *an* 'can it be that
...' introduces a surprised direct qu. (*OLD* 1). *male* 'not quite' is a
polite quasi-negative (*OLD* 6), less emphatic than *non* or *in-*.

32 gratia 'goodwill' (*OLD* 2). The metaphor is of an incompletely
healed wound; cf. Petr. 113.8 *ueritus ne inter initia coeuntis gratiae recentem
cicatricem rescinderet* (*OLD coeo* 5).

33 calidus sanguis hints at the dangers of *ira* discussed in II,
natural enough in the young, esp. in a company of ambitious men
surrounding an important figure.

rerum inscitia 'general inexperience', cf. Ter. *And.* 911 *imperitos
rerum* (of young men), Sen. *Ep.* 90.45 *ignorantia rerum*; but some take
it to mean 'a misunderstanding'; for the indefinite use of *rerum* see
Nägelsbach 96–7. As Morris noted, this tactful reproach should make
them see sense (they might be proud of hot-bloodedness).

34 indomita ceruice feros: the metaphor of untamed bulls or stal-
lions recalls by contrast 1.39–40 and 2.64 (a link between these two
poems to young men) and so suggests the need for correct training.

locorum, partitive gen., recalls the opening enquiries (1–5); the
plur. here seems to be somewhat stylized, cf. N–H on *C.* 1.38.3 *quo
locorum*.

35 uiuitis 'are' (2.10n.). For *fraternum ... foedus* see 18.44n.; the bond of brotherhood is proverbial (Otto §714; of course, there were famous exceptions, cf. N–H on *C*. 2.2.6).

rumpere is complementary infin. with *indigni* 'too good to ...' (*OLD* 3). H. tactfully puts the observation that the breach is unworthy of their natures in an off-hand way.

36 < Virg. *G*. 3.219 *pascitur in magna Sila formosa iuuenca* (a bold intertext: see p. 275). A heifer (*iuuenca*), vowed as sacrifice (*uotiua*; cf. *C*. 1.36.2 *uituli sanguine debito*) in order to secure his friends' safe return, will be eaten at the celebratory *cena aduenticia*.

in 'in anticipation of' (*OLD* 22c); *uestrum* hints that H. takes their reconciliation for granted.

The previous epistle was addressed to a young man preparing to take his place in public life; yet he was not depicted within society. This epistle enlarges the horizon. Florus too is beginning to make his way in the world, but we see him in an altogether wider context, not at Rome but abroad, not alone but in company, indeed, in the highest company. It is noteworthy that this group of young aspirants variously combine poetic activity with civic duty. As usual, H. was concerned with the poet's function in society; he interests himself in these young men not simply because they are poets but because they are active in public life as well. Hence the patriotic note is sounded, esp. at 29 *patriae*. Conformably to this, H. sees epic verse as panegyric of Roman achievements and he praises Titius for advancing Latin poetry into new territory, Pindaric lyric. He places his young poets in a civic ambience because poetry is rightly a part, not the whole of, their lives. (Similar is the more specific advice to Lollius in XVIII concerning his poetic activities. He is to lay them aside if his superior friend has other amusements in view (40–7).) H. knows that society makes just claims upon our time, even if we happen to be poets and so addicted to solitude (*Ep*. 2.2.77 *scriptorum chorus omnis amat nemus et fugit urbem*). West's argument (29–39) that H. uses bee imagery to urge upon Florus the realization of his full potentialites as a poet is unduly restrictive; he must realize himself as a man in society.

But company can chafe and so guidance is needed on behaviour. (In VIII H. uses the Muse, as guardian of civility, to give Celsus a warning on how to behave in company.) For all Florus' accomplishments there will be a hole at the heart without attention to *caelestis sapientia*. (Strikingly similar in tone and the pattern of argument is the letter of Pliny to Caninius, 1.3, which begins with questions about his garden and his enjoyment of it. Or is he perhaps busied with other property interests? If so, he is no better than most men. Pliny therefore advises him 'quin tu (tempus enim) *humiles et sordidas curas* aliis mandas, et ipse te in alto isto pinguique secessu studiis adseris? Hoc sit negotium tuum.') An object lesson in the need for understanding is Florus' estrangement from Munatius. H. uses the letter as a means to encourage, even to enforce with an invitation to dinner, their reconciliation. He has learnt his lesson from the behaviour of Nestor in the *Iliad* (cf. 2.11–12).

Epistle IV

1–5 H. asks what work Albius is currently engaged upon. Is he writing or meditating in his country retreat?

1 Albius is also the addressee of *C.* 1.33, from which it appears that he writes elegies (*decantes elegos* 3). This has prompted his identification with the contemporary elegist Albius Tibullus. Unfortunately Albius is a common name (*S.* 1.4.28, 109), composing elegy was the fashion, and Tibullus always refers to himself by his cognomen. In short, the identification of the two is unproven (J. P. Postgate, *Selections from Tibullus*[2] (London 1910) 179–84).

sermonum refers to all H.'s hexameter writings on moral matters (B. on *Ep.* 2.1.250). H. singles them out rather than the lyrics to prepare for the question of 4–5.

candide 'good-natured' (*OLD* 8), perhaps with a pun on the addressee's name: *Albius < albus* (R. Flores, *R.A.A.N.* 37 (1962) 59–62). Literary works were usually handed round a circle of friends to secure critical comment (*S.* 1.10.81–4, *AP* 438–52).

2 quid ... te dicam facere = *quid facis?*; this periphrasis with a deliberative subjunc. is found in tragedy, and was common in colloquial speech (Lindsay on Pl. *Capt.* 533, Jocelyn on Enn. *scen.* 300 J., Ruckdeschel 161, *TLL* v 1.985.62–70). H. hints at a desire for a reply, but the invitation at the close offers a more intimate opportunity for chat. The *regio Pedana* was east of Rome in the hill country not far from Praeneste. The retreat suits Albius' supposed activities.

3–4 scribere ... reptare: sc. *dicam te.* C. Cassius of Parma, one of Caesar's assassins, died at a time that cannot now be determined, certainly before this epistle; his literary works, whatever they were, have not survived (*RE* III 1743–4; A. La Penna, *Fra teatro, poesia e politica romana* (Turin 1979) 143–51).

3 uincat 'surpass' (*OLD* 9); for the subjunc. see 1.12n. In antiquity as nowadays writers looked upon each other as rivals, and composition was seen in terms of competition.

4 tacitum: Albius appears to be alone with his moral reflections (*S.* 1.6.123 *quod me tacitum iuuet*, *Ep*. 2.2.145 *tacitusque recordor*).

siluas inter ... salubres: a variant of the word order noticed at 2.6n. Clearly the health Albius seeks in the woods is as much spiritual as physical. For *reptare* 'stroll', cf. Plin. *Ep*. 1.24.4 *reptare per limitem* (of Suetonius on his little estate).

5 curantem: 1.11n. *sapiente bonoque*, united, present the ideal combination of *sapientia* and *uirtus* (1.41, 2.17). Cicero uses the pair to embody, without philosophical colour, his exemplary Roman citizen (*TLL* II 2084.21–5); H., however, seems to be redefining that ideal for private life (cf. 7.22, 16.20, 32, 73).

6–14 Albius has the right notions about putting his life in order; yet perhaps, H. hints, he overdoes it and should enjoy his blessings a bit more.

6 Non ... eras 'you didn't use to be (and aren't now)'; the imperf. referring to present time seems to be a Grecism (N–H on *C.* 1.27.19 *laborabas*, B. on *AP* 19). *pectore* 'intelligence' (*OLD* 3b).

6–7 di tibi ... di tibi: anaphora and alliteration in 7 emphasize the abundance of heaven's blessings. Beauty and wealth are *fortuita*, as is the knack for enjoying them.

7 dederunt: the prosody is characteristic of dactylic poetry and is not found in the *Odes* (Plautus has it only at the end of a line or hemistich, so it is already for him a metrical convenience; M. Platnauer, *Latin elegiac verse* (Cambridge 1951) 53–4 n. 1).

fruendi: the keynote is now struck. H. hints that we must make use of our gifts, esp. if we know how to.

8–11 The protasis (9–11) is a rel. clause, its verbs in the potential/ generic subjunc. (cf. 1.49–51n.). The sentence illustrates a characteristically Horatian technique for advancing a thought. Prosaically we would say, 'The gods have given you looks, wealth, wisdom, eloquence, etc. What more could a nursemaid wish for her charge?' H. says, 'The gods gave you looks and wealth. Could a nursemaid wish more for a charge, if he have wisdom, etc.' See N–H on *C.* 1.7.10 and Introduction p. 26 n. 95. The nursemaid's prayers for conventional forms of success are a moral commonplace (Mayor on Juv. 10.289–97).

8 dulci ... alumno < *C.* 3.23.7 *dulces alumni*; dat. of advantage.

9 sapere picks up *sapiente* 5. *fari possit quae sentiat* suggests eloquence; Obbar compared Thuc. 2.60.5 'better than anyone else Pericles knows what is necessary and can explain it', and Professor Kenney notes that it is the source of the Walpole family's motto.

10 gratia 'popularity' (*OLD* 5). For the sing., *contingat*, see 1.84n.

11 mundus uictus 'stylish way of life'; the epithet is colloquial in tone (Axelson 106) and used often by H. to suggest a mean between luxurious superfluity and sordid lack.

non deficiente crumina 'thanks to a never-failing purse'; the abl. phrase is causal (> Juv. 11.38). *crumina* is used by the figure metonymy to mean 'money' for the first time here.

12–14 After the enumeration of Albius' blessings H. obliquely exhorts him to make the most of them. The sentence forms a paratactic condition.

12 timores inter et iras: the word order is characteristic of poetry (*TLL* vii 1.2147.28–34). These emotions need not describe Albius, they are common to all men (cf. *inter* 12.14).

13 diluxisse, as distinct from the commoner *illuxisse*, suggests the light of dawn breaking *through* darkness or clouds, which well suits the context of encouragement to Albius.

supremum: take predicatively, 'each day that dawns is the last'. The sentiment is a moralist's commonplace (Summers on Sen. *Ep.* 12.8).

14 grata: take predicatively, 'the unhoped for hour will come in addition, and welcome too'. For the fut. *sperabitur* see 2.34n.

15–16 H. offers Albius a standing invitation. The reference to Epicureanism hints that H. at any rate practises what he has just preached.

15 Me counterbalances *te* (2); *pinguem et nitidum* is attached to it somewhat elliptically, for Latin, unlike Greek, had no present part. of *esse* (cf. 5.12n.). A prose writer would probably have used an appositional phrase: 'me, uirum pinguem et nitidum' (cf. K–S i 226–8).

bene curata cute: causal abl. H. looks after himself, as he encourages Albius to do, but unlike the Phaeacians, not *plus aequo* (2.29n.).

uises 'be sure to come and see'; the fut. often conveys an urbane command or exhortation (G–L §243, Roby §§1466, 1589, Bo 260–1), but it can also generalize: 'you will come whenever you want to laugh at ...' (H–S 621–2).

16   ridere may recall that H.'s *Sermones*, which Albius enjoyed, used laughter to expose folly and reveal truth (cf. *S.* 1.1.24–5, 10.14–15; J. den Boeft in J. den Boeft and A. H. M. Kessels (edd.), *Actus: Studies in honour of H. L. W. Nelson* (Utrecht 1982) 21–41); he should therefore be able to see the joke in H.'s overstated self-portrait. For *uoles* see 2.34n.

porcum   is the object of *ridere*, and not in apposition to *me*. For H. as a figure of fun cf. 14.39. Because of their reputed hedonism the Epicureans were branded as swinish (Nisbet on Cic. *Pis.* 37 *Epicure noster, ex hara producte, non ex schola*); *grex* puns on this, since it means both 'herd' and 'philosophical school' (*S.* 2.3.44 *Chrysippi ... grex*).

In substantial (but not complete) contrast to the preceding epistles, we are presented here with a solitary friend who has no public ambitions (though he clearly aims to shine in his chosen line). Like the men of III, he is a poet. And once again poetry is seen not to be altogether enough for happiness. A right disposition is wanted, so that the good things of life do not go unenjoyed. H. takes it upon himself to remind his young friend of his blessings and to encourage him – if necessary by ocular demonstration – of the need to make much of them. In effect the epistle is an invitation (*uises* 15), which links it to the next letter, written to one who is very much in the thick of things. H. also opens up for the first time in the collection the notion of himself as the model of one who uses his opportunities.

Epistle V

1–11   An invitation to Torquatus to enjoy a simple dinner with H. The wine, however, will be special. All is ready if only the guest will oblige; he has no excuse since the next day will be a holiday. Torquatus was a member of the patrician family of the Manlii Torquati; he was clearly a hard-working barrister (9). Both details recur at *C.* 4.7.23 *non, Torquate, genus, non te facundia*.

1 potes 'can bring yourself to' (*OLD* 3), a polite formula in invitations, cf. Pl. *St.* 619 *si poteris accubare*, Mart. 5.62.2 *si potes in nudo ponere membra solo*. Archias was presumably a maker of simple furniture. *conuiua* 'as a guest', predicative.

2 modica i.e. not gold, reinforces *Archiacis*; the simplicity of H.'s own domestic economy often points a moral (*C.* 1.20.1 *modicis … cantharis*). *times* 'disdain, refuse' (cf. *metues* 18.1n.); the acc. *holus* with *cenare* is archaic and perhaps colloquial (B. on *Ep.* 2.2.168).

omne 'nothing but', a sense unknown to lexicography, is illustrated by Sonnenschein on Pl. *Rud.* 500 *omnes tui similis hospites habeas tibi*; it is usually taken to mean 'all kinds of'. The salad dinner is typical of H. (N–H on *C.* 1.31.15) and again has emblematic status (cf. 17.13–15; *S.* 2.2.70 on the value of *uictus tenuis*): simple fare suits him.

3 supremo … sole 'at the end of the day' (*OLD supremus* 3, *sol* 2c, poetic), a latish time for a Roman dinner (7.47n.), and so chosen out of courtesy to Torquatus, since it leaves him time to complete his pleading and have a bath. Moreover, since the guest of honour could hardly be expected to travel for several hours after his day's work, the meal will be given in H.'s town house (*domi*).

manebo 'wait for' with a personal object is colloquial (*OLD* 3b).

4 uina: poetic plur. *iterum Tauro*, without *consule*, appears to be unique in literature and so avoids the normal expression. T. Statilius Taurus was consul for the second time in 26 B.C.

diffusa 'racked off' from the *dolium* into the *cadus* in which it was sealed; this was only done for good wine that would keep. The names of the consuls were painted on the sides of the jars to indicate the year of the vintage.

5 The wine seems to be Massic from Campania (Paget 233–5). In this same country in 340 B.C. T. Manlius, *cos.* 347 B.C., defeated the Latins; if the addressee belongs to that family then the wine is a compliment to him (N–H on *C.* 1.20, p. 245). Petrinum is hard to place; Porphyrio says it was a village in the Falernian plain.

6 si '*but* if' taking up *si* (1) by adversative asyndeton (K–S II 431–2). H. avoids *sin*, even in the conversational hexameters, whereas Virgil uses it in the *Georgics* and in the speeches of the *Aeneid*, but not in the *Eclogues* (yet B. on *AP* 125 calls it 'prosaic').

arcesse 'have it sent', a causative use.

imperium: the immediate reference is to H. as 'master of the feast', but it may also refer to the cognomen *Imperiosus* bestowed on the same T. Manlius. It is picked up at 21. *fer* 'put up with' (*OLD* 20). The closing rhythm is not unusual in H.'s hexameters, cf. 6.39, 16.6, 68 (B. on *AP* 139).

7 Construe ἀπὸ κοινοῦ: *iamdudum tibi ⟨mundus⟩ focus et munda supellex splende⟨n⟩t.* The hearth is clean in case the late September evening (9n.) prove cool. *tibi*, dat. of advantage, hints at the trouble H. has taken for Torquatus. The theme of preparations, common in invitation poems, recurs at 21–4 (cf. *C.*1.36, 4.11 and above all 3.29).

8 mitte 'drop' (*OLD* 4); cf. *C.* 3.8.17 *mitte ciuiles super urbe curas,* 3.29.5 *eripe te morae* after announcing that all is ready to receive Maecenas. The 'trifling' (*OLD leuis* 13) hopes may be his own or those his clients repose in him. The struggle for wealth (*certamina diuitiarum*) is Torquatus' (but not his alone); cf. *C.* 4.12.25 *pone moras et studium lucri* in an invitation to Vergilius. Barristers could not legally take fees or gifts thanks to the *lex Cincia* of 204 B.C. (*OCD* s.v. *Aduocatus*).

9 Moschi causam: Volcacius Moschus, a rhetorician of Pergamum, though defended by Asinius Pollio as well as Torquatus, was condemned for poisoning and fled to Marseilles to teach; he became a citizen there and left his estate to the city in A.D. 25 (Sen. *Con.* 2.5(13).13; Tac. *Ann.* 4.43.5). This trial is referred to not to fix the date (which is now unknown) but to compliment Torquatus for the grand cases he has to deal with.

nato Caesare 'by reason of Caesar's birth'; causal abl. with *festus*; for the abstract form of expression see 2.7n. The birthday of Augustus fell on either 21 or 22 or 23 September (Housman on Manilius v, p. 112); Suetonius, *Aug.* 57, mentions celebrations, but this is the only reference to a legal holiday. The month would suggest that H. is in the country (16.16), but see *domi* 3n.

9–10 festus ... dies: a sensible man enjoys a holiday and a proper Roman respects the civil calendar when it enjoins a cessation of legal business (N–H on *C.* 2.3.6).

10 ueniam somnumque 'permission to lie in', hendiadys.

impune licebit parodies legal language and leaves Torquatus with no excuse for refusal.

11 benigno 'friendly' (*OLD* 1, cf. Livy 28.6.6 *benigno uoltu ac sermone*) confirms H.'s disinclination to gossip (*S.* 2.6.70–2); it could also mean 'abundant'. *tendere* 'prolong' (= *extendere*, *OLD* 2).

12–20 H. anticipates a charge of imprudence and praises insobriety; the underlying lesson applies to Torquatus too.

12 Quo mihi fortunam 'what's the use of wealth to me'; the idiomatic ellipse of a verb is common in prose and poetry (*OLD quo*¹ 2, H–S 424, Heinsius on Ov. *Ep.* 2.53). For *uti* cf. 2.50.

13 parcus: understand *nimium* ἀπὸ κοινοῦ; the qualification is necessary, since it is not frugality itself but an excess of it that H. faults (cf. *S.* 1.4.107–8, quoted at Introduction p. 30).

heredis: objective gen. with *curam*. The alien heir is prominent in H.'s poetry, not least perhaps because he appears to have had no legal relatives himself (N–H on *C.* 2.14.25); cf. Sen. *Ep.* 123.11 *quanta dementia est heredis sui res procurare et sibi negare omnia.*

14 adsidet 'resembles', a novel sense (*OLD* 5), perhaps encouraged by *dissideo* 'differ'; to amuse Torquatus, H. plays with legal concepts, here the *cura furiosi* and the *cura prodigi* (1.102n.).

potare implies serious drinking (N–H on *C.* 2.11.17); garlands and scattered flowers (*spargere flores*), esp. roses (*C.* 3.19.22 *sparge rosas*), were an essential ingredient of the after dinner symposium.

15 patiar ... haberi 'I shall allow myself to be regarded (*OLD* 24) as being ...' The infin. with *patior* is complementary, not a Grecism (so N–H on *C.* 1.2.43–4). The predicate of the infin. naturally has the same case as the subj., hence the nom. *inconsultus* (Roby xxii–xxiii and §1350, K–S 1 702, with ref. to 679). *inconsultus* 'reckless' again evokes legal terminology; cf. *furere, insanire* in the less restrained *Odes* (N–H on *C.* 2.7.28).

16–20 H.'s self-defence is generalized. The praises of drink were a proverbial theme of symposiastic song; cf. esp. Bacchylides, fr. 20b S–M and Pindar, fr. 124a–b S–M (Otto §1899). But philosophy had to take a more judicious stand on the issue: Does the good life admit of relaxation? Seneca offered a cautious answer at *Dial.* 9.17.8–9. (At *Ep.* 89.16 he hints that this was a theme for declamation too.) H.'s position is clear: *dulce est desipere in loco* (*C.* 4.12.28), where emphasis falls on the last words of the poem, 'on the right occasion' (cf. 15.18–21). That such an occasion exists now is clear from 9–11. The style of the lines is discussed at Introduction p. 12.

16 dissignat 'manage'. Editors print this verb, lexicographers are reluctant to allow its existence (see McGlynn s.v., and Martin on Ter. *Adel.* 87). One of its radical senses is 'unseal' so there may perhaps be a pun on the *signum* 'seal' set on the jar (*Ep.* 2.2.134).

recludit 'lays bare' (*OLD* 5), in the sense of confiding secrets, not betraying them (25); a poetic verb (B. on *Ep.* 2.1.103). Cf. *S.* 1.4.89 *condita cum uerax aperit praecordia Liber*.

17 Cf. 15.19–20, *C.* 4.12.19 *spes donare nouas largus* of wine jars; the hopes of 8 are now confirmed. *inertem* 'coward'; cf. Bacchyl. fr. 20b.7 'straightway he is stripping cities of their diadem of towers'.

18 animis … eximit: cf. 15.19, *C.* 1.18.4 *mordaces … diffugiunt sollicitudines* (with the n. of N–H), 2.11.17–18 *dissipat Euhius | curas edaces*.

addocet: a coinage, encouraged by *addisco*; the prefix implies increase or progress (Roby §1833).

20 solutum puns on a Greek title for Dionysus, Lyaeus 'the releaser' (whence *Liber*), cf. *Epod.* 9.37–8 *curam metumque Caesaris rerum iuuat | dulci Lyaeo soluere*. The thought again is a commonplace: cf. Bacchyl. and Pind. (16–20n.), Aristoph. *Equit.* 93. The struggle for wealth (8) is satisfied, for a time.

21–9 The wine will do its job, I have mine. Notice of preparations is resumed from 7 and H. offers Torquatus final inducements to accept.

21 Haec points forward to the final clauses, 22–6; cf. *S.* 2.5.36–7 *haec mea cura est, | ne …*

procurare suggests official oversight, like that of an aedile (Heinze). The infin. depends on *imperor* 'I am under orders', a rare passive (used here reflexively: G–L §218) of an intrans. verb, perhaps modelled upon *iubeor* (B. on *AP* 56 *inuideor*) or even upon Greek, ἐπιτάττομαι + infin. The elision at the main caesura is remarkable; there are many instances in the *Sermones*, but only one more in this book at 11.9 (Nilsson 94–5).

idoneus 'competent' may also hint at a legal sense, 'solvent' (*OLD* 2), and so pick up H.'s reference to his prosperity (12) in a way to tease his legal friend. The litotes *non inuitus* precludes any sense of constraint in *imperor*.

22–6 H. ticks off his check-list of chores with a host's attention to detail for a special guest. The four clauses are carefully balanced by pairs. The first pair concern the furnishings, the second the company. Negative and positive clauses alternate.

22 toral … mappa: their function is unclear but the first is taken to be a coverlet for the couch, the second a napkin. The emphasis on cleanliness is not only characteristic of H. but perhaps of symposiastic verse, cf. Xenophanes 1.1–2 'for now the floor is clean and everyone's hands and the cups'.

23   corruget 'make *you* wrinkle'; for the sense see 1.100n.; the verb may be a coinage, as Quintilian seems to suggest at *IO* 11.3.80.

24   ostendat tibi te: for silver polishing cf. *C.* 4.11.6 *ridet argento domus* (for Maecenas' birthday).

fidos inter amicos: take with *dicta* 25 and cf. *S.* 2.1.30 *fidis ... sodalibus. fidus*, not a word of common speech, belonged more to the elevated style of high poetry (J. N. Adams, *B.I.C.S.* 20 (1973) 139 n. 22). H. now moves from the furnishings to the company, a more important attraction.

25   eliminet 'broadcast', a unique sense of an archaic verb; for the subjunc. cf. *personet* 1.7n.

25–6   Construe ἀπὸ κοινοῦ *ut par pari coeat iungaturque*; *coeat* refers to the invitation, *iungatur* to the place on the couch. It was a rule of the symposium that all were equals round the mixing bowl; there is also a clear allusion to the proverbial fondness of like for like (Otto §1335).

26   tibi, as in 7, emphasizes the guest's pleasure. Butra, Septicius and Sabinus cannot now be identified. Is it possible that even the first readers would not have known who they were? In that case, the impression is enhanced of a party of close friends, rather than of celebrities.

27   prior 'earlier' (temporal) rather than 'preferable' (qualitative); it was socially acceptable to go from one party to another on the same evening. *-que* 'or', disjunctive (*OLD* 7).

28   adsumam: understand *Sabinum* from the rel. clause.

umbris: companions brought by a guest, though not directly invited by the host (*S.* 2.8.22 *quos Maecenas adduxerat umbras*). A further courtesy and inducement, Torquatus may bring some cronies.

29   nimis arta ... conuiuia resumes the modest note of the opening; H.'s dining room is as small as its furniture. *premunt* 'oppress' (*OLD* 8); H. offers a tactful caution in a sententious line, so that his friend does not pack in too many extras.

olidae, first here, perhaps as metrically handier than *olens* or *foetidus*, is not uncommon in later prose so may have had colloquial tone. *caprae* 'rank smell', a unique metaphorical use of the fem., encouraged by the use of *caper* and *hircus* (*TLL* VI 3.19–23). Despite pre-dinner bathing, perfume and the *alipilus*, sweaty armpits remained a nuisance, esp. noticeable since Romans shared the couches on which they reclined (cf. *iungatur* 26).

30–1   Torquatus has so much less to do than his host, how can he refuse?

30   Tu)(*ego* 21.

   quotus: lit. 'the howmanyeth' as in *S*. 2.6.44 *hora quota est?*; to which the answer will be an ordinal, e.g., 'it is the fifth (hour)'. The slave who delivers this note will wait for Torquatus to pen an answer, hence *rescribe*.

   rebus omissis 'dropping (*OLD* 5) everything else' varies the colloquial expression, *relictis r*. 'instantly' (McGlynn s.v. *relinquo* V; Lucr. 3.1071; cf. Duff on Sen. *Dial*. 10.7.4), perhaps in order to recall *mitte* 8.

31   seruantem 'occupying', a poetic sense (cf. 10.6, *OLD* 3). Clients assembled in the *atrium* (here in poetic plur., cf. 1.88n.) to consult their patron at his convenience in the morning; evening was not the proper time to pay a call.

   postico falle 'elude (*OLD* 7) by the backdoor', instrumental abl.; cf. Sen. *Dial*. 10.14.4 *quam multi per refertum clientibus atrium prodire uitabunt et per obscuros aedium aditus profugient, quasi non inhumanius sit decipere quam excludere.* But there is also a humorous sense to *falle*, 'deceive', the last thing, of course, that a worthy barrister like Torquatus would consider doing (cf. N–H on *C*. 2.18.24, p. 305).

Epistles IV and V are juxtaposed in order to cast different lights on a similar theme (cf. the placing of XVII and XVIII). Both are invitations, a popular form of poem inherited chiefly from the Hellenistic epigram (N–H on *C*. 1.20, pp. 244–5). Yet the approach in each is subtly different.

   Albius is well-to-do, a literary figure who does not neglect moral reflections when alone in the country. What he appears to neglect – and H. is not crudely explicit – is the use of his many blessings. H. reminds him of these, and offers a picture of himself as Epicurean hedonist to serve as a model. Now a further point is that the Epicureans set great store by friendship and the sharing of pleasure. It is that above all which H. offers Albius when he gives him a standing invitation to visit.

Torquatus is different. A patrician of ancient family, he is actively pursuing an honourable career at the bar in Rome, engrossed in the world's affairs. H. like a good friend wants him to relax and so organizes a dinner party just for Torquatus. Every detail, especially the wine, conspires to allure him. H. stresses the simplicity of his arrangements, a commonplace in some invitations from social inferiors, most notably *C*. 3.29 to Maecenas – a poem which opens with language very similar to this (N–H on *C*. 1.20, p. 245). Once again H. himself serves as a model when he insists that his prosperity is pointless if unused. The praises of wine reinforce the message. (J. C. Scaliger faulted these lines as irrelevant '*praeter propositum*' in his *Poetices libri septem* (Lyons 1561) 337D; more drastically Ribbeck deemed them an interpolation.) The cycle of work and business must be broken, and it is a friend's duty to act. But pleasure is not in its turn to become a round. So the party is to be an interruption only, justified by the celebration of the emperor's birthday (a patriotic note is struck, as in III). H. has done all he can, all Torquatus has to do is accept; indeed, he is offered no alternative.

Many of the details of H.'s preparations suggest the literature of etiquette, especially for parties, which was pretty extensive. We know that Varro, for instance, gave advice on the most suitable number of guests at parties (Gellius 13.11). Much later Plutarch put together some similar reflections in his *Quaestiones conuiuales*. It seems that once again H. presents model behaviour in his own activities.

Epistle VI

1–27 H. offers Numicius, a now unknown addressee, a motto to guide him to happiness. Originally applied to remove the fear of natural phenomena (3–5), it works equally well on the objects of desire (5–8) and of dread (9–11). All unreasonable emotions and pursuits (even that of virtue) are based on a spiritual paralysis (12–16). Our aspirations (17–23) end after all in death (24–7).

1 Nil admirari 'idolize nothing': the motto is as old as Pythagoras' μηδὲν θαυμάζειν (Plut. *Moral.* 44B). Democritus took up the theme (*athambia*), which then found its way under various names into the major schools: Epicurean imperturbability (*ataraxia*) and the Stoic's lack of emotion (*apatheia*). H. is not urging indifferentism, but self-reliant composure; the theme recurs frequently: 1.47 *miraris*, 10.31 *mirabere*, 14.18 *miramur*.

prope: urbane qualification, cf. 9 (B. on *AP* 432); the lack of it is significant at *una* 30, *sola* 47.

res ... una 'the one thing' (1.106n.; *OLD res* 3); separation from *solaque* by the line end and the insertion of the voc. give additional force (Wickham).

2 possit: cf. *personet* 1.7n. *facere et seruare beatum* is echoed ironically at 47; cf. Milton *PR* 4.362 'What makes a Nation happy, and keeps it so.'

3–16 back up the opinion just enunciated and unpack the sense H. gives to *admirari*. He of course assumes that men covet (*cupiens* 10) what they idolize. Lines 3–5 form the protasis of a paratactic condition; 5–8 the apodosis. The argument moves from greater to lesser, from our attitude to the grand spectacle of heaven to the mundane world around us.

3 hunc 'yonder', deictic; Dillenburger compared Cic. *Tusc.* 1.60 *hoc nebuloso et caliginoso caelo*, where the weather is not the issue, though the conversation is held out of doors. *decedentia* 'passing' (Ellis on Catull. 66.4 *ut cedant certis sidera temporibus*) goes with *solem et stellas* ἀπὸ κοινοῦ.

4 tempora 'seasons' (*OLD* 3); *momentis* 'degrees' (*OLD* 4d). The philosophical study of natural phenomena freed men from dread (*formidine nulla*) by establishing the fixed (*certis* 3) laws which govern them.

5 spectent strikes a keynote, viewing, cf. 8, 11, 13, 14, 18, 19, 24, 26, 49, 60. For the subjunc. see *personet* 1.7n.

5–8 quid censes ... quo spectanda modo: the kernel of the question is *quomodo spectanda* [*esse*] *censes*. But *quid censes* was itself so common (*OLD censeo* 4c) that it became idiomatic to attach to it an acc. and infin. giving the substance of the question, which *quid* merely served to introduce; cf. Cic. *S. Rosc.* 49 *quid censes hunc ipsum Sex. Roscium, quo studio et qua intellegentia esse in rusticis rebus?* (Holden on Cic. *Off.* 2.25). So prolonged is the present sentence that *credis* 8 is inserted to resume *censes*.

5 munera terrae: developed at 17–18, 24–5.

6 maris: sc. *munera* ἀπὸ κοινοῦ; *extremos* goes ἀπὸ κοινοῦ with *Indos* (cf. 1.45).

Arabas: Greek acc. plur., obj. of *ditantis* 'enriching', gen. sing. with *maris*, an expressive verb, hardly found outside poetry before Livy (B.

on *AP* 57). H. has in mind the pearls that proved a mania among Romans (Mayer on Sen. *Phaed*. 391–2 *niueus lapis* | ... *Indici donum maris*). The notion of foreign trade is developed at 32–5.

7 ludicra quid 'what of the shows'; for the word order cf. 11.3. To gain popularity Romans spent huge sums on the provision of public spectacles (plays, gladiators, beast fights); cf. the anecdote of Lucullus, 40–4. The popular and successful were greeted at the theatre with spontaneous applause, *plausus* (N–H on *C*. 1.20.3–4 *datus in theatro* | *cum tibi plausus*); Marcus Aurelius also used applause as a symbol of faulty human values (6.16.2 τί οὖν τίμιον; τὸ κροτεῖσθαι; οὐχί). *dona* refers to public office, a theme developed at 49–55. Both forms of ambition, as Préaux noted, are in Seneca's mind at *Ep*. 94.60 *non est quod tibi compositae mentis habitum et sanitatem plausus excutiat, non est quod tibi tranquillitatis tuae fastidium faciat ille sub illis fascibus purpura cultus*.

Quiritis: the sing., here used collectively, is poetic diction (*OLD Quirites* 2, N–H on *C*. 2.7.3).

8 sensu ... et ore: internal and external manifestations of interest, cf. 14.

9–16 Instead of answering the question, H. moves to a further definition of his understanding of *admirari*, and asserts that dread (of the loss of what we idolize) is like desire; both emotions produce a paralysing fixation. Such fixation is bad however worthy its object.

9–10 timet ... cupiens: 2.51n. *fere* offers a necessary qualification: dread 'overvalues' in 'much the same way' as desire certain conditions which it is anxious to avoid (cf. 1.43).

miratur picks up the motto, but may here have the sense 'gaze at in wonder' (*OLD* 3), as at 18; thus it includes the keynote theme of 'viewing'.

eodem quo ... pacto < *S*. 1.4.55–6; phrases built with *pactum* are common in prose and in the argumentative style of Lucretius (L. on *S*. 1.4.99).

10 pauor 'thrill' (*OLD* 2c) is elevated and archaic; found in tragedy (Jocelyn on Enn. *scen*. 17 J.) and in history, elsewhere too it maintains its distinction, e.g. Pl. *Epid*. 530 *paupertas, pauor territat mentem animi*; *S*. 2.7.57 *tremis ossa pauore*, *Epod*. 5.96 (in an unearthly imprecation).

11 improuisa: emphatic by position. The Stoics especially enjoined a mental preparation for events, cf. Cic. *Tusc*. 3.30 *ergo id quidem non dubium, quin omnia, quae mala putentur, sint improuisa grauiora. itaque quam-*

quam non haec una res efficit maximam aegritudinem, tamen, quoniam multum potest prouisio animi et praeparatio ad minuendum dolorem, sint semper omnia homini humana meditata. et nimirum haec est illa praestans et diuina sapientia, et perceptas penitus et pertractatas res humanas habere, nihil admirari, cum acciderit, nihil, ante quam euenerit, non euenire posse arbitrari (N–H on *C*. 2.10.14 *bene praeparatum*).

simul = *simulac* (*OLD* 11); *exterret* 'dismays', as at Lucr. 2.1040 (*TLL* v 2027.31).

12 gaudeat ... metuatne: an alternative indir. qu. commonly requires no introductory particle, e.g. *utrum* (K–S II 528); for *-ne* see *OLD* 5c. The subj. is supplied from *utrumque* 11. The fourfold division of the irrational emotions was developed by the Stoics (L–S §65), but had probably become a commonplace, cf. Virg. *A*. 6.733 *hinc metuunt cupiuntque, dolent gaudentque.*

quid ad rem: understand *interest* (*OLD res* 12b).

13 melius peiusue sua spe: prose prefers *opinione*, which does not fit the hexameter (*OLD opinio* 2); H. picks up the handier *spe* from the historians, Sallust and Livy (K–S II 470, L. on *S*. 1.10.89); the monosyllabic ending is softened by the close adherence of the possessive pronoun.

14 animoque et corpore torpet: cf. 8; paralysis of mind and body (a polar expression) betokens the complete loss of independence in those who idolize. *-que et*, an archaic equivalent to τε καί, is found in comedy, in Catullus (28.5, 44.15, (?)76.11; D. O. Ross, *Style and tradition in Catullus* (Cambridge, Mass., 1969) 65–7), and in historians (*TLL* v 2.887.36–80); one metrical advantage is the avoidance of hiatus, as here (B. on *AP* 196, 444).

15–16 An extreme, even paradoxical instance of crucial importance (resumed at 29–31) concludes this section and introduces the next (concerned with lesser objects of aspiration). Not just external goods, but even *uirtus* as an object of pursuit can prove damaging. Moderation is the watchword; cf. Cic. *Tusc*. 4.62 *etiamsi uirtutis ipsius uehementior adpetitus sit, eadem sit omnibus ad deterrendum adhibenda oratio.*

15 ferat: apodosis to *si petat*. With *iniqui* understand *nomen* ἀπὸ κοινοῦ.
16 For *ultra quam satis est* see Introduction p. 43.

17–27 Possessions, prestige, wealth – the order of the list recalls the opening, 5–7 – all the objects we desire and perhaps overvalue will not free us from death.

17 I nunc, a common ironical exhortation, sets the tone of the rest of the epistle (*OLD eo*[1] 10b). As elsewhere the addressee fades out to be replaced by an indefinite second pers.

argentum 'silver plate' (*OLD* 2). *uetus* belongs to all the nouns ἀπὸ κοινοῦ (Introduction p. 26); *aera* 'bronze statuary' (*OLD* 7); *artes* 'works of art' (*OLD* 8b). For the list cf. 1.38n.

18 suspice 'esteem' (*OLD* 2), but the radical sense of looking up in wonder is reinforced by *mirare*, the topical word.

Tyrios: Tyre and Sidon (cf. 10.26) in the Lebanon were the sources of the best purple dye used on luxurious dress (there were many counterfeits of which H. names a surprising number: African *C.* 2.16.35, Laconian *C.* 2.18.8, Coan *C.* 4.13.3, Aquinate 10.26 below, Tarentine *Ep.* 2.1.207, Gaetulian *Ep.* 2.2.81; *RE* XXIII 2008). These items recall the *munera terrae et maris*, 5–6.

19 spectant: 1.2n. *mille* serves as an indefinite number (L. on *S.* 1.6.111).

loquentem 'chatting'; *loquor*, never used of formal public speaking (*TLL* VII 2.1673.39–49, 63–74), here evokes a prominent citizen whose lightest word is of general interest, cf. Sen. *Con.* 5.2 *tot serui sequuntur, tot liberti, tot clientes ut quidquid dixerit rumor sit.* (It is hardly likely that it forms a contrast with *Mutus*; the proper name should have preceded.)

20 nauus: adverbial (cf. 1.24). *uespertinus* is also adverbial; this use of an adj. of time is chiefly poetic, a syntactical Grecism = ἑσπέριος (Eden on Virg. *A.* 8.30). Since the Roman business day ended in the early afternoon (cf. 7.46 and Martial 4.8.3 *in quintam* [*horam*] *uarios extendit Roma labores*), not to leave the Forum until evening showed ruthless industry. The Forum was the heart of Rome's business and legal life, cf. 7.48, 16.57, 19.8. The man works in town to earn enough to buy the sort of country estate that Mutus (a κωφὸν πρόσωπον) acquired easily as part of his wife's dowry.

21 emetat 'reap off', apparently a coinage = ἐκθερίζω, ἐξαμάω (the last a poetic verb).

22 et continues the negation (K–S II 211, cf. 18.58).

indignum: acc. of exclamation (G–L §343), in apposition to the thought of 23; *quod* 'seeing that ...' (*OLD* 10); *sit* is a subjunc. of reported reason (G–L §541, Roby §1740).

peioribus: sc. *quam tu*, abl. of origin (G–L §395).

23   tibi … illi: dat. of agent. *mirabilis* strikes the keynote and denotes the standard men set for their self-esteem, the admiration of others.

24–5   form a paratactic comparison: '*just as* time … , *so* will it bury …' Only the grave is certain. The proverbial sentiment recalls Soph. *Aj*. 646–7 'all things the long and countless years first draw from darkness, then bury from light' (Otto §1756). As Jebb observed, the emphasis there as here is on time's destructive power, which the first clause only serves to bring into relief. The metaphorical language recalls the shining metals and stones, all products of the earth, listed at 17–18.

24   apricum 'the light of day', an unusual sense (*OLD* 2), but adopted to fit in with the notion of viewing (*spectent* 5n.).

25–6   Construe ἀπὸ κοινοῦ: *cum te bene notum porticus Agrippae ⟨et⟩ uia Appi conspexeri⟨n⟩t.*

26   porticus: built in 25 B.C., decorated with paintings of the adventures of the Argonauts, it became a popular resort (Richardson 312); since its usual name was either *p. Argonautarum* or *p. Neptuni* H. not only avoids a precise term but obliquely flatters the builder, M. Agrippa. The *uia Appi* – the expression deliberately avoids *u. Appia* – had been built by Appius Claudius Caecus in 312 B.C. As the main road to Campania and the resorts around the bay of Naples, it evokes the life of success and pleasure. But the highway was lined with the tombs of the rich, so we are prepared for the thought of 27.

   conspexerit: fut. perf. indic.; for the sing. see 1.84n.

27   ire … restat: the infin. as subject is poetic syntax (Ter. *Ph*. 85, Lucr. 1.1005, 5.227, Ov. *F*. 5.369); the prose construction is found at 1.27. Numa Pompilius, the second king of Rome, was credited with founding the city's religious institutions (Ogilvie on Livy 1.18–21). Ancus Marcius was the fourth king (Ogilivie on Livy 1.32–4). (Their heads appear together on coins of *c*. 86 B.C.) It was a commonplace of the literature of consolation in antiquity to remind the bereaved or those upset at the prospect of death that better men in the past had had to die (N–H on *C*. 1.28.7; it is by design that in an epistle Roman rather than mythological *exempla* are chosen). Ancus is first referred to as a type of the good king who died none the less at Lucr. 3.1025 *lumina sis* [= *suis*] *oculis etiam bonus Ancu' reliquit*; cf. *C*. 4.7.14–15 (discussed at Introduction p. 11).

28–66   The inevitability of death does not, however, rule out attention to physical health; just as we look after our mortal bodies, so we must seek health for our spirit. But where does it lie? The traditional analogy between physical and spiritual health helps to advance the argument in a new direction, the rehearsal of various other views of what constitutes the *summum bonum*.

28 temptantur 'are afflicted', medical terminology (*OLD* 10).

29 uis ... non? '*if* you wish to be happy – well, who doesn't?' forms the protasis of an interrupted paratactic condition. (The belief that *uis* alone introduces a simple qu. (so, e.g., H–S 461) is not supported by Livy 39.42.11 or Petr. 111.12, for they begin *uis tu*, a different idiom, illustrated by Bentley on *S.* 2.6.92; cf. *OLD* 8.) The suppressed apodosis might have been a piece of practical wisdom, expressed by an imperative to match *quaere*. But H. has already given his view at 1–2, so here he changes tack. He acknowledges that the desire for happiness is universal (*quis non?*) and goes on to show that it has generated a bewildering diversity of opinion about how to secure it. Behind his illustrations lies a long tradition of moral thought that had neatly divided men's pursuits into life-styles, be it wealth (31–48) or prestige (49–55) or pleasure (56–66) (see N–H on *C.* 1.1, p. 2). Each proposed ideal is announced conditionally: *si uirtus* 30, *si res* 47 (the proposition concludes rather than initiates the argument), *si ... species et gratia* 49, *si bene qui cenat* 56, *si ... sine amore* 65.

recte 'in a desirable manner' (*OLD* 9), not 'with moral rectitude' (*OLD* 6, where this passage is cited; see 2.41n.); the focus throughout this section is on the human craving for happiness rather than on goodness; cf. 47, 49, 56, 66.

30–1 A paradoxical start. Virtue might well be thought likely to produce happiness (and some commentators believe that it is not one of the implicitly rejected options), but H. sows doubt, following Aristotle; cf. *EN* 1.5, 1095B30–1096A2. The section is not as fully developed as the later ones, because virtue is itself a good; H. focusses rather upon the monomaniac's pursuit of it.

30 una echoes 1 but the lack of qualification is too dogmatic for H. (cf. *prope* 1 and 47); the unbending Stoics are in his mind. *fortis* is adverbial (cf. 15.27).

omissis ... deliciis: too uncompromising, if the doctrine of IV and V is heeded. The ideal of pleasure will close H.'s list.

31 hoc age 'get on with it' (*OLD* 22). This way of getting at happiness through virtue alone runs foul of the warning at 15–16.

31–48   The longest section is devoted to the belief that wealth brings happiness (hence the ambiguous *beatum* 47).

31–2   Virtutem: repetition forms a transition to the topic of wealth. The sentence *uirtutem ... ligna* is itself a paratactic comparison, introducing a paratactic condition: '*if, just* as you think a sacred grove mere firewood (*TLL* VII 2.1385.78–80), *so* you regard virtue as empty words (*OLD* 11), *then* ...'. (Indeed *ut* replaced *et* in some MSS.)

31   uirtutem uerba: the sarcasm, pointed by the alliteration here and with *lucum ligna*, was proverbial, cf. 17.41 (Otto §1909); Brutus as he was dying at Philippi (where H. fought) quoted a line from a now unidentifiable Greek tragedy about Hercules: 'o miserable virtue, you were but a word all along, yet I respected you as a reality' (*TGF*² 374 = (!) Diogenes Sinop. fr. 3 Snell–Kannicht).

32–3   For the traditional figure of the merchant cf. 1.45n.

33   Cibyra, a Phrygian town, exported iron ore and hams (*RE* XI 1.374–7). Bithynia, a province of Asia Minor on the Black Sea, had considerable trade; cf. *C.* 3.7.3 *Thyna merce beatum.*

34   rotundentur 'round off the sum', apparently a colloquial expression (or founded on one), cf. Petr. 76.8 *centies sestertium corrotundaui* (Trimalchio is speaking).

   totidem altera 'as many again', cf. Catull. 5.8 *mille altera.* For the enjambment with *et* see Introduction p. 24; it goes closely with *et* in 35 'both ... and'.

35   et ... : construe: *et ⟨succedat ea⟩ pars quae quadret* (final subjunc. in rel. clause). For *aceruum* see 2.47n.

36   scilicet 'obviously' ironically introduces the benefits wealth confers. The list is constructed by polysyndeton, i.e. connectives are piled on (*-que et ... et ... et*), here to enhance an impression of abundance. H. recalls the scene in Hesiod, *Op.* 63–76, in which the gods and goddesses (esp. Aphrodite and Persuasion) adorn (*decorat* 38) Pandora. For *uxorem cum dote* cf. *beata ... uxor* 2.44–5 and *dotalibus* 21 above; for *fidem* see 1.57n.

   amicos ... formam: the thought is derived from Sophocles' *Aleadae*, fr. 88 P. 'money gets friends for men ... it makes even the ugly beautiful to look on'.

37   regina Pecunia < Hes. *Op.* 73 πότνια Πειθώ 'queen Persuasion'. The personification of money is found in Varro, *gram.* 150; for its status cf. *S.* 2.3.94–6 *omnis enim res* | *uirtus, fama, decus, diuina humanaque pulchris* | *diuitiis parent* and Juv. 1.112–3 *sanctissima diuitiarum* | *maiestas*. At bottom, the notion is proverbial, cf. 10.47n. and Publ. Syr. 458 *Pecunia ... regimen est rerum omnium*. *donat* alludes to the name Pan*do*ra, as Dr M. B. Trapp points out.

38 bene nummatum, a colloquial phrase (*TLL* II 2126.3–5), undermines the tone of the grand personifications.

Suadela 'Persuasion', personified as *Suada* by Ennius, *Ann.* 308 Sk., = Πειθώ. H. artfully puts Venus in place of the Graces because Hesiod had mentioned earlier that Zeus ordered Aphrodite to give Pandora a gift (*Op.* 65–6).

39 aeris: the gen. with *egeo* had been replaced with the abl. by Cicero, but the older usage may still have been colloquial (*TLL* v 2.233.44–5). The reference appears to be to Archelaus, a recent king of Cappadocia, notorious for lack of cash (*RE* II 451–2, n. 15). For the final rhythm cf. 5.6.

40 ne fueris: the negated perf. subjunc. serves as a prohibition (G–L §263.2 (b), LS §46). The long final syllable retains the original quantity (Austin on Virg. *A.* 1.388). *hic* 'like him', cf. 15.42 and *OLD sum* 16.

ut aiunt announces an anecdote (*OLD aio* 4b). L. Licinius Lucullus, *cos.* 74 B.C., an able general and administrator, was famous above all for his spectacular wealth. Plutarch's biography of him mentions this anecdote as derived from H. (*Lucull.* 39.5).

41 si ... 'whether' is like an indir. qu. (*OLD* 13; H–S 543; Roby §1754 notes that *possim* is frequently found in such conditions, and §1755 shows that the idiom is colloquial). The request is in keeping with the gigantism of Roman stage productions (*ludicra* 7); three thousand statues adorned the stage in 58 B.C. (Plin. *NH* 34.17.36) and Cicero protested at the extravagant inauguration of Pompey's stone theatre in 55 B.C.: *quid enim delectationis habent sescenti muli in Clytemestra aut in equo Troiano creterrarum tria milia?* (*Fam.* 7.1.2).

centum: an indefinitely large number (L. on *S.* 1.1.50); *scaenae* 'for the theatre', dat.

42 Anecdotes typically follow this pattern of an indirect qu. and an answer in direct speech.

qui 'how' (*OLD qui*²1), used here as for the most part in prose with *possum*; it is avoided in higher genres such as the *Odes*, but finds a natural home in H.'s hexameters (Waltz 49, L. on *S.* 1.1.1). With *possum* understand *praebere*.

habebo 'I find that I have'; potential fut. (H–S 311, but cf. 2.34n.).

43   paulo: take with *post*, abl. of measure of difference (*NLS* §82 (iii), Roby §1204).

scribit: historical pres. as the imperf. subjunc. *tolleret* indicates.

quinque: its position emphasizes Lucullus' own, perhaps feigned, surprise.

44   domi 'available' (Fordyce on Catull. 31.14; *OLD* 7b is less satisfactory).

tolleret, ἀπὸ κοινοῦ with *partem*, is an indir. command (*NLS* §§139, 142), the subject being the addressee of Lucullus' letter, the praetor or aedile who is putting on the show.

45–6   The rich man's home is described in three cola of two words each; the repetition of *et* produces polysyndeton, which here suggests that H. is ticking off the basic requirements.

45   supersunt: for H., whose watchword is *satis* (1.2n.), superfluity (both in possessions and in poetic style) is undesirable.

46   fallunt 'escape his notice' (*OLD* 6). The master's inability to keep watch over his possessions prompts the deflating joke of the last clause.

ergo: for the enjambment see Introduction p. 24. H. concludes the section on wealth as the means to securing happiness.

47   res 'money' (1.65n.) spells out the implication of the idea behind 30–1. The line ironically parodies 1–2, but the unqualified *sola* spoils the claim, cf. 30.

48   hoc … opus: moneymaking.

primus … postremus 'be the first to … the last to' recalls the advice of 20; the form of the advice parodies proverbs, e.g., *postremus dicas, primus taceas* (Marcius, *poet.* 1), *primus cubitu surgat, postremus cubitum eat* (Cato, *Agr.* 5.5).

repetas … omittas: jussive subjunctives.

49–55   The pursuit of happiness through prestige comes next. It is presented in its most notorious form, canvassing (*ambitus*) before an election, so as to recall 7 *amici dona Quiritis*. H. thus depicts in concrete Roman terms what Aristotle had presented as a theoretical objection at *EN* 1.5, 1095B23–6 'honour seems too superficial to be what we are looking for, since it is thought to depend on those who bestow honour rather than on him who receives it, but the good we divine to be something proper to a man and not easily taken from him'.

49 fortunatum implies dependency on *fortuna*, which plays a large role in electoral success (Cic. *Pis*. 3 *sit sane Fors domina Campi*). *species* 'pomp' (*OLD* 4); for *gratia* see 4.10n.

50 mercemur: less an exhortation than a polite command in which the speaker, here ironically, includes himself (*LS* §39; N–H on *C*. 2.9.18 and 16.17). *seruum* refers to the *nomenclator* (*OCD* s.v. *candidatus*); he walked to the left side (*laeuum*) of his master, whose right was protected by the housewalls (L. on *S*. 2.5.17). For *dictet, fodicet* and *cogat* (51) see *possim* 1.12n.

51 trans pondera 'across the stepping-stones' (*OLD* 5d), huge blocks set in the street to allow passage between the raised pavements. The candidate must make an effort to greet someone influential. (Other interpretations of the phrase are reviewed by H. Musurillo, *Class. World* 67 (1973–4) 199 n. 18.) *cogat* hints at his reluctance to woo a vote; he has forfeited his independence, esp. since it is the slave who makes him stretch out his hand.

52 The liveliness of the slave's remark is enhanced by its lack of introduction. The Fabia and Velina were two of the thirty-five tribes into which Romans were distributed for voting purposes; both were rustic tribes, in which individual votes counted for more than those of the four vast urban tribes. For *multum* see 3.15n.

53 cui libet: understand *dare*. *hic* = a third person. The *fasces* were rods bound around an axe so as to form a bundle; carried before those who held *imperium*, they symbolized that power.

53–4 curule ... ebur: the magistrate's ivory throne; a poetic synecdoche supplants the technical term, *sella curulis*.

54 cui uolet: understand *eripere* from *eripiet* which takes the dat. 'of disadvantage', common with verbs of depriving (*NLS* xvii, §61; Bo 207–8; cf. *generi* 20.22n.); for the fut. see *noles* 2.34n. *importunus* 'disobligingly' (*OLD* 2) is adverbial.

55 facetus 'deftly', adverbial, though *facete* was available. The candidate neatly varies the form of address to suit the age of the voter.

56–66 The path of pleasure comes last, the complete antithesis of the first option, *uirtus* (30–1); it is subdivided into two pursuits, gluttony and love (curtly dismissed).

56   bene = *iucunde* (*TLL* ii 2113.60–3), but with overtones perhaps of *recte*.

lucet 'the moment it's light' serves as the protasis of a paratactic temporal clause. For the subjunc. in *eamus*, *piscemur* and *uenemur* see *mercemur* 50n.

57   ducit hints at the loss of self-determination; the gourmand is in thrall to his appetite. His hunting and fishing are of course done in the marketplace, as H.'s illustration, an anecdote (*olim* 1.73n.) reminiscent of those in the *Sermones* ridiculing a named (but now unknown) person, shows.

59   Campum: the *C. Martius* (7.59n.); the emendation of Bentley is here accepted. The MSS reading *populum*, a pointless repetition of 60, gives impossible syntax with *differtum Forum* (cf. *S.* 1.5.3–4 *forum Appi* | *differtum nautis*); it does not conform to any known type of hendiadys, the usual defence. Bentley also pointed out that *mane* indicates that Gargilius is *returning* from hunting and has ordered his slaves to take a roundabout way home through the Campus and the now packed Forum; he set out at first light, when the Forum was empty.

60   unus ... e multis 'just one of the many', a common expression (L. on *S.* 1.9.71, adding Catull. 68.36, Virg. *A.* 5.644). The intent gaze of the crowd recalls 19 and 23 *mirabilis*.

ut introduces a type of final clause in which the actual result is ironically described in terms of a purpose, the 'rhetorical pseudo-final clause' (H–S 642; it is characteristic of Juvenal's satires).

61   emptum: sarcastic.

crudi 'without having digested' (*OLD* 3b). For the subjunc. *lauemur* see *mercemur* 50n.; the first conjugation form is less common in poetry than the third (N–H on *C.* 2.3.18). Bathing just after finishing a meal was a token of luxury since it was reckoned to assist digestion (Pers. 3.98, Juv. 1.141–2); M. Aurelius praised Antoninus Pius for avoiding 'early bathing' (1.16.8 with Farquharson's n.).

62–4   In his review of notions about what produces happiness H. openly criticizes only pleasure just because it seems to most people the key to it (cf. Arist. *EN* 1.5, 1095b14–16).

62   quid deceat, quid non: the indir. questions recall 1.11 and the *uirtus* of 30.

Caerite cera: 'the wax of Caere' is a poetic way of referring to the wax-filled tablets (*tabulae Caerites*) in which were recorded the names of disfranchised citizens; H. alludes to an episode of Roman history when the citizens of Caere were rewarded with *ciuitas sine suffragio* (Gell. 16.13.7; Ogilvie on Livy 4.24.7). The reference suggests impaired or incomplete political and legal status, i.e. the loss of some independence. Full citizens, e.g., those who at 52–4 bestow or withhold prestige by their vote, might lose this enabling right through bankruptcy or loss of reputation (*infamia*). The life of pleasure was just the sort of thing to bring this about (cf. Maenius at 15.26 and the warning *exempla* of *S.* 1.4.109–15).

63 remigium '*like* the crew' (7.74n., Introduction pp. 28–30). The proper sense of *remigium* is 'oarage', but it was given a poetic sense (found later in Livy) because the word for oarsman, *remex*, which could be used as a collective sing., is unsuited to hexameter verse in a number of its forms. Still, 'crew' is dismissive, cf. *sociis* 2.21. H. now applies the doctrine of II, and uses Homer as a guide; he may have in mind either the episode of the Lotus-eaters or of the cattle of the Sun (*Od.* 9.82–102, 12.313), but cf. 2.24.

Ithacensis stresses Ulysses' love of his homeland. *Vlixei*, gen. sing. (G–L §65 s.v. *Achilles*), is quadrisyllabic, but the last two syllables are pronounced together by synizesis. H. preferred to use the older fifth decl. form here and at 7.40 for the sake of euphony; the third decl. gen. sing. in *-is* would have unpleasantly echoed the termination of the preceding word (see H. Maas (ed.), *The letters of A. E. Housman* (London 1971) 437).

64 For *cui* see 2.30n., for *patria* 1.106n.

interdicta: Ulysses himself forbade the eating of the lotus.

65–6 Against Homer H. sets the doctrine of Mimnermus of Colophon, a sixth-century poet whose most famous elegy is here parodied; it began 'what is life (= *uiuas*), what is enjoyable (= *iucundum*), without golden Aphrodite (= *sine amore*)?' There seems also to be a polemical reference to the recently published first book of Propertius, cf. 1.9.11 *plus in amore ualet Mimnermi uersus Homero*. H. clearly found the attitude of the elegists too self-regarding (cf. *C.* 2.9). At any rate, we have come full circle, since the thought of these lines recalls *deliciis* 31.

66 uiuas 'pass your life', jussive subjunc. The mocking echo, *in amore iocisque*, urges us to sense the triviality and limitations of the life of pleasure.

67–8 A two line signing-off, cf. 10.49–50.

67   siquid ...: a polite request for reply is both traditional (cf. Eur. *Hipp.* 298–9, Plat. *Crat.* 426B, Isocr. *Nic.* 38, Pl. *Epid.* 263–4 *si placebit, utitor | consilium; si non placebit, reperitote rectius,* Cic. *Tusc.* 5.82) and consonant with H.'s tendency to qualify dogmatic statement. He is himself after all *docendus adhuc* (17.3).

istis 'than the things I've just been talking about', cf. Ov. *Am.* 2.18.39–40 *si bene te noui, non bella libentius istis | dicis*; G. Grassi assembles more examples of *iste* and *hic* referring to the same thing in *Maia* 21 (1969) 159–60. A different interpretation by O. Skutsch in *Hermes* 88 (1960) 504–5 disjoins *istis* from the comparative and takes it to be an instrumental abl. with *imperti* 'present ⟨me⟩ with a share of (*OLD* 2) your views'; for the supplied object *me*, to be understood from *mecum*, see F. Leo, *Ausgewählte kleine Schriften* (ed. E. Fraenkel, Rome 1964) I 101. But the violent disjointing would hardly have been possible for the Roman reader of an unpunctuated text. Emendation has also been tried, e.g., *istic* (G. Wagner; R. G. M. Nisbet, *M.D.* 26 (1991) 89–90).
68   si: 5.6n. *candidus* 'kindly' (4.1n.), adverbial; *candide* would not fit the hexameter.

his 'these views of mine' refers to the substance of 1–27. *utere* is the imperative of a deponent verb. H. emphasizes that he is not theorizing for its own sake; indeed he personally has put his reflections into practice (*mecum*).

Up to now H. has shown no interest in a systematic approach to the search for the good life. He referred in I, II and IV to some of the leading sects, Stoics, Academics and Epicureans, but after all he refrained from attaching himself to any school and clung rather to the guidance of poetry (II), to which he reverts in this epistle with reminiscences of Hesiod, Sophocles, Homer and Mimnermus. It is clear from the argument of the poem (which formally owes much to Aristotle) that a single-minded attachment to any thing as an ideal possession or goal is bound to prove partial and so deny the many-faceted quality of life. The only 'thing' that matters is not a thing at all, but a disposition of the spirit to overvalue nothing, *nil admirari*. This conviction of H.'s has not always been easy for his readers to accept. It is, for instance, perfectly clear that H. regards the pursuit of virtue itself as liable to excess (15–16). Kiessling sees the point of this when he has to account for 29–31, but the philosophically more committed Heinze, among others (e.g., Cruquius), struggles against the obvious run of the argument; he cannot believe that H. might be belittling *uirtus* as a panacea and so starts the list of false ideals at 31, rather than at 30. But, after all, the most H. hoped for was a rule of thumb, hence the need for frequent qualification of otherwise sweeping generalizations. In effect, the letter justifies the eclectic stand enunciated at the beginning of the first epistle. H.'s own motto, *nil admirari*, is not in fact owed to any contemporary school, another indication (like his attachment to Aristippus) of his independent approach.

This epistle is least like a letter in form, and seems to make very little direct appeal to its unidentifiable addressee.

Epistle VII

1–13 H. apologizes for misleading Maecenas about the length of his absence and proposes a new date in the spring for their meeting.

1 Quinque dies 'for a few days' (*S*. 1.3.16 *quinque diebus*), acc. of extent of time.

pollicitus '*though* . . .'; a concessive idea may be understood (G–L §609, cf. N–H on *C*. 2.8.20); the local abl. *rure* is metrically handier than the locative *ruri* (K–S 1 485–6).

2 Sextilem totum 'for the whole of August' (acc. as in 1). The sixth month counting from March, the first month of the Roman year (which did not start with January until 153 B.C.), was renamed 'August' in 8 B.C.

mendax: a prompt avowal of fault secures a favourable hearing for H.'s defence, cf. *Ep*. 2.2.25 *expectata tibi non mittam carmina mendax*. For the enjambment see 2.33–7n.

3 uiuere: 2.10n.

sanum . . . ualentem: cf. 16.21; *recte ualere* is a colloquial expression (*OLD recte* 9c). H. paves the way to developing a concern with his health in VIII and XV; Maecenas the hypochondriac (*C*. 2.17) will have sympathized.

4 quam: the antecedent is *ueniam* 5. *aegro* '*when* unwell'; for the fut. *dabis* see *uises* 4.15n.

aegrotare timenti: sc. *mihi* ἀπὸ κοινοῦ; the infin. where a *ne*-clause would be regular is an innovation of H.'s and it remains largely poetic syntax (*OLD timeo* 4b). H.'s fears for his health in the autumn (16.16) were reasonable; fever-laden breezes from the Pomptine marshes passed through Rome (N–H on *C.* 2.14.15–16 *frustra per autumnos nocentem | corporibus metuemus Austrum*). It was moreover at about this period that H. excused himself from Augustus' service (see Introduction p. 6).

5 Maecenas: the friend's name is emphatically sounded within the urgent request. M. Aurelius learned from his adoptive father, Antoninus Pius, 'social tact and permission (= *ueniam*) to his suite not invariably to be present at his banquets nor to attend his progress from Rome as a matter of obligation, and always to be found the same by those who had failed to attend him through engagements' (1.16.2). H. expects similar courtesies from Maecenas.

ficus prima calorque: for the vivid combination of concrete image and abstract concept cf. *C.* 2.14.3 *rugis et instanti senectae. prima* is answered at 13.

6 dissignatorem 'marshal'. Lictors did not necessarily attend only upon those holding *imperium*; for their presence at funerals see Cic. *Leg.* 2.61.

decorat: for the idiom see 1.100n.

atris)(*pallet* 7; dingy togas were worn as a sign of mourning.

7 pueris: dat. with *pallet* (= the notion of fearing *for* someone, K–S I 339). H. hints that a patron's interest in his client must be no less than a parent's for his child (cf. *pater* 37).

8 officiosa ... sedulitas 'attentive diligence'; e.g., visiting a sick friend (*S.* 1.9.17–18) or the *salutatio*; Seneca seems to recall the phrase, *operosa sedulitas* (*Dial.* 10.2.1). *opella forensis* refers rather to legal duties, e.g., standing bail, or to H.'s own as a *scriba quaestorius* (*S.* 2.6.66–7); the diminutive, found only at Lucr. 1.1114 before H., belittles the jobs, perhaps because at that time of year they were usually petty (contrast Cic. *Mur.* 41 *forensis opera*). The unusual rhythm of the line with only a fourth-foot caesura may be expressive of anxiety (Nilsson 84) or restlessness (Heinze).

9 testamenta resignat: a humorous way of saying that the fevered die.

10 illinet 'will powder' vividly describes the light snow showers of early winter.

11 ad mare: cf. 15.5, 18 for a winter journey to the seacoast for his health (not necessarily the one referred to here).

uates 'bard' is a grand word for the Augustans, who use it to imply poetic inspiration and a public voice (N–H on *C.* 1.1.35). But the intimate possessive *tuus*, stressing an undiminished strength of personal affection (cf. *C.* 2.6.24 *uatis amici*; 1.105), tugs in the opposite direction (cf. N–H on *C.* 2.6, p. 96).

12   contractus 'huddled up' suits the picture, but the meaning is variously explained (B. on *Ep.* 2.2.80); there may be a hint that H. wants to live a more restricted life (*OLD* 2; cf. 5.20, *macra* 33, *paruum* 44 and *C.* 2.31), or that his mind is concentrated on his reading)(*distractus*.

dulcis amice: cf. *dulce decus meum C.* 1.1.2 of Maecenas; no one is ever more warmly addressed by H., cf. *Epod.* 1.2 . . . 4 *amice . . . Maecenas.*

13   si concedes politely solicits an encouraging reply. The West wind (*Zephyrus*) and the swallow are first found together as harbingers of spring in Leonidas of Tarentum (*AP* 10.1 = *HE* 2490–1), who is taken up by Virgil (*G.* 4.305–7).

14–24 coheres with 25–8. H. has given as yet no grounds for prolonging his absence through the winter. Nor does he, at once. Instead he anticipates a charge of ingratitude towards Maecenas (without of course attributing such thoughts to Maecenas himself), and works his way round to a profession of indebtedness at 24. In doing so he opens up the theme of the ideal benefactor and the ideally grateful beneficiary. Then he turns to his reason for absence (25–8): not ingratitude but a way of life changed with the years.

14–19 From an amusing anecdote, launched asyndetically, a general moral crystallizes at 20–3; H. applies it to himself in 24. (The progression of 40–5 is exactly similar.) Characteristic of the lively conversational style is the dialogue between host and guest. There are no verbs of speaking, as there would be in heroic epos (there is only one exception to this practice in the whole of the *Aeneid*, 6.719).

14   Non is placed to emphasize the contrast with Maecenas' behaviour; the focus is here on the giver, not the receiver. H. often uses a geographical epithet, here *Calaber*, to lend a story reality (N–H on *C.* 1.27.10 *Opuntiae*). Hosts gave their guests little presents, *apophoreta*, such as fruit (*piris*) or trinkets at the end of the evening; they were not supposed to be worth much, though in the later empire they became quite luxurious.

uesci ... iubet: sc. *hospitem* as acc. subj. of the infin. The pres. is historic, not unusual in a subord. clause in poetry (L. on *S.* 1.6.13).

15 locupletem 'rich *in land*', the etymological sense (cf. N–H on *C.* 2.18.22). Maecenas gave H., not trinkets, but an estate; reasonable prosperity is implied, not vast wealth (Holden on Cic. *Off.* 2.63, B. on *Ep.* 2.1.137). For *uescere* see *utere* 6.68n.; for *sodes*, 1.62n.

16 at has strong expletive force with the pronoun and an imperative (*OLD* 11c). *benigne* 'no, thank you' is pointedly echoed at 62.

17 non inuisa ... munuscula < Catull. 64.103 *non ingrata tamen frustra munuscula diuis*; though H. abjured Catullus (*S.* 1.10.19), the music of his verses (esp. in this most highly regarded poem) stuck with him.

18 tam 'so much' (*OLD* 4b). *dimittar* 'I were being sent away'; the pres. subjunc. has unreal force in a clause of conditional comparison (G–L §602, *LS* §151(b)).

19 ut libet 'just as you like', a formula of mere assent (*TLL* VII 2.1325.38–43; McGlynn s.v. *lubet* I). The host stupidly depreciates the gift. The dat. *porcis* may serve both as agent with the gerundive *comedenda* and as the indir. obj. of *relinques*.

hodie, not exactly temporal, adds immediacy, perhaps a tone of exasperation (*OLD* 3; J. B. Hofmann, *Lateinische Umgangssprache*[3] (Heidelberg 1951) 41–2).

20–3 The sentences enunciating the moral are symmetrically balanced (Fraenkel 329–30), and marked off from one another by adversative asyndeton.

20 prodigus et stultus)(*uir bonus et sapiens* 22. H.'s *prodigus* is Aristotle's ἄσωτος at *EN* 4.1; he is also *stultus* (Aristotle's ἠλίθιος, 1121A25–7) because in his inability to discern true values he gives ill-advisedly (cf. 1121B3–7). *donat* ...)(23.

odit 'has no use for' (Fordyce on Catull. 68.12, N–H on *C.* 1.38.1; the *OLD* is inadequate); the rhyme with *spernit* is characteristic (B. on *AP* 110).

21 seges 'field' (*OLD* 2) metaphorically alludes to the proverb 'whatsoever a man soweth, that shall he also reap' (Otto §1104).

ingratos)(*dignis* 22. Aristotle's liberal man not only gives to the right people, he takes as well only what he needs and from the right people (*EN* 4.1, 1120B30–1). The *prodigus* on the other hand attracts bad sorts (spongers, flatterers) who only set store by acquiring money.

tulit et feret: for the polyptoton cf. Ov. *Am.* 3.6.18 *nec tulit haec umquam nec feret ulla dies*, C. 2.13.20 *uis rapuit rapietque gentis* (B. on *AP* 70). **omnibus annis** 'annually', abl. of time, sustains the metaphor of harvest.

22   uir bonus et sapiens: 4.5n.; Aristotle's ἐλευθέριος 'the generous man'. There may even be an inverted echo of what Nausicaa says of Ulysses, that he seems neither bad nor foolish (*Od.* 6.187 = 20.227).

dignis 'the deserving', masc. dat. with *paratus*, a syntactical Grecism = ἑτοῖμος + dat., handier than the native construction, *ad* or *in* + acc. Moralists from Theognis (1161–2 W.) on had stressed that benefactors must assure themselves that the beneficiaries were good and worthy men; cf. Arist. *EN* 4.1, Cic. *Off.* 2.62 *in deligendis idoneis iudicium et diligentiam adhibere* and Sen. *Dial.* 7.23.5 *donabit aut bonis aut eis quos facere poterit bonos. donabit cum summo consilio dignissimos eligens* (A. R. Hands, *Charities and social aid in Greece and Rome* (London 1968) 74–5). So Maecenas chose his friends, *S.* 1.6.51 *praesertim cautum dignos adsumere*.

paratus: the nom. subj. of the infin. after an active verb of speaking is a syntactical Grecism (G–L §527 N2, Roby §1350, K–S 1 702). Unlike the Calabrian, the *uir bonus* does not force his generosity on the reluctant.

23   tamen 'besides', an idiomatic use where two co-ordinated statements are affirmed, but the second is affirmed irrespective of the truth of the first (cf. 14.26; Powell on Cic. *Sen.* 1.1 *et tamen*, p. 99 and 6.16, p. 138). However ready the good man is to be of service, he is still not blind to the value of his gift, unlike the *prodigus* who gives unthinkingly what he has no use for.

lupinis 'lupine seeds' were apparently used on the stage as pretend money (Pl. *Poen.* 597).

24   dignum praestabo me 'shall continue to show myself worthy' (*OLD praesto*² 7) marks the return from the general reflections of 20–3 to the immediate issue, H.'s satisfaction of his debt of gratitude (not yet complete, as the fut. hints). By implication, then, Maecenas is *bonus et sapiens*.

etiam 'as well' goes with the following phrase, for H. takes for granted his gratitude *pro benefactis* 'in the light of gifts received'.

pro laude merentis 'considering the renown of my benefactor' (*OLD pro* 13, *laus* 2, *mereo* 6b). The best commentary is found in *Ep.*

2.1.245–7 *at neque dedecorant tua de se iudicia atque | munera, quae multa dantis cum laude tulerunt | dilecti tibi Vergilius Variusque poetae*. Augustus shows commendable judgement in supporting those poets; at 238 Alexander the Great is called *prodigus* for throwing his money away on the verses of Choerilus.

25–8 H. acknowledges Maecenas' continuing generosity (*merentis* not *meriti*), for which he professes gratitude; urbane and candid, he lists the qualities that attracted Maecenas to him in the first days of their friendship, qualities well suited to that life of pleasure in which Maecenas still indulges. H. here develops the theme *non eadem est aetas* (1.4). Tactfully he does not draw attention to his change of heart (*non mens*), but insists that Maecenas must restore to him his vanished youth if he wants his constant attendance for the future. (This interpretation is derived from Lambinus.)

25   noles: the fut. shows that the issue of H.'s attendance is still open; Maecenas has yet to decide.

25 ... 27   reddes: for the fut. see 4.15n. A triple anaphora pathetically underscores the impossibility of the task; cf. 95.

26   latus suggests sexual stamina (*TLL* VII 2.1027.24–39, where this line might have been cited; J. N. Adams, *The Latin sexual vocabulary* (London 1982) 49); cf. also 1.9. *nigros*)(*praecanum* 20.24.

angusta fronte: a low hair line on the brow was admired in both sexes, but in men especially it betokens youth (N–H on *C.* 1.33.5 *insignem tenui fronte Lycorida*).

27   reddes ... loqui ... ridere ... 28   maerere: the infin. as substantive ('talking, laughing, weeping') serves as dir. obj. of *dare*, its compounds, synonyms and antonyms: poetic syntax (K–S I 681, H–S 345).

dulce ... decorum: poetic adverbial acc. (G–L §333 R6, Roby §1096, K–S I 281). Sweet talk and graceful laughter reflect Sappho, 31.3–5 *PLF* 'he listens nearby to your sweet voice and your lovely laughter', a thought incompletely rendered by Catullus, 51.5 *dulce ridentem*; H. improved upon it: *C.* 1.22.23–4 *dulce ridentem Lalagen amabo, | dulce loquentem*. The words could be a motto for the life of pleasure. For the enjambment with *et* see Introduction p. 24.

28   inter uina 'in the midst of (*OLD* 7) the drinking (*OLD* 1d)' goes with *maerere*; *uina* is poetic plur. (5.4n.).

proteruae: cf. the *grata proteruitas* (*C.* 1.19.7) of Glycera, like Cinara, a wanton.

29–39 A fable, similar to Babrius 86, is introduced, as usual by asyndeton; its relevance is revealed later (34–9), as at 46–95, a characteristic strategy (cf. 10.34–8, 15.26–46; B. on *Ep.* 2.2.81–6).

29 Forte commonly announces an anecdote or fable (L. on *S.* 1.1.1).

angustam tenuis: the pointed juxtaposition is emphasized by the diminutive *uulpecula*, itself sandwiched between the words for the 'narrow chink', an example of concrete poetry (T. A. Hayward, *Class. World* 80 (1986–7) 19). The poor vixen was driven from the text by Bentley on the grounds that foxes do not eat grain; he replaced her with *nitedula* 'a dormouse'. But it is the vixen's cunning, not her diet, that matters to the fabulist; nor are dormice at all usual in the cast of characters in fables.

30 pasta 'having fed herself' (*OLD* 6).

31 pleno ... corpore: descriptive abl. *tendebat* 'was striving' (*OLD* 13b) governs the complementary infin. *ire*.

frustra: dramatic at the end of the verse and period, cf. *C.* 3.13.3–6 *cras donaberis haedo, | cui frons turgida cornibus | primis et uenerem et proelia destinat | frustra.* Good feeding has led to imprisonment.

32 procul 'hard by' (Fordyce on Catull. 64.108; the *OLD* is inadequate). Pseudo-Acro believed that the sibilants were a fine imitation of the weasel's hissing (if that is what they do).

33 macra ... macra: repetition sharpens up the advice and recalls *tenuis. cauum* 'chink' (*OLD* 3). For the fut. *repetes* see 4.15n.

34 compellor imagine 'I am arraigned by this parable' (*OLD compello* 3b, *imago* 7), a legal metaphor. The charge comes not from Maecenas but from what H. feels the malicious might think, namely that he battened on Maecenas only to desert him after securing what he wanted in the first place. There is no hint that Maecenas expected the return of his gifts, as if they were a *depositum*.

cuncta resigno 'I hand over everything' without exception including even the Sabine estate, though H. is careful not to specify at this stage that Maecenas' gifts are what he restores. The uncompromising assertion is at once justified by 35–6 and further clarified at 39 *donata. resigno,* a synonym of *rescribo* 'pay back' (*OLD* 5), according to Festus (352.4), suggests bookkeeping; cf. *C.* 3.29.54 *resigno quae dedit* [*Fortuna*], addressed to Maecenas.

35 somnum plebis: humble folk were thought to sleep easily because of a supposed freedom from cares and a healthier diet; cf. *C.* 3.1.21–3 *somnus agrestium | lenis uirorum non humilis domos | fastidit.* The expression in 35–6 implies an elliptical antithesis, viz. *somnus ⟨et fru-galitas⟩* : *⟨insomnis et⟩ satur* (Introduction p. 26 n. 95; B. on *Ep*. 2.1.41).

satur altilium 'full of fattened fowls' (cf. *pleno ... corpore* 31); the gen. with *satur* is poetic (K–S 1 442). H. praises the simple life as a consistent policy, not because he is sleepless after too rich a meal; even when less well looked after he avows its merits.

nec: a special type of anaphoric enjambment; in Virgil the whole of the sixth foot is used, e.g., *G*. 3.428 *dum amnes ulli rumpuntur fontibus et dum ...* , so H.'s practice is distinctive of the non-heroic hexameter.

36   Arabum: in antiquity their proverbial wealth was founded upon the re-export of eastern merchandise (N–H on *C*. 1.29.1, Otto §148). For the sentiment cf. *C*. 3.1.47–8 *cur ualle permutem Sabina | diuitias operosiores?*, where the Sabine valley corresponds to leisured freedom here. The latent antithesis is: *otia liberrima ⟨et paupera⟩ : diuitiae ⟨operosae⟩* (Introduction p. 26 n. 95).

37–8 H. needs a guarantor for his claims. Who better than Maecenas himself?

37   saepe, emphatic, leaves no doubt. *uerecundia*, a notion important to H. (9.12, 17.44, 20.3), is broadly 'moral sensiblility', above all that consideration of others that amounts to modesty (Holden on Cic. *Off*. 1.93, *ibid*. 99 *homines non offendere* and 148).

laudasti 'you have commended me for being ...' (*OLD* 1f), sc. *me*. The acknowledgment has been public.

rex 'patron', in colloquial language (*OLD* 8); *pater* too could be used in this sense, but has greater warmth (*OLD* 5).

-que ... -que: the archaic idiom, perhaps modelled on τε ... τε, raises the tone to epic level here, its only occurrence in the collection (it is not uncommon in *S*. or *AP* (B. on *AP* 11, with addenda)). The first *-que* no more connects the verbs of this sentence than at *S*. 1.1.76; this idiom commonly joins two nouns, esp. at the end of the line (Skutsch on Enn. *Ann*. 170 Sk.).

38   audisti 'have heard yourself called', a lexical Grecism, perhaps employed to flatter Maecenas' Hellenizing tastes (so Coleman 137, see Introduction p. 22 n. 79; *OLD* 5); *uerbo* 'by a single word', for the abl. see 6.43n. Others will confirm H.'s avowal of indebtedness to Maecenas.

39 H. has worked back round to an amplified restatement of the claim at 34 *cuncta resigno*, but he now has Maecenas and others as witnesses to his attitude.

inspice, another bookkeeping term, implies official scrutiny of accounts (*TLL* VII 1952.37–41, 47); for *si* see 6.41n.; the indic. in the indirect qu. is quite regular (K–S II 426, but cf. 17.4–5).

donata: more specific than *cuncta* 34; Maecenas' gifts are now the issue; the following lines make it clear, as Heinze saw, that H. has chiefly in mind the position in high society which he owed to Maecenas. *reponere* keeps up the bookkeeping metaphor (*OLD* 5).

laetus, to be understood adverbially, is emphatic; restoration must not cost a pang (contrast 16.35 *tristis*).

40–5 The argument advances asyndetically. H., following his doctrine in II, illustrates the return of gifts from Homer, *Od*. 4.601–8, and introduces a fresh theme, appropriateness.

40 Haud male was a set phrase in Plautus and perhaps still in conversational use, though *haud* itself had largely disappeared from the spoken language (*TLL* VI 2.2560.60–1; Axelson 91–2). The ellipse of a verb of speaking is also conversational and conforms to the usual pattern of introducing the sentence with an adverb (Roby §1441).

sapientis is preferred to *patientis* since it suggests that Telemachus inherited his father's practical wisdom, a point made in Menelaus' reply to his refusal of the gift: 'My son, from what you say, you come of good stock' (*Od*. 4.611). For the form *Vlixei* see 6.63n.

41–2 A paratactic causal sentence.

41 aptus equis < *C*. 1.7.9; *aptus* is a keyword, echoed at 43 (there is no equivalent in Homer). *ut* 'being as it is' (*OLD* 21, 'usu. without vb').

42 spatiis 'over ground for racing' (*OLD* 1); the abl. is local, cf. Sen. *Nat*. 3.8 *ingenti spatio maria porrecta sunt*.

43 Atridē 'son of Atreus', i.e. Menelaus. *tibi* belongs to both *apta* and *relinquam* (cf. 19).

44 paruum parua decent recalls, formally at least, Callimachus, *Aetia* 2, αἰεὶ τοῖς μίκκοις μίκκα διδοῦσι θεοί 'the gods always give small things to the small' (*Supplementum Hellenisticum*, edd. H. Lloyd-Jones and P. J. Parsons, 253.11). A generally applicable moral is drawn from the Homeric story. The alliterative repetition in *paruum parua* is emphatic (L. on *S*. 1.8.3, 2.6.81). Here, as at 3.28, *paruus* refers to economic and social status; elsewhere it characterizes H.'s poetic genres (Fraenkel 335–6); his use of *tenuis* is similar. *decent* picks up *aptus* and *apta*; cf. 1.11.

mihi applies the moral to himself and *iam* draws attention to his changed situation, cf. 25–8, *nunc* 1.4, *iam* 10.11.

regia Roma: alliteration enhances the phrase. Rome's monarchical quality conflicts with H.'s own reign in the country (10.8).

45 uacuum 'quiet' (of Athens at *Ep.* 2.2.81); *Tibur*, modern Tivoli, is eighteen miles east-north-east of Rome. At some time H. acquired a villa there (Suet. *uita Hor.* 65 Rostagni); he is not referring to the *Sabinum* which Maecenas gave him (N–H on *C.* 1.7.13).

imbelle Tarentum: the modern Taranto was an elegant resort for Romans (16.11, N–H on *C.* 2.6, pp. 94–5). H. emphasizes the retired nature of his now favoured residences (cf. 11.7–10).

46–95 An anecdote concerning an inappropriate gift (and its attendant life-style) dramatizes the leading themes; its relevance to the first part of the epistle is set out in the final lines, 96–8, though details within the story itself reflect by contrast the relationship between H. and Maecenas (McGann 53–4).

46 Strenuus and its common companion *fortis* (*OLD* 1b) mark a contrast with H.'s favoured retreats.

causis ... agendis: causal abl. with *clarus* 47, cf. *S.* 2.3.194 *seruatis clarus Achiuis*. L. Marcius Philippus, *cos.* 91 B.C., was often referred to in glowing terms by Cicero (*RE* XIV 1562–8, *Marcius* 75), but it has been doubted that he is to be identified with the Philippus of this anecdote (Shackleton Bailey 58 n. 29).

47 octauam ... horam: this fell somewhere about twelve forty-five in winter and two thirty p.m. in the summer; Philippus has prolonged his toils past noon, a reasonable hour to finish (Fraenkel 337 n.1). The ninth was the dinner hour (71).

48 Foro: the simple abl. of separation, where prose would use *ab*, is chiefly poetic (K–S I 371). Trials were held in the open air in the Forum. The fashionable residential neighbourhood known as the *Carinae* 'Ships' Keels' lay on the western end of a southern spur of the Esquiline (Richardson 71–2); the distance from the Forum is not great, it only seemed so to an old man who had done a day's work and wanted his dinner.

49 ut aiunt: 6.40n.

50 adrasum 'close shaven'; *ad* is intensive (Roby §1834).

uacua: barber-shops attract the idle for masculine gossip (Porphyrio on *S.* 1.7.3); it recalls H.'s description of Tibur (45), and points up the contrast between two ways of life.

51 proprios = *suos*, chiefly poetic diction (*OLD* 2b). Leisure, simplicity and perhaps frugality are suggested by the scene; he has time and inclination to clean his own nails rather than pay the barber to do them. Soon they will become broken and dirty (90).

52 The scene is set, and the drama begins with direct speech unintroduced (14–19n.), though the voc. at the head of the line clearly marks the change of direction. A slave-boy, *puer*, always attended a Roman gentleman when out of doors, to fetch and carry.

non laeue: litotes; the adverbial form, found only here in the whole of extant Latin, is a loan-shift from σκαιῶς, not inappropriately used of a Greek boy.

53 abi ... refer: the crisp commands are matched by the brisk description of the lad's action: *it, redit et narrat* (55).

unde domo 'where he comes from', an idiomatic expression, lit. 'whence in respect of home?' Take *sit* (54) ἀπὸ κοινοῦ with all the indirect questions.

54 cuius fortunae 'of what status' (*OLD* 11b), i.e. slave or free or freedman; gen. of description.

quo ... patre: cf. *S.* 1.6.58 *non ego me claro natum patre* where H. describes his background to Maecenas on their first meeting.

quoue patrono: he may be a freedman; his former owner would now be his patron. Maecenas, it should be recalled, did not socialize with freedmen (*S.* 1.6.7–8 *cum referre negas, quali sit quisque parente | natus, dum ingenuus*).

55 it, redit: a common asyndeton, perhaps colloquial (*TLL* v 2.630.46–8, Norden on Virg. *A.* 6.121f.); cf. 72n.

narrat: sc. *eum esse*. Mena, now immortal, is otherwise unknown. His name betrays a freedman, once simply Mena (from Menas, a shortened form of Menodoros; Bentley explained why Romans omitted the final *s* from such freedmen's names in his *Epistola ad Joannem Millium* (ed. A. Dyce, London 1836) 342–9). On manumission the *nomen* of his previous owner, Volteius, was added, slaves having no legal father.

56 praeconem: auctioneers held low status but had good prospects for self-advancement (N. K. Rauh, *Historia* 38 (1989) 451–71); H. himself might have ended up following that trade, like his father before him (*S.* 1.6.86). The point here is that, then as now, auctioneers need considerable charm and address; they must have above all a way with words (72). A *praeco* could be a *scurra* (15.28n.), like Granius in Lucilius (412 M.) or Sex. Naevius (Cic. *Quinct.* 11).

tenui censu: descriptive abl.; *tenui* echoes 29 (cf. 44) and may even by contrast recall 1.43, in that Mena appears to be content. *sine crimine* 'blameless' is a stereotyped phrase (Pease on Virg. *A.* 4.550).

notum governs the four infinitives.

57   properare 'work energetically' (*OLD* 1b); *loco* 'on the right occasion' (*OLD* 21b, K–S II 567), an important proviso, that applies, as Dacier noted, to all the infinitives ἀπὸ κοινοῦ, cf. *C.* 4.12.28 (quoted at 5.16–20n.). Elision of iambic words is strictly regulated in Augustan verse; here, as usual, the elided syllable is followed by a (generally monosyllabic) connective (Winbolt §137).

cessare 'take it easy' (*OLD* 4); *quaerere* 'acquire money' (*OLD* 7b); *uti* 'spend' (Holden on Cic. *Off.* 2.71 *utentior*). By contrast with the old man of *AP* 170 who *quaerit et inuentis miser abstinet ac timet uti*, Mena fulfils an Horatian ideal of well-balanced activities; his flaw is his ignorance of his own felicity (so too Virgil's farmers: *fortunatos nimium, sua si bona norint*, *G.* 2.458) and so he is prepared to exchange his happy state for uncertainty.

58   paruis: 3.28n. For *-que et* see 6.14n.; here the metrical advantage of *-que* is the addition of the short syllable, cf. *C.* 4.9.35 *rerumque prudens et secundis. lare certo* shows that Mena is a respectable householder, not a vagabond like Maenius at 15.28.

59   ludis: cf. 14.15.

post decisa negotia 'after concluding business' (> Suet. *Vesp.* 21), that is to say, at the right time; for the idiom see 2.7n. and cf. *Ep.* 2.1.140 *condita post frumenta, C.* 1.3.29–30 *post ignem ... subductum.* In the afternoon Romans resorted to the open spaces of the Campus Martius for exercise or amusement (18.52–4, Richardson 65–7).

60   Again direct speech appears without introduction.

scitari 'enquire about' appears in Plautus, *Capt.* 263, and then in Virgil, *A.* 2.105, 114 (in the speech of Aeneas); perhaps it had a place in conversational use, though it is never found in classical prose.

dic governs the indir. command *ueniat* (*OLD* 2c); for the enjambment see Introduction p. 24.

61   sane intensifies the negative, and reproduces Mena's actual thought: 'non sane credo' (15.5; B. on *Ep.* 2.1.206).

61–2   credere ... mirari: the historic infin., used in excited narrative, is common in *S.*, but only found here in *Ep.* (Bo 269–70, *NLS* §21).

62   quid multa? 'in short' (*OLD multus* 3b). For *benigne* see 16.

63   neget 'can *he* refuse *my* invitation?' (*OLD* 3b); *ille mihi* are emphatic; for the subjunc. in an indignant qu. cf. 1.49–51n. (*LS* §84).

improbus 'the inconsiderate fellow' (*S.* 1.9.73); the slave takes his cue from his master's tone.

63–4   te neglegit = *C.* 3.21.10.

65   tunicato ... popello 'the rabble in working dress' (> Tac. *Dial.* 7 *tunicatus ... populus*) had no patron to visit and so no need to wear the toga. The tone of the diminutive (first found here, Bo 218) is hard to pin down; it may be either contemptuous or sympathetic.

66   occupat 'catches unawares' (*OLD* 11). Philippus puts Mena in an awkward position, since etiquette required that an inferior be the first to greet (*OLD salue*¹ 2, *iubeo* 7b) his social superior (see Martial 3.95).

67   excusare 'allege as a reason' (*OLD* 2); for the historic infin. see 61–2n.

mercennaria uincla: i.e. Mena is constrained to earn his fee (*merces*); cf. *S.* 1.6.86–7 *si praeco paruas ... mercedes sequerer*.

68–9   uenisset ... prouidisset: subjunc. because the verbs are virtual indir. speech. Mena ought to have attended the early morning *salutatio* at Philippus' house.

69   sic 'on this one condition' anticipates the *si*-clause, a colloquialism appropriate to direct speech (*OLD* 8c, G–L §590 N1).

putato: the fut. imperative is normal when the action is determined by a subord. clause referring to the fut. (Roby §1603).

70   ut libet: the ungracious tone hints at embarrassment (Fraenkel 338); as at 19, the speaker merely falls in with another's wishes.

ergo 'well, then', a colloquial sense with the fut. or imperative (*TLL* v 2.768.5–24); for the enjambment see Introduction p. 24.

71   post nonam: mid-afternoon, the usual time (47n.) For the fut. *uenies* see 4.15n.

nunc i ≠ *i nunc* (6.17n.).

rem ... auge: cf. 16.68; Philippus approves of Mena's industry. *strenuus* is adverbial; *strenue* would not fit an hexameter.

72   dicenda tacenda, i.e. 'anything that came into his head, whether worth saying or not', a polar form of proverbial expression (Otto §642); Mena is a chatterbox, not perhaps fit for an aristocratic dinner table. The pairing of contrasted words in asyndeton is common in early Latin (N–H on *C.* 2.3.26), but the use of the gerundive as a noun is chiefly poetic at this time and confined to the neuter pl. (K–S 1 229, H–S 371).

73 tandem ... dimittitur: Philippus could not bring himself to dismiss the engaging Mena. For *dormitum* see *repetitum* 3.18n.

74 uisus 'was seen to', sc. *est* (the ellipse in a subord. clause is rare except in Virgil, cf. Leo (1878) 188–9).

piscis '*like* a fish', a metaphor instead of simile (6.63n., Introduction p. 29), alluding to the proverbial 'hook' (Otto §781). As Bentley noted (on 96) the image points up Philippus' awareness of the effect he is having on the dazzled freedman.

75 iam 'by now' (*OLD* 3). In the same way H. became the *conuictor* of Maecenas, cf. *S.* 1.6.47.

75–6 iubetur ... comes ire: the nom. is here a predicate referring back to the subj. (5.15n.). It was usual for a client to be invited on a journey to relieve its tedium and to show the patron's prestige (17.7–8, 52, *S.* 1.6.101–3 *ducendus et unus | et comes alter, uti ne solus rusue peregreue | exirem* and 2.6.41–6); that is the situation in *S.* 1.5 (H.'s journey to Brundisium).

76 rura 'estates' (*OLD* 2); the bare acc. is a poetic extension of the usage with *rus* (K–S 1 486).

indictis ... Latinis 'when the religious festival of the Latins had been appointed'. The *feriae Latinae* (or simply *Latinae*) were celebrated at the Alban Mount every spring, once the consuls had appointed the date (*indicere*), which was not fixed (*OCD* s.v. *Jupiter* §5); the Senate attended and public business in Rome was suspended.

77 impositus: i.e. in the carriage drawn by the ponies, *mannis* (a word Munro believed was owed to Lucr. 3.1063 *currit agens mannos ad uillam*, 3.937n.).

caelum 'climate, air', esp. with reference to change of scene (*OLD* 7, N–H on *C.* 2.7.4). Like many less well-to-do citizens Mena had probably never been out of Rome.

79 sibi: Philippus is not interested, as a friend should be, in Mena's welfare (Heitland 234 speaks of his 'scurvy trick'); he may be *rex*, he is clearly not *pater* (37).

dum ... dum: 2.21n.; *dum* (80) has gerundial force, 'by giving ...' *requiem* 'amusement' (*OLD* 3).

80 mutua 'on loan', sc. *sestertia*. Philippus was not as generous as Maecenas, who gave H. his *Sabinum* as an outright gift. The sum apparently would have secured only a fairly small property. What is worse, no provision is being made for labour. On top of that the Sabine country was not specially fertile (cf. 14.23 and 16.8–11); that mattered less to H.: his larger estate was chiefly a retreat and he had other sources of income.

82–3 ne ... morer: a transitional formula (B. on *Ep.* 2.1.4, p. 39); for *ultra quam satis est* see Introduction p. 43.

83 ex nitido 'from being stylish' (*OLD ex* 13, *nitidus* 6b); the expression appears to compress a fuller thought: *ex nitido ⟨et urbano⟩ fit rusticus ⟨et horridus⟩* (Introduction p. 26 n. 95). For the enjambment with *atque* see Introduction p. 24.

84 crepat 'harps on' (*OLD* 4); its internal acc. obj. is poetic syntax and common in H. (K–S 1 278, Roby §1123, B. on *AP* 247). *mera* 'nothing but', to be understood ἀπὸ κοινοῦ with *sulcos*, has a colloquial tone (*OLD* 2; *TLL* VIII 846.35).

praeparat ulmos: until their recent adoption of French or mixed techniques of viticulture, central Italians used to train vines up into elm trees, which were pruned into tiers, *tabulata* (16.3; cf. Virg. *G.* 2.361 *summasque sequi tabulata per ulmos*; K. D. White, *Roman farming* (Cambridge 1970) 232–6, N. Belfrage, *Life beyond Lambrusco* (London 1985) 9–11).

85 immoritur: a coinage along Greek lines = ἐναποθνῄσκω (ἐνθνῄσκω is used metaphorically at Eur. *Hec.* 246). It governs the dat. *studiis* (B. on *Ep.* 2.2.82). The hyperbole makes a contrast with his former life, esp. *cessare* (57).

senescit: first here in the metaphorical sense (*OLD* 1b).

habendi 'gain', cf. Virg. *G.* 4.177 *innatus apes amor urget habendi*, *A.* 8.327, Ov. *AA* 3.541, *Met.* 1.131. No one denies that a farmer works for gain (Tibull. 1.9.7–8 *lucra petens habili tauros adiungit aratro | et durum terrae rusticus urget opus*). But, as pseudo-Acro noted, Mena had never been interested in gain before now, so 'possession' might be the sense (Shackleton Bailey 58 n. 31, cf. *TLL* VI 2.2401.1–5).

86–7 Mena's efforts come to nought; for the sake of variety there is no further reference to the vineyard, but disaster doubtless struck there too.

86 periere goes ἀπὸ κοινοῦ with *oues*, but in a slightly different sense, 'vanished'. This and the next clause are arranged chiastically.

87 mentita 'falsely promised' is used transitively in poetry (*OLD* 2);

supply *est* ἀπὸ κοινοῦ. Harvests are of course unreliable, hence *C.* 3.1.30 *fundus mendax.*

88   offensus 'troubled by' (*OLD offendo* 4).

media de nocte, cf. 2.32n., suggests first that Mena, unable to sleep for worry, decided to throw in the towel at dead of night, and secondly that he set off so as to catch Philippus at his *salutatio.*

caballum 'riding horse' is colloquial (L. on *S.* 1.6.59).

89   arripit: the diaeresis and slight pause after the first dactyl (Winbolt §8) depict Mena's urgency.

iratus: H. leaves it open whether the rage is directed at himself, at Philippus, or at both.

90   simul: 6.11n.

scabrum intonsumque: a bitter contrast with the first sight Philippus ever had of him, *adrasum* (50) and *nitido* (83); Mena has had neither time nor perhaps money for barbering. His condition is the more striking since appearance at the *salutatio* demanded a formal neatness.

91–5 The use of direct speech indicates that the anecdote is drawing to a close.

91   durus: 16.70. *Voltei* scans as two syllables by synizesis (cf. *Pompei* at *C.* 2.7.5 and 2.70n.); *nimis* belongs with *attentus* 'frugal' (*OLD* 3) ἀπὸ κοινοῦ.

92–3 Mena's tone has the pathos of tragedy (Leo (1912) 135 n. 3); cf. Eur. *IT* 499–500 'What name did your father give you? :: We might fairly be called "Wretch"' and Siegmund's reply to Sieglinde in Act I Scene II of Wagner's *Die Walküre*: 'I can't call myself "Peaceful"; I wish I were called "Cheerful"; but "Woeful" has to be my name.' Though no Roman bore the cognomen *Miser*, Mena, as a Greek, might have been punning on the proper name Ἀθλίας > ἄθλιος 'wretched' (this name is attested along with the pun in Diog. Laert. 6.44).

93   ponere = *imponere* (*OLD* 16b, Bo 388); cf. Ov. *Tr.* 3.6.36 *nomina si facto reddere uera uelis.*

94   quod 'wherefore' introduces a wish or adjuration (*OLD* 1b, K–S II 321), esp. in poetry, so the pathetic tone is sustained. The list after *per*, alliteration, and the synonymous verbs of beseeching also enhance the urgency of his prayer. For *Genium* see *genialis* 1.87–8n.; for similar requests in its name see Pl. *Capt.* 977, Ter. *An.* 289, [Tibull.] 4.5.7; for requests by the right hand (symbol of honour) see Pl. *Am.* 923, Virg. *A.* 4.314; for an oath by the Penates see *CIL* I 582.

95 obsecro et obtestor: paired also in Pl. *Aul.* 716, Cic. *Quinct.* 91 and *Fam.* 2.1.2. Elision of final *ō* in a word of cretic shape $(-\cup-)$ before *ĕt* is strictly confined by Augustan poets to the first foot (cf. Virg. *Ecl.* 4.12 *Pollio et, A.* 1.391 *nuntio et,* 11.503 *audeo et).*

uitae 'way of life' (*OLD* 7a).

redde echoes 25, 27. Only Philippus can waive the loan with which the farm was bought.

96–8 The moral is drawn in two stages, which relate back to the whole of the epistle. *repetat* recalls the advice to the vixen at 33, and *metiri* embraces all references to size, whether physical (*tenuis* 29, *macra* 33) or metaphorical (*paruum* 44, *tenui* 56, *paruis* 58).

96 semel agnouit: Holder's emendation *agnouit* (later withdrawn) is accepted *exempli gratia*. The main MS tradition offers *simul aspexit*, an inadvertent recollection of 90; all editors adopt *semel* from the *recentiores*. The word *aspexit* ousted may be beyond recovery.

dimissa = *relicta* (97).

petitis: the objects of our striving can prove unsatisfying.

97 mature 'speedily'. The triple repetition of the prefix *re* is exceptional and drives home the advice.

98 A proverbial *sententia* concludes the poetic argument (Otto §1107). The view was also given philosophical sanction by Panaetius, a second-century Stoic who lived for a time in Rome. His work on proper behaviour is the basis of Cicero's *De officiis*. In discussing *decorum*, what is appropriate for a man, Cicero says: *sic enim est faciendum, ut contra uniuersam naturam nihil contendamus, ea tamen conseruata propriam nostram sequamur, ut, etiam si sint alia grauiora atque meliora, tamen nos studia nostra nostrae naturae regula metiamur* (*Off.* 1.110, cf. L–S I 427–8, II 420). Even the Epicureans held that ambitious men must follow their natures if they were to achieve happiness (Plut. *Moral.* 465f).

se quemque suo: emphasizes personal responsibility in the conduct of life.

pede 'footrule' apparently, a unique usage (*OLD* 9).

uerum est = *decet*, cf. *S.* 2.3.312, quoted in 18.28n. (1.11n.).

Just as VI gave a fuller justification for H.'s refusal to toe a systematic philosophical line in his search for happiness, so this epistle starts by elaborating an issue latent in the refusal in the first epistle to compose more lyric poetry. What that entailed was also abandoning the life of pleasure that he had enjoyed with Maecenas. He begins this letter by pursuing the matter and accounting more fully for the change of heart that the years have brought. But from this opens out an altogether more pressing issue, the right relation between patron and client, focussed above all on the patron's obligation to keep an eye on the client's best interests and so respect his aspiration towards independence and self-determination. But the burden of striking a balance falls above all upon H. himself, as three of the four illustrative passages show by focussing upon the recipient (if the vixen may be included) of benefits, real or imagined.

It is remarkable that pseudo-Acro finds the tone of this letter harsh and severe. He introduces the poem thus: *hac epistola asperius ac destrictius* [more uncompromisingly] *Maecenati praescribit libertatem se opibus non uendere*; and on 37 he says *nunc paulo asperior est*. This view Shackleton Bailey is inclined to share – he speaks of the abrasiveness of 29–39 (55) and the aggressive assertion of independence (56), a message not compromised to spare Maecenas' feelings. It may be that the original author of the scholia lived, like Suetonius, at a time when the relations between friends of unequal financial means required greater servility on the part of the inferior (cf. Fraenkel 15–16).

Further reading: T. Berres, '"Erlebnis und Kunstgestalt" im 7. Brief des Horaz', *Hermes* 120 (1992) 216–37; Nicholas Horsfall, *La villa sabina di Orazio: il galateo della gratitudine. Una rilettura della settima epistola del primo libro* (Venosa 1993).

Epistle VIII

1–2 H. asks the Muse to carry greetings and a message to Albinovanus Celsus, now unknown, though his poetic aspirations (which here prompt invocation of the Muse) are clear from 3.15–20. His unusual *(ag)nomen* may link him to Albinovanus Pedo, the poet and friend of Ovid (and perhaps *praefectus equitum* under Germanicus, so *RE* I 1314.12–20). He may also be the Celsus, friend of Cotta Maximus, whose death Ovid mourns at *Pont.* 1.9.

1 **Celso** is dat. with *refer*, which governs the infinitives (K–S I 683);

but beside *gaudere* it suggests a parody of a Greek epistolary greeting, Κέλσωι χαίρειν (as pseudo-Acro noted; Roman salutations differed: see 10.1). That would be an appropriate form of salutation from a *Musa* (rather than a *Camena*). The parts of his name are reversed to suggest a verbal point (17n., cf. 2.1n.) and belong together ἀπὸ κοινοῦ.

bene rem gerere 'to fare prosperously', a common greeting (*TLL* VI 2.1943.66–71), here perhaps chosen for a moral colour to be applied to both correspondents.

2   rogata 'at my request'; cf. Catull. 35.2 *uelim Caecilio, papyre, dicas* for a similar use of an intermediary.

refer 'duly tell him' (*OLD* 5); *re* often implies that the action is appropriate or expected (Page on Virg. *Ecl.* 3.21), though some assume Celsus had written to H. and that this is his reply.

comiti scribaeque: the pairing may reflect his official titles; C. Cichorius, *Römische Studien* (Leipzig and Berlin 1922) 387 compares the reference of Germanicus to Baebius as his 'friend and secretary' (§320.11 in V. Ehrenberg and A. H. M. Jones (edd.), *Documents illustrating the reigns of Augustus and Tiberius* (Oxford 1976)). Like Florus in III, Celsus has a place in the *cohors* of Tiberius. What is more, he has secured a staff appointment (*RE* IV 1.623.24–5). The *scriba* was a personal secretary with charge also of accounts and records; he was of equestrian rank, but not so elevated that he should expect to rise much further (S. Demougin, *L'ordre équestre sous les julio-claudiens* (Collection de l'école française de Rome 108, 1988) 710–12). This has a bearing on the advice at the end; nor should it be forgotten that H. himself was a *scriba quaestorius* (B. on *Ep.* 2.2.51–2), whom Augustus wanted for personal correspondence (Introduction p. 6).

3–12   H. gives some account of himself, by way of preparing the ground for his advice to Celsus. He is not well in spirit, but at least he can analyse the grounds for his indisposition. This sets up a contrast between himself and Celsus (*nec recte*)(*recte*), and softens the implied warning that true self-knowledge must back up our assessment of our situation.

3   quid agam both 'how I am' and 'what I'm up to' (*OLD* 21f. and see 3.15n.).

multa et pulchra minantem '*though* promising many fine things' (*OLD minor*[1] 3; cf. *pollicitus* 7.1n.) < *S.* 2.3.9 *multa et praeclara minantis* (for both cf. Patrocles fr. 1.3 N. τί δῆτα θνητοὶ πόλλ᾽ ἀπειλοῦμεν

μάτην). The language sounds doubly Greek, and so again is appropriate to the Muse's way of speaking. First, *et* is superfluous in Latin, since
multa is here used as a noun (cf. 2.21 *aspera multa*), but the expression
evokes πολλὰ καὶ καλά. Secondly, the sense of *minor* is unusual (Servius
noted this on *A.* 2.96); it is another calque, on ἀπειλέω (as Cruquius
saw), which means either 'promise' or 'threaten', but usually the latter.
(In the satire from which this phrase is recalled, the speaker is a Greek,
Damasippus.) For the moral colour of *pulchra* see 2.3n.

4 uiuere: sc. *me* (2.11n.). *recte* refers to moral ideals (6.29n.), *suauiter*
'agreeably' to inclinations (cf. *S.* 1.6.130 *uiuere suauius*).

4–7 haud quia ... nec quia ... sed quia: the carefully repeated
articulation of the colloquial *quia* suits the argumentative style (12.10–
11, B. on *Ep.* 2.1.76–7). For *haud* see 7.40n. and Introduction pp.
18–19. The subjunc. (*contuderit, momorderit, aegrotet*) is regular in rejected reasons (G–L §541 N2, *NLS* §243).

4 grando: cf. *C.* 3.1.29 *uerberatae grandine uineae*. H.'s farm did not
produce wine (14.23); this and the following disasters have nothing to
do with him but perhaps recall Mena's misfortunes (7.86–7).

5 momorderit 'nipped' (*OLD* 6b), cf. *C.* 3.1.30–2 *arbore ... culpante
nunc torrentia agros sidera.*

6 A reference to transhumance, the pasturing of herds in different
places at different seasons; *longinquis* suggests that the beasts are too far
away to be easily tended.

7–11 sed quia ... uelim etc.: all the verbs in the clause giving the
real reasons are also part of the indir. speech begun with *dic* (3), hence
the subjunc. (6.22n.).

corpore toto answers obliquely the question of 3: H.'s health is
completely (*toto*) sound. His suffering is not financial or physical, but
spiritual (*mente*), a malaise of aimless dissatisfaction, not uncommon
among the successful middle-aged. This theme will be developed later.
The thought and even perhaps expression echo Lucr. 3.109 *cum miser ex
animo laetatur corpore toto.*

8 nil ... nil: 1.88n. *audire* and *discere* are keywords picked up from
1.48. H. refuses to be receptive to well-intended advice, another pallia-
tive for the warning he is about to offer Celsus.

leuet 'alleviate' (B. on *Ep.* 2.2.212); see *possim* 1.12n.

9 fidis ... medicis: to be understood literally, not figuratively of
philosophical texts (cf. *S.* 2.3.147 *medicus ... fidelis*; *fidos* 5.24n.); the

restless and discontented rail at (*OLD offendo* 7b) their unnecessary doctors (Plut. *Moral.* 466c τὸν ἰατρὸν αἰτιῶνται). For the combined interest of doctors and friends in a person's well-being cf. Catull. 41.5–6 *propinqui, quibus est puella curae,* | *amicos medicosque conuocate. fidis* goes with *amicis* ἀπὸ κοινοῦ.

10 cur suggests reproach, rather than a genuine question; cf. *C.* 1.8.2–3 *Sybarin cur properes amando* | *perdere* (*TLL* IV 1451.61–8).

me ... arcere ueterno: cf. *AP* 64 *classes Aquilonibus arcet,* (1.31n.). *ueternus* = ληθαργία (*S.* 2.3.145) 'coma', a term of wide meaning, but a potentially fatal symptom, hence *funesto* (Cels. 3.20). H. need not be exaggerating the seriousness of his listlessness; a letter from Augustus refers to his uncertain health (Suet. *uita Hor.* 29 Rostagni), and active men find depression harder to deal with.

11 nocuere: the indic. is retained in a subord. clause in *O.O.* when it is a circumlocution for what might have been expressed substantivally, here, e.g., *res iniuriosas* (*NLS* §§286–8, esp. 287). The sentiment is a pre-echo of Ov. *Met.* 7.20 *uideo meliora proboque, deteriora sequor*.

12 uentosus: inconstancy of purpose clearly lies at the heart of H.'s malaise, cf. *S.* 2.7.28–9 *Romae rus optas, absentem rusticus urbem* | *tollis ad astra leuis. Tibure* is locative (B. on *Ep.* 2.2.3); see 7.45n.

13–17 H. now turns to Celsus, with a warning about the dangers of complacency amid success.

13 ut ualeat: cf. 3.12n. For *quo pacto* see 6.10n. *rem gerat* picks up the opening greeting, but the addition of *se* ('how he conducts himself', *OLD gero* 7) makes a transition to H.'s real concern.

14 iuueni: Tiberius was in his early twenties.

percontare: cf. *utere* 6.68n. That Celsus has found favour with Tiberius is clear from his appointment. His standing with the other *amici* might well prove harder to be sure of; from III we see the tensions that exist among them. Celsus' new position opens him up to envy and even slander.

15 recte: a reasonable enough answer to the questions about his health and personal affairs, but uncertainty would be a more prudent response concerning his relations with Tiberius and the rest of the *cohors*.

gaudere 'to display your delight', almost 'congratulate' depends on *memento* ἀπὸ κοινοῦ. The Muse is told to be pleased on Celsus' behalf, to soften her friendly warning.

16   instillare: the warning is to be as gradual as the infusion of oil into clogged ears (for the metaphor cf. 2.53), so that Celsus may come to understand the real pitfalls of his situation (esp. since he should try to hear what will from now on be said of him).

memento 'be sure to' (*OLD* 4a), a colloquial usage, popular with poets (*TLL* VIII 653.64–78; N–H wrongly regard it as formal at *C.* 2.17.31). Of course, as a daughter of Mnemosyne (Greek for memory), the Muse will have no difficulty.

17   fortunam sc. *feres*, cf. *C.* 3.27.74–5 *bene ferre magnam | disce fortunam.*

Celse: the unusual repetition of the name in an emphatic position points to the danger to which the addressee is now exposed. He is indeed 'exalted', but it would not do to rub his friends' noses in his own success. H. likes to play with the meaning of names, e.g., *pauper Opimius S.* 2.3.142, *immitis Glycerae C.* 1.33.2, *Scaeua* 17.1n. The advice to use self-restraint in prosperity recalls *C.* 2.10.23–5 *sapienter idem | contrahes uento nimium secundo | turgida uela.*

H. returns to society in general, with his eye again on the circle of Tiberius, introduced in III. Having introduced the theme of the right relationship between patron and client in VII, he can focus on another aspect of it here and in the next epistle. In both he is concerned for young men who are making their way upwards in Roman society. Celsus has arrived, but needs to be made aware of the dangers of complacency both towards his patron and other aspirants. Müller suggested that the letter was placed here because it too develops the theme of H.'s unreliable mood, which was put down to fears of sickness in VII, but now seems due to spiritual malaise.

Epistle IX

1–9 H. explains to Tiberius why Septimius has chosen him to write this letter of recommendation. The emphasis is clearly laid upon Septimius' appraisal of H.: *intelligit, censet, uidet, nouit* (1–6). H.'s own self-appraisal is less assured (7–9). Septimius is probably the addressee of *C.* 2.6, and may also be the *Septimius noster* mentioned in a letter from Augustus to H. (Suet. *uita Hor.* 31 Rostagni). Nothing is known of his background, but from this epistle it is clear that he aimed to improve his status, and that H. thought well enough of him to lend a hand. Its publication shows that H. secured his wish.

1 Claudi: the Romans at this time had no formal address equivalent to our 'sir'; the son of a freedman uses the nobleman's given name.

nimirum ... unus 'better than anyone else, it would seem' (*OLD unus* 8; L. on *S.* 2.2.106); *nimirum*, a colloquial word (and so found only in a speech in Virg. *A.* 3.558), is here ironical.

2 quanti: gen. of value; *facias* 'esteem' (*OLD* 18c).

cum 'in that' (*OLD* 9); the apodosis is in 6.

rogat et prece cogit: cf. Plin. *Ep.* 9.21.4 *uereor ne uidear non rogare sed cogere, si precibus eius meas iunxero. cogit* shows that H. acts under compulsion. The abl. sing. of *prex*, rarely encountered outside poetry, is common in H. to whom its two short syllables recommend it; the usual plur. serves for other cases.

3 scilicet 'actually' (*OLD* 2) goes with *cogit. tradere* 'recommend' (*OLD* 7).

coner: a qualification; H. should make the attempt at least and leave the decision to Tiberius; cf. *experiar S.* 2.6.39.

4 '*as being a man* worthy of the character and household of a Nero, who selects *only* what is honourable' (*OLD mens* 4e, *domus* 6, *lego*[2] 6). For the attachment of the attributes to *se* see 4.15n. Latin often does not express the idea of 'only' (Kenney on Lucr. 3.144 with addenda). For the thought see *S.* 1.6.62–3 *magnum hoc ego duco,* | *quod placui tibi* [Maecenas], *qui turpi secernis honestum.* The rhythm of the line is noteworthy for the complete harmony of word accent and verse ictus (cf. 2.43, 14.30; Waltz 218–9) and for four successive trochaic caesurae (generally avoided: Waltz 214, Winbolt §70). Commentators fancy a variety of reasons for these unusual features.

honesta: generalizing neuter plur. as at *C.* 1.34.14 *obscura promens.*

5 Construe: *cum ⟨me⟩ fungi munere proprioris amici censet; cum* 'because' (*OLD* 6); *me* is to be supplied from *coner.* With *proprioris* cf. *S.* 2.6.52 *deos quoniam propius contingis. censet* 'supposes' carries the nuance of holding possibly mistaken views (*OLD* 2).

6 possim 'am capable of' (2.17n.). For the abl. of comparison *me ... ipso* see 1.106n.

ualdius, colloquial and common in Cicero's letters, is unusual in poetry (B. on *AP* 321).

7 quidem 'to be sure' (*OLD* 3a). For *cur* see 8.10n. *excusatus* 'released from the duty' (*OLD* 3), *abirem* 'I might get off with impunity', a judicial metaphor (*OLD* 7b, L. on *S*. 2.3.246).

8   mea 'what is in my power' (*OLD* 7).

putarer: it is not suggested that the notion had occurred to Septimius. At *S*. 2.6.38–9 H. depicts himself as not being believed when he fails to guarantee that he can secure Maecenas' agreement to a document.

9   dissimulator = εἴρων: 'the mock-modest man ... disclaims what he has or belittles it' (Arist. *EN* 4.7.3.1127A22). But since to belittle one's capacities may be polite (as it is for Aristotle; cf. *S*. 1.10.13–14 *urbani parcentis uiribus atque | extenuantis eas consulto*), H. adds a phrase that leaves no doubt.

commodus 'obliging' (*OLD* 5b); *uni* 'alone' (1.106n.).

10–11   His effort to be let off having failed, H. is reduced to what he regards as a lesser evil than failing a friend, effrontery.

11   'I have stooped to the privileges of town-bred assurance' (*OLD* *descendo* 8b, *frons*[2] 3). Modesty has long been attributed to country-folk (Cic. *Fam*. 5.12.1); the town dweller exercises a breezy informality.

11–13   H. at last makes his request briskly. For the enjambment with *quodsi* see Introduction p. 24.

12   depositum ... pudorem 'the laying aside of my modesty' (2.7n.).

laudas: H. leaves it to Tiberius to decide whether his recommending Septimius is after all acceptable.

ob amici iussa: the request of a friend brooked no refusal, unless it was morally reprehensible (cf. 18.45 *imperiis* and the commonplace of literary exordia in antiquity, that composition and publication have been ordered by a friend; E. R. Curtius, *European literature and the Latin Middle Ages* (Eng. trans. London 1954) 85). This phrase explains and justifies H.'s suppression of scruple, but does not force Tiberius' decision one way or the other.

13   scribe 'enroll' (*OLD* 7); *tui gregis* 'as one of your set (*OLD* 3)', a partitive gen. used poetically with the verb (K–S 1 453). Septimius wants to be more than just a member of the *cohors* which would disband when its business was completed.

fortem ... bonumque: the only words in praise of Septimius are purely conventional; cf. Cic. *Fam*. 13.77.2 *M. Bolanum, uirum bonum et* *fortem et omnibus rebus ornatum meumque ueterem amicum, tibi magno opere commendo*; C. 4.4.29 *fortes creantur fortibus et bonis* (*TLL* VI 1.1150.3–4). It may be that here and in the ode just cited (it is dedicated to Nero Drusus) H. alludes to the meaning of *nero* in the Sabine dialect, viz. *fortis* (Suet. *Tib.* 1.2; so Obbar). *crede* 'regard him as' (*OLD* 6 with pred. acc.).

One of the commonest kinds of friendly *patrocinium* 'brokerage' in antiquity entailed the writing of letters of introduction. Cicero collected a whole book of them, *Ad fam.* XIII (H. Cotton, *Documentary letters of recommendation*, Beiträge zur klassische Philologie 132 (Königstein 1981) and *A.J.P.* 106 (1985) 328–34). Now a Cicero had no doubt, given his status, that he could effect introductions and that his recommendations would be acted upon. The *parvenu* H. is in quite a different position, not least because only his talents have brought him into contact with the highest in the land. On the one hand it is his duty to do something for a worthy aspirant who is attached to him (17.11 *tuis* n.), on the other he must not seem to presume on his acquaintance with the great. With reserved affability he leaves the issue fairly in the hands of the aristocrat to decide, a classic moment in his intercourse with the great. This letter thus opens up the theme of associating with the socially superior, to be justified in XVII. Professor Kenney further observes that there is also an implicit message for young men on the way up like Septimius; they must for their part be realistic in what they expect of their seniors.

Epistle X

1–11 H. writes from the country to Fuscus at Rome; his desire to express his happiness in his choice of residence introduces the deeper contrast between city and country that makes up the bulk of the epistle.

1–2 Vrbis)(ruris: a contrast enhanced by the placing of the words at the head of each line. M. Aristius Fuscus, *mihi carus* in *S.* 1.9.61 (though he lets H. down maliciously) and one of H.'s preferred readers at *S.* 1.10.83, is the dedicatee of *C.* 1.22. He is said by the scholiasts to have been a notable schoolmaster (45), and to have been a poet (not a point ever noticed by H. himself); it has been suggested that he inclined to Stoicism (S. J. Harrison, *C.Q.* 42 (1992) 543–7). For *saluere iubemus* see 7.66n.

2–5 The punctuation of these lines diffidently follows Klingner and Shackleton Bailey; numerous variations have been proposed by editors (interpolation or the loss of a line does not seem to explain the difficulty).

3 multum, adverbial (3.15n.), is common with words expressing difference, e.g. *Ep.* 2.2.62 *multum diuersa. cetera* 'in other respects' (*OLD* 4) is adverbial acc. with *gemelli*.

4 animis 'feelings' (*OLD* 10b), causal abl. *et* 'too', sc. *negat*.

5 adnuimus, the sign of assent, paves the way to the metaphorical doves, birds proverbial for shared affection (Otto §414). The diminutive *uetuli* conveys a note of affection; the apposition of *columbi* produces metaphor instead of comparison (Introduction pp. 28–30).

6 nidum preserves the metaphor; for *seruas* cf. 5.31n.

7 circumlita 'bestrewn'; H. crisply enumerates the most agreeable features of the countryside, water and shade. For mossy rocks cf. Lucr. 5.951 *umida saxa, super uiridi stillantia musco*, Catull. 68.58 *muscoso ... e lapide*.

8 quid quaeris? 'in short' (*OLD* 8c); a colloquial formula, common in Cicero's letters, for introducing a general statement.

uiuo 'I really live' (*OLD* 7 (in emphatic sense)). *regno* associates the independence theme with life in the country (contrast 33, 40–1 and 7.44n.); cf. 1.107n. and *OLD* 1d. For *simul* see 6.11n.

9 uos 'you, Aristius and other cityfolk'; Latin almost never uses the second pers. plur. of one person (Roby §2297).

ad caelum effertis 'extol' (*OLD caelum* 3d, *TLL* v 2.149.79). Many editors print *fertis* (*TLL* III 91.10–22), but this is likely to be an ancient emendation designed to provide the line with a normal caesura; *effertis*, however, produces a 'quasi-caesura' (2.20n.).

rumore secundo 'with cries of approval', a stereotyped phrase (Skutsch on Enn. *Ann.* 244 Sk.), but Lambinus detected a reference to popular opinion ('ex opinione et consensu uulgi'), in which case H. is as usual asserting his independence.

10 H. rejects ⟨urban pleasures⟩ as the runaway slave (*fugitiuus*) refuses sacrificial cakes; the comparison is so blended with the main sentence that *liba* passes into metaphor as the obj. of *recuso* (Introduction pp. 28–30). He feels himself a slave in town, in implicit contrast with his kingship in the country (8); to be free he runs away from a luxury that has palled (though slaves often absconded because of inadequate fare (*S*. 1.5.67–9)). The gen. *sacerdotis* may be possessive, though not so taken at *TLL* VI 1.1496.1–2 (cf. 30–1); it is instead perhaps a Grecism (cf. Herod. 3.137.2 ἄνδρα βασιλέος δρηπέτην 'a runaway *from* the king'; K–S I 439, N–H on *C*. 2.16.19 *patriae . . . exul*).

11 pane suggests a return to basics. For emphatic *iam* see 7.44n.

potiore placentis: alliteration and unusual syntax. In prose a comparative governing an abl. chiefly agrees with the subj. (whether nom. or acc.) or the acc. obj. of the sentence to avoid the ambiguity of annexing one abl. to another. Yet here and, designedly, at 39 a comparative agrees with an abl. and governs one itself (K–S II 465–6, 469; in fact, the usage is only found in H.).

12–25 A new section, as usual introduced asyndetically but also signalled by ring-composition (12, 24), develops the theme of the countryside's superiority by stressing its conformity to the demands of *natura* and its latent appeal to the town dweller.

12 Viuere 'spend one's life' (*OLD* 9). The Stoic *summum bonum* was *conuenienter naturae uiuere* (Cic. *Off*. 3.13; *OLD natura* 5a), but H. exploits the ambiguity of *natura* to suggest not only man's natural needs (e.g., the bread of 11) and satisfactions but also the countryside which so readily supplies them. *conuenienter* will be picked up by *conuenit* 42. For *oportet* see 2.49n.

13–14 form a paratactic comparison: '*just as* we need a cleared site for our house, *so* the country is best, don't you think, for our 'natural' way of life'.

13 ponendae ... domo: 2.44n. The dat. form *domo* is common in early Latin, esp. the elder Cato; poets tried to avoid all *ui* terminations. The gerundives are specially weighty (B. on *Ep*. 2.1.55).

14 -ne colloquially invites a negative answer (K–S II 505–6). Even Fuscus will admit the countryside's superiority, for it has its riches (not the obvious ones of the city, cf. *C*. 3.29.11–12 quoted on 31–2), hence *beato*.

15–21 A string of questions enumerates the *laudes uitae rusticae*. In all of them a comparative word form (*plus, gratior, minus, deterius, purior*) hints at the town's inferiority.

15–16 For mild winters and cool summers as a convention in encomia of places see N–H on *C.* 2.6.17–18 *uer ubi longum tepidasque praebet* | *Iuppiter brumas.*

tepeant ... leniat ... 18 diuellat: generic subjunc. (B. on *Ep.* 2.1.63, p. 115).

16 Canis 'the dog-star, Sirius' (*OLD* 3) rises in late July, when the Sun is in his house, the sign *Leo.* H. devotes more description to the summer's heat since the advantages of the country over the town are most obvious then, cf. *C.* 3.29.17–20.

momenta 'movements' (*OLD* 2), perhaps like *impetus* at *C.* 3.1.28.

17 semel 'once' (*OLD* 4 'indicating a single occurrence upon which some consequence ensues'). *furibundus* is predicative; the Lion raves after receiving (*OLD accipio* 7) the sharp sun's rays (*solem acutum* < Hes. *Op.* 414 ὀξέος ἠελίοιο (see West *ad loc.*)).

18 minus: take with *diuellat*, a vividly pictorial verb; cf. Virg. *G.* 3.530 *nec somnos abrumpit cura salubris.* cura is *inuida* 'mean' in robbing us of sleep (cf. N–H on *C.* 1.11.7–8 *inuida aetas*).

19 Libycis ... lapillis: *tesserae*, mosaic cubes (cf. *C.* 3.1.41 *Phrygius lapis*), were pieces of coloured marble, of which some of the most prized came from Africa (*C.* 2.18.4–5 *columnas ultima recisas* | *Africa*). H. makes a point also found in Virg. *G.* 2.463–6 that imported luxuries are unnecessary; he may also be faulting their artificiality, since stone only shines when cut and polished, it only smells when sprinkled with scent, as was the stage (*Ep.* 2.1.79).

20 uicis: the streets of Rome. *tendit* 'strives' (*OLD* 13b) takes a complementary infin. Water from aqueducts was conveyed to houses under pressure (hence *rumpere*) in pipes made either of clay or of lead; H., being himself fussy about what he drank (15.15n.), specifies lead because it was notorious for producing a foul taste and for being injurious to health (Vitruvius 8.6.10–11).

21 trepidat 'purls' (*OLD* 2).

22 nempe 'obviously: for ...' (Hand IV 157); H. answers his own questions by noting the town dweller's fondness for gardens.

uarias 'mottled' picks up *lapillis* (19); exotic marble columns were typically a mark of luxury (N–H on *C.* 2.18.4). Only the wealthy could afford peristyles and roof gardens in the city (*C.* 3.10.5–6 *nemus* | *inter pulchra satum tecta*, Sen. *Con.* 2.1.13 *quin etiam montes siluasque in domibus* and 5.5 *in summis culminibus mentita nemora*).

23 A town house (*domus*) on one of Rome's hills, esp. if equipped with a tower (1.100n.), would command a view of the surrounding country-side; cf. *C*. 3.29.6–7 *ne semper udum Tibur et Aefulae | decliue contempleris aruum* (P. Grimal, *Les jardins romains*³ (Paris 1984) 133).

24–5   A paratactic concessive sentence.

24   furca: a proverbial instrument for brusque removal (Otto §743; Ellis on Catull. 105.2 *Musae furcillis praecipitem eiiciunt*).

25   perrumpet furtim: an oxymoron, since the action of the verb could hardly be performed unobtrusively, yet that is how *natura* meta-phorically breaks through an opposing force of disdain (as the country-side's imported water strives to break the city's confining lead, 20); for *fastidia* cf. Sen. *Con*. 2.1.13 *fastidio rerum naturae laborantibus* 'men struggl-ing with their distaste for what is natural'. *uictrix* powerfully concludes both sentence and section; cf. Sen. *Ep*. 119.2 [*natura*] *contumax est, non potest uinci, suum poscit*.

26–33   The sham countryside nurtured within the wealthy city proves the value of the real thing; yet the sophisticated are blind to the difference. When it is a question of being imposed upon by a cheat, the need for discrimination is clear, if we are to avoid pecuniary loss, but moral discrimination is more important than commercial, if genuine wants are to be recognized and satisfied.

26–9   Construe: [*is*] *qui uellera quae Aquinatem fucum potant Sidonio ostro callide contendere nescit, non certius damnum accipiet* ... To the moralist dyeing falsified nature (Virg. *G*. 2.465 *alba neque Assyrio fucatur lana ueneno*). H. uses here an argument *a fortiori*. If we admit the need for discrimination in what is after all an unnecessary refinement (*C*. 3.1.41–3 *dolentem* ... | *nec purpurarum sidere clarior* | *delenit usus*), how much more necessary is it to distinguish true from false in our way of life.

26   contendere 'compare' (*OLD* 9), so as to distinguish between them, governs the dat. *ostro*, a Grecism found chiefly in poetry. *callidus* is adverbial; *callide* would not fit an hexameter.

   ostro: an abbreviated comparison. For purple dyes see 6.18n.

28   medullis: dat. with *propius*.

29   poterit 'shall prove unable' (6.42n.); for the simple abl. of sepa-ration *uero* see 7.48n.

30–2   The penalties of false assessment are exemplified.

30   plus nimio: abl. of measure of difference. The idiomatic phrase (N–H on *C*. 1.18.15, quoted at 18.22n.) makes an essential qualification; good fortune must be used moderately and its alteration is to be anticipated (N–H on *C*. 2.3.1).

31–2 The doctrine of VI is recalled; we overvalue the extraordinary but unnecessary things in life, which are usually to be found in the city (*C*. 3.29.11–12 *omitte mirari beatae | fumum et opes strepitumque Romae*). For the indef. second pers. sing. see 1.28–40n.

31 pones: 1.10n.; H.'s own position is clear from 7.39 *reponere laetus*.

32 inuitus, emphatic by position at the end of its sentence and the beginning of a line, stresses the subjugation of our wills to the objects of our desire. (Ovid picked up the phrase at *Rem*. 719.)

fuge magna 'avoid (*OLD* 10) anything grand'; *fuge* echoes *fugitiuus* 10. For the brisk two-word injunction see 2.55–63n.; H. may here be parodying Aristius' schoolmasterly form of admonition.

33 reges 'grandees' (they live in *regia Roma*, 7.44) and *uita* pick up *uiuo et regno* 8; of course, H. himself was in the class of 'regum amici'. *uita* (7.95n.) is abl. of respect with a word indicating superiority (G–L §397 N2, but cf. 12.28n.). For the metaphorical notion of outstripping in a race (*praecurrere*) see G–H s.v. Wettlauf.

34–41 A fable, introduced asyndetically, illustrates the danger of aspiring to more than one needs, the topic of the previous warnings. But it also introduces the notion that such aspiration may entail loss of independence. Stesichorus, according to Aristotle, *Rhet*. 2.20.5, told the fable of the stag and the horse to the Himereans, who were considering giving Phalaris a bodyguard, to warn them not to seek revenge on their enemies at the risk of losing their political freedom. H. gives the tale an entirely personal moral. (Phaedrus 4.4 and Aesop 238 Hausrath–Hunger are similar fables.)

34 Ceruus equum: fables often begin with the characters' names (e.g., Phaed. 1.1 *ad riuum eundem lupus et agnus uenerant*).

pugna: abl. of respect with *melior* (see *uita* 33n.).

35 minor 'inferior' (*OLD* 7b), referring to the horse.

36 opes 'assistance', a sense more usually found in the sing. (*TLL* XI 2.816.7–33).

37 uictor ... discessit 'went away victorious' (*OLD discedo* 4). *uiolens*, as Bentley showed, is an unacceptable addition to this idiom but editors cannot agree on an improvement; it is, however, defended as a surprising transformation of the common intrumental abl. *ui* with the verb *uincere* into an adjective with its nominal derivative *uictor* (O. Skutsch, *C.Q.* 10 (1960) 195 n. 5 = *Studia Enniana* (London 1967) 60 n. 24).

38 non ... non: anaphora stresses the completeness of the loss of freedom.

39–41 The application of the moral is stated, as often (but not invariably) at the end (7.29–39n.). *pauperiem* echoes *paupere* 32, the starting-place of the fable.

39 potiore recalls 11 (n.); the plur. *metallis* is unusual, but ensures that there is no ambiguity. For the thought cf. 1.52–3.

40 libertate recalls the freedom suggested by *regno* 8. *uehit* preserves the image of the fable; *improbus* 'in his greed' (*OLD* 4). For the position of *atque* see Introduction p. 24.

41 aeternum, adverbial acc., is poetic (7.27n.; cf. Virg. *A.* 6.617 quoted on 2.43); prose (at least from Livy on) preferred *in aeternum*.

paruo ... uti: a commonplace (*uiuitur paruo bene C.* 2.16.13), recalling by contrast *fuge magna* (32).

42 cui 'if a man ...', conditional rel. clause; sc. *eum* as antecedent and as obj. of the verbs in 43. The sentence offers another blended comparison (Introduction pp. 28–30); fully expressed, it would run: 'if a man's circumstances do not suit him, they will either trip him up, like too large a shoe, or chafe him, like one too tight'. The main verbs are used ἀπὸ κοινοῦ and apply literally to the thing compared (*calceus*), metaphorically to *res*. (As Müller says, it is the early reference to the thing compared that generates the metaphorical expression.) The thought recalls 1.19: circumstances must be fitted to the person, not *vice versa*, if one is to avoid trouble. The image of the shoe is proverbial and found in other moralists (Otto §297; Epict. *Ench.* 39). Strictly speaking only the notion of small resources is relevant to what has preceded; the notion of large resources is added to give the observation the widest application.

conueniet: recalls *conuenienter* 12; cf. 7.44. *olim* 'sometimes' (*OLD* 4).

43 maior 'too big for' expresses disproportion (G–L §298); the use of the simple abl. of comparison instead of the more cumbersome *quam pro* or a periphrasis appears to be a syntactical innovation of H.'s (K–S II 474–5; *S.* 2.3.310–11 *corpore maiorem ... spiritum*).

si minor: sc. *pede erit* ἀπὸ κοινοῦ. *uret* 'will chafe' (*OLD* 10).

44–8 H. implicitly aknowledges at the close that where we live is of less importance than a cheerful acceptance of what we have (the theme of XI); discontent is the cancer that attacks our happiness.

44   Laetus '*if* you are happy with . . .'. As Fuscus is happy here, so is H. at 50, an example of ring-composition.

sorte tua: H. does not impose the country on Fuscus. *sapienter* 'sensibly' (Palmer on *S*. 1.1.38).

45   dimittes 'don't let me off' (for the fut. see 4.15n.).

incastigatum, a coinage = ἀνεπιτίμητος, perhaps alludes to Fuscus' supposed profession of schoolmaster (R. G. M. Nisbet, *C.Q.* 9 (1959) 74). H. urbanely gives his friend the right to discipline him, in case he falls short of his own ideal of behaviour. He needs advice too.

46   cogere 'gather' (*OLD* 5b). For *satis est* see 1.2n.

ac 'and so' subdivides the sentence (*et* would not); *non* is closely joined with *cessare* (Roby §2235, B. on *Ep*. 2.2.143). H. asks Fuscus to do for him what he himself did for Torquatus in V, thus softening his own advice. For the sense of *cessare* see 7.57n.

uidebor 'I shall be seen . . .' (B. on *Ep*. 2.1.51).

47–8   Personal freedom is at the heart of the moral. *imperat* suggests *regina Pecunia* 6.37; cf. 2.62–3; *seruit* recalls *dominum* 40, but here it is the money which is to be the slave; cf. Sen. *Dial*. 7.26.1 *diuitiae enim apud sapientem uirum in seruitute sunt, apud stultum in imperio* (a proverbial notion: Otto §1369). *collecta* 'amassed' (B. on *Ep*. 2.2.26).

48   Cf. *S*. 2.7.20 *qui iam contento, iam laxo fune laborat*. In both passages the image seems to be of an animal being led on a rope against which it sometimes struggles.

tortum: a standing epithet of ropes, which are made by twisting fibres (Pease on Virg. *A*. 4.575).

digna 'deserves to . . .' (B. on *AP* 183); *sequi* is to *seruit*, as *ducere* is to *imperat*; for the infin. see 2.64n.

49–50   This two line signing-off (6.67–8) is one of the closest imitations of epistolary convention in the collection (H. omits the date).

49   tibi: 5.7n. *dictabam* 'I was dictating', i.e. to a slave-secretary. The tense is owed to the Romans' practice of putting themselves in the place of the addressee, esp. at the beginning and end of their letters (G–L §252, Roby §1468).

post 'beyond' (*OLD* 1b (topog.)). Vacuna was a Sabine goddess of victory whose crumbling shrine was perhaps near H.'s estate; such a shrine may have been restored by Vespasian (*CIL* XIV 3485). Her name suggested a connection with idleness, *uacare* (*cessare* 46).

50   excepto quod …: abl. absolute in which a rel. clause serves as the subject (G–L §410 N4, Roby §1252, H–S 141).

simul 'together with me', a conversational sense (*OLD* 1); *esses* gives the writer's own reported reason (*NLS* §242 n. 1, Roby §1744).

cetera: 3n. Despite the ample blessings of the countryside, H. misses his friend, a fine compliment to Fuscus.

The epistle starts with what appears to be the conventional praise of the countryside, as found for instance in *Epode* 2. But the contrast with the city as usual prompts H. to consider in more depth the quality of life offered by the alternatives. Contrasts are subtly worked into the fabric of the poem. For instance, the mossy rocks and woods (7) are not purely descriptive but are implicitly preferred to the variegated marbles and the counterfeit *silua* (22). What H. praises (6) is not what townsfolk praise (9, 23); what he has relinquished (8), others may find hard to do without (31–2). The country will provide bread (11) under a poor roof (32), the city has its honeyed cakes (11) and columned palaces (22–3). But the choice between these contrasted ways of life is not to be made on grounds of taste alone. The city's grandeur (32) poses the moral temptation of overesteem (31). What the countryside offers above all (to H. at any rate) is independence (8). To be sure, the city has its grandees (33) and, a significant addition, their hangers-on; but they are not true 'kings', albeit called *reges*. For their position is founded on wealth and prestige, and they must dread the change of fortune (31) or poverty (39) that deprives them of it. Only in the country then is true freedom to be found (8, 40). H. most artfully draws this conclusion by bringing the bread he now yearns for (11) into close relation with the freedom that outweighs cash (39–40) through the repetition of *potiore*, used in a syntactical relation never found outside H.'s own poetry. Freedom is associated with *pauperies* (39–40); under a humble roof (32) the most enduring freedom is to be found (33). Money too has its role to play, but that must be established in relation to freedom; it either rules us or serves us (47), and the only sure goal is sufficiency (45–6). As Macleod pointed out, the poem's concern with the insufficiency of conventional notions of success is symbolized in the image of the crumbling temple of Victory (49).

The epistle seems to have been placed here to conclude the first half of the collection with a major theme, the symbolic value of life in the countryside. So far H. has only hinted at it (8.13). It will be developed, even corrected, in various ways as the book progresses.

Epistle XI

1-10 Bullatius (otherwise unknown; for the name see *CIL* VI 13660) is or has been travelling in the East and H. wonders how he found the famous tourist attractions of Asia Minor and the Greek islands. Since men travelled chiefly on business, whether private or official (Bullatius might be a *comes* of Tiberius), journeys were something of a chore; tourism, much indulged in by Romans, was seen as a relief from duty.

1 quid tibi uisa 'what sort of place did it strike you as being', sc. *est* (*OLD quis* 3, *uideo* 20g; L. on *S.* 1.6.55 *quid essem*). Chios, Lesbos and Samos are all islands off the coast of Asia Minor; Sardes, Smyrna (mod. Izmir) and Colophon were notable cities. Apart from the beauty of their sites, the towns of the Greek East, unlike old-fashioned Rome, were elegantly planned and equipped with public amenities, hence their attraction.

2 concinna 'elegant'. The chief town of the island, also called Samos (mod. Pithagorio), is laid out on a grid plan and has a specially fine stone harbour wall, still in use.

   regia 'capital city', appositive to *Sardes* (Greek nom. plur.); it remained important and splendid in Roman times (Akurgal 124-32). Croesus, the last king of Lydia (*c.* 560-546 B.C.), had become shortly after his death a semi-mythical figure.

3 Zmyrna quid: for the word order cf. 6.7. The city was refounded by Alexander the Great, and became one of the wealthiest and most beautiful on the coast (Akurgal 119-24). Colophon too had its claims to attention (Akurgal 133-6), though a much smaller place.

   maiora minorane 'are they things greater or less ...?'; the neuter plurals are substantives, not adjectives referring to all the place names (cf. *grandia* at *C.* 1.6.9; H-S 434-5). *-ne* in poetry introduces an alternative dir. qu. (*OLD* 2). For abl. *fama* see 1.106n.

4-6 After politely soliciting Bullatius' opinion, H. moves to his main interest: how was Bullatius affected by what he saw? Is home still best? For *ne ... an ... an* cf. 3.3-5.

4 prae 'compared to' (*OLD* 4). The Campus Martius, esp. with its new porticoes, offered some amenities to set beside those of the Greek East; at any rate it was the favourite resort of Rome's fashionable young (cf. *C.* 1.8.4 and 8).

Tiberino flumine: the periphrasis poeticizes the local river (*TLL* VI 1.958.69–82), nor can it be accident that the expression occurs in the as yet unpublished work of H.'s friend Virgil (*A.* 10.833, 11.449). *sordent* 'are inferior' (*OLD* 2).

5 uenit in uotum: cf. *S.* 2.6.1 *hoc erat in uotis.* The Attalid kingdom had the famously beautiful cities of Pergamum and Ephesus.

6 odio < *C.* 2.6.7 *lasso maris et uiarum.* The discomforts of travel might induce a man to plump for the nearest refuge, however paltry its charms.

7–10 H. unexpectedly voices his own discontent and a desire to get away from it all, even in a one-horse town like Lebedus (cf. 7.44). Since antiquity, however, the lines have sometimes been taken to be an imagined reply of Bullatius to the question in 6. But 'was H. likely to mention Lebedus unless he had been there himself? In which case, could he make Bullatius tell him what he already knew?' (Shackleton Bailey 66 n. 47). Moreover Dr Johnson's criticism of Pope would apply to H. as well: 'Pope seems to have written with no very distinct idea, for he calls that an *Epistle to Bathurst*, in which Bathurst is introduced as speaking' (*Life of Pope*, Everyman edn, p. 190). The addressee cannot speak in an epistle, as he can in a *sermo*; the introduction of an imaginary interlocutor at 16.31–3 and 41–3 is not similar.

7–8 scis … sit: ironical, for Lebedus was so insignificant at this time, that Bullatius is most unlikely even to have heard of it, let alone paid it a visit (*RE* XII 1052–3); H. may have seen it (along with other places named here) when he served under Brutus (cf. *S.* 1.7). For *quid sit* see 1n. Gabii and Fidenae were old Latin towns (paired by Virgil, *A.* 6.773), all but abandoned in H.'s day. For *atque* see 7.83.

8 uellem 'I'd have been prepared' (*OLD* 5, so Lambinus), not 'I would love' (Fairclough); potential subjunc.

9 Pope imitated the polyptoton of this emotional line in *Eloisa to Abelard* 208: 'The world forgetting, by the world forgot'. For the elision at the main caesura 5.21n. *-que* connects *uiuere* and *spectare*. *et* 'as well', adverbial. For *illis* see *mihi* 1.1n.

10 Neptunum 'the sea'; the metonymy sheds grandeur on the concept (*OLD* 2). The thought is proverbial (see Pearson on Soph. fr. 636 P.), and formally indebted to Lucretius 2.1–2 *suaue, mari magno turbantibus aequora uentis | e terra magnum alterius spectare laborem* (Munro *ad loc.*).

11–16 H. rejects his wish (8) as an unreasonable whim; circumstances must not tempt us into accepting a temporary relief from discomfort as a permanent good. The sentence forms a paratactic comparison: '*just as* 11–14, *so* neither would you 15–16' (for the three illustrations cf. 1.20–3n.); cf. the same use of *nec … nec* at 18.39–40, *C.* 1.6.5–9, 3.5.27–30.

11 H. envisages someone's returning to Rome from abroad, or from vacation in southern Italy.

12 **adspersus** '*because* …', a causal idea may be understood (G–L §666). The inn, *caupona*, as image of a staging-post, not the ultimate goal, is also use by Epictetus (Arr. *Epict.* 2.23.36–7).

uiuere (10.12n.) is highlighted both at the end of its clause and foot (= a light diaeresis pause, because followed by *nec qui* which continues the sense from *neque qui*; cf. Winbolt §21). The main caesurae are the same as in *S.* 1.4.111.

13 **frigus collegit** 'has stiffened with cold', rather than 'has caught a cold' (so *OLD frigus* 3, cf. *TLL* III 1614.44–51 s.v. *colligo*), though the unique expression is hard to analyse; at any rate, *furnos* 'bake-houses' (*OLD* 2) will quickly dispel the sensation of cold but not the malady.

14 **ut:** 7.41n. The qualification in *plene* points up the unsuitability of these places for a long-term stay.

15–16 **te … uendas:** H. could have written *quem … uendat*; the shift to the indef. second pers. (1.28–40n.) provides variety.

15 **iactauerit** 'it should have tossed', perf. subjunc. in a remote condition (*LS* §142).

16 **idcirco:** 1.29n. The notion suggests something like our 'burning one's bridges' to nullify a change of heart.

17–21 Travel is put into perspective; it should be unnecessary to the wholly healthy.

17 **incolumi** 'for one unimpaired in health (physical and mental) or position'; masc. substantive, dat. of advantage. To Roman ears *incolumis* might have been suggestively ambiguous, since it was used both of sound health and of one whose citizen status was fully operative. This hint H. develops at 20, and it becomes clear that he has in mind the exile or voluntary retirement which prominent Romans might have to endure, often on islands (cf. his unknown friend Pompeius, who at length returns a full citizen to Italian skies, *C.* 2.7.3–4, or Agrippa, who had recently returned from Mytilene).

pulchra should be understood ἀπὸ κοινοῦ with *Rhodos*, the chief town of its eponymous island, famous for its wealth, beauty and for one of the seven wonders of the world, the Colossus. (Yet the reference is odd, for H. ought to have recalled that it had been plundered by Cassius in 42 B.C. (*CAH* x 23, *RE Suppl.* v 806–7).) Mytilene is one of the chief cities of Lesbos.

facit: sc. *idem* 'just as much'.

18–19 are elaborately finished (for the implied negative comparison cf. 2.52–3n.). Four objects make up the list of things whose desirability depends not on themselves but upon our circumstances. The list is ordered chiastically around reference to the seasons, themselves chiastically disposed (summer : winter :: winter : summer). There are echoes of what has gone before. The travelling cloak (*paenula*) picks up 11–12, *caminus* 13. *campestre* (sc. *uelamentum*) refers to a garment worn whilst exercising on the Campus Martius, after which a swim in the Tiber was usual (*C.* 1.8.8, 3.12.6), a chime with 4. Moreover the objects listed contrast with one another; in summer we want no additional clothing or heat, in winter just the reverse. The application to travel is clear. It cannot make good deficiency or enhance sufficiency.

20 > Ov. *Tr.* 1.5.27 *dum iuuat et uultu ridet Fortuna sereno. dum licet ...* develops *incolumi* 17 and sounds a recurrent warning to seize opportunities: *S.* 2.6.96, *C.* 2.11.16, 4.12.26.

21 Romae: home is best, if all is well. The rhythm of the line enhances the advice. The weighty initial spondee is emphatic; the Greek place names, by contrast all pyrrhics placed in the unaccented part of the foot, are rattled off. Their repetition from earlier lines indicates a summation of the argument.

laudetur 'may be politely rejected' (cf. Virg. *G.* 2.412 *laudato ingentia rura*, a calque on ἐπαινέω).

absens 'distant' (*OLD* 3), a use of the word invented by H. at *S.* 2.7.28 *absentem ... urbem.*

22–30 Bullatius is now directly addressed again, and the value of travel is plainly assessed.

22–3 Cf. *C.* 1.9.14–16 *quem Fors dierum cumque dabit, lucro | adpone, nec* *dulces amores* | *sperne puer neque tu choreas* and 2.16.25–6 *laetus in praesens animus quod ultra est* | *oderit curare*.

22 Tu: 2.63n. Since *fortuno* is found in Plautus and in Cicero's letters, its tone may be colloquial; the subj. is always a divinity (*TLL* VI 1.1195.78–82).

23 neu, instead of *nec*, adds a prohibition to a positive command in poetry (K–S I 203–4, where this line is accidentally unattributed; cf. 13.16n.). For *in* see 2.39n.

24 fueris: perf. subjunc. (cf. 15n.). *libenter* = *ut libet*; though it occurs in Enn. *Ann*. 268 Sk. and *scen*. 284 J., it was felt to be too conversational for elevated poetry – H. never uses it in lyric (L. on *S*. 1.1.63) – and was replaced by *libens* (cf. 14.44). For the thought cf. *C*. 3.29.42–3 *cui licet in diem* | *dixisse 'uixi'*.

25–7 H. develops the notion that place (*locus* 26 picks up *loco* 24) is immaterial to true happiness. The humanist puts his trust in reason and foresight.

25–6 curas: understand *auferunt* ἀπὸ κοινοῦ from *aufert*.

26 arbiter 'viewer', a striking metaphor for a place; the sea prospect recalls 10.

27 caelum: 7.77n. This famous line, echoed at Sen. *Ep*. 28.1 *animum debes mutare, non caelum*, encapsulates a commonplace as old as Aeschines, *In Ctes*. 78 'for he did not alter his character (τρόπον), only his situation (τόπον)'; cf. 14.13, N–H on *C*. 2.16.19–20 *patriae quis exul* | *se quoque fugit?*, Cic. *Quinct*. 12 *fit magna mutatio loci non ingeni*, Lucr. 3.1059 *commutare locum, quasi onus deponere possit*, Sen. *Dial*. 9.2.13 *scire debemus non locorum uitium esse quo laboramus, sed nostrum* (Otto §285; E. Skard, *S.O*. 40 (1965) 81–2).

28 strenua ... inertia: oxymoron, > Sen. *Dial*. 9.12.3 *inquietam inertiam* and, neatly reversed, 10.12.2 *desidiosa occupatio* (G. Bruno, *A. & R*. 30 (1985) 17–25). *exercet* 'harasses' (*OLD* 2b).

28–9 nauibus atque quadrigis: understand literally, since travel is the theme; the abll. are instrumental. The phrase, imitated at Juv. 9.132 *et carpentis et nauibus*, vividly replaces the standard polar expression *terra marique* (cf. N–H on *C*. 1.6.3 *nauibus aut equis*). For *atque* see Introduction p. 24. *quadrigis* is a pointed exaggeration, since a two-horse carriage was usual; four horses suggest ostentation and restless speed (N–H on *C*. 2.16.35, p. 269).

29 petimus governs the complementary infin. For *bene* see 6.56n.; cf. Sen. *Ep.* 28.5 *quod quaeris, bene uiuere. hic* 'here at home in Italy'.

30   Ulubrae (mod. Cisterna di Roma) is a small town in Latium near the marshes; an argument *a fortiori* for indifference to place.

animus ... aequus: a common expression (18.112, also the last line of its poem), perhaps derived from the adverbial *aequo animo*, rather than from a Greek philosophical term (N–H on *C.* 2.3.1). Composure depends on us, not on our circumstances, hence its central role in happiness; cf. Pl. *Aul.* 187 *pol, sist animus aequos tibi, sat habes qui bene uitam colas.*

Well-to-do Romans enjoyed travel and sightseeing, especially in Asia (cf. Catull. 45.6 *ad claras Asiae uolemus urbes*). The *pax Augusta* enhanced their opportunities for visiting the famous cities of the Greek East. But to a moralist travel could be seen as a running away from the self, at least if it was unnecessary (hence the importance of *incolumi* in 17; it leaves the door open to necessary travel, on public business as in III or for health as in XV).

The placement of this letter may be significant, for it opens the second half of the collection. Some see it as designed to correct the attitude of X (McGann 60, G. Maurach *Acta classica* 11 (1968) 73–124, esp. 104). But this seems to miss the point of the previous letter, in which H. nowhere says that anyone has to live in the country to be happy. The country there is an emblem of simplicity and 'naturalness' and as such it is in marked opposition to the city, but that does not rule the city out as a place for contented living. That is the point made at line 44 *laetus sorte tua*. The country helps, but no exclusive claims are made for it. The eleventh letter is, however, connected to the previous in its focus upon the theme of place as bearing on contentment. Here H. is concerned to overset a common view, that travel relieves the spirit. What gives this epistle its peculiar poignancy is the poet's own evident unease, seen in the sighed wish, quickly corrected, of 8–10. As Lejay says in his introductory note, 'Cette lettre pose le même problème que la précédente. On ne sait encore si Horace veut corriger Bullatius d'une inquiétude qui le pousse en d'incessants voyages, ou si plutôt, sous couleur de prédication morale, H. ne confesse pas le mal dont lui-même souffre et qu'il a souvent avoué (8.12; S. 2.7.28).'

Epistle XII

1–11 Iccius, the dedicatee of *C.* 1.29, has complained of his lot (3), so H. braces him up with practical advice. He is the manager (*procurator*) of the Sicilian estates of M. Agrippa, who, with Maecenas, had long been Augustus' closest ally and was now his son-in-law (Syme, *RR* 228; G. Fabre and J. M. Rodez, 'Recherches sur la "*familia*" de M. Agrippa', *Athenaeum* 60 (1982) 84–112). In short, he fails to appreciate that he has found a good billet, like Seneca's friend Lucilius (*NQ* 4. *pr.* 1 *delectat te . . . Sicilia et officium procurationis otiosae*).

1 Fructibus 'produce' (both 'revenue' and the fruits of the earth, cf. *fruges* 28). Sicily was the bread-basket of Rome (until Egypt supplanted it), so Iccius must be imagined as living amid plenty; the picture reappears in the closing lines.

2 si: displacement of the conjunction helps to emphasize *recte*, which in the context has a legal sense, 'as is your right' (*OLD* 7), as well as a moral one, 'aright'. *frueris* pointedly echoes *fructibus* and both hint at the legal concept of *ususfructus*, which went beyond *usus* (4) 'the legal right to use another's property' in allowing a right to receive profits from it as well (*OLD* s.v. *usus* 4b). Iccius is failing to exploit his prerogative; cf. Sen. *Ben.* 6.3.2 *quid tamquam tuo parcis? procurator es.*

non est ut 'it is not possible that . . .' (*OLD sum* 7). *copia* is picked up in the personification at 29, as *maior* is echoed by *maius* 6 (both at line-end).

3 ab Ioue donari possit: cf. *poterunt regales addere* 6.

tolle 'away with' (*OLD* 14c, N–H on *C.* 2.5.9). Iccius may have complained of being poor or of his dependence on another's bounty; in *C.* 1.29 he seemed to be planning to improve his fortune by going on campaign to the East.

4 suppetit 'is available at need'. H. knows that *usus* alone would suffice, but has suggested above that Iccius could go well beyond that. His insistence on Iccius' legal rights makes a moral point (2.49n.; there is a full discussion with special ref. to H. by B. on *Ep.* 2.2.158–79, pp. 367–9).

5 bene . . . est: take both ἀπὸ κοινοῦ; health is a prerequisite for happiness (2.49–50). The thought may be borrowed from Solon, fr. 24.1–4 W., where the contrast between physical well-being and wealth is also drawn; it was also a point stressed by the Epicurean Metrodorus

(Cic. *Off*. 3.117). The apodosis begins with a highly emphatic enjamb-ment of *nil* (Introduction p. 24).

7–11   On the other hand, Iccius may choose not to take full advan-tage of the resources at his disposal.

7   si: 5.6n. *forte* 'as may be the case' (*OLD* 3a); H. makes no claim to know how Iccius really lives his life.

   in medio 'available to all' (*OLD medium* 4a) goes with *positorum*, as at *S*. 1.2.108 (N–H on *C*. 1.31.17 *paratis*).

   abstemius governs the gen., a poetic Grecism (*NLS* §73(2) n. (i), K–S I 436).

8   uiuis ... uiues: emphatic repetition. *urtica* 'nettle' (a good salad herb if picked young) is a specific type of *herba*, and the connective *et* 'for instance' is epexegetic or explanatory (Hand II 475, N–H on *C*. 1.2.15, B. on *Ep*. 2.2.137 *morbum bilemque*; *eruis*, conjectured by N. Schmidt *apud* O. Zwierlein, *Kritischer Kommentar zu den Tragödien Senecas* (Wiesbaden 1986) 195, is unnecessary nor is there a plur. of *eruum* in use).

   protinus 'uninterruptedly' (*OLD* 1b) underscores the continuance of his practice. *ut* 'even though' (*OLD* 35); for the enjambment see Introduction p. 24.

9   riuus: probably not in allusion to the mythical gold-bearing rivers, Pactolus and Tagus, which have no connection with Fortuna. On the famous and often copied statue of the *Tyche* (=Fortuna) of the city of Antiocheia by Eutychides the infant river Orontes was depicted at her feet, and numerous riverine cities adopted the image on their own coins (Roscher V 1364–5); H. may have had this in mind, unless his expression is proverbial.

10–11   uel quia ... uel quia: the repetition proposes a coolly ratio-nal appraisal, reminiscent of Lucretius, e.g., 3.820–2 *quod ... aut quia ... aut quia* (8.4–7, *S*. 2.7.25–6). The second makes a transition to Iccius' philosophical interests.

10   nescit 'cannot' (*OLD* 3); H. uses *nequeo* in *S*., but not in *C*. or *Ep*. 1. The sentiment is not necessarily ironic. Money brings out the worst in us, but a shower of wealth will not affect the constitutionally moder-ate (as Iccius may prove to be).

11   cuncta 'all else' (*OLD* 2c); for *una* see 1.106n. The Stoic colour of *uirtute* is confirmed by *C*. 1.29.14 where Iccius was a reader of Panae-tius. In addition to his character, his Stoic principles enjoin an ascetic life. His unmoderated striving is unlikely, however, to secure H.'s approval (cf. 6.30).

minora, as last word of the sentence and section, makes a sharp contrast with the 'more' that Iccius appears to want (2, 6). H. shows his friend that after all more would not be suitable for him personally, so he has no grounds for complaint.

12–20 The next section is asyndetically introduced. Iccius is praised for his higher studies (yet he attends to Agrippa's business), but not without a subtle irony. For his researches are confined to one field, natural philosophy (16–20). It is implied that attention to the ethical branch might go some way to removing his discontents (cf. 18.97–103). (Marcus Aurelius counted himself fortunate not to have studied physics and dialectic (1.17.9).)

12–15 An argument *a fortiori*: Democritus' neglect of his property in favour of scientific speculation is surpassed by Iccius' devotion to study amid the world of affairs, which he handles without contamination. Democritus was a fifth-century Greek philosopher, chosen here as a representative of pure research into the nature of matter, since he devised with Leucippus a theory of atoms later exploited by Epicurus (*OCD* s.v.); a variant of H.'s story, which suits Iccius' situation on Agrippa's estates, is also found in Cicero, *Fin.* 5.87.

12   si 'that' (*OLD* 12b); *ēdit*: perf. of *ĕdo*.

13   peregre 'abroad'; an ironical hit. Democritus, so tradition ran (Diog. Laert. 9.38–9, Cic. *loc. cit.*), had bankrupted himself whilst travelling in pursuit of wisdom. But *animus* points rather to an intellectual voyage, a variant of the commonplace theme of the flight of the mind (R. M. Jones, *C.P.* 21 (1926) 97–113). From the previous epistle it is clear that H. finds travel unnecessary for what is most important, happiness. A warning to Iccius is implied.

14   cum 'whereas' (*OLD* 7b).

scabiem … et contagia 'contagious itch for …', hendiadys. Since *contagio* did not fit into verse, Lucretius coined *contagium* to be used in the plur. by poets, as here. As a *procurator* Iccius could not afford to neglect Agrippa's business interests; yet whilst engaged in them he has not abandoned his researches (cf. *inter* 4.12n.).

15   nil paruum sapias 'you have no trivial knowledge' (*OLD sapio* 6b); *nil* is an internal limiting acc. (*C.* 3.25.17–18 *nil paruum aut humili modo,* | *nil mortale loquar*).

adhuc: take with *sapias* ἀπὸ κοινοῦ (Fairclough); it emphasizes that his interest in philosophy has not been interrupted by business.

sublimia 'elevated matters' = τὰ μετέωρα, a lexical Grecism refering specifically to heavenly phenomena; the word is 'noble and antique' (B. on *AP* 165).

16–20 Indirect questions clarify *sublimia* and so are governed by *cures* (1.11). Contemporary interest in physical science is attested in Virg. *G.* 2.477–81 and Prop. 3.5.25–38, where, as here, it forms a contrast with some other pursuit. The fashion is attributed to the renown of Posidonius, a Greek philosopher admired by Cicero among others (A. D. Nock, *J.R.S.* 49 (1959) 1–15, esp. 14 = *Essays on religion and the ancient world* (ed. Z. Stewart, Oxford 1972) 1 852–76).

16 compescant means either 'check the movement of' (*OLD* 3), with reference to tides as at Virg. *G.* 2.479–80, or 'suppress the growth of' (*OLD* 2), concerning why the sea does not increase despite the constant flow of river water into it, cf. Lucr. 6.608–38.

temperet 'regulates' (N–H on *C.* 1.12.16).

17 sponte sua (poetic word order) suggests that the movement of the planets (*stellae*), which Aristotle and the Stoics agreed were divine beings, was *uoluntarius* (Cic. *ND* 2.44, and *ibid.* 43 [*sidera*] *ipsa* sua sponte *suo sensu ac diuinitate moueantur*); *iussae* may point to another common Stoic theory that they follow a divine plan, perhaps Jupiter's (Arat. *Phaen.* 10–13). (Some impose an Epicurean interpretation on one or the other expression, but to the Epicurean the movement of the stars was purely *fortuitum* and Iccius was anyway a Stoic, cf. 11n.) H. hints that such nice details have little to do with right conduct here below.

-ne introduces an alternative only in an indirect question (*OLD* 5c).

uagentur et errent: cf. Cic. *Rep.* 1.22 *earum quinque stellarum quae errantes et quasi uagae nominarentur*.

18 obscurum 'into darkness', predicative, in reference to the moon's phases (Prop. 3.5.27–8), not eclipse. *lunae ... orbem* belong together ἀπὸ κοινοῦ.

19 uelit ... possit 'means (*OLD* 17) ... effects (*OLD* 8b)'.

concordia discors: oxymoron (> Ov. *Met.* 1.433). A discordant harmony recalls esp. the teaching of Empedocles concerning the two basic causes of movement, strife and love.

20 Empedocles, a fifth-century philosopher from Sicily (hence per-

haps a reason for mentioning him to Iccius) investigated above all the
nature of the universe rather than man's place in it. For H. he seems
to be the very type of mad philosopher, because of his supposed leap
into the volcano Etna whereby he hoped to secure a reputation for
immortality (*AP* 464–6). A contemporary work by one Sallustius was
entitled *Empedoclea*, further evidence of the interest in natural science.

Stertinium ... acumen = 'clever Stertinius', a mockingly high-
flown periphrasis (B. on *Ep*. 2.1.191); he was a contemporary Stoic
preacher (*S*. 2.3). The personal name serves as an adjective, a poetic
extension of a usage confined in prose to official designations, e.g.
Roscia ... lex 1.62, *uia Appia*.

21–4 Raillery at philosophical whimsies is brushed aside for practical
concerns, first, the introduction of H.'s friend Grosphus.

21 Verum: a strong transition back to the theme of diet (7–8), as a
thing philosophically regulated. Friendship on the other hand was a
practical good, and universally encouraged.

pisces: Empedocles himself? One of his doctrines concerned escape
from the wheel of birth; he allowed that he had once been a sea fish
(Diog. Laert. 8.77).

porrum ... trucidas: a hit at the Pythagorean doctrine about the
transmigration of the soul into other living things, which made all
akin. Hence Pythagoreans avoided meat and beans (W. K. C.
Guthrie, *A history of Greek philosophy* (Cambridge 1962) I 184–95). On
the other hand, fish was a delicacy and onions cheap, so H. may only
be saying 'however you choose to treat yourself ...'

22 utere 'be a friend to' (*OLD* 9b; for the form see 6.68n.) intention-
ally echoes *usus* (4); H. continues to encourage Iccius to make use of
any available good. Pompeius Grosphus, a Sicilian land-owner and
eques, was the dedicatee of *C*. 2.16.

ultro 'readily' belongs with *defer* (Catull. 68.40 *ultro ego deferrem,
copia siqua foret*, Cic. *Fam*. 4.13.2 *quod non ultro mihi Caesar detulerit*).

23 uerum: 1.11n.

24 'The retail price of friends is cheap, when good men need something.' The commercial metaphor suits Iccius as an agent, and implies
that a good man's wants are not likely to be excessive, so his friendship
can be secured for a small service. The proverbial thought adapts an
opinion of Socrates (Xenophon, *Memor*. 2.10.4 'thanks to present circumstances acquiring good men as friends at a bargain rate is now
possible'; Otto §89).

annona 'current price', esp. of corn (*OLD* 4), not only recalls *fructibus* 1, but forms a gliding transition to 28-9.

bonis: dat. of disadvantage with *deest* which scans as one syllable by synizesis (2.70n.).

25-9 To conclude H. widens the perspective to embrace current affairs, which brings him back to the opening theme of bounty (*fruges* = *fructibus*). His news concerns affairs abroad (26-8) and at home (28-9), a concealed polar expression; it is cast into three sentences linked asyndetically. In substance and style the section reflects the sort of reports which annalistic historians like Livy and Tacitus append to the end of their accounts of individual years. The themes of military success and bounty are sculpturally represented on the cuirass of the Prima Porta Augustus (P. Zanker, *The power of images in the age of Augustus* (Ann Arbor 1988) 189-92, esp. fig. 148b).

25 Ne: 1.13n. *tamen* either effects a simple transition with no adversative sense, like δέ (E. J. Kenney, *C.Q.* 29 (1979) 400-1, 410, 423; the same phrase is common in Ovid), or suggests a contrast with the limited topics that have gone before.

quo ... loco 'in what condition' (Austin on Virg. *A.* 2.322, *OLD* 22). *Romana res* 'the Roman state' evokes, without exactly duplicating, Ennian phraseology, e.g., 156 Sk. *moribus antiquis res stat Romana uirisque*, 495 Sk. *qui rem Romanam Latiumque augescere uoltis*, continued by Virg. *A.* 6.857 *hic rem Romanam magno turbante tumultu* and Livy. In a lyric, H. reverts to the Ennian pattern: *CS* 66 *remque Romanam Latiumque*.

26-7 A polar expression emphasizes Rome's imperial successes in the East (*Armenius*) and in the West (*Cantaber*).

Cantaber ... Armenius: the collective sing. is a colloquial way to speak of an enemy (N-H on *C.* 1.19.12 *Parthum*). Agrippa, Iccius' patron, had gone to Spain to complete the work of Augustus in 19 B.C. (cf. 18.55; R. Syme, 'The conquest of north-west Spain', *Legio VII Gemina* (1970), 103-4 = *Roman papers* (ed. E. Badian, Oxford 1979) II 849). Tiberius' success (3.2n.) was owed to pure diplomacy, which the unspecific *uirtute* may acknowledge (but see Josephus, *Ant.* 15.4.3); *armis* would have stretched the point to breaking. Another court poet, Crinagoras, also hailed this 'victory' (*A.Pl.*(A) 61 = *GP* 1929-34).

26 Agrippae goes with *uirtute* ἀπὸ κοινοῦ (he really did fight). The periphrasis, *uirtus* + gen., sounds an epic note, cf. *S.* 2.1.72 *uirtus Scipiadae*, *C.* 3.21.10-11 *Catonis ... uirtus*.

27   ius imperiumque: a dignified phrase found in the historians
(Sall. *Iug.* 14.1; Livy 6.23.9, 22.27.6; Tac. *Ann.* 3.71.2). Phraates was
the then king of Parthia who on 12 May 20 B.C. restored the eagles
captured from Crassus in 53 B.C. at Carrhae (18.56, *C.* 4.15.6–8 *signa
nostro restituit Ioui | derepta Parthorum superbis | postibus*); for the correct
Latin orthography of his name see N–H on *C.* 2.2.17.

28   genibus: abl. of respect with *minor* (cf. *uita* 10.33n., *TLL* x
1.567.49–60); the unusual phrase was devised to suggest what was not
in fact the case, that Phraates humbled himself by kneeling; Augustus
himself called the Parthians *supplices* (*Anc.* 5.42) and so they are represented on contemporary coinage. The metaphorical expression throws
a veil of patriotic sentiment over a diplomatic solution.

   aurea recalls *inauret* 9, but implies correction; peace and abundance
are true riches.

29   Italiae: dat. of advantage.

   Copia: cf. *CS* 59–60 *adparetque beata pleno | Copia cornu*; Plenty's horn
is a common attribute (*Lexicon iconographicum mythologiae classicae* III
1.304, Otto §441). There had been a severe famine in 22 B.C. (Dio
54.1.1), so H. stresses the return of Nature's bounty. Historians often
comment upon the corn supply, e.g., Tac. *Ann.* 2.87, 4.6.4, 6.13.

Epistle XIII

1–9   H., worried that his messenger may not have heeded earlier
advice, sends after him a note with more urgent admonitions. The
addressee, Vinnius, is otherwise unknown; the scholiasts guessed at an
identity to incorporate the *cognomen* referred to at 8–9. It has been
attractively suggested that he was a centurion of the pretorian cohort
renowned for his strength, Vinnius Valens, who served under Augustus, though it is not known when (R. G. M. Nisbet, *C.Q.* 9 (1959)
75–6). If the identification is correct, much of the military language
(e.g., *uictor* 11) receives added point.

1   saepe diuque: commonly paired (*TLL* v 1.1558.54–5).

2   Augusto: emphatic by position. *reddes* 'duly deliver'; see 4.15n. for
the fut., and *refer* 8.2n. for the force of the prefix.

   signata = *obsignata* (1.10n.); *uolumina* were protected by parchment
wrappers (*membranae*); these or perhaps the rolls themselves were secured with leather strings (*lora*; see Fordyce on Catull. 22.7) and then

sealed with the owner's ring to guarantee that they had not been tampered with.

3 A tricolon crescendo, i.e. each limb of the sentence is longer than the preceding (Fraenkel 351, N–H on *C*. 1.21.1). The great expected to have petitions and the like thrust upon them at the *salutatio*, and poets esp. could make nuisances of themselves (Plut. *Caes*. 65; *Ep*. 2.1.219–21; Cic. *Arch*. 25). The prudent and polite took precautions to ensure a favourable reception (*S*. 2.1.18–19 *nisi dextro tempore Flacci | uerba per attentam non ibunt Caesaris aurem*; Ov. *Met*. 9.610–12 *forsitan et missi sit quaedam culpa ministri: | non adiit apte nec legit idonea, credo, | tempora nec petiit horamque animumque uacantem*).

ualidus: Augustus' health gave cause for alarm in 23 B.C. (Suet. *Aug*. 81–2). *denique* 'lastly' (*OLD* 2).

4 ne ... pecces: either a rare form of prohibition (*S*. 2.3.88 *ne sis patruus mihi*, 5.16–17 *ne ... recuses* (*LS* §46)) or a final clause. The sense 'stumble' for *pecces* (1.9n.) would pave the way to the joke on Vinnius' name. *nostri* is an objective gen.

5 importes 'inflict, cause' (*OLD* 2), only here in Augustan poetry. Vinnius' fault is likely to be a counter-productive enthusiasm (*sedulus*, see B. on *Ep*. 2.1.260), and H. himself would be blamed for having chosen a clown as agent.

6 grauis: ironic, since the three papyrus rolls in their box (*capsa*) would not be unmanageable. For *uret* see 10.43.

7 ābicito: 7.69n. Prefixes of *iacio* that end in a consonant scan long (L. on *S*. 1.6.39). H.'s advice suggests that of Aristippus, recalled at *S*. 2.3.99–102, who bade his slaves throw away the gold that hindered their progress.

quo: understand *ibi* as antecedent.

8 ferus: adverbial (there was no adverbial form); the comparison is presented metaphorically (Introduction pp. 28–30).

8–9 Asinaeque paternum cognomen: Vinnius' father had the *cognomen* (or perhaps more correctly *agnomen* 'nickname') *Asina*, but he himself does not appear to have inherited it (M. J. McGann, *C.Q.* 13 (1963) 258–9); like many Roman *cognomina* it was of agricultural origin. If the son behaves doltishly at court the *cognomen* will prove all too applicable (*nomen omen*), and he will be an 'ass'.

10–19 H. recapitulates the sort of advice he pretends to have given Vinnius when he first set out. What it boils down to is management of oneself appropriately to circumstances: vigour on the road, tact in the imperial presence.

10 uteris: 4.15n. The list of obstacles to be overcome is amusingly exaggerated, since the journey, presumably from the Sabine hills to Rome, along the *uia Tiburtina*, was hardly irksome. (It is, however, always possible that Augustus was further away, say, on his Campanian estates.)

lamas 'bogs', a rare word found twice in Ennius (Skutsch on *Ann.* 580 Sk.), and perhaps chosen to enhance the humorous description of Vinnius' epic route-march. It has been suggested that the word, of Illyrian origin, might have been current in the parts of southern Italy from which H. and Ennius came (C. Hernando Balmori, *Emerita* 3 (1935) 74–85); regional words were certainly not discreditable, for Catullus took *ploxenum* (97.6) from his own territory according to Quintilian, *IO* 1.5.8.

11 propositi: gen. of definition, as in *belli uictor*.

12 sic … ne: a result may be seen as willed, so blurring the distinction between consecutive and final ideas (*LS* §51, G–L §552 R3, Roby §1650, N–H on *C.* 2.11.14, B. on *AP* 152). For *seruabis* see 4.15n.

13–15: for three illustrations cf. 1.20–7n.

14 It is generally assumed that H. has in mind a scene from a mime or comedy. Unfortunately the proper name *Pirria* is an impossible formation and must be deemed corrupt.

15 A scene from town life balances the first simile, but the situation is now unclear. A fellow tribesman (*tribulis*), clearly of slender means since he has no slave to carry the slippers he will wear in the dining room, has been invited to dinner, perhaps when his host has an election in view.

16 neu: first used by Virgil to negate a jussive subjunc. after a positive command: poetic syntax (K–S I 193, cf. 11.23n.). Its rarity may account for the variant *ne* here (Eden on Virg. *A.* 8.582). Some take the clause to depend on *oratus*. *uulgo* is indir. obj. of *narres*.

17 carmina refers to the first three books of *Odes*, published in the latter half of 23 B.C., not to the *Epistulae* (Introduction p. 4).

possint: potential. *morari* 'hold' (*OLD* 3).

18 Caesaris: for the diaeresis pause see 7.89n., but this, the last word of a clause/sentence, is more emphatic yet (cf. Virg. *G.* 3.46–7 *mox tamen ardentis accingar dicere pugnas | Caesaris* and *Ep.* 2.1.4 where

Caesar is last word of the four-line introductory sentence). H. was proud of the attention his poems secured him among the *principes ciuitatis*, and shows neither false modesty (cf. the boasts of 19.33–4, 20.23) nor presumption.

oratus: by H. For *prece* see 9.2n. For *nitere* cf. *utere* 6.68n.

19 cauĕ: the final syllable of some iambic words is commonly shortened, but not invariably (cf. 6.32; L. on *S*. 2.3.38).

mandata is the participle, meaning 'what has been entrusted to you', i.e., the poems, not the noun 'commissions', as Porphyrio saw.

That the epistle is fictive is clear to most. Wilkins said that the real purpose of the letter was to indicate to Augustus that H. had no intention to thrust his trifles upon him; Fairclough, that instead of writing a formal note to the Emperor H. indulges in the fiction of sending a letter of instructions to the messenger. They are not alone in taking the point that H., rather than parade his relationship with Augustus by addressing him directly (a thing he had not done in the first collection of lyrics), prefers to hint at it by making clear that his works interest the emperor (cf. 19.43–4). So this epistle looks at another facet of a social issue, tactful handling of the great, and above all the danger of presuming upon one's relationship with them (this is the difficulty in IX).

Epistle XIV

1–5 H., who has obligations in Rome (6–9), writes to his bailiff, contrasting their attitudes to his Sabine estate. The bailiff's is glanced at (*fastidis* 2), whilst H.'s own pride of ownership and sense of relief are stressed. The first sentence thus sets the tone of the whole epistle. A *uilicus* was the chief slave on an estate (H. had a good half dozen 'hands' *operae* (*S*. 2.7.118)), who was charged with general superintendence of activities and purchases; his responsibility was therefore considerable.

1 mihi me reddentis 'allows me to be myself', cf. *uiuo et regno* 10.8, *reficit* 18.104 and Sen. *Dial*. 10.8.5 *te tibi reddet* (*OLD* 2b). H.'s evaluation of his farm's true worth to himself is plain from the outset. M. Aurelius may have had this passage in mind when he spoke of a retreat into the hermitage that is oneself (see Farquharson on 4.3.4).

2 habitatum '*because*...' (11.12n.) 'by *only*...' (9.4n.); *focis* 'hearths'

by the figure metonymy refers to their households. For the enjambment with *et* see Introduction p. 24.

quinque: the repetition boasts of the size of his holding. Varia is
now Vicovaro, the market town of the region.

patres = *patresfamilias*; obviously free men, H.'s tenants, they went
to the local market-town perhaps to perform their civic duties as well
as to buy and sell (Heitland 215–6).

4 certemus governs a double indir. qu. (*TLL* III 897.8–24) introduced by *ne* (*OLD* 5a). The notion of a contest puts H. and his slave on
a morally even footing, which will be fairly kept up, cf. *uterque* 12.
Moreover, as Müller observed, H. politely quashes the bailiff's hope of
return to Rome.

spinas: used literally of the estate, figuratively of the soul; cf.
Catull. 64.72 *spinosas ... curas, S.* 1.3.35–7, *Ep.* 2.2.212 *quid te exempta
iuuat spinis de pluribus una?* For the metaphor cf. *culturae* 1.40n.

-ne is attached to the word that carries the weight of the question
(cf. *animus* 13) even at the price of hyperbaton (cf. *Ep.* 2.2.65–6 *praeter
caetera me Romaene poemata censes | scribere posse*). With *ego* understand
euellam.

5 melior 'in better shape'. H. is in fact more concerned to reconcile
the bailiff to his situation, but he begins his approach indirectly, with
his own need for 'psychic husbandry' (1.40n.).

rus 'his estate'; a conjecture of D. Heinsius, supported by Bentley
with the citation of Sidon. *Ep.* 8.4.1 *difficile discernitur domini plusne sit
cultum rus an ingenium*. The MSS reading, *res* 'property', is insufficiently
concrete; it is moreover the sort of word to intrude where it is not
wanted, e.g., at 11, where it has supplanted *sors* in part of the tradition.

6–9 The reference to the death of Lamia's brother goes some way to
accounting for the need for a letter. But we also glimpse the depth of
his attachment to the farm and all it stands for. His thoughts ought to
be all for his grieving friend, yet (*tamen* 8) he cannot help wanting the
country.

6 quamuis governs the indic. on the analogy of *quamquam*, chiefly
poetic syntax (L. on *S.* 2.2.29, *OLD* 4a, K–S II 443).

Lamiae pietas et cura 'my tender concern for L.'; the gen. is
objective and the nouns form a single idea by hendiadys. Three odes
honour men named Lamia, whom we can neither distinguish nor iden-

tify (1.26, 36, 3.17; Syme, *AA* 394–5). It is equally impossible to say who the dead brother was or of what age (E. J. Kenney in *I.C.S.* 2 (1977) 29–39 argues that he was young, silly and in the clutches of a courtesan).

7 fratrem ... fratre: the repetition and the rhyme between *maerentis* and *dolentis* imitate the pathetic cries of the grieving. *maereo* refers to the manifestation of grief by tears, etc., *doleo* to the feeling (R. Ogilvie, *Horae Latinae* (London 1901) 119–20).

8 insolabiliter: a coinage = ἀπαραμυθήτως. *mens* and *animus* are commonly paired in poetry to stress the harmony of judgement and inclination (*TLL* 1 96.27; see Jocelyn on Enn. *scen.* 198 J.).

9 fert 'inclines, tends' (*OLD* 7). *auet*, Bentley's conjecture, provides the right sense; *amat* of the MSS can only mean 'find pleasure in' (*OLD* 9) or 'is accustomed to' (*OLD* 12).

  spatiis: 7.42n.; *claustra* 'the bolts' that secure the starting-gates. H.'s longing is depicted metaphorically as a racehorse (1.8–9) eager to run.

10–17 The argument runs thus: the point at issue is defined (10), and a general reason for it is offered, discontent with one's position (11). H. then passes judgement on both contestants (12) and locates the cause of discontent not in circumstances but in the heart (13). He restates the point at issue in the light of what has gone before (14–17), but with the new insight that the bailiff is inconsistent (14–15), whereas he knows that after all H. himself is not (16–17).

10 Construe with ἀπὸ κοινοῦ: *ego ⟨dico⟩ rure uiuentem ⟨beatum⟩, tu dicis in urbe ⟨uiuentem⟩ beatum*. For *rure* see 7.1n. *dicis* 'call' (*OLD* 9, with pred.). For *in urbe* cf. *S.* 1.1.12 *solos felicis uiuentis clamat in urbe* of the farmer.

11 For the thought see 2.57n. For *cui* understand *ei* as antecedent and as dat. of possessor with *est ... sors*. Take *sors* as subj. of *placet* ἀπὸ κοινοῦ.

  alterius: used instead of the gen. of *alius*; its juxtaposition with *sua* enhances the contrast; *sua* refers to the implied dat. *ei*, not the grammatical subject, *sors* (*OLD* 2).

  odio 'disagreeable' (cf. 7.20n.), predicative dat. (*NLS* §68 n. 1).

12 stultus balances *inique*, which gives the effect of folly. *locum immeritum* resumes by contrast the theme of XI, in which places were praised.

13   in 'in (a specified state or condition)' *OLD* 37. *effugit* recalls the thought of Lucr. 3. 1068–9 *hoc se quisque modo fugit, at quem scilicet, ut fit,* | *effugere haud potis est* (cf. 11.27n. and *animo* 4).

14   mediastinus 'factotum'; his move to the villa was a promotion. *tacita prece* (9.2n.) suggests that H. must have guessed what the slave had been yearning for all along (*petebas*).

15   Like Mena in VII the bailiff wants his old life back, not that his grounds for complaint are as serious. What he misses are the amusements (*ludos*, 7.59) and the places of resort (*balnea*). He will not be more prosperous in town.

16   constare 'to be consistent' (*OLD* 10). But at 8.12 H. was fickle about place, as he will apparently be in the next epistle. Hence ironical self-mockery has been detected (B. on *Ep*. 2.1.108). But in VIII the fickleness was the result of malaise (*ueterno* 10), in XV H. has the excuse of doctor's orders; here, however, he insists upon a settled disposition and appeals to the bailiff's own awareness of his master's true feeling (*scis*).

17   negotia: to H. Rome represents business, not the pleasures sought by the bailiff (15). The visit he is now paying is not, however, 'business', but an *officium*, motivated by affection.

18–30   An analysis of the grounds for disagreement about the villa, largely from the bailiff's point of view.

18   Non eadem miramur 'we have different ideals', cf. *Ep*. 2.2.58 *non omnes eadem mirantur.* H. warned in VI that idealizing leads to trouble; the doctrine was reiterated at 10.31. Still H. himself is not free of the tendency.

   eo 'consequently' (*OLD eo*³ 1); the logical particle suits the conversational tone (Introduction p. 16). *disconuenit* 'there is a disagreement', impersonal, but cf. 1.99. For *inter* see Introduction p. 24.

19   -que et: 6.14n. *deserta*)(the thronged places of resort he misses (15).

   inhospita: a poetic synonym for *inhospitalis*, which does not fit hexameters; *tesqua* 'heath', a very rare word of uncertain origin; there is no evidence for its currency among country-folk.

20   amoena: cf. 16.15, *C.* 1.17 1 *amoenum … Lucretilem* (a hill near H.'s estate). *sentit* 'agrees' (*OLD* 6b); for *odit* see 7.20n.

21–6   The bailiff's missed pleasures are again referred to but now in less creditable detail than at 15, where his express wish was, as it were, quoted.

21 uncta 'savoury' (*OLD* 1b) to the bailiff, to H. merely 'greasy' (*OLD* 1a). The brothel and cook-shop are what he really wants.

22 uideo 'I perceive' (*OLD* 14), parenthetic, is colloquial (H–S 528). *quod* ... adds another subject to *incutiunt* (*OLD* 4).

23 angulus suggests remote seclusion rather than snugness (N–H on *C*. 2.6.14). H. adopts the point of view of the bailiff (*OLD iste* 2), who is imagined as using a familiar device, the *adynaton* (impossible) (N–H on *C*. 1.29.10): pepper and incense came from the East, the farm could obviously never produce them. For the abl. *uua* see 2.4n.

24–5 Not only does the estate not produce wine, there is none to be had in agreeable surroundings nearby.

24 subest 'is close at hand as a refuge' (*OLD* 4). Take *uinum praebere* with *possit* 25.

25 possit: 1.12n.; *cuius* as last word effects enjambment.

26 strepitum: the hostess plays the castanets, as in the pseudo-Virgilian *Copa*; there is no pejorative colour (cf. 2.31, and *C*. 4.3.17–18 *testudinis* ... | *dulcem* ... *strepitum*).

salias implies less refined dancing than *salto*, cf. Virgil's rustics at *G*. 2.384 *unctos saluere per utres*; for the subjunc. see 1.7n. *terrae* is dat. of disadvantage with *grauis*, cf. *C*. 3.18.15–16 *gaudet inuisam pepulisse fossor* | *ter pede terram*. For *tamen* see 7.23n.

27 iampridem: take with *non tacta*; the bailiff found the estate in need of rehabilitation.

28 disiunctum: even when the ox is unyoked the bailiff still has to oversee the work of those who feed the cattle. Leaves were stripped (*strictis*) from the branches to provide fodder in summer, cf. Virg. *Ecl*. 9.61 *agricolae stringunt frondes*.

29 pigro 'unoccupied' (so Dacier, *OLD* 4); rain prevents some tasks, but adds to the bailiff's duties.

30 mole 'toil' (*OLD* 8), though 'dyke' would be possible (cf. Virg. *A*. 2.496–7 *amnis* ... *oppositas* ... *euicit* ... *moles*); the sense of toilsomeness is enhanced by alliteration and the self-contained spondee in the first foot. The rhythm of the rest of the line is remarkable, not only for the trochaic caesurae in both second and third feet (9.4n.), but also for the false ending produced by *aprico* (Introduction p. 14).

docendus: rivers (unlike irrigation ditches) are naturally untamed and so need 'training' (N–H on *C.* 2.14.4), cf. *AP* 67–8 *amnis | doctus iter melius*.

aprico parcere prato: alliteration again emphasizes the thought. A dry period bakes surface soil hard; the first rains do not soak in but, aided by an overflowing torrent, gouge channels down which the valuable top soil is washed away.

31–6 H. now comes to the kernel of the epistle and gives his view of the grounds for disagreement. But in describing his present frame of mind, he covertly advises the bailiff.

31   Nunc age: a formula of transition (B. on *Ep.* 2.1.214); we pass to H.'s assessment of the situation.

concentum: H. and his slave agree that they want to be elsewhere; but H. now calls upon the principle of right time to justify his present attitude.

32–4 Three descriptive clauses touch on the distinctive features of the life of pleasure that H. used to live (the perf. tense is important). The anaphora of *quem* hammers in the identity (Fraenkel 311).

32   tenues: i.e. made of finer wool; for the imagery of dress cf. 1.95–6n.

nitidi: because anointed with perfumed oil, cf. *nitidum caput C.* 1.4.9.
33   scis: again an appeal to the bailiff's personal knowledge as at 16.

immunem '*though* giftless'. H.'s charm (he is proud to report) outweighed his poverty in the eyes of a courtesan, however grasping; cf. Prop. 2.20.25 *nec mihi muneribus nox ullast empta beatis*.

34   quem bibulum: sc. *scis* ἀπὸ κοινοῦ and *fuisse*. The adjective is itself poetic, and its government of the gen., *Falerni*, is poetic syntax (K–S I 443). This Campanian wine was emblematic of all that was most refined in the life of pleasure.

liquidi 'clear', because strained; ancient winemaking was somewhat rough and ready, and bits of stalk or pips had to be filtered out before drinking (N–H on *C.* 1.11.6 *uina liques*).

media ... luce: i.e. the drinking began rather early (*S.* 2.8.3); for *de* see 2.32n.

35   cena: a family meal, not a feast (*dapes*); *breuis* enhances the notion: his meal is not prolonged, instead of a *commissatio* he naps on the lawn (the fragrance of which he likes, 10.19, and cf. *C.* 2.3.6 *in remoto* *gramine*). Behind the phrases lies a tradition of moralizing on the simple life (B. on *mensae breuis AP* 198).

36 The clinching judgement recalls *ludicra* 1.10 (cf. B. on *lusisti Ep*. 2.2.214). H. is no prig; it is not the life of pleasure as such that disgraces but an inability to give it up. A similar thought appears in Philodemus (3.18–20n.), *AP* 5.112 = *GP* 3269–73.

non incidere: understand *pudet* ἀπὸ κοινοῦ.

37–44 H. stresses the positive merits of a country life both for himself (37–9) and for the bailiff (40–2), and briskly concludes with allusion to a fable and a proverb.

37–8 For rural goodwill see Cato, *Agr. praef.* 4 *minime ... male cogitantes sunt qui in eo studio* [farming] *occupati sunt*. That H. personally was the object of envy and backbiting in Rome is clear from a number of passages (N–H on *inuidia maior C.* 2.20.4).

37 obliquo oculo: envy's sideways glance is a commonplace (N–H on *C.* 2.2.23, 20.4); another common way of describing such a glance (not necessarily envious) was *limis*, and it seems H. had this in mind when he chose the verb *limat* 'files away', used metaphorically to produce a sort of implicit etymology. The elision of the long *o* into the short is unusual (Winbolt §134).

mea commoda: above all his friendship with Maecenas, and latterly, Augustus, cf. 19.33–4 and *S*. 2.6.47–8.

38 odio ... morsu 'the bite of secret hatred'; hendiadys.

38–9 uenenat)(rident: adversative asyndeton contrasts the open amusement of the countryside with the guarded malignancy of the town. As obj. of *rident* understand *me* from *mea*. For H. as a figure of fun in the country cf. 4.16.

40–2 H. reminds the bailiff of the inconveniences of town service, and hints that a replacement will not be hard to find.

40 cum seruis: though himself a slave, in the country the bailiff can at least lord it over the others. *rodere* suggests hard fare, which, in town, was measured out (*S*. 1.5.68–9, Sen. *Ep*. 80.7 *seruus est: quinque modios accipit*), unlike the produce of farm and garden (*horti* 42). With *mauis* understand the emphatic *tu* (41) ἀπὸ κοινοῦ.

41 uoto: 2.56n.; the bailiff's inconstancy of purpose is pinpointed.

inuidet usum ... tibi: colloquial syntax (*TLL* vii 2.193.41).

42 lignorum: firewood is scarce in towns. *argutus* hints to the bailiff to 'wise up'.

43 Behind this thought lies Pindar, fr. 234 S–M 'the horse is for the chariot, the ox for the plough'; Plutarch quoted it with the same purpose as H.'s, to encourage contentment with one's lot, *Moral.* 472c.

ephippia 'saddle cloth', a Greek loan word; the saddle may be included.

piger goes ἀπὸ κοινοῦ with *bos* and *caballus* (7.88n., H. H. Huxley, *G. & R.* 19 (1972) 187–9). The ox, tired of ploughing, thinks that carrying a man on his back is preferable, and the horse, fed up with supporting weight, reckons it easier to draw a plough. This is the sort of discontentedness with one's lot mentioned at 11.

44 Construe: *censebo, uterque [eam] artem quam scit libens exerceat.* The proverb from Aristoph. *Vespae* 1431 is rendered by Cicero (*Tusc.* 1.41) *quam quisque norit artem, in hac se exerceat* (cf. *Off.* 1.114 *ad quas igitur res aptissimi erimus, in eis potissumum elaborabimus*; Otto §167). H. applies it to the *calo* and the *uilicus*.

libens: adverbial, though *libenter* was available (cf. 11.24n.); the notion, *not* found in the proverb, is central to the epistle: contentedness with one's lot. It is emphasized by its separation from *exerceat* by the parenthetic *censebo*.

censebo 'my advice would be' (B. on *AP* 235 *amabo*), as at Pl. *Mil.* 395 *narrandum ego istuc militi censebo*; the fut. is politer than the more decided pres. (H–S 850, *addendum* to 311).

As with the previous letter there is here too some agreement that the epistle is fictive: 'nominally addressed to H.'s farm-bailiff' (Wilkins), 'professedly addressed to the slave' (Fairclough); Wickham concurs.

The epistle brings together the theme of contrast between town and country, with that of contentedness with one's lot (10.44), especially where that 'lot' was the object of one's own aspirations (be careful in what you aspire to: you may get it!). Important too are the notions of consistency and of right time. Presumably the bailiff was a man of mature years (H. was too sensible to put a boy in charge of his estate), so he like his master ought to act his age.

Yet the doctrine is somewhat unexpected. H. has stressed his love of the country, his need for it, but remains convinced in principle that place should be a matter of indifference to the well-regulated spirit (10–11, cf. 11.27). There is a fundamental inconsistency in his attitude, which he tries here to justify up to a point.

The fact that this epistle was conceived in the first place is to the poet's credit. He presents himself as a humane master, who, though he has no intention of granting the bailiff's wish to return to town, would not leave him to stew in his discontents. Rather, he shows that he can put himself mentally into the slave's position (though of course he does not approve of it) and would try to argue him out of it, using his own attitude as a model. This is, in the best sense of the word, condescension and remarkable in a free-born Roman's treatment of a slave. H.'s behaviour becomes exemplary for his readers. (There is no such letter in Pliny's collection.)

Epistle XV

1–25 A series of indirect questions (1–2, 14–16, 22–3) concerning the amenities of sites in southern Italy for a proposed winter holiday (cf. 7.11) is interrupted by parenthetic explanations, clearly signposted by *nam* 2–13, 16–21; the first gives the reason for the visit, a cure, the second balances it with the hint that it is not only H.'s body that needs restoration. The main clause comes last at 25. Digressions, inserted with consummate art, lead us to the poet's hidden goal under the guise of inconsequence (L. on *S*. 1.7.10–18).

1–2 Quae ... quod ... quorum 'what kind of' (*OLD qui*[1] 2). Velia, chosen by Aemilius Paulus as a place to recuperate on doctor's advice in 160 B.C. (Plut. *Aem*. 39.1), is now Castellamare di Veglia, Salernum is Salerno.

1 caelum: 7.77n. The addressee, Vala, is unknown. The scholiasts add the name Numonius; inscriptions confirm that such a family lived in the part of Italy to which H. was thinking of going.

2 quorum hominum: descriptive gen., not possessive. The *uia Popilia* led to Salernum from Naples.

nam: the explanatory parenthesis was much affected by Callimachus (Hopkinson on Callim. *H*. 6.70), but H. inflates his in a chatty way that parodies epistolary rambling, yet introduces the sickness theme indirectly. For *Baias* see 1.83n.

3 superuacuas goes with *facit* ἀπὸ κοινοῦ; preferred by H. as metrically handier than *superuacaneus* (N–H on *C*. 2.20.24), the word reappears often in the medical writer Celsus, hence the supposition that he parodies his doctor's jargon. H.'s casual reference to Antonius Musa

(3.26n.) shows in what circles he now moves; for the order of his names see 2.1n.

tamen: Musa is the culprit, 'yet' H. is blamed.

4 cum 'seeing that' (*OLD* 6) gives the reason for their hostility; the indic. is usual (K–S II 329).

unda ≠ *aqua* (an Ovidian poeticism); H. is to be immersed in a body of water (Kenney on *Moret*. 43).

5 sane: 7.61n. *relinqui* 'are avoided' (*OLD* 10,11), depends, as does *contemni*, on *gemit* 7 (*OLD* 4b).

6–7 'the sulphur, said to drive out of the muscles the lingering ailment (? rheumatism)'. The volcanic neighbourhood of Baiae abounds in sulphur springs. Both *cessantem* (*TLL* III 960.38–40) and *elidere* (*OLD* 4a) are medical terminology.

7 sulpura: poetic plur. (K–S I 83). Since Baiae was not a municipality (*OCD* s.v.), it is strictly correct to call it a *uicus* (*OCD* s.v.).

aegris: dat. with *inuidus*.

8 caput et stomachum: cf. 16.14, where these parts of the body are well served by the stream on H.'s estate.

9 Nowhere else are springs attested at Clusium, now Chiusi, in Etruria; Strabo on the other hand refers to those at Gabii in Latium (5.3.11). For *-que* 'or' see 5.27n.; *Gabios . . . et . . . rura* form hendiadys.

10–13 Riding southwards on the Appian way H. would have taken a right fork for Baiae. But he must now stay on that road, bypassing the usual stopping-off places, so he tugs at the left rein (12) to keep the horse on the highway.

10 deuersoria: acc., governed by the prefix *praeter*.

11 praeteragendus: a coinage, found only here, = παρελαύνω.

11–13 A lively realization of the scene at the crossroads when the journey takes an unwonted turn. Cumae, once a considerable power, had become another resort near Naples (*OCD* s.v.).

12 stomachosus 'testily'; with it (as the word order shows) goes *habena* as instrumental abl.

13 sed: elliptical, correcting *dicet*: 'but ⟨what's the use of talking, since⟩ horses only "hear" through the mouth'. *sed* has not, however, seemed wholly satisfactory (Introduction p. 15 n. 51); it might, on the other hand, have had colloquially a weakened sense, like δέ, and thus introduced a reason (so E. Löfstedt, *Philologischer Kommentar zur Peregrinatio Aetheriae* (Uppsala 1911, repr. Darmstadt 1970) 33–4).

equis: possessive dat.; the plur. generalizes so as to describe horses as a species.

14–15 H. returns to his questions, focussing on diet.

15 Water was (and still is) a concern to the traveller, cf. *S.* 1.5.7, and H. is specially interested in its quality (10.20–1, 16.12–14). Where there were no springs or wells, reservoirs or tanks (*collectos*) were needed, but their water lost freshness.

-ne ... -ne 'whether ... or', a form of double indir. qu. found chiefly in poetry (K–S II 528, *OLD* 5b).

16 nam uina: the second parenthesis is generated by the concern for drink, but H. develops it into a small encomium of wine (5.16–20), hinting at inner needs, to complement the physical ailments of the first parenthesis.

nihil moror 'I have no time for', a colloquial form of dismissal (*OLD* 4b, B. on *Ep.* 2.1.264).

17 rure: 14.5n. The pairing of alliterative synonyms, *perferre patique*, is colloquial; cf. 16.74, Ter. *Andr.* 35 (H–S 786).

18 ad mare: adversative asyndeton; *cum ueni* 'whenever I come', the indic. generalizes (*NLS* §233).

generosum, first used here of wine (then Ov. *Rem.* 567, [Tibull.] 3.6.5), enters oenologists' language in the seventeenth century (*OED* s.v. *generous* 5). The literal meaning is to the fore, the wine shows its breeding.

lene 'mellow' (*OLD* 3). Seneca too recommends an occasional journey with better feeding to tone up the spirit (*Dial.* 9.17.8 *aliquando uectatio iterque et mutata regio uigorem dabunt conuictusque et liberalior potio*).

19–21 quod ... : anaphora enhances the sense that H. has a list of requirements of his wine, and ticks each one off. The subjunc. in each rel. clause is final.

19 curas abigat: cf. 5.18 and *C.* 4.12.19–20 *spes donare nouas largus amaraque | curarum eluere efficax* (where the style is appropriate to lyric).

mănet ≠ *mānet*.

20 quod uerba ministret: cf. 5.19. The poet's basic tools which wine seems to provide. But it may be that the artificial inducement hints at an anxiety, the loss of powers.

21 Lucanae: Velia was in Lucania. H. intends to slip back entirely into the life of pleasure he had put behind him, with the excuse that he is following doctor's orders.

iuuenem: '*as if I were* …'

22–3 H. returns to his questions, again focussed on food, for which land and sea (a concealed polar expression) are to be scoured.

22   pluris: take with *apros* ἀπὸ κοινοῦ.

23   utra: take with *aequora*.

24   pinguis: cf. 4.15. *Phaeax* (2.28n.) suggests that H. is happy to mitigate his strictures if occasion requires.

25 The Roman reader would have been waiting for this, the main clause, after all the dependent subjunctives.

accredere: the *ad-* prefix points to a colloquial form (Wölfflin 123); *par* 'reasonable' (*OLD* 14).

26–46 An illustrative *exemplum* is introduced asyndetically; as usual its application (here self-defence) is delayed (7.29–39n.).

26   Maenius: a notorious wastrel in the time of Lucilius; H. unusually reverts to a practice of his *Sermones* (1.3.21–3) in referring to the butts of an earlier satiric tradition. Yet this Maenius shows something of an exemplary, Aristippean adaptability.

27   fortiter 'stoutly' is ironic; *urbanus* 'a wit' (*OLD* 4).

28   scurra 'a clever parasite'; for this characterization see P. Corbett, *The scurra* (Edinburgh 1986) 61–5 or the careful account of their way of life in L. pp. 551–3. *uagus*, developed in the rel. cl., shows that the *scurra* aims to preserve some independence by not having a steady patron (cf. *certus* 7.75).

non qui 'not the sort'; the subjunc. here and at 29 is generic.

praesepe 'manger'; perhaps a colloquial metaphor (Bo 337).

29   impransus '*if* unfed'; common in Plautus, the word may be characteristic of the *scurra*.

dinosceret: a coinage = διαγιγνώσκω; *hoste* is abl. of separation (7.48n.). The contrast with *ciuem* is proverbial, cf. Pl. *Trin.* 102, Manil. 5.494 (*TLL* vi 3.3060.73–6).

30 'vicious at devising any insult you like against anyone at all'. The infin. is complementary with *saeuus*.

31   macelli goes with all three nouns ἀπὸ κοινοῦ. The metaphorical language recalls (without exactly reproducing) the abusive terms found in comedy.

32   auaro: his appetite is indiscriminate, and he trims his morals to the contents of his plate.

33–4 ubi ... abstulerat 'whenever he had got from' (18n.); for the datives, *fautoribus* and *timidis*, see 6.54n.

nequitiae: the gen. understood ἀπὸ κοινοῦ with *timidis* is poetic syntax, first found in H. (B. on *AP* 28).

et 'or' (*OLD* 13); Maenius gets a meal either as a reward for wit or to buy his silence.

nil aut paulum: the division of this common phrase (Fordyce on Catull. 68.131) produces a conversational enjambment.

35 et is postponed (Introduction p. 21); *uilis* belongs only with *agninae* (tripe, after all, is cheap food). *esset* is a generic subjunc.

36 scilicet ut 'so that he actually', expresses surprise.

lamna < *lamina*, which loses its short vowel by syncope. Heated metal plates were applied to the peccant part of the miscreant's body as a form of punishment (Galen v 584 K.).

37 correctus Bestius '*like* a reformed Bestius'; by a common idiom the proper name stands for a class of person (English uses the indef. art.; B. on *AP* 450); here it is used in apposition instead of comparison (Introduction pp. 28–30). Bestius is unidentifiable, but reformed miscreants notoriously make savage moralists.

idem 'yet this same man' commonly introduces contrasting behaviour in one and the same person (*OLD* 10; cf. 44).

38 quidquid is picked up by *omne*; *praedae* is a gen. of rubric.

39 uerterat: cf. 33–4n. *in fumum et cinerem* picks up the metaphor of rapine in 38, and suggests epic destruction (cf. Ov. *Met.* 2.215–6 *incendia gentes | in cinerem uertunt*); the expression may be proverbial (Otto §731).

40 si: 12.12n. *qui* is nom. pl. of the indef. pronoun *quis*.

comedunt bona: a common metaphor (*TLL* III 1767.38–42).

41 nil ... nil: anaphora enhances his enthusiasm (1.88). *turdo* and *uolua* (sow's womb was a delicacy) are abll. of comparison.

42–6 H. now applies the story to himself, not without ironical overstatement (*nimirum* 9.1n.).

42 hic: 6.40n. Maenius is a moral relativist, his view of what is right changes with his circumstances. The same inconstancy is ascribed to H. by his critical slave, Davus, at *S.* 2.7.29–32, where H. is said to praise a simple meal at home, until Maecenas suddenly invites him to a dinner party.

tuta et paruula laudo: e.g. at 7.44. The neuter pl. is abstract, and generalizes H.'s position; food is not his chief concern, though it created a useful link between his questions to Vala and the tale of Maenius.

43   satis: typical qualification.

44   quid: from the indef. pronoun *quis*. *contingit* 'falls to my share' (*OLD* 8); Maenius had sought his rewards (32, 38). It makes a difference that H.'s are an accident, thanks here to doctor's orders (albeit flexibly obeyed).

unctius (14.21n.) keeps up the gastronomical tone of the letter. *idem* recalls 37 and points up H.'s similarity to Maenius.

45   uos: understand *solos* ἀπὸ κοινοῦ. *sapere* 'are sensible' (*sapienter* 10.44n.); for *bene* see 6.56n. and for *quorum* Introduction p. 24.

46   nitidis ... uillis 'well-maintained country seats' advertise the solid wealth of rich landowners (Heitland 235). H.'s inconsistency appears less extreme when it is remembered first, that a *uilla* is necessarily in the country and secondly, that he only adopts this line when doctor's orders put him in the way of taking advantage of it. The reference to good maintenance forms a contrast to the description of H.'s own estate in the previous letter.

At the outset of the collection H. had declared that he was a natural follower of Aristippus, one to make the circumstances in which he found himself serve his turn (1.19). This epistle is an object lesson in that doctrine. (It may also be worth suggesting that H. pretends as well to be angling for an invitation to come and stay at Vala's place in the region he has fixed upon to visit for his cure.) H. usually takes a winter break on the coast (7.11), or in the warm South, but uncertain health and doctor's orders (and what a doctor! the imperial physician no less) demand a change in habit and H. is not one to stick doggedly to a simple regime. This is not inconsistency, since H. knows that what he likes and what is best for himself are usually but not always the same. Here is a case in point, and so he will not let slip the chance to abandon his usual practices. (We all use our holidays for this purpose, and indeed it is just the sort of situation he creates for the overworked Torquatus in V.) In the end, we return home (24) to the habits we approve.

Epistle XVI

1–4 Forestalling enquiry about the produce of his farm, H. describes it. Quinctius is unidentifiable (though he seems prominent, 17–18); perhaps he is also the recipient of *C.* 2.11. That he is addressed as *optime* not only shows H.'s regard for him, but paves the way to the definition of the *uir bonus*.

1 **Ne etc:** H. anticipates an interest in the farm's produce and its financial value. The following description, however, concentrates on other merits. For the indirect alternative qu. without introductory particle see 6.12n.

2 **erum** 'master', in relation to servants or property (N–H on *C.* 2.18.32), introduces an important theme, independence: cf. *dominum* 10, *liber* 63, 66 (cf. *regno* 10.8). For *er(um) an* see 7.57 n.

   opulentet: a coinage perhaps, stressing the note of abundance that will be sounded later (8, 10).

4 **scribetur** 'will be described' (*OLD* 15).

5–16 This description should be compared with that of *C.* 1.17, in which a rustic divinity, Faunus, appears as guardian and musician; the lyric and the epistolary landscape are different.

5 **Continui montes:** supply *sunt*. The logical apodosis is suppressed (Roby §1574, *LS* §145): the mountains form a chain running east–west, unbroken but for the valley, which is cut by the Digentia (18.104), flowing southwards (see Dilke's edn, pp. 9–12).

   ni dissocientur: the pres. subjunc., usually in neg. conditionals, was still used, though less frequently than the imperf., to express present unreality (*LS* §137).

6 **sed ut ...** seems to qualify *opaca* (12n., 20.25n., B. on *AP* 257 *non ut*, H–S 641). The descriptive point would be that the valley is shaded by the mountain sides, but they are not so steep as to keep the morning and evening sun from parts of the estate; of course, the valley itself is sunny at midday, but H., who is *solibus aptus*, wants as much sunshine as he can get. For the final rhythm see 5.6n.

7 **curru fugiente:** cf. *C.* 3.6.44 *abeunte curru*; *uaporet* 'heats' (*OLD* 2).

8 **temperiem** covers more than climate in H.'s moralized landscape. *si* 'supposing' (*OLD quis*[1]13a, Roby §1578, 1579).

9–10 ferant ... iuuet: the subjunc. suggests the thought in the mind of the reader of the letter: 'suppose you knew that ...'

10   multa ... multa: anaphora enhances the sense of abundance. Acorns were turned into mash for the pigs.

dominum 'owner' (cf. *S*. 2.6.14 *pingue pecus domino facias*) picks up *erum* 2; H. feels the security of ownership (cf. *meus* 1).

umbra: cf. *Ep*. 2.2.78 *somno gaudentis et umbra* of poets.

11   dicas ... Tarentum 'you'd say that leafy T. (7.45n.) had come nearer home'; the Latin participle often carries a greater emphasis than the leading verb of its sentence (here *frondere*) (B. on *Ep*. 2.2.168; K–S I 781).

12–14   See 15.15n., and cf. 18.104.

12   dare: complementary infin. with *idoneus*.

ut: understand either *talis* or *tam frigidus et purus*; H. is inordinately fond of this concise form of qualification (B. on *AP* 3 (not on *Ep*. 2.2.87, p. 317, where this passage is incorrectly analysed), K–S II 248–9).

13   ambiat 'wind through' (not 'round' as *OLD* 9b); cf. 3.3. The descriptive adjectives, not the verb, carry the weight of the sentence.

14   infirmo goes with *aluo* ἀπὸ κοινοῦ. The anaphora of *utilis* emphasizes the benefits to health, cf. 15.8. H. is less concerned with an economic return.

15   latebrae: herein lies the chief merit (1.5n.); for the estate's charm see 14.20n.

iam si 'if after all', a rare variant of concessive *si iam* (*TLL* VII 1.128.38–48; *OLD iam* 7d is less satisfactory).

16   incolumem ... praestant 'keep (*OLD praesto*² 13) ... safe and sound'; another benefit is health at a bad time of the year (cf. 7.4).

tibi 'you'll be glad to hear' (Rudd), either an ethic dat. or one of advantage, but not indir. obj. of *praestant*. It subtly forges a link with the next section: Quinctius is interested in H.'s health and happiness; the poet gives explicit assurances on those points and turns to reciprocate his friend's concern.

horis 'season', a poetic sense introduced by H., perhaps a loan-shift (*TLL* VI 2.2964.1–9).

17–24   The description of the estate closed with a picture of H., presumably contented and healthy in retirement. H. now turns to Quinctius, who is not in retirement (far from it), but the issue remains the same, health (21–4), to be understood, as usual, of both physical and spiritual well-being.

17   recte uiuis: 6.29n.; a more moral concern emerges in the development of the argument. *esse* 'to be in reality'. For *audis* see 7.38n.

18 iactamus 'speak confidently of' (*TLL* VII 1.60.50–1) explains *audis*; *omnis ... Roma* is in apposition to the subj. (H–S 439).

beatum: 'often used ... for a happiness vouched for by public opinion' (Wickham on *C*. 3.29.11), an interpretation confirmed by the use of *Roma*; though the town is in contrast with H.'s *latebrae*, yet here he adds his voice. The hint is that after all each man can only know himself best; others are deceived by appearances.

19 Moralists agreed that we should be slow to assent to a favourable popular assessment of reputation, esp. our own. Self-esteem must be founded upon self-knowledge; cf. Persius 1.7 *nec te quaesiueris extra*, 4.46–7 *egregium cum me uicinia dicat,* | *non credam?*, Sen. *Ep*. 7.12 *multi te laudant. et quid habes cur placeas tibi si is es quem intellegant multi? introrsus bona tua spectent*, 80.10 *si perpendere te uoles, sepone pecuniam, domum, dignitatem, intus te ipse considera: nunc qualis sis, aliis credis* (Otto §65).

uereor initiates a tricolon crescendo.

20 alium with comparative abl. is perhaps colloquial (K–S II 467).

sapiente bonoque: resumed at 73 (4.5n., 7.22). H. corrects the definition of happiness as at *C*. 4.9.45–50 *non possidentem multa uocaueris* | *recte beatum; rectius occupat* | *nomen beati, qui deorum* | *muneribus sapienter uti* | *duramque callet pauperiem pati* | *peiusque leto flagitium timet*, where the notions of prudence and goodness are developed.

21 populus resumes *omnis ... Roma*, but H. has now detached himself out of mistrust in popular judgement (1.7on.).

sanum ... : cf. 7.3. The common analogy between physical and spiritual health is introduced as a metaphor. Just as we know better than anyone else how we feel, so we should not trust another's favourable opinion of our moral health, lest it blind us to our faults.

22 dictitet: the frequentative suggests unreflecting repetition; one comes to believe what is heard so often.

occultam: predicative; he pretends that the fever does not exist, in order to preserve his reputation for sound health. *sub* 'just before' (*OLD* 23).

23 incidat: the subjunc. in the *dum*-clause has lost any sense of intention (*NLS* §224 Nii).

unctis: the dinner has begun. Romans usually ate with a knife and their fingers, which were presumably washed throughout the meal (cf. Petron. 34.4).

24 stultorum: emphatic by position; the plur. tactfully generalizes the observation; Quinctius will not want to find himself in this class.

incurata 'untreated', probably predicative; a Horatian coinage = ἀθεράπευτος.

pudor malus 'false shame', cf. *S*. 2.3.39, *AP* 88 and Phaedra's αἰδώς at Eur. *Hipp*. 385–6, where it is the shame that too readily falls in with what others say or believe; it prevents self-reliance and independent action (Barrett).

25–40 H. develops the theme of the unreliability of popular assessment as it touches ourselves. We know when praise does not belong to us (25–9). Moreover people are fickle and deprive us of it (33–5), or even blame us unfairly (36–8). In this section the second pers. becomes indefinite. The metaphor of health is sustained (*medicandum* 40).

25–31 A paratactic concessive sent.: '*though* you would prove capable of recognizing extravagant praise for martial achievements as inappropriate to you, would you *still* welcome an exaggerated reputation for probity?'

25   tibi: dat. of agent with *pugnata*.

26   dicat: 1.1n. *uacuas* 'unoccupied' (*OLD* 11c), of ears that have nothing better to listen to, as at Ov. *Met*. 4.41, 12.56.

27–9 H. devises an encomium that could only apply to someone as important as Augustus. Tastefully oblique flattery of the ruler (as at 18.56–7) appears to be a Callimachean invention; cf. *H*. 4.165–90 for the praise of Ptolemy insinuated into the hymn to Delos. Pseudo-Acro's notion that the lines came from a panegyric by Varius must be repudiated, since the rhythm of 27 is only suitable to the looser hexameter of an epistle. (Scholiasts make it a rule to attribute lines which appear to be quotations to some known author, for instance the supposed lines of Nero's in the first satire of Persius.)

27 The indirect qu. depends on *in ambiguo* (*OLD* 2).

29   Iuppiter: for the diaeresis pause see 7.89n.

30   cum pateris 'in allowing yourself . . .' (Roby §1729). For the rest of the syntax see 5.15n. *sapiens emendatusque* echoes 20, but *emendatus*, first used here in a moral sense (cf. *mendosum* 40), suggests the successful completion of a course of improvement.

uocari, picked up by *dici* (32), marks the possible gulf between our reputation, what men say of us publicly, and the reality (cf. *esse quod audis*).

31   -ne = *nonne*, a colloquial usage that strengthens the emphasis by only seeming to ask an open question, when really an affirmative answer is expected (cf. 10.14n.).

tuo ... nomine: instrumental abl. At a census or levy of troops a man repeats his name when it is called (*OLD nomen* 21), a practice H. may be metaphorically alluding to here (whilst avoiding any technical phrase). But the meaning could be 'on your own responsibility' (*OLD* 14b), i.e. having made up your own mind that the praise is warranted, you subscribe to it.

nempe 'well, to be sure' (*OLD* 4); H. avoids the impression of hounding his reader by conceding that he too delights to have his reputation publicly acknowledged (*dici*), an unexceptionably Roman attitude. (This is the interpretation of Lambinus, endorsed by Hand IV 159. But the scholiasts, followed by some editors, took the sentence to be an imaginary objection raised by H.'s addressee.) For the enjambment see Introduction p. 24.

32 bonus et prudens = *sapiente bonoque* 20, *sapiens emendatusque* 30. *delector* takes a complementary infin. first here.

ac 'as much as' expresses similarity, though no term, e.g. *aeque*, precedes (K–S II 20, *TLL* II 1083.63–7; *OLD atque* 13c is inadequate); since the usage is found earlier only in Plautus (but rarely), it may have colloquial colour.

33–5 A warning (asyndetically pointed) that the people remove their approval either as easily as they do public office (33–4, a reference to *abrogatio*) or as a man reclaims what is rightfully his (35).

33 qui: see *cui* 1.85n.; *hoc* = *uirum bonum et prudentem dici*.

34 detulerit: fut. perf. For *fasces* see 6.53n.

indigno: to be understood also with *detrahet* ἀπὸ κοινοῦ; for the dat. see 6.54n. For the thought that popular esteem is not only fickle, but also faulty cf. *S*. 1.6.15–16 *populo, qui stultus honores | saepe dat indignis*. For *idem* see 15.37n.

35 A paratactic conditional sentence. *meum est* parodies the claim to ownership (*uindicatio*) as made in a Roman court (cf. Gaius, *Inst*. 4.5); it has no specific reference in the context, as Morris saw.

pono: 1.10n.; more polite than the second pers., but H. is using himself as an example, not suggesting biographical facts.

tristisque recedo < Lucr. 3.995 *tristisque recedit* (also describing electoral defeat); contrast 7.39, which really refers to H.

36–8 A further objection: if consistent, we should have to accept the people's bad as well as good opinion about ourselves. But their baseless charges should not affect us any more than their undeserved praise.

36 idem (= *populus*, implied in the preceding) **si** introduces a tricolon crescendo in which the crimes are of increasing gravity. The charges of *furta* and *libidines* are found together at Cic. *Dom*. 93, *Pis*. 38; both would, if proven, lead to *infamia* (39).

pudicum: sc. *me* here and as subj. of *pressisse* 'throttled' (*OLD premo* 26). As applied to a man *pudicus* meant that in sexual relations he played a man's part, not that he abstained altogether; the *impudicus* was the passive partner in homosexual acts, a typical Roman slander (cf. Catull. 16, 25, 29, 112).

37 Parricide was the worst of crimes, cf. *C*. 2.13.5–6 *parentis ... sui | fregisse ceruicem, Epod*. 3.1–2 *parentis olim siquis impia manu | senile guttur fregerit*.

contendat 'allege' (*OLD* 6).

38 mordear ... mutem 'am I to be upset ... to change ...', repudiating questions (*LS* §83, cf. 1.49–50n.); for the metaphor in *mordear* see 18.82n.

falsis: a crucial point, to be echoed in 39.

39–40 The strands of the argument are now drawn together; just as lying accusations (36–7) should not dismay, so by implication unmerited renown for goodness (30, 32) cannot satisfy.

39 infamia 'ill repute' was no trifling matter, for it imposed grave civil disabilities on the citizen (*OCD* s.v.).

40 quem ... quis: the interrogative is emphatically postponed as at 18.19 (cf. *S*. 2.3.187 *ne quis humasse uelit Aiacem ... uetas cur?*, 7.104 *obsequium uentris mihi perniciosius est cur?*).

mendosum)(*emendatus* 30; there is also a chime with *mendax* 39. *medicandum* resumes the metaphor of health, and holds out the prospect of cure.

40–62 We need then to define the *uir bonus* (T. Sinko, 'De Romano uiro bono', *Acta Acad. Cracoviensis* 36 (1903) 251–300). The first definition, offered by popular opinion (41–3), is not wrong, but, as in a Socratic dialogue, incomplete. The good man as popularly conceived is seen in his public and, above all, legal capacity; we are not, however, always on display, our failings may be revealed only in private (44–5). This is best seen at the opposite end of the social scale: a slave's attempt to establish his own goodness is after all self-interest (46–56). H. then returns to the conventionally defined 'good man' to expose his hypocrisy (57–62).

41–3 The analysis of the good man's qualities under five aspects, articulated by anaphora of *qui*, is characteristic of H. (B. on *AP* 312–16).

41 consulta patrum = *senatus consulta* avoids the technical term; understand *seruat* 'heeds' (*OLD* 4, B. on *AP* 86) ἀπὸ κοινοῦ. The advice of the senate was not a legal enactment, but was increasingly held to be binding.

leges 'laws' duly passed by the *comitia*; *iura* 'rights, privileges' in the widest sense.

42–3 quo ... iudice ... quo ... sponsore ... quo ... teste 'by whose verdict, surety, testimony'; abl. of manner. The concrete nouns have a virtually abstract sense (N–H on *C.* 1.35.22 and 2.18.32).

42 secantur 'are resolved' (*S.* 1.10.15, an Horatian, not a technical sense). The *iudex* (*OCD* s.v.) was not a magistrate, but a senator or an *eques* of good repute (i.e., not *infamis*), whose name was inscribed in the *album iudicum* (Cic. *Cluent.* 121). His civic standing entailed certain other *officia* and made him a model of acceptable behaviour, the sort appealed to by H.'s father (*S.* 1.4.123 *unum ex iudicibus selectis obiciebat*); H. himself was probably a *iudex* (*S.* 2.7.54).

43 tenentur with *res* ἀπὸ κοινοῦ has the sense 'are retained' (*OLD* 13); with *causae* the sense is 'are won' (*OLD* 16b). H., as a citizen of good standing, expected to act as *sponsor* (*S.* 2.6.23, *Ep.* 2.2.67), an *officium* basic to civic life (cf. the story of M. Lutatius Pinthia, who *sponsionem fecisset ni uir bonus esset* (Cic. *Off.* 3.77)). The closing alliteration clinches the definition.

44–5 Out of the Forum he is transparent to his family and neighbours (17.62), and what they see is ugly. The civic criterion of the good is shown to be inadequate, as usual.

44 For the pairing cf. *S.* 1.1.84–5 *non uxor saluum te uult, non filius; omnes | uicini oderunt, noti, pueri atque puellae.* The earlier satire's copious expression is here crisply compressed.

45 An allusion to the fable of the ass in the lion's skin (*S.* 2.1.64–5 *detrahere et pellem, nitidus qua quisque per ora | cederet, introrsum turpis* of Lucilius' satire; Otto §1377); for dress imagery see 1.95–6n.

turpem)(*speciosum* (a word of strong approval usually, B. on *AP* 319) has great force (2.3n.).

46–56 H. turns from a *iudex selectus* to a slave; in effect, a polar analysis: high and low, free and slave are all alike hypocrites.

46 Theft (*furtum*) and flight (*fugi*) were the commonest faults of slaves, to be declared by the owner before sale (Cic. *Off.* 3.71). The slave at first defines his merit negatively. Direct speech enlivens this section.

46–7 si ... dicat ... aio 'supposing he says ... my answer is', an ideal protasis and an unconditional apodosis, as at *AP* 438–9 *siquid recitares ... aiebat* (the verb of the protasis is usually, but not invariably, the ideal second pers. sing.; cf. Ov. *Tr.* 4.3.77–8 *ars tua, Tiphy, iacet, si non sit in aequore fluctus; | si ualeant homines, ars tua, Phoebe, iacet*; G–L §596.1). It is, however, possible that the subjunc. has been intruded into the protasis, cf. the capital MSS of Virgil at *Ecl.* 2.27 and 73 (*fastidiat* P, *fastidat* R); then *dicit* of some MSS should be read.

48 non ... coruos: a proverbial expression (Otto §447).

49 frugi: the stock word of praise for a slave, as *nequam* is of blame. His final claim to positive worth is also invalid.

renuit 'throws back his head' as a gesture of denial; though the meaning 'refuse' is attested earlier (*OLD* 1), the literal sense appears to be first found here instead of *abnuo*, probably for metrical convenience.

Sabellus i.e. H. himself; in his eyes, the Sabelli, who had dwelt near his birthplace, Venusia, preserved the stricter morality of old Italy (cf. *S.* 2.1.36 *pulsis ... Sabellis, C.* 3.6.37–41; Salmon 32, 125 n. 4).

50–6 H. accounts for his severity. The slave is like the irrational beasts, whose caution is instinctive; the truly good have a rational love of virtue, which does not reckon with penalties. However trifling his crime, the slave is still a sinner.

50–1 The sentence is analysed in the Introduction pp. 27–8.

50 accipiterque: an unusual rhythm, a single word occupies both the last feet.

51 miluus 'gurnard' scans as a dactyl.

52–3 Cf. Ben Jonson, *Epode* 87–9 'He that for love of goodness hateth ill | Is more crown-worthy still | Than he which for sin's penalty forbears.'

53 tu nihil admittes in te '*you* won't be likely to commit a crime' (*OLD* 13); for the fut. see 6.42n. *formidine* picks up *metuit* 50.

54 sit is a jussive subjunc. forming the protasis of a paratactic conditional sentence in a form popular with poets (Leo (1878) 223–4; G–L §593.4); the apodosis is in the fut. The sentence is joined to the preceding by adversative asyndeton.

fallendi 'of escaping detection' (*OLD* 6c).

miscebis 'confound' (*OLD* 11d); cf. *S.* 2.7.73–4 *tolle periclum:* | *iam uaga prosiliet frenis natura remotis* (the whole context is similar to the present).

55   nam: elliptical: the exaggerated crime just mentioned may after all not be what you have in mind, but you are still a thief if you only filch a bushel of beans. It is a question of moral disposition, not of the value of the loss. This is not the Stoic paradox that all sins are equal.

fabae 'beans', collective sing. (G–L §204 N8a, L. on *S.* 2.6.115).

56 'in my view, the loss is more tolerable (*OLD lenis¹* 6) on that account, not the crime'. *mihi,* dat. of person judging (cf. 66), rather than possessive, draws attention to the fact that morality cannot depend on opinion. A man may be able to endure a loss by theft, but the thief has still committed a crime.

pacto ... isto: the second pers. demonstrative applies here strictly to the slave, whose policy is to commit a petty theft which, if detected, is lightly punished. H. concludes that guilt is not to be measured on the slave's terms; any wrongdoing invalidates a claim to goodness. For *pacto* see 6.10n.

57–62 H. now reverts to the *uir bonus* as popularly conceived and shows that he is on the same level as the slave in his desire to avoid being detected in wrongdoing.

57   uir bonus: an ironic reversion to 40–3. H. recapitulates his definition by naming the commercial (*forum*) and legal (*tribunal*) spaces of Rome. There the standard is public, civic, external; it does not reach the private interior of the man, so *sapiens* is left out of the equation.

omne 'every' (*OLD* 5), repeated for emphasis. There was more than one *forum* in Rome, e.g., the *f. boarium* (Richardson 162–4) and the *f. holitorium* (Richardson 164–5), just as there were several places where the praetors erected platforms from which to administer justice (Richardson 401). For *spectat* see 1.2n.

58–62 Men's unspoken prayers were a moralist's commonplace from the time of Pythagoras (Smith on Tibull. 2.1.84). The 'good man's' prayer exposes his finished hypocrisy.

59   pater: an honorific title of gods and men (*OLD* 6, 5); take *cum dixit* ἀπὸ κοινοῦ. The repetition of *clare* stresses the deliberate and repeated fraud.

60   metuens = *nolens* (*TLL* VIII 905.48); this *uir bonus* is no better than the slave after all. Laverna was an Etruscan goddess of thieves; *pulchra* is cajoling.

61   da 'grant' (*OLD* 3) + complementary infin. is poetic syntax (K–S 1 681, L. on *S*. 2.3.191; cf. 1.2–3n.); .

fallere: see 54n., not 'cheat' (Rudd); a man needs a god's help less for trickery than for its concealment.

iusto sancto 'scrupulous' (*OLD* 4) go with *mihi* ἀπὸ κοινοῦ; the predicates are attracted into the dat. of the indir. obj., again poetic syntax (K–S 1 680). It is remarkable that what seems to reproduce ordinary speech is phrased so artificially (Introduction p. 23).

62   noctem ... nubem form chiasmus with the datt., *peccatis* and *fraudibus*. They express metaphorically the notion of 54 and 61. For *ōbice* cf. *ābicito* 13.7n.

63–72   Still dismantling the conventional definition of the *uir bonus* H. rules out the previous candidate for his hypocrisy, revealed in his secret prayer to the goddess of theft. His true condition is enslavement to wealth (67–8), and yet even that may be condoned as at the very least useful to others (69–72).

63   Qui 'in what respect' (*OLD qui*² 1d, cf. 6.42n.) introduces an indirect qu. dependent on *uideo* 65. H. seems to borrow a Stoic technique of argumentation on many of the occasions when he uses *qui* (Lejay p. 359; he also observed on *S*. 1.1.1 that H. commonly attaches it to a comparative). Take both *seruo* (abl. of comparison) and *sit auarus* ἀπὸ κοινοῦ.

64   The scholiast on Persius 5.111 explains that boys fixed a coin with melted lead to a paving stone and laughed at anyone who stooped to retrieve it. Their mockery of course entailed loss of self-esteem.

65   nam ... quoque: 2.51n. For enjambment with *porro* see Introduction p. 24.

66   liber: the point of comparing the conventional *uir bonus* to a slave emerges sharply. As popularly defined, he appeared as a citizen performing his duties (41–3). But at 46–56 a slavish trait was suggested. This is now developed thanks to the exposure of the *auaritia* of the hypocrite. Morally considered he is a slave, whatever his civic status. Here H. does glance at a Stoic paradox, that only the virtuous man is free; this was treated of by Cicero, *Parad*. 5 (cf. 40 *an non est omnis metus seruitus?*). This reminds us that H. is master on his humble estate (2, 10). For *mihi* see 56n.

67–72 H. now explains how the greedy hypocrite has become servile in status.

67 perdidit ... deseruit: gnomic perfects. The loss of arms was a supreme disgrace (N–H on *C.* 2.7.10), as was desertion: hence the defeat and enslavement. The metaphor of the moral life as soldiering, recalled from 1.17, was long established and especially popular among Stoics (exx. in Powell on Cic. *Sen.* 73).

locum 'post' (*OLD* 8, cf. *TLL* v 1.675.82–4). The 'post of bravery' is the front rank (cf. Sen. *Dial.* 2.19.3–4), but here *uirtutis* also has the sense of moral excellence. For *qui* see Introduction p. 24.

68 semper: a crucial qualification, emphatically placed; increase of wealth is not absolutely bad (7.71; H. took pride in it himself at *S.* 2.6.6 *si neque maiorem feci ratione mala rem*). But a pursuit of gain so unremitting as to overwhelm (*obruitur*) is slavish. The warping of a sense of proportion in any pursuit is condemned (6.15–16). *et* connects only the two verbs. For the rhythm of the end of the line see 5.6n.

69 captiuum continues the metaphor of the deserter (67), who is to be sold into slavery after capture. Morally worthless, the avaricious have some commercial value to society at large.

70 seruiet: see 6.42n. The condition is now accounted for; one who abandons the struggle to be good for gain sells himself into slavery.

sine 'let', imperative of *sino* + subjunc. (*OLD* 6b). The farmer and the merchant (71) form a polar expression ('on land and sea'), to stress the universality of the pursuit of gain. But here the farmer is imagined as being one of his own labourers.

durus 'the sturdy fellow'. For *-que* see 5.27n.

71 mercator '*as a* merchant', for slaves could trade on behalf of their masters. Sailing stopped during the winter storms, so this merchant must be very devoted to gain to risk his ship and life.

72 annonae prosit: i.e. his labour will serve to keep down the cost of our food (*OLD annona* 4).

portet: either literally of a porter or = *importet*, the simple for the compound (so Bo 388).

73–9 The question at 40 is answered at last, but unexpectedly, not with a definition but with a dramatic picture of the good and wise man in action. The scene contrasts with that of the captive and slave just described (though the notion of the constraint of the person is common to both sections). H. borrows from and freely adapts Euripides'

Bacchae, 492–8 (of which there was a Latin version by Accius); he may have used the scene because the truly good man is as hard to recognize for people generally as Dionysus was for Pentheus.

73 Vir bonus et sapiens recalls 20, for H. is not satisfied with the mere *uir bonus* as popularly defined; he offers instead his vision of the true *beatus*. The speaker in the *Bacchae* is the Lydian stranger (Dionysus in disguise); he has been apprehended on the orders of Pentheus, king of Thebes, who interrogates him. Another attraction of the myth to H. may have been that the god's Latin name was *Liber* (cf. 5.20n.).

74 perferre patique: 15.17n.

75 indignum agrees with *quid* 74.

  adimam bona: the situation is similar to that imagined at 7.39, our attitude to the loss of possessions; cf. Cic. *Parad.* 1.8 *neque ego unquam bona perdidisse dicam si quis pecus aut supellectilem amiserit.*

  nempe 'you mean, I suppose' (*OLD* 3b) is ironical because the speaker does not believe such things to be true *bona.*

76 lectos: couches could be luxurious, made of exotic woods, inlaid ivory and precious metal. For *argentum* see 6.17n. and for the enjambment with *et* Introduction p. 24.

78 ipse deus: ironical in the *Bacchae*, where the speaker is the god. (Plutarch too cited this line, *Moral.* 476B.) *uolam* (2.34n.) points to suicide; the context refers only to the loss of goods and freedom, which was not felt by Stoics to be a sufficient ground for ending one's life (Summers on Sen. *Ep.* 77).

  soluet perhaps hints at the god's nickname, *Lyaeus* 'the releaser' (Wickham on *C.* 3.21.16, cf. 5.20n.).

  opinor: in the same position in the line and, though parenthetic, at the head of its sentence at *S.* 1.3.53 (*TLL* IX 2.723.65–74).

79 sentit 'means' (*OLD* 9). *moriar*, as Lejay suggested, reinterprets the hint of the last speaker in a less forbidding light; H. is not concerned with suicide, the Stoic's ultimate proof of self-determination, but with death, sooner or later, as the end of all.

  linea 'the finishing line' of death introduces the metaphor of life as a race (cf. Cic. *Tusc.* 1.15 *calx*, *Amic.* 101); cf. the common metaphorical sense of γραμμή (LSJ II). These closing words were Erasmus' motto, as it appears on the medal by Massys.

H. addresses himself to a common dilemma. Society always sets the moral agenda, which in Rome was enshrined in the unassailable *mos maiorum*. But there could be gaps in the civic system of morality; this was specially true of antiquity when success in public life established the moral standard for all free male citizens. The moralist nevertheless had to point out that civic duties adequately performed could not be the whole story. The private life and the individual character counted for something, and had to be assessed by standards other than those considered adequate for public affairs. In order to restate this fundamental moral consideration H. places himself outside the city with its dominant (but partial) moral stance; in the country he can better take stock of the whole man. From this vantage point he warns Quinctius, who is as H. himself admits a fortunate fellow, against believing popular opinion where its judgement is either without foundation or too partial in its application. The civic code is not undermined, but shown to fall short of completeness. Nor after all is it philosophy which provides the supplementary standard. As in II H. relied upon Homer for moral guidance, so here he turns to the philosopher among poets, Euripides, for a dramatic picture of the good and wise man. He does not want a definition, but an example. The shifting arguments and tones of the letter, which Schütz deemed one of the finest examples of poetic paraenesis in antiquity, are analysed in the Introduction pp. 36–9.

Further reading: R. F. Thomas, *Lands and peoples in Roman poetry: the ethnographical tradition* (Cambridge Philological Society Supplement 7. Cambridge 1982) 8–34.

Epistle XVII

1–5 H. deprecatingly proposes to offer Scaeva advice on self-advancement. The addressee is unknown; T. P. Wiseman hesitantly identifies him with P. Paquius Scaeva (*New men in the Roman Senate* (Oxford 1971) 180). Some assume the name was chosen because of its sense 'gauche' (*OLD scaeuus* 3; cf. Celsus 8.1). But it also means a favourable omen (*OLD scaeua*[1] 2, a point forgotten by students of Lucan as well). What is more H. uses the proper name for nobody in particular at *S*. 2.1.53.

1 **Quamuis ... per te:** a polite formula, used when offering advice; cf. 18.67, *AP* 366–7 *quamuis ... per te sapis*, Longin. *Subl.* 1.3, [Q. Cic.] *Comm. Pet*.1.1 *etsi tibi omnia suppetunt*; failure to recognize the formula has led many to misconceive H.'s attitude to his addressee. For the indic. see 14.6n.

2 tandem 'please' is retained from Scaeva's implied direct question (*OLD* 1b; cf. Austin on Virg. *A.* 1.331); H. appears to be replying (for once) to an appeal for advice, which is not thrust unsought upon his addressee. For *quo pacto* see 6.9–10n.

deceat strikes the keynote; our concern is not simply access to the eminent (*OLD maior* 6), but proper behaviour in their company (23, 42). For *uti* see 12.22n.

3 docendus goes with *amiculus*; H. politely regards himself as still learning, cf. 1.27, 6.67–8. The diminutive insinuates a touch of ironic self-deprecation; Scaeva had supposedly pestered H. for advice, seeing his success in securing and maintaining friendship with the great. For the enjambment with *ut si* see Introduction p. 24.

4 caecus: the comparison, which exploits a proverb (Otto §277), continues the irony against himself. *adspice* 'consider' (*OLD* 9b); for *si* see 6.41n.

5 et 'even' (more irony). For *cures* see *personet* 1.7n.

fecisse: the perf. infin. refers to a completed action (cf. 18.59); Scaeva may want to appropriate this advice and keep it for good (Wickham on *C.* 3.4.51); others suppose it to have been chosen solely for its metrical convenience (B. on *AP* 98).

6–42 The advice is unexpectedly deferred for a discussion of the importance of choosing the right way of life. Of course, H. knows which one Scaeva proposes to follow, but the implicit warning tactfully suggests the need to know one's own mind and it prepares for the defence of H.'s own way of life later on.

6–12 If stress and strain dismay you, then a quiet life is best (6–10); but if you aim higher, you need patronage. The form of the argument, two conditional clauses linked by adversative asyndeton, is also used at *Ep.* 2.1.64–8.

6–7 Si ... si ... si: the anaphora produces a tricolon *de*crescendo and emphasizes the list of difficulties to be faced.

6 primam ... horam: in summer, about 4:30, in winter, 7:30. A client would be expected at his patron's *salutatio* at that hour (cf. 7.68, 18.34). For *in* see 2.30n.

7–8 Cf. 7.75–6n. With *puluis strepitusque* understand *laedit* ἀπὸ κοινοῦ.

8 caupona: cf. *S.* 1.5.4 *cauponibus ... malignis.* Ferentinum was a small town in Latium, in the country of the Hernici (Paget 217).

iubebo strikes a didactic note, appropriate to the role assumed at Scaeva's request; cf. *AP* 317, Virg. *G.* 3.329 and Ov. *AA* 1.51.

9–10 Though not rich or famous, one may still be happy and good. A quiet way of life is not disparaged, indeed it has its attractions. But the ambitious man must yield to the imperatives of his nature.

10 natus moriensque fefellit 'whose birth and death have passed unnoticed' (*OLD* 6c); the construction is a syntactical Grecism = λανθάνειν + participle, perhaps designed to recall the motto of the Epicureans, λάθε βιώσας. For the sentiment cf. 18.103, Ov. *Tr.* 3.4.25 *bene qui latuit bene uixit*, Eur. *IA* 16 *apud* Cic. *Tusc.* 3.57 *nec siletur illud potentissimi regis anapaestum, qui laudat senem et fortunatum esse dicit, quod inglorius sit atque ignobilis.*

11 si = *sin* (5.6n.). *tuis* forestalls a charge of selfishness. A man improved his position not just for himself but for the sake of those who depended on him (46; cf. Lucr. 3.897–8 *tuis ... praesidium*); in this spirit H. recommended Septimius in IX. Alexander the Great was supposed to have said that the advantage of a surplus was that it could be distributed among friends (Plut. *Moral.* 181E).

paulo: 6.43n. The typical qualification warns Scaeva not to overdo it. Take *ipsum* with *te* 12.

12 tractare 'treat' (*OLD* 4, cf. *S.* 2.2.85 *tractari mollius*); for *accedes* see *uises* 4.15n. *siccus* 'thirsty' (*S.* 2.2.14 *siccus, inanis*).

unctum 'a rich table', probably neuter as at *AP* 422, rather than masc.; cf. 14.21n. The metaphor forms a gliding transition to the opening sentence of the following anecdote.

13–32 An illustrative anecdote is introduced asyndetically (it is found in Diog. Laert. 2.8.68, and, with its point reversed, in Valerius Maximus, a first-century A.D. collector of moral *exempla*, 4.3 *ext.*4). It begins abruptly with direct speech; the unnamed speaker turns out to be Diogenes, founder of the Cynic sect (*OCD* s.v. Diogenes (2)). His belief that our needs are few and must be satisfied as cheaply as possible confronts the adaptability of the aspiring Aristippus, who is here presented as a model of Roman behaviour (1.18–19n.). Thanks to his adaptability he may secure an agreeable life (13–22) without forfeiting his ability to live as an ordinary citizen (23–32); but above all his aspirations are honourable to him (33–42).

13   patienter: 25n.

regibus: Aristippus was at the court of Dionysius I of Syracuse; but there are overtones of the colloquial sense (cf. 43; 7.37n.). For *uti* see 2n.

14   regibus uti: a mocking repetition (B. on *Ep.* 2.2.150).

15   notat suggests the Roman censor, who put a mark, *nota*, in the album (16.42n.) by the name of any who fell below an acceptable standard of behaviour. The vignette thus blends Greek and Roman.

utrĭus introduces an indir. qu. dependent on *doce* 16.

16   uel 'or rather' (*OLD* 3b); *iunior 'as being* the younger'.

17   namque as last word effects enjambment, cf. *S.* 1.3.36, 5.39.

18   mordacem alludes to the origin of the name Cynic from κύων 'dog', an animal which fawns upon its benefactor, barks at the niggardly, and bites the bad (Diog. Laert. 6.60).

eludebat 'used to baffle', perhaps a technical term of gladiatorial combat (cf. *elusus Ep.* 2.1.47); the tense suggests repeated encounters of the antagonists. For *ut aiunt* see 6.40n.

19   scurror 'I play the hanger-on'; the belittling verb, apparently a coinage, ironically adopts Diogenes' imagined reproach against Aristippus.

ego ipse mihi, populo tu: Aristippus acts by deliberate choice 'for his own benefit' (cf. 1.27n.); Diogenes only fawns 'for the people's sake' since they laugh at his exhibitionist antics.

hoc 'this way of mine' (*TLL* VI 2.2713.46–7). For *et* see 2.30n.

20   multo: 6.43n.

equus ... rex: a Greek proverb lies behind this formula (Diogenianus 5.31 ἵππος με φέρει, βασιλεύς με τρέφει). Since *equites* were unofficially styled *splendidus* (*OLD* 4b), a hint at that rank here would unobtrusively reinforce the image of the censor at 15. Aristippus is behaving like a good Roman of the better class.

21   officium facio '*I* do what I am bound to do as a friend'; no *ego* balances emphatic *tu*. This corrects *scurror*, as Porphyrio saw. Aristippus recommends his position by speaking in the character of a Roman gentleman.

poscis: the sequel will show (43) that the prudent courtier or client, like Aristippus here, demands nothing, whereas Cynics prided themselves on their begging (Sen. *Ben.* 2.17.1, Diog. Laert. 6.60).

uilia rerum: in this form of expression the emphasis falls upon the epithet (L. on *S.* 2.2.25 *uanis rerum*). The better-attested *uerum* gives no satisfactory connection of thought.

22   dante minor 'inferior to the giver', a predicative phrase; Diogenes deludes himself, since for all his protests he is still a dependant, however slight his needs, however humble his patrons.

fers te 'pose as' (*OLD* 34b); for the indic. see 14.6n. *nullīus* is masc., rather than neuter (> Ov. *Tr.* 1.5.15).

23   decuit: 2n. *color* 'life style' (*OLD* 5; *TLL* III 1720.24, 1721.18); *status* 'social position'; *res* 'degree of prosperity'.

24   temptantem 'making a bid for' (*OLD* 8; cf. 34); Aristippus' example validates proper aspiration and H.'s own practice (15.42–3).

fere 'as a rule', characteristic qualification. Aristippus was not radically discontented, but he did not disdain to better his position. (The word order is against taking *fere* with the preceding phrase.)

aequum 'equal to' takes the dat. (*OLD* 8b); cf. *C.* 3.29.32–3 quoted at 1.12n. The doctrine is found in Isocrates, *Dem.* 29 'be content with what you have, aim for the best'.

25   quem = Diogenes; sc. *eum* as antecedent and as direct obj. of *decebit* 26.

duplici panno: Diogenes reckoned an undergarment unnecessary since he had only to fold his ragged cloak for extra covering (Diog. Laert. 6.22); hence Cynics were called διπλοείματοι 'double-covered' (Cercidas 1.3). For clothing imagery see 1.95–6n.

patientia = καρτερία 'endurance', a Cynic virtue (cf. 13).

26   mirabor 'I'd be surprised', the fut. indicates likelihood (G–L §242 R3 N2, B. on *AP* 424).

uitae uia ... conuersa 'a change of life style' (for the idiom see 2.7n.); *uitae uia* is a long-established metaphor (B. on *AP* 404).

decebit: the pointed echo of 23 contrasts the men. Diogenes cannot adapt at all, let alone fittingly.

27–8   There were two specific stories about Aristippus' dress. Either Strato or Plato said that only Aristippus could wear either a fine wool cloak (χλανίς) or rags (Diog. Laert. 2.67, cf. Plut. *Moral.* 330c, where the woollen cloak is specified as Milesian); Dionysius bade him dance in purple (*id.* 2.78, cf. Sext. Emp. *P.* 3.209).

28   quidlibet indutus 'after donning anything at all'; the acc. with the part. is a syntactical Grecism (*NLS* §19(iii)).

uadet 'he will proceed' ('walk' is too tame), without trying to avoid the public gaze. He keeps his dignity, however garbed.

29   personam ... feret 'he will sustain (*OLD* 17) either role (*OLD* 3)'. The theatrical metaphor (cf. Diog. Laert. in 23n.) reassures us that role-playing does not compromise our essential personality: behind the mask we remain the same.

non inconcinnus: litotes. Another way of saying *decenter*, and so sustaining the keynote.

30 Mileti textam: clearly related to the observation by Plutarch (27–8n.), but transferred to Diogenes. Miletus, on the coast of Asia Minor, was famous for its fine wool (Gow on Theocr. 15.126); *Mileti* is locative.

cane ... et angui: comparative ablatives; for the form *angui* see *OLD* s.v. *orthog*. For *et* 'or' see 15.33n. Both animals, if encountered, could prove bad omens, cf. Ter. *Ph*. 706–7, but fear of snakes is, of course, proverbial (Otto §108).

peius colloquially adds force to expressions of repugnance (*OLD* 2, to which add *C*. 4.9.50, quoted at 16.29n.).

31 chlanidem: the χλανίς (27–8n.) was sometimes contrasted with the philosopher's cloak (LSJ s.v.). This rare word is the conjecture of Cruquius; it is likely to have been replaced by the more common loan-word, *chlamydem*. For *si non* in the last foot see Introduction p. 24.
32 rettuleris: fut. perf., the second pers. is indefinite. For *sine* see 16.70n.

ineptus 'misfit that he is', a term of social disapproval, applied by H. to the butts of his satire (*S*. 1.4.91, 10.79), by Cicero and Catullus to those who misconceive a situation (Fordyce on Catull. 8.1, 12.4). Its position as last word of its sentence and paragraph is forceful (at *Ep*. 2.1.270 it is the last word of the poem). The ragged Diogenes is dismissed with contempt because his values are false: a mere change of clothes amounted in his eyes to a loss of personality (cf. 1.19, 18.31–6).

33–42 A third line of defence opens asyndetically. In essence, it is not unlike the argument for moral improvement offered at 1.28–32: you can achieve something honourable, even if not the highest.

33 gerere ... ostendere: subjects of *attingit* 34. H. specifies success in arms (*OLD gero* 9), since it was on that above all that the Romans prided themselves; Aristippus' patron, Dionysius, had also extended his empire.

34 attingit: cf. *C*. 3.3.9–10 *hac arte Pollux et uagus Hercules | enisus arcis attigit igneas*; indeed, the Roman *triumphator* embodied a god-king in the course of his triumph (*OCD* s.v. Triumph).

solium Iouis = Διὸς θρόνος, a pictorial expression for 'heaven' first found in Aeschylus, *Eum*. 229, then in Theocritus, 7.93; H. may have imported it into Latin, but the phrase has a colloquial or proverbial tone, for it is found at Petron. 51 *putabat se solium Iouis tenere.* The *triumphator* offered up his crown at the temple of Jupiter on the Capitoline.

35 principibus ... uiris: the leaders of society are meant, not just generals; cf. 2, 20.23, for which this line prepares. There is a distinction in associating with the conspicuously successful, as Aristippus did (N–H on *C.* 1.1.2). Adversative asyndeton links this to the previous sentence.

non ultima: litotes.

36 cuiuis ... contingit adire: the syntax (dat. and infin.) is poetic (K–S II 240). A Greek proverb provides a fancied objection to the stand H. has just taken (Aul. Gell. 1.8.4 οὐ παντὸς ἀνδρὸς ἐς Κόρινθον ἔσθ' ὁ πλοῦς; Otto §431). A famous courtesan, Lais, lived at Corinth, where she exacted so high a price for her favours that the less wealthy were deterred, in spite of the obvious attraction. The proverb thus suggests that not everyone can succeed in associating with *principes uiri*; pleasing them requires its own *uirtus*.

37 sedit 'did nothing' (*OLD* 7); gnomic perf. (as is *timuit*).

succederet: impersonal (*OLD* 7b).

esto 'granted' (*OLD sum* 8b) concedes the point that some are too shy to improve their status. But does that bear on our opinion of those who aspire and succeed?

38 quid: 1.91n. *peruenit* 'attained his objective' (*OLD* 7, whence the mod. French *parvenir*, past part. *parvenu*) preserves the metaphor of *adire* (36).

uiriliter: emphatic; cf. Sen. *Ep.* 124.3 *contemnimus illos qui nihil uiriliter ausuri sunt doloris metu.*

atqui 'well' anticipates a doubtful answer to the question: 'suppose you aren't sure that it is a manly thing to do, yet this is the very point at issue between the opinions of Aristippus and of Diogenes'.

39 hic 'here' (*OLD hic*² 5); cf. Ter. *Hau.* 279–80 *hic sciri potuit aut nusquam alibi, Clinia,* | *quo studio uitam suam te absente exegerit.*

39–41 hĭc 'the one' (= *qui timuit*), **hīc** 'the other' (= *qui peruenit*); in prose the latter would be *ille* (*TLL* VI 2.2717.44–52, to which this example may be added).

39 horret 'shudders at' (*OLD* 5).

40 ut 'as being' (*OLD* 10).

paruis ... paruo: emphatic repetition with differing verse ictus (Bo

399); *animis* and *corpore* form a polar expression referring to the whole man. For *maius* see 10.43n.

41   subit 'shoulders' (*OLD* 2), understand *onus* ἀπὸ κοινοῦ. The prefix *per-* deliberately echoes *peruenit*.

uirtus 'resolution' and 'moral excellence' in one (1.17n.); its etymology is emphasized by *uiriliter* 38 and *uir* 42. For the sentiment see *uerba* 6.31n.

42   decus recalls 2 and 23, but *pretium* adds the notion of material reward, the issue floated at 11–12 and elaborated from 43–66. H. tacitly declines to believe that virtue is its own reward.

recte petit 'he is right to seek'; the adv. 'of judgement', which recalls *rectius* 19, carries the weight of the sentence (N–H on *C.* 1.2.22 *melius perirent*, K–S 1 795).

experiens 'enterprising'; *uir* emphatically concludes its sentence and paragraph; for the rhythm see 5.6n.

43–62   The promised advice is offered, now that the defence of self-advancement through clientship is validated. It warns against certain ploys in the pursuit of financial support (the central issue in clientship). First (43–51), avoid begging openly. Secondly (52–62), avoid indirect begging through complaints.

43   rege: 7.37n. *sua*) (*poscente* 44 (recalling 21); asking for help is bad form, since it implies either that the patron fails to keep an eye on the client's needs or that the client is rapacious.

44   plus poscente 'more than the one who asks', cf. N–H on *C.* 2.12.27.

ferent 'will get' (*OLD* 34 'esp. as a consequence of one's action').

distat 'it makes a difference' + indir. qu. (*OLD* 4). This sentence picks up the opening question, *quo pacto deceat* (2), esp. with *pudenter* 'in moderation' (*AP* 51 *sumpta pudenter*), which restates the theme of propriety (cf. 7.37 *uerecundum* and *C.* 2.18.12–13 *nec ... largiora flagito*).

45   hoc ... hic refer less to *plus ferent*, self-enrichment (cf. 11–12), than to the way we achieve it; anaphora emphasizes the point. For the gender of the pronouns see 1.6on. *caput* and *fons* are commonly paired (Cic. *Planc.* 18, *De orat.* 1.42, 195, *Tusc.* 4.83).

erat 'was all along' 'always has been', a common use of the imperf. extending to the present and beyond (G–L §233 N3; cf. 4.6n.).

46–7   A lively vignette of a client impudently intruding his financial woes upon his patron's notice. The client is plainly the head of his family (there is no reference to a living father) and needy. The publication of his woes will prove ill-judged.

46 indotata: an undowered girl might prove *illocabilis* or at any rate unlikely to secure a husband of her own status; hence the friends or patrons of her male relatives would supply or supplement the dowry (Cic. *Off.* 2.56; Treggiari 342–4). The diminutive *paupercula* imports a wheedling tone.

47 pascere: complementary infin. with *firmus*; once again speech is given a poetic cast (Introduction p. 23).

48 uictum date: the plur. suggests that H. parodies a beggar's plea to bypassers. *succinit* 'chimes in'.

49 et mihi refers back to the plea in 46, rather than to *date*; he too has a sister, etc.

diuiduo ... munere 'as a divided gift'; this common abl. is hard to define: it may be felt as predicative (cf. *TLL* VIII 1667.23–33), or modal (cf. Fordyce on Catull. 101.8, 65.19), or even in apposition to the idea of the sentence (cf. H–S 429). For *findetur* see *eris* 1.58n.

50 tacitus: understand adverbially. This seems to be a glance at a fable.

51 inuidiaeque: for the rhythm see 16.50n.

52–7 The client is his patron's *comes* (7.76n.). Complaints of discomfort and loss are ruses for securing recompense and depress his relations with his patron to the level of a whore's with her clients. What is worse, his motive is transparent.

52 comes ... ductus: take together, *aut* simply connects the names of the towns.

Surrentum ... amoenum: the attribute attached directly to the town name is poetic (K–S I 479; Introduction p. 22, cf. *C.* 1.35.1 *gratum ... Antium*). Brundisium (mod. Brindisi) was the port of embarkation for Greece; Surrentum (mod. Sorrento) is still attractive to travellers. The implication of the latter is that the companion is on holiday with his friend (always a test of character), and should be the more agreeable.

53 qui: a remarkable hyperbaton, but the proximity of the rel. pron. to its verb mitigates the dislocation.

salebras: and yet the *uia Appia* was the best maintained of the Italian highways. The companion invents grievances.

54 cistam effractam ... subducta uiatica: for the idiom see 2.7n.

plorat 'bewails', a strong verb (B. on *Ep*. 2.1.9), suggests an exaggerated reaction to loss; its trans. use begins with H. (poetic syntax).

55   refert 'reproduces' (*OLD* 16).

acumina 'tricks' (*OLD* 4, an unusual sense) strictly speaking applies only to 54 (cf. 3.25n.). For the wiles of the mistress see Smith on Tibull. 2.4.13–20, p. 435; cf. Ov. *AA* 1.431–2 *quid, cum mendaci damno maestissima plorat, | elapsusque caua fingitur aure lapis?*

56   periscelidem 'anklet', a Greek loan word first found here in Latin; for the dat. *sibi* see 15.33–4n.

uti gives the result of trick; for *mox* see 1.12n.

57   fides 'credence' (*OLD* 12). *ueris* belongs with *damnis* ἀπὸ κοινοῦ.

58–62 A warning example closes the section of advice and the epistle.

58   nec ... 'for the once-deceived cannot be bothered'; the conjunction is emphatic and seems to have causal force (K–S II 42).

59   fracto crure: 2.64n. The ruse is that he has fallen and apparently broken his leg. Anyone engaged in lifting him, he (or perhaps an accomplice) robs. Quintilian knows a proverb along the same lines: *homini nequam lapso et ut adleuaretur roganti 'tollat te qui non nouit'* (*IO* 6.3.98).

planum 'impostor', a Greek loan-word, first found in fourth-century comedy; it was perhaps introduced into Latin in the mimes of Laberius (Aul. Gell. 16.7.10, a discussion of his use of the word) and is then found at Cic. *Clu.* 72 (where it is intended to sting) and in Petronius. It seems therefore to have a colloquial ring.

licet 'although' (*OLD* 4), virtually a conjunction governing *manet* (15.19n.) and *dicat. illi* is dat. of disadvantage.

plurima: an epithet with the collective sing. *lacrima* (60) is poetic style (K–S I 70).

60   Osirim: an Egyptian deity; either the impostor is himself foreign, or he uses the unusual oath to impress.

61   ludo 'deceive' (*OLD* 9b). The appeal for help in an emergency ought to impose a duty on the citizens (B. on *AP* 460), but the neighbourhood knows better (cf. 16.44).

62   rauca: adverbial (no adverbial form was in use). The alliteration crisply concludes the poem.

In VII H. had focussed on the ideal treatment of a client by his patron. In this and the following complementary letter he turns to the more pressing matter of the client's disposition towards support. Here he clears the ground of objections to clientship as such, showing that it is not an obligation upon anyone, but that, once undertaken, it must be done properly (*deceat*). Hence his concern is not only to justify clientship but to instil a sound attitude to the honourable pursuit of the goal. In effect, he is defending his own way of life, and that of the young men (like Celsus and Septimius) in whom he took an interest.

None the less, H.'s tone has often been misapprehended and the theme of the letter has been found unattractive. The critical responses are discussed at some length in the essay referred to at Introduction p. 5 n. 18.

Epistle XVIII

1–20 H. feels sure that Lollius, the addressee of II, will steer a middle course in his friendships between servility (an unlikely failing in him) and truculence. These faults are illustrated, fawning from 10–14, intransigence from 15–20. The extremes are noticed by Aristotle too in *EN* 4.6.1–4, 1126B6–11; he characteristically recommends the mean (9n.), which is not exactly friendship, but like it. H., however, is clearly concerned with true friendship.

1 Si bene te noui 'knowing you as I do', a formula expressing assurance, not uncertainty (Sen. *Ep.* 16.7, 18.3). *metues* 'will disdain' (N–H on *C.* 2.2.7, cf. 5.2 *times*, 16.60nn.).

liberrime 'most candid' announces the theme of the epistle, true independence in friendship; alliteration draws attention to the phrase. Candour is a virtue (cf. *liber amicus S.* 1.4.132) but it can chafe (*libertas* 8), if exercised imprudently.

2 scurrantis: 15.28n.; the unusual verb, found at 17.19, forges a programmatic link between the letters. Words of opposed sense enclose the line.

professus amicum 'after claiming to be a friend'; omission of the reflexive pronoun (*te*), usually expressed in prose (*OLD profiteor* 4b, with refl. pron. and pred.) produces poetic syntax and so brings *professus* into line with the Virgilian construction *confessa deam* (Austin on *A.* 2.591). There is no need to take *amicum* in an abstract sense, 'friendship' (16.42–3n.).

3–4 The comparison to a whore forges another link with XVII (55), though its tone here is different. The thrice-repeated prefix *dis-* emphasizes H.'s point.

3   merētrici: the lengthened second syllable is unusual (cf. 17.55), found elsewhere only in Bibaculus, fr. 4 Morel. The caesuras in the line, weak in the second foot and strong in the fourth with none in the third, are remarkable; cf. 19.14n.

3–4   erit ... distabit: gnomic futures (B. on *AP* 68).

4   discolor refers to *color* 'way of life' (17.23n.), but a powdered complexion (*OLD color* 3; Jocelyn on Enn. *Medea exul*, p. 361 n. 2), or different-coloured clothing are also possible.

   infido scurrae: cf. 15.28–30; the dat. with *disto* is a syntactical Grecism originating with H. (cf. *C*. 4.9.29–30 *paulum sepultae distat inertiae | celata uirtus*; G–L §346 N6).

5   diuersum governs the dat. *uitio*, another syntactical Grecism related to that in 4. For the pattern of repetition in *uitio uitium* cf. *AP* 133 *nec uerbo uerbum curabis reddere, C*. 3.1.9 *est ut uiro uir latius ordinet*, Cic. *Off.* 3.26 *errat in eo quod ullum aut corporis aut fortunae uitium uitiis animi grauius existimat* and Sen. *Ep.* 13.12 *uitio uitium repelle*.

   prope 'almost' (*OLD* 6e), because it is more likely to offend.

6   asperitas agrestis 'uncouth truculence', cf. *Ep.* 2.1.129 and Cic. *De orat.* 3.44 *rusticam asperitatem*, the bluntness of country speakers, as opposed to *urbanitas*. Müller believed that the caesura after the third trochee enhanced the sense of the booby's awkwardness.

   inconcinna: a link to 17.29 (cf. its opposite, *ineptus* 17.32); adaptability in relationships is a virtue, cf. *S*. 1.3.50–1 *concinnus amicis | postulat ut uideatur. grauis* 'oppressive' (*OLD* 10).

7   se commendat 'seeks to recommend itself'; the present may indicate attempt or endeavour (G–L §227 N2). The notion is ironical, since the truculent man would scorn the action. But he mistakes external appearance for spiritual reality, the accidents of independence for its essence.

   tonsa cute: close-cropped hair betokened parsimony (Theophr. *Char.* 10.14), or philosophical interests (Pers. 3.53, Juv. 2.15), but here perhaps suggests indifference to good grooming (cf. 1.94), as the unclean teeth confirm.

8   dum: 2.21n.; for *uera uirtus* see 1.17n.

9   uirtus: adversative asyndeton introduces the definition of true moral excellence; the repetition of the leading term, called anadiplosis, is similar to *C.* 3.3.59–62 *rebusque fidentes auitae | tecta uelint reparare Troiae. | Troiae renascens alite lugubri | fortuna tristi clade iterabitur* (Bo 402).

medium 'a mean' (*OLD* 6, *TLL* VIII 592.60); the gen. *uitiorum* is crisper than the usual construction, *inter uitia*. The definition is owed to Aristotle and his school, the Peripatetics: *EN* 2.6.15, 1106B36–1107A2 'virtue is a state of character concerned with choice, lying in a mean relative to us ... it is a mean between two vices, one an excess, the other a defect'. H. found the doctrine congenial (N–H on *auream mediocritatem C.* 2.10.5).

utrimque reductum < Lucr. 5.839 *utrimque remotum*.

10–14 The *scurra* described; he illustrates a deficiency of independence of character by toadying for a meal.

10 obsequium 'compliance' is not *per se* a bad thing, so the qualification *plus aequo* (2.29n.) justifies the criticism.

10–11 imi ... lecti 'on the lowest couch', descriptive gen. In a Roman dining room three banks of couches were arranged round the table (the fourth side was left free for the service of the meal). Each bank, and indeed each couch, had a name and function. The host took the lowest, where he might be flanked by his parasites (like Nasidienus in *S.* 2.8.40). They provided amusement for the company, but also made the host look good, e.g., by praising the meal as in *S.* 2.8.25–6.

derisor = the *scurra*, since it is always amusing to run down others (*deridere*; so Rudd on *AP* 433, cf. *S.* 1.4.87–8 *unus amet quauis aspergere cunctos | praeter eum qui praebet aquam*), but the word is puzzling, since the allusion to mockery seems scarcely in point here: Shackleton Bailey 101).

11 nutum: the nod betokens domination, the *scurra* has forfeited his independence, cf. *Ep.* 2.2.6 *uerna ministeriis ad nutus aptus eriles*, Lucr. 4.1122 *adde quod alterius sub nutu degitur aetas* (of the lover in thrall to his mistress), Cic. *Parad.* 39 *quem nutum locupletis orbi senis non obseruat?*

12 cadentia 'as they pass unregarded'. The usual interpretation 'falling from his lips; as they are spoken' (Fairclough, *OLD* 14) assumes that here *cado = excido* (*OLD* 5). When words 'fall', *cado*, unlike the English, implies that they fail to make an effect (so Dacier here, Postgate on Prop. 1.16.34 and the other examples gathered in *OLD* 14, with which cf. 7c; it is under that head, not 14, that Prop. 1.5.14 belongs; again, Postgate *ad loc.* sees the point). The parasite retrieves (*tollit*) the 'fading' words from oblivion by repeating them; like the plagiarist (3.15–20) or the literary imitator (19.19–20), he thus advertises his inferiority.

13–14   Neither a boy in school nor the 'second fiddle' have any self-determination, both ape their superiors.

13   saeuo 'severe' (B. on *Ep.* 2.2.21–2), dat. of agent with *dictata* (for which see 1.55n.).

14   tractare 'perform' (*OLD* 7b); the second actor in the mime, a salacious form of dramatic entertainment, usually did no more than support the *archimimus*, perhaps by parodying his or her movements and utterances (W. Beare, *The Roman stage*[3] (London 1964) 153).

15–20   The crosspatch displayed in action balances the previous description; his behaviour is more developed and enlivened with direct speech because his is the fault to which Lollius might lean.

15   de lana ... caprina: he comes to blows over unimportant terminology: is a goat covered in wool or hair or fur?

16   nugis, dat. with *propugnat*, is poetic syntax; prose repeats the prefix as a prep. to govern the noun (*OLD* 1b and c).

16–18   scilicet 'if you please', highly ironical (*OLD* 4b).

   ut non sit ... ut non ... elatrem: subjunc. in protesting/indignant questions introduced by *ut* (1.49n., L. on *S.* 2.5.18, *LS* §82, *OLD ut* 44). The repetition of *ut non* and its emphatic placement underscore the speaker's exasperation.

17   uere quod placet 'my real opinion'.

18   elatrem, a coinage = ἐξυλακτέω, suggests the 'bark' of the Cynic (17.18n.).

   pretium ... sordet: lit. 'another lifetime as reward is not good enough' (*OLD sordeo* 2), i.e. if he has to suppress his opinion; *pretium* is in apposition to *aetas*. The sentiment derives from Homer, *Il.* 9.444–7, where the aged Phoenix says that he would not leave Achilles even if Zeus were to make him young again.

19   ambigitur quid enim 'well, what is at issue?' *enim* introduces a remark qualifying the previous speaker's words; cf. Pl. *Am.* 694 *quid enim censes?* (*OLD* 1). *ambigo* has legal overtones (B. on *Ep.* 2.1.55), suggesting something weighty; it virtually governs the following indir. questions.

   Castor ... an Dolichus: they may have been actors or gladiators or even *grammatici* (*RE* v 1251.12–40). For *Dolichus* 'Longfellow', an unusual Greek name, some MSS offer *Docilis*, a known Roman one, and so a less preferable reading.

sciat 'is more skilled' (*OLD* 8).

20 Minuci ... uia ... Appi: for the expression see 6.26n. The Minucian Way ran across Samnium, its actual route still something of a mystery (Salmon 21 n. 3); presumably it was shorter than, but inferior to the Appian Way.

21–36 Asyndeton marks a shift in the argument. H. moves on to the moral character of the inferior friend as seen by his superior (they are revealed to be men of unequal resources), especially in the use of money. Once again, it is a matter of keeping to the middle way, and not 'getting above oneself'.

21–4 Quem: sc. *eum* as antecedent and as obj. of *odit et horret* 25.

21 damnosa: i.e. incurring *damnum* 'waste of money' (*Ep*. 2.1.107 *damnosa libido*); *praeceps* 'risking sudden disaster' (*OLD* 4b, cf. *C*. 2.1.6 *periculosae ... aleae*).

nudat)(*uestit* 22; take with *uenus* ἀπὸ κοινοῦ.

22 gloria 'vainglory' (*C*. 1.18.15 *et tollens uacuum plus nimio gloria uerticem*); *uires* 'financial resources' (*OLD* 26b).

uestit et unguit: perfumes bespoke luxury (B. on *Ep*. 2.2.183), as did some clothing, the dangers of which H. elaborates at 30–6.

23 argenti: 2.44n. *sitis* is a common metaphor for *cupiditas* (N–H on *C*. 2.2.14); *importuna* 'unremitting' (*OLD* 2c) goes ἀπὸ κοινοῦ with *fames*.

24 quem: supply *tenet* ἀπὸ κοινοῦ. *diues amicus* at last introduces patronage into the argument.

25 decem uitiis instructior 'though himself better equipped by some ten vices'; the number is indefinite, suggesting a lot (*OLD decem* 1b, B. on *AP* 294); the abl. indicates measure of difference. For *odit* see 7.20n.

26 regit 'puts him right' (*OLD* 9); cf. *rex* 7.37n.

pia mater: cf. *custodia matrum* 1.21; the client's behaviour is not his own choice.

27 sapere: 15.45n.; understand *eum* as subject. What lies behind this notion is the view that some friendships are founded upon dissimilarity of tastes (Cic. *Amic*. 82).

28 prope: characteristic qualification; *stultitia* is never good, but its degree of harmfulness depends on circumstances. That clients foolishly ape their patrons is an observation H. applied to himself at *S.* 2.3.312–13 *an quodcumque facit Maecenas, te quoque uerum est* [= *decet*], | *tanto dissimilem et tanto certare minorem?*, and drove home with the fable of the exploding frog.

contendere 'argue' against this advice (so Torrentius; *OLD* 8e); not 'rival me', for that command comes later (30–1).

29 stultitiam 'imprudence'; *patiuntur* 'allow' (*OLD* 8).

30 sanum: 1.8n.; the thought is similar to 7.44. The choice of clothing as an index of temperament recalls 1.95–6; cf. Juv. 3.177–81 on extravagant dress among the less well-to-do.

31–6 After the lively warning, the practice of P. Volumnius Eutrapelus is adduced. He was a noted social figure of Cicero's day (*RE* IXA 878–9), whose *cognomen* means 'witty' in Greek. His view (nastier than Philippus' in VII) was that you should give a man enough rope with which to hang himself.

31 cuicumque: sc. *ei* as antecedent, and as indir. obj. of *dabat* 32.

32 uestimenta explains the patron's reference to the *toga* at 30, but also recalls XVII, in which Aristippus, unlike Diogenes, did not fear a change of character and aspirations with a change of clothing. On the other hand, all clothing advertisements in our own day endorse Eutrapelus' view that we are what we wear.

beatus 'the lucky fellow', sarcastic as at *AP* 425; *iam* 'all too soon' (N–H on *C.* 1.4.16), is also the emphatic last word at *AP* 468.

33–6 sumet, dormiet, postponet, pascet, erit, aget: historic futures, used by a narrator who adopts the point of view of someone in the past who foresees the result of his own action (H–S 310); it is not appropriate therefore to enclose the sentence in quotation marks.

33 consilia et spes: see 1.23n.; take *noua* ἀπὸ κοινοῦ.

34 dormiet in lucem: i.e. to the neglect of other duties, e.g. the *salutatio*, or even moral improvement (2.35n.).

35 officium: not specified, but again the sort of duties a citizen might be expected to perform, e.g., appearance in court.

nummos alienos sidesteps the technical term for borrowed money, *aes alienum*; *pascet* 'will feed' (*OLD* 4d), viz. by paying interest. For *ad imum* 'in the end' (*OLD* 5) see Introduction p. 18.

36 Thraex: a gladiator armed like a Thracian (*OLD* 2); for the loss of independence involved see 1.1–19n. *mercede* 'for pay' is abl. of price (*OLD* 1b, G–L §404); for *caballum* see 7.88n.

37–8 H. offers specific advice: don't pry, don't blab. The drift of the following admonitions urges against egotism, as Wickham noted.

neque ... -que '*just as* not ... *so* also'; for this unusual form of paratactic comparison see K–S II 48. For the postponed connective *neque* see Introduction p. 21; in contrast with the general observation there, it is remarkable that *neque* is not postponed anywhere in *S*. (see Klingner's index, p. 337).

37 tu: 2.63n.; Lollius is addressed, because H.'s advice now begins. For this fut. (and those which follow) see *uises* 4.15n.

illius brings Lollius' own superior friend down to the footlights; though he is never named, his position is indicated later. (Bentley reckoned he was Tiberius.)

38 commissum: probably a noun as at 70. The ability of a friend to keep a secret weighed with the Romans (N–H on *C*. 1.18.16); likewise the dangers of *garrulitas* were stressed (Bömer on Ov. *Met*. 2.688). Maecenas was especially prized by Augustus for his *taciturnitas* but had slipped from favour in 23 B.C. through inability to keep to himself what he knew of the danger hanging over his unsatisfactory brother-in-law, Murena (he told his wife! (Suet. *Aug*. 66.3)).

et ... tortus 'even (*OLD* 6) *though* ... '; cf. *AP* 434–6 *reges dicuntur multis urgere culillis | et torquere mero, quem perspexisse laborent | an sit amicitia dignus*. For the second *et* see 15.33n. and for the dangers of *ira* see 2.59–63.

39–66 Again, one's favoured pursuits must take a back seat if they clash with those of the superior friend; poetry and exercise provide concrete instances. Simo's praise of his son in Terence's *Andria* 63–6 is in point: *cum quibus erat quomque una îs sese dedere, | eorum obsequi studiis, aduersus nemini, | numquam praeponens se illis; ita ut facillume | sine inuidia laudem inuenias et amicos pares*.

39–40 Nec ... nec: 11.11–16n.

40 uenari: chosen *exempli gratia*, and then developed with reference to Lollius. Only at 67 are the *praecepta* resumed.

poemata panges: alliteration lends a sarcastic note (B. on *AP* 416).

41–4 Appealing to Lollius' learning, H. drives home the message with the story of Zethus and Amphion from Euripides' *Antiope*. The play was famous (and the Latin version was still known to Cicero, *De orat.* 2.155 *Zethus ille Pacuuianus*); Callicles had used it to justify his own depreciation of philosophy in Plato's *Gorgias* 484c–486c. H. reasserts the place of poetry, but makes it clear that it is the more civilized brother, Amphion, who yields.

41   gratia: 3.32n. For *atque* see 7.83n.

42   dissiluit: livelier than *dissoluitur*. *seuero* is dat. of agent with *suspecta*.

43   cessisse: proverbial wisdom endorses Amphion: *non uincitur, sed uincit qui cedit suis* Publ. Syr. 398 Meyer (= N22) (Otto §1897). *putatur* shows that the story is traditional, a myth (N–H on *C.* 1.7.23 *fertur*).

44   tu: emphatic (2.63n.); *cede* echoes *cessisse* 43, so that the sentence forms a paratactic comparison. The bond of brotherhood is to be the model for the relationship between friends, cf. 3.35.

potentis amici develops *illius* 37; H. refers to Maecenas as his *potentem amicum* at *C.* 2.18.12.

45   lenibus: either the friend's character is well known to H. or he has in mind an ideally courteous relationship. For *imperiis* cf. 9.12 *iussa*.

46   Aeoliis: i.e., made from flax grown at Cumae, an Aeolian colony, cf. Gratt. *Cyn.* 34–6 *optima Cinyphiae, ne quid cunctere, paludes | lina dabunt; bonus Aeolia de ualle Sibyllae | fetus.* This is a conjecture of Ulitius (J. Vliet); the MSS offer *Aetolis*, which can only be explained as a purely decorative allusion to the Calydonian boar hunt in Aetolia. *Aeoliis* would also appeal to Lollius' learnedness.

47   inhumanae ... Camenae 'the unsociable Muse', an oxymoron, since she was the patron of *humanitas* 'civilization'; but it was well known that the poet shuns company in order to compose (*Ep.* 2.2.77, quoted on p. 132 above). *senium* 'gloom' (*OLD* 3).

48 The shared meal is at the heart of the relationship; hence the double meaning of *conuictus*, both 'living on intimate terms' and 'banquet'. *pariter* hints at an equal partnership.

laboribus alludes to a charge Zethus brought against Amphion, laziness (Zethus needed a helping hand to kill Dirce and deal with Lycus).

49   Romanis ... uiris: an appeal to *honestum*, patriotism and masculinity.

sollemne ... opus 'customary task'; syntactically a so-called acc.

in apposition to the idea of the sentence (*NLS* §15, H–S 429; cf. *C*. 3.20.7 *grande certamen*, *AP* 65 *regis opus*). H. stretches a point, since the elaborate style of hunting which he describes was imported from Greece only in the second century (J. Aymard, *Essai sur les chasses romaines* (Paris 1951) 54–7).

49–50   famae uitaeque et membris: an appeal to *utile*. A Roman's chief moral concerns centred upon his *res*, *fama* and *uita* (or *salus*); cf. *S*. 1.2.33 *ne nummi pereant aut puga aut denique fama*, 4.118 *uitam famamque tueri* | *incolumem*, 2.7.67 *committes rem omnem et uitam et cum corpore famam*; Tac. *Ann*. 6.51.5 *egregium uita famaque* (*TLL* VI 1.213.3). All were to be kept in sound condition and, in the case of property and reputation, if possible improved. Hunting maintains Lollius' reputation and health because it is a manly tradition; unlike the pleasure-loving he has not succumbed to *mollitia*. The huntsman is up betimes and leaves his bedfellow (*C*. 1.1.26, Ov. *Rem*. 199–200).

50   praesertim, only found in H.'s hexameters (L. on *S*. 1.6.51), suits the argumentative style of Lucretius and of Virgil's *Georgics*. For *et* see Introduction p. 24.

51   cursu: the Romans did not hunt on horseback, but ran after the hounds. *superare* goes ἀπὸ κοινοῦ with *uiribus aprum*.

52   Construe: *adde quod non est qui uirilia arma speciosius tractet*. Advice now shades into praise of Lollius as an embodiment of the ideal Roman youth. The hunt and athletics prepare him for service to the state under arms.

adde ... quod: an argumentative transition, found predominantly in poetry (McKeown on Ov. *Am*. 1.14.13).

uirilia, emphatic by position, echoes *uiris* 49.

53   tractet 'can handle'; for the subjunc. see 1.7n. *clamore* is abl. of attendant circumstance (K–S 1 410); *coronae* refers to the circle of spectators (*OLD* 4a).

54   proelia ... campestria: contests in the Campus Martius, cf. *AP* 379 *campestribus ... armis* and *C*. 1.8.1–12 (the lovelorn Sybaris has given up exercise).

54–7   Lollius' greatest claim to fame is his service in Spain under Augustus, who is thus obliquely praised (56–7, cf. 16.25–9). The conclusion of the Cantabrian war and the conquest of Spain were celebrated late in 25 B.C. with the closure of the gates of the temple of Janus, but Agrippa still had work to do there (12.26n.). As Heinze noted, reference to Spain in the West and Parthia in the East forms a polar expression which embraces the whole world.

54–5 saeuam militiam puer < *acri militia puer C.* 3.2.2; cf. 2.68n. A Roman became liable to military service from his seventeenth year. For *et* see 12.8n.

56 templis: dat. (6.54n.). For the *signa* see 12.27n.

57 nunc: 20 B.C. *abest* 'is wanting' (*OLD* 13). *Italis ... armis* (dat.) = *Romano imperio* and provides a concluding patriotic flourish, cf. *C.* 4.15.13–14 *Italae ... uires*, *Ep*. 2.1.2 *res Italas*.

  adiudicat 'assigns', a legal term often used of land disputes.

58–66 Just as Lollius was encouraged to fall in with his superior friend's amusement, so he is assured of compliance (*consentire*) on the friend's part.

58 ne ... et: 1.13 and 6.22nn. *te retrahas* 'back away' (*OLD* 5b), i.e., from hunting in particular, from compliance in general.

  inexcusabilis: a coinage = ἀναπολογήτως.

59–60 quamuis ... curas excuses what follows, esp. *nugaris*; even at play, Lollius observes decorum. For the indic. *curas* see 14.6n. The musical metaphor in *extra numerum ... modumque*, applied to propriety of behaviour as at *Ep*. 2.2.144 (quoted at 1.10n.), may allude to Amphion (E. K. Borthwick, *C.Q.* 17 (1967) 46 n. 1). For *fecisse* see 17.5n.

60 Lollius unbends, but only now and then (*interdum*) and discreetly retired from public view (*rure*).

  nugaris: at *S.* 2.1.71–4 H. described how Lucilius, Laelius and Scipio amused themselves *ubi se a uulgo et scaena in secreta remorant*; clearly it was important not to lay aside one's *grauitas* except in private, among family or friends. Cicero notes that these frolics took place in the country (*De orat.* 2.22 *Laelium ... cum Scipione solitum rusticari eosque incredibiliter repuerascere esse solitos, cum rus ex urbe tamquam e uinculis euolauissent*).

  rure: 14.5n.; *paterno* stresses Lollius' respectability.

61–4 Lollius and his brother re-enact the battle of Actium of 31 B.C. Mimic sea battles were popular entertainments in Rome (*OCD* s.v. naumachia), but something much smaller is here intended.

61 Actia: the poetic form for *Actiaca*.

62–4 te duce ... aduersarius ... alterutrum: H. tactfully declines to say who drew the short straw and played Antony.

62 pueros 'slaves' (*OLD* 5). For *refertur* see 17.55n.

hostili more: *mos* is usually qualified by a gen., but the cretic scansion of *hostium* is inconvenient in hexameters, hence the use of the epithet.

63 Hadria: poetic for *Hadriaticum* (*mare*) (Fordyce on Catull. 36.15). *donec* in last position produces enjambment as at *S.* 2.1.73; the subjunc. *coronet* (64) suggests that this is a real fight and its issue is in doubt (contrast 16.23n.).

64 uelox: the goddess Victory was depicted with wings.

65 consentire picks up the notion of compliance broached at 39 (contrast *inconcinna* 6); *studiis* echoes *studia* 39 to conclude the section with ring composition. For the rhythm of the line-end see 5.6n.

66 utroque ... pollice: a proverbial expression (Plin. *NH* 28.25); at gladiatorial games the audience indicated its verdict for or against a defeated contestant by some gesture of the thumb, to which this is the first extant reference (and the only reference to the use of both thumbs); it is uncertain how exactly the thumb was held, despite the common English phrase 'thumbs down' (Courtney on Juv. 3.36).

67–85 H. resumes his *praecepta* after the digression of 41–66.

67 ut: expresses H.'s intention (*OLD* 29, cf. 1.13n.). *quid* 'at all' is acc. of respect.

   tu: highly emphatic, and suggesting that he does not.

68 de quoque = *et de quo*, referring to the superior friend; Lollius is not to gossip about him.

68–9 uideto 'take care' (*OLD* 17) **... fugito** (10.32n.)**:** the fut. imperatives strike a didactic note as in Virg. *G.* 2.408–13 *fodito ... cremato ... referto ... metito* (*NLS* §126 n1).

69 percontatorem: a nonce-word derived from Pl. *Men.* 933 (Gratwick *ad loc.*). At *S.* 2.6.51–8 H. describes how he was bombarded with enquiries from those who assumed that his acquaintance with the great provided him with privileged information.

70 fideliter: take with *retinent*.

71 emissum '*if* ... '. The sentiment is proverbial; cf. *AP* 390 *nescit uox missa reuerti* (Otto §1871). *uolat* suggests the 'winged words' of Homer; *irreuocabile* is predicative.

72–5 The only advice on sexual conduct in the whole collection: prudence, not continence.

72 Non in an emphatic position and to be taken with *ulla* (also emphatic thanks to assonance) negates the optative subjunc. *ulceret*, a gentler form of prohibition than *ne* + jussive (Tibull. 2.1.9 *non audeat ulla*, K–S I 192).

iecur: to the ancients more than to us a seat of the emotions (N–H on *C.* 1.13.4); H. is practically alone in referring love to the liver (*C.* 1.25.15 *iecur ulcerosum*, 4.1.12).

ulceret 'make sore'; blunt diction trivializes erotic sentiment. The lover speaks of his heart or breast as 'wounded' (cf. Ov. *AA* 1.21 *Amor ... mea uulneret arcu | pectora*); H. sees nothing more than a sore liver. So far as the 'sore of love' is concerned, he agrees with the satirical attack of Lucretius on the passion at 4.1068, *ulcus enim uiuescit et inueterascit alendo*.

73   uenerandi hints that such an attraction is after all bad form.

74   pulchri caraeue: understand both ἀπὸ κοινοῦ since each slave is pretty and so dear.

75   beet: an archaic verb, found in comedy, but then only in H. in the classical period (N–H on *C.* 2.3.7, B. on *Ep.* 2.2.121). The wealthy friend 'enriches' his lovelorn dependant at small cost, an oxymoron; the prudent dependant holds out for a more valuable gift than a pretty slave (which, after all, will age). In the case of a Lollius, this ought to be a magistracy or other significant post.

incommodus may be either conditional or adverbial; as Müller notes, it should also be taken with the preceding ἀπὸ κοινοῦ.

76–85   Advice on personal recommendations follows (cf. H.'s practice in IX and XII). The basic notion is as old as Theognis 963–4 'never praise a man until you have accurate knowledge of his temper, character and disposition'. Cicero, for example, had difficulties with Trebatius, whom he had recommended to Caesar (*Fam.* 7.17).

78   quondam 'at times' (*OLD* 3) goes with *fallimur* ἀπὸ κοινοῦ. For *tradimus* see 9.3n.; for *ergo* 6.46n.

79   deceptus '*if* ... '; *omitte* = *noli* (*OLD* 5b).

80   ut: final.

crimina: cf. *S.* 1.4.82 *qui non defendit* [*absentem amicum*] *alio culpante*; backbiters attempt to bring down favourites and advance themselves.

81   For the enjambment with *qui* see Introduction p. 24; for the rhythm 5.6n.

82   dente Theonino: the allusion is no longer known, though the tooth of envy or malice is a common metaphor (*OLD* 1b, Otto §507). *ecquid* has the nuance of *nonne* (K–S I 657).

83   post paulo: 6.43n.

84   res agitur 'interest (*OLD* 13) is at stake (*OLD* 39b)'.

proximus ardet < Virg. *A*. 2.312 *proximus ardet Vcalegon* (with Austin's careful note). As Professor Kenney points out, Ucalegon's name could be derived from οὐκ ἀλέγων 'taking no care', and that gives the astute reader a fuller understanding of *neglecta*.

85   neglecta '*if* ... '; this is a variant of the proverb (Otto §666) that smoke will lead to fire if not dealt with.

86–95   H. now offers advice on keeping the friendship alive and reflects that attendance on the great is never easy, for it demands vigilance.

86   The sentiment parodies Pindar, fr. 110 S–M 'a sweet thing is war to the inexperienced, the experienced man dreads its approach greatly at heart' (the opening phrase became proverbial, Otto §616).

inexpertis: for the dat. see 2.30n.

cultura   'cultivation of someone's acquaintance' (*OLD* 4, a novel and unique sense), sc. *est*; *potentis amici* recalls 44.

87   expertus metuet: adversative asyndeton.

dum ... est: i.e. 'while it's plain sailing' (Smith on Tibull. 1.5.76 *in liquida nat tibi linter aqua*; Otto §962).

88   hoc age: 6.31n.; i.e. concentrate on the business in hand, don't be complacent.

mutata ... aura 'a change in the wind' (for the idiom see 2.7n.).

89–93   A crisp list of four character types covers two lines, then a fifth (the boon companion) spreads out over another two (after pruning 91–2). The hinted advice to be adaptable reverts to the notion of harmony (39–40) and the proverbial fondness of like for like (5.25–6n.); cf. an Attic drinking-song, *scol*. 19 'rave with me when I'm raving, be sensible when I am', the symposiast's traditional appeal for good fellowship. To be sure it could be overdone, cf. Cicero on Catiline, *Cael*. 13 *uersare suam naturam et regere ad tempus atque huc et illuc torquere ac flectere, cum tristibus seuere, cum remissis iucunde, cum senibus grauiter, cum iuuentute comiter, cum facinerosis audaciter, cum libidinosis luxuriose uiuere*.

89   oderunt: 7.20n.

91–2   The textual difficulties of the transmitted lines are notorious; Pottier's elegant excision is here accepted, though accounting for the interpolation is not easy (Jachmann 403–14; R. J. Tarrant in J. N. Grant (ed.), *Editing Greek and Latin texts* (New York 1989) 132).

92   quamuis in the sixth foot effects enjambment.

93 formidare: perhaps still colloquial, but contemporary prose favoured *reformidare* (Ruckdeschel 27).

tepores 'fevers'; wine is 'heating' (*S*. 2.8.38 *feruida ... uina*, *C*. 2.1.19 *ardentis Falerni*).

94 supercilio: abl.

nubem: for the common metaphor see Nisbet on Cic. *Pis*. 20 *nube-culam* and Wilamowitz on Eur. *HF* 1140.

94–5 H. warns that one's unexceptionable qualities may be misinterpreted. It was a commonplace that virtues could be taken for vices (Henderson on Ov. *Rem*. 315–30, Pinotti on Ov. *Rem*. 323–4).

plerumque 'as a rule' (*OLD* 2), a down to earth word, rare in poetry outside Lucretius (Axelson 106).

95 occupat 'assumes' (*OLD* 5), unintentionally of course.

obscuri 'secretive' (*OLD* 7b); *acerbi* 'uncongenial, morose' (*OLD* 8); understand *occupat speciem* ἀπὸ κοινοῦ.

96–103 The advice refocusses now on Lollius' moral disposition, not on his relationship to his friend.

96 Inter cuncta refers to all the activities, esp. physical, that have been discussed hitherto. H. now turns to the things of the mind and spirit. They are kept till last as being most important, and ease the transition to the close, which concentrates on H. himself.

leges et percontabere: cf. Cic. 2 *Acad*. 1.2 *partim in percontando a peritis, partim in rebus gestis legendis* (how Lucullus became a successful general); for the tense see *uises* 4.15n.

doctos: take ἀπὸ κοινοῦ with both verbs. Its sense is unspecific, and points generally to the cultivated and well-read, not necessarily to the philosophical (though they are not excluded either). Some assume here as at 7.12 *leget* that only philosophers and their texts are meant. But this is advice to the same young man to whom Homer was commended as a moral guide superior to philosophers; who was encouraged to call for his book (2.35); a young man who composes poetry himself (40). His preferred reading becomes obvious. H.'s advice moreover is not typical of the philosophically committed; cf. the Stoics M. Aurelius 2.2 'put away your books', 2.3 'away with the thirst for books' and Seneca, *Ep*. 106.12 *paucis satis est ad mentem bonam uti litteris*.

97–103 A list of the sort of issues to which Lollius should be seeking answers for his own good.

97 qua ratione = *quomodo* as at *S*. 2.5.10 (B. on *Ep*. 2.2.96); *ratio* is not 'system'. *leniter* 'moderately' (*OLD* 5).

98, 99   num introduces indir. questions in which the verbs (to be taken ἀπὸ κοινοῦ) may be original deliberatives, i.e. *agitet* 'is to harass' (*NLS* §182(2)). (It is, however, attractive to read here either *ne ... ne* with Bentley and Madvig or *ne ... neu* with Müller.)

98   semper inops: take together (2.56n.), cf. Claud. *In Ruf*. 1.200 *semper inops, quicumque cupit*.

99   pauor 'anxiety' (*OLD* 2; 6.10n.); understand *rerum mediocriter utilium* ἀπὸ κοινοῦ.

mediocriter: things that are not the highest good, e.g., material goods, were called by the Stoics 'indifferent', cf. Cic. *Fin*. 3.53 *quod sit indifferens cum aestimatione mediocri*.

100   paret: from *păro*. For *-ne* see 6.12n. The issue, hitherto neglected by H., was the theme of Plato's *Meno* and *Protagoras* (which Cicero translated); cf. Sen. *Dial*. 8.4.2 *natura an ars bonos uiros faciat*.

101   quid te tibi reddat amicum 'what renders (*OLD* 17) you a friend to yourself'; cf. 3.29n., *S*. 1.2.20 *quam sibi non sit amicus*, 2.2.97 *te tibi iniquum* (*TLL* 1 1903.78–1904.4). The notion was much discussed, and has a proverbial aspect too ('charity begins at home'). Aristotle reckoned that the true 'friend to himself' is not selfish, but wants what is truly best – justice, temperance and honour (not wealth and power) – both for himself and for his friends (*EN* 9.8, 1168A28); reason, not passion, is his guide (1168B30, 1169A17–18). Plato concluded his *Republic* by saying that we pursue justice with wisdom that we may be friends to ourselves and to the gods (10.621C). The notion became widely diffused, cf. Sen. *Ep*. 6.7 for Hecato of Rhodes (K. Gantar, *A.Ant.Hung*. 12 (1964) 129–35).

102   pure 'absolutely' (*OLD* 6), a crucial qualification. For *tranquillet* cf. Cic. *Tusc*. 4.10 *tranquillitatem, id est placidam quietamque constantiam*.

102–3   Three alternatives are offered in a tricolon crescendo, a device to influence the reader's decision.

102   honos 'public office' is a *praemium uirtutis iudicio studioque ciuium delatum* (Cic. *Brut*. 281); but the citizens sometimes erred (Cic. *Pis*. 1 *obrepisti ad honores errore hominum*), and virtue had to endure *repulsa*. So ambition cannot calm absolutely. The archaic form in *-ōs* is adopted as at *AP* 69 *metri gratia*.

dulce lucellum: the epithet and diminutive ironically present the point of view of the acquisitive (cf. *S*. 2.3.95–6 *pulchris | diuitiis*). Public office and wealth might be avoided because of the toil they cause (1.42–4).

103   et does not add a new idea, but a clarification (12.8n.). For *fallentis* see 17.10n.

semita 'side-path' (not a *uia* 'highway' (17.26n.)) suggests retirement; Juvenal picked up the phrase, 10.363–4. This alternative, clearly the preferred choice, and perhaps reminiscent of the one made by Ulysses for a quiet life (cf. Plat. *Resp.* 10.620c), points to H.'s own circumstances and paves the way to the personal conclusion.

104–12 H. has opted for the course described in 103, and pushes the argument forward to show (by citing his own view) that the essential things are within our power. The moral overtones of the section are discussed by J. Bramble, *Persius and the programmatic satire* (Cambridge 1974) 62–3.

104   Me is so placed often in the *Odes* to introduce a personal close (e.g., 1.1.29, 31.15), esp. where there is a contrast between H. and his addressee (e.g., 2.17.27; see N–H on *C.* 2.16.37).

reficit (cf. 14.1) suggests a medicinal cure (*Ep.* 2.2.136–7 *opibus curisque refectus|expulit ... morbum*).

gelidus Digentia riuus: the interlaced apposition is highly artificial (Thomas on Virg. *G.* 2.146–7 *maxima taurus|uictima*). For the cold cf. 16.13.

105   quem Mandela bibit: an epic phrase elevates the suburban locality (N–H on *C.* 2.20.20 *Rhodanique potor*); the village is now Bardella, the stream Licenza. H. delights to introduce these local names into his verse (e.g., *Lucretilis C.* 1.17.1, *Vstica ibid.* 11, *Varia* 14.3), and the care he here expends on their description testifies their value to him.

rugosus frigore pagus imaginatively evokes the compound epithet + noun phrases used by Homer to describe towns and countries in the catalogues of *Il.* 2. *pagus* 'community' is distinct from a *uicus* (*OCD* s.vv.).

106 The eloquent conclusion is approached solemnly through the notion of prayer, itself a matter of philosophic debate (N–H on *C.* 1.31, pp. 347–8). H., however, knows what to pray for, and what to manage for himself.

amice: the appeal heightens the grave intimacy of tone (Virgil uses this vocative but twice in the whole *Aeneid*, when Deiphobus and Aeneas address one another, 6.507, 509).

107–10 The prayer conforms to an old type which gives thanks for blessings received and asks, not for more, but for secure enjoyment of them (Fraenkel 138 n. 4).

107 **et** is preferable to *ut* (which = *dummodo*, a conditional-restrictive use (*OLD* 31)), since it produces a choicer parataxis, favoured in poetry, e.g., Virg. *Ecl.* 3.104 *dic quibus in terris ... et eris mihi magnus Apollo* (G–L §475 N2, Nägelsbach 798).

mihi uiuam (fut.) sounds the independence theme; cf. Ov. *Tr.* 3.4.4 *uiue tibi*, Sen. *Dial.* 10.4.2 *aliquando se uicturum sibi* (the wish of Augustus), *Ep.* 48.2 *alteri uiuas oportet, si uis tibi uiuere*, 55.4–5 and the Ambrosian life of Pindar, βούλομαι ... ἐμαυτῶι ζῆν, οὐκ ἄλλωι 'I want to live for myself, not for someone else' (the poet had been asked why he was not going to live in the court of a Sicilian tyrant, as Simonides had done). This is not selfishness, but modesty.

108 **quod superest aeui:** a common phrase (Lucr. 3.904, Prop. 3.17.19, Ov. *F.* 6.416), here the internal obj. of *uiuam*. The monosyllable *di* is emphatically placed.

109 **bona:** take with *copia*, both ἀπὸ κοινοῦ. The need for books is characteristic (96, 2.35, 7.12, *S.* 2.6.61 *ueterum libris*), and points to a commonplace in prayers, that the gifts of the mind should be an object of aspiration. (At *S.* 2.3.11–12 H.'s vacation reading-matter is listed: Plato, Menander, Eupolis, Archilochus (they suit a writer of satires and epodes); from 11 we know that Homer is now his staple.)

prouisae 'supplied in advance' (*OLD* 5); bodily needs must be seen to also.

in annum 'to last the year' (Fairclough, *OLD* 23b). As Lambinus noted, H. does not look beyond the very near future; *annos* would give an entirely different sense.

110 **neu:** 11.23n. *fluitem*, metrically handier in hexameters than *fluctuo*, had been endowed with the same metaphorical sense at *S.* 2.3.269. *spe* is causal abl. with *pendulus* 'wavering' (*OLD* 4), which is predicative.

horae: see *OLD* 5b 'with ref. to the ... transient nature of time'.

111 **sed:** H. revokes the final part of the prayer; material goods depend on the gods, curtailing our hopes is up to us.

quae: it was perhaps ignorance of the fact that *oro* may govern two objects that prompted the variant *qui* (which may also be, as Wilkins suggested, a false assimilation to *Iouis*). *ponit* 'provides' (*OLD* 5).

112 **det ... det:** anaphora stresses that these are the matters over which the gods have control. Adversative asyndeton then introduces what H. reckons he must manage for himself; cf. Sen. *Ep*. 41.1 *facis rem optimam ... si ... perseueras ire ad bonam mentem, quam stultum est optare, cum possis a te impetrare.* For *aequum ... animum* see 11.30n.

mi ... ipse: emphatic as at 1.27. The elision of the long monosyllable into a short vowel is exceptional in this collection. The tense of *parabo* hints that the process is incomplete.

H.'s advice on the use of the great continues from the previous letter but from an unexpected angle. H. now looks at the issue from the point of view of the prosperous and well-connected, who none the less need the help of a superior friend for further advancement. The dangers here are subtler, since men like the addressee are less inclined to compliance (which, if anything, they expect to exact from their many inferiors).

The warning H. offers could well have been heeded by the poet Gray when making the Grand Tour with Horace Walpole. The prime minister's son undertook all expenses; he sought pleasure in company. Gray, however, pined for study and the improving side of tourism. His subordinate position galled, and he would not enter fully into his benefactor's pursuits (though Walpole tried somewhat to realize Gray's own). In the event, there was a terrible breach, not healed for some four years.

Further reading: R. L. Hunter, 'Horace on friendship and free speech', *Hermes* 113 (1985) 480–90.

Epistle XIX

1–20 H. addresses Maecenas, his ideal critic, on what appears at first to be a discussion of the literary value of *ars*, represented by 'water drinkers', and *ingenium*, extolled by 'wine drinkers'. Bacchus and the arch-poets of Greece and of Rome are cited as proof that drink and song go together (5–8). H. sides with them and alleges that he has set the tone among his contemporaries (8–11). From 10 on a broader theme, self-reliance, gradually emerges. Further objects of imitation are offered (one moral and Roman, Cato, the other literary and Greek, Timagenes), on a yet more satirical note. A general observation concludes (12–17). The theme of independence is at last clearly enunciated and dominates henceforth (19–20).

1 prisco: cf. *S*. 1.4.1–2 *Eupolis atque Cratinus Aristophanesque poetae | atque alii quorum comoedia prisca uirorum est*. In Cratinus' *Wine jar*, produced in 423 B.C., the poet as character spoke what became a famous line: 'no water-drinker can produce anything clever' (*Poetae comici Graeci* (edd. Kassel–Austin) 203); it became a proverb in Greek, cf. Nicaenetus *AP* 13.29 = *HE* 2711–16 (H. may have known that poem too (Otto §139)). What is more, the play, perhaps his last, was composed in self-defence; Cratinus answered the abusive charges of the young Aristophanes in the *Knights* of 424 B.C. Thus the links between H. and Cratinus are more numerous than they at first sight appear; the opening sentence contains more than one clue to the drift of the poem, which will be less concerned with inebriation than with independence and self-reliance in the face of criticism.

docte gives the ground of his appeal: Maecenas has the learning to appreciate what H. is up to (cf. *C*. 3.8.5 *docte sermones utriusque linguae*).

2 diu: take with *uiuere* ἀπὸ κοινοῦ; cf. *C*. 1.32.1–3 *siquid ... lusimus tecum* [the lyre], *quod et hunc in annum | uiuat et plures*, 4.9.10–12 *spirat adhuc amor | uiuuntque commissi calores | Aeoliae fidibus puellae* (where *adhuc* goes ἀπὸ κοινοῦ with *uiuunt*; for *uiuere* of poetry see N–H on *C*. 2.2.5).

3 aquae potoribus: dat. of agent; the phrase = ὑδροπότης (cf. 1.76n.). For the thin-blooded mannerisms of 'water-drinking' poets cf. Antipater of Thessalonica *AP* 11.20 = *GP* 185–90. (There is as yet no evidence what stand, if any, Callimachus took on this issue; see N. B. Crowther, *Mnem*. 32 (1979) 1–11, esp. 5.)

ut 'ever since' (*OLD* 27). For *male* 'not quite' see 3.31n.; it is commonly used to negate *sanus* (Pease on Virg. *A*. 4.8 with addendum). *sanos* hints at the notion that the higher genres of poetry at any rate (e.g., lyric) were the product of *insania*, cf. *C*. 3.4.5–6 *amabilis | insania*, *AP* 296–7 *excludit sanos Helicone poetas | Democritus*, 455 *uesanum ... poetam*.

4 adscripsit 'enrolled' (*OLD* 3, cf. B. on *Ep*. 2.2.78 *cliens*). The Roman god Liber assumed Bacchus' role as inspirer of poets, a largely Hellenistic notion (N–H II p.316). Satyrs were Greek goat-men often found as attendants of Bacchus; fauns, Italian spirits of the wild wood, were their equivalent but in addition represent early song (Enn. *Ann*. 207 Sk.). The mixture of Greek and Roman divinities in this composite picture is another clue to the development of the epistle.

5   uina (5.4n.) is internal acc. with *oluerunt* 'smelled of'. For *dulces ...
Camenae* cf. *C.* 1.26.9 *Piplea dulcis*, Virg. *G.* 2.475 *dulces ... Musae, Catal.*
5.12 *dulces Camenae*.

6   laudibus ... uini: cf. *Certamen Homeri et Hesiodi* 80–94, where
Homer, replying to Hesiod's challenge to name what was best for
mortal hearts, recited *Od.* 9.6–11, the description of a feast. (Virgil
never uses the gen. sing. of *uinum*, preferring *Bacchi* or some other
phrase; H. sees no harm in it.) *uinosus* is predicate, giving the nature of
the charge; the argument was employed by the historian Timaeus (cf.
Polyb. 12.24).

7   pater is not only reverential (16.59n.), it also suggests Ennius'
originality within an imitative tradition. He claimed to have suffered
from gout, an ailment often associated with indulgence (*Sat.* 64 *nun-*
quam poetor nisi si podager).

7–8   ad arma ... dicenda 'to sing of (1.1n.) combat', for the idiom
see *NLS* §206. The theme of Ennius' master work, *Annales*, was the
second Punic war (218–202 B.C.).

8   prosiluit: the poet performs the action he describes (3.14n.);
dicenda, coming last, undeceives.

puteal ... Libonis: a stone well-head in the Forum, decorated
in relief with citharae between which swing garlands of laurel (an
appropriate decoration for H.'s water-drinking poets). It was also the
gathering-place of money-lenders and orators, thirsty from their
pleading (Richardson 322–2).

9   mandabo ... adimam: the fut. parodies the style of the magis-
trate (B. on *AP* 235). *siccis* 'sober' (*OLD* 7).

cantare: either complementary infin. with *adimam* (K–S 1 681) or a
substantive, 'singing', serving as dir. obj. (7.27n.). For the dat. *seueris*
with *adimam* see 6.54n.

10   edixi evokes the magistrate's *edictum* (*OCD* s.v.), whereby he
stated the principles on which he proposed to govern. This tone suits
the didactic poet too; cf. *S.* 2.2.51 *siquis nunc mergos suauis edixerit assos*,
Virg. *G.* 3.295 *edico*, 300 *iubeo*. Unobtrusively H. ranges himself among
the leaders.

cessauere 'have (not) been slow to' governs complementary infini-
tives, *certare* and *putere*; poetic syntax (K–S 1 670).

11 For the form of the line cf. *AP* 269 *nocturna uersate manu, uersate*
diurna and for the adverbial use of the adjectives see 6.20n.

mero: instrumental abl., cf. *C*. 4.1.31 *nec certare iuuat mero*.

putere, stronger than *oluerunt* (5), introduces a note of censure that will prevail. Such poets after their previous night's carouse do not actually produce poems, only a stink of stale drink.

12–14 The misguided imitator, having chosen a first-rate model, errs in aping only the externals of expression or dress, cf. Cic. *De orat*. 2.91 *nihil est facilius quam amictum imitari alicuius aut statum aut motum*. It is not clear which Cato is meant, but, given his moral authority, the younger seems more likely; he became a proverbial type of Roman excellence (Otto §358) and he did have such a follower in M. Favonius (Dio 38.7.1).

pede nudo: philosophers traditionally went unshod, as did the younger Cato (Plut. *Cat. min*. 6). Dr M. B. Trapp observes that Socrates set the fashion among his followers, e.g., Aristodemus (Plat. *Symp*. 173B, Aristoph. *Nub*. 102).

13 exiguae: a flowing toga suggested luxury and effeminacy; for clothing imagery see 1.95–6n.

textore 'with the help of a weaver of ...'; the abl. is instrumental (cf. 1.94n. *tonsore*) since the weaver is not so much the agent as the means employed by someone else for his own ends.

14 -ne = *num* (10.14n., Summers on Sen. *Ep*. 11.7); *repraesentet* 'revive' (*OLD* 6). The caesuras are similar to those at 18.3; but here as at *Ep*. 2.1.147 *libertasque recurrentes accepta per annos* the suffixes -*ne* and -*que* may have been felt to be separable, producing a strong caesura in the second foot (Waltz 202–3, cf. Introduction pp. 14–15).

Catonis: the repetition focusses on the real person, not the eccentricities of his behaviour. Roger Ascham tells a similar story in *The scholemaster* (ed. J. E. B. Mayor, London 1863) 180: 'one here in England did follow Syr Tho. More: who, being most unlike unto him in wit and learnyng, nevertheless in wearing his gown awrye upon the one shoulder, as Syr Tho. More was wont to do, would needs be counted like unto him'.

15 rupit 'destroyed' (*OLD* 8). Though Timagenes was a notorious rhetor in early Augustan Rome (M. Sordi, *A.N.R.W*. II 30.1.775–97; *RE* VIA 1063–71), it is now impossible to be sure which of his traits may have proved his rival's undoing. His wit (*urbanitas*) verged on the saucy (*dicacitas*) – he was prepared to mock the imperial family; Iarbitas (now unknown) perhaps went a step too far. *aemula* here takes obj. gen.

16   dum ... haberi: the thought is presented analytically (Introduction p. 28): he aims and strives to be seen as witty and eloquent. For *dum* see 2.21n., for the infin. 1.2–3n., for the nom. 5.15n.

17   uitiis: abl. of respect with *imitabile*. This alludes to one of art's eternal truths, restated in our own century by Henry James, writing to Hugh Walpole about Russian novelists (*Henry James Letters* IV (ed. L. Edel, London 1984) 619): 'we see how great a vice is their lack of composition, their defiance of economy and architecture, directly they are emulated and imitated; *then*, as subjects of emulation, models, they quite give themselves away'. Others have warned that defects (moral and literary) attract the mindless imitator more strongly than virtues; cf. *S.* 2.2.52 *praui docilis Romana iuuentus*, Cic. *Or.* 171, Sen. *Ep.* 114.17 *haec uitia unus aliquis inducit, sub quo tunc eloquentia est, ceteri imitantur, et alter alteri tradit* (exx. then given from contemporary imitators of Sallust), Quint. *IO* 10.1.25 *summi enim sunt, homines tamen: acciditque his, qui quidquid apud illos reperietur dicendi legem putant, ut deteriora imitentur (id enim est facilius) ac se abunde similes putent, si uitia magnorum consequantur,* Juv. 14.40–1 *dociles imitandis | turpibus ac prauis omnes sumus.*

18   casu: his pallor is accidental, unintended and meaningless; hence the folly of the imitator of external qualities. *poetae* (10) is the subj. of *biberent*.

 exsangue: the effect of the drink is ascribed to its chief ingredient.

19   o imitatores: hiatus after the interjection is common (G–L §720.2). H.'s main concern is now clearly announced.

 seruum pecus: both emphatic)(*libera* 21, *dux* 23 (applied to H. as literary model) and *ingenuis* 34. The themes of independence and self-reliance in the life of letters, touched on at 3.15–20, are now developed.

20   bilem suggests anger; not used in higher genres (N–H on *C.* 1.13.4), it is emphatic thanks both to enjambment and to the isolation of the spondee in the first foot.

21–34 Literary imitation has taken centre-stage, apparently to its discredit. But, since it was the universally agreed path to be trodden by writers in antiquity, H. must clarify his position. Disapproving of both excessive reliance on a model and the aping of its defects, he links his own practice to the sounder imitative procedures of his own models. He begins, asyndetically and obliquely, by boasting of his innovations (21–4), but then identifies his model (24–5). To answer a charge of imitating (26–7), he cites the equally imitative practice of Sappho and of Alcaeus, who in his turn (32) proves to be another of H.'s models. He concludes with reference back to his innovations and to his audience. (He has perforce to leave his *Sermones* alone, since all he claimed to add to the Lucilian tradition was a superior artistry; he was not otherwise an innovator.)

21 Libera)(*seruum* 19, strikes the keynote; it is reformulated by *uacuum, princeps* and *ingenuis* 34.

per uacuum)(*aliena* 22: legal terminology for land *sine possessore*. Poets often speak metaphorically of their originality as treading virgin soil, cf. Lucr. 1.925–6 *auia Pieridum peragro loca, nullius ante* | *trita solo*. For poetic footsteps cf. *Ep.* 2.2.80 *contracta sequi uestigia uatum, AP* 286 *uestigia Graeca*; H. borrowed the image from the famous prologue to Callimachus' *Aetia* 1, fr. 1.26 Pf. ἑτέρων [= *aliena*] ἴχνια.

princeps: cf. *C.* 3.30.13 (24n.) of his introducing lyric to Italy.

22–3 qui … examen: a *sententia* enunciates the self-reliance theme. *fido* belongs (apart from the pres. part.) exclusively to high poetry (see *fidos* 5.24n.); for the fut. (and *reget*) see 2.34n.

dux '*as* leader', predicative. *examen* is an appropriate metaphor since poets are often likened to bees, cf. 44, *C.* 4.2.27–8 *ego apis Matinae* | *more modoque*.

23–5 H. refers first to his *Epodes*, poems of scathing attack, modelled on those of Archilochus of Paros, but with significant alterations, a point H. will make much of.

23 Parios … iambos: 3.13n. The metres of Archilochus' poems were not exclusively iambic, but the word came to be used of any lampoon, even in hendecasyllables (Fordyce on Catull. 36.5 *iambos*; *Epod.* 14.7 *inceptos … iambos, Ep.* 2.2.59 *hic delectatur iambis*).

24 ostendi 'introduced' (*OLD* 6b); cf. *S.* 2.8.51–2 *ego primus …* | *monstraui* (a smug gourmet, cf. B. on *AP* 74).

Latio sounds a patriotic note, cf. 32; H.'s poetic activity widens the empire of Latin literature, adding new provinces from the Greek world, cf. *C.*1.32.3–4 *Latinum … carmen*, 3.30.13–14 *Aeolium carmen ad Italos* | *deduxisse modos*.

animos 'spirit' both in the general sense, 'disposition', and with particular reference to Archilochus' 'angry temperament'. This, along with the metre, H. admits he owes.

secutus: cf. *S.* 1.4.6 *hinc omnis pendet Lucilius, hosce secutus* (the old comedy of Athens), 2.1.34 *sequor hunc* (H.'s debt to Lucilius).

25 res 'subject matter' (cf. 29, B. on *Ep.* 2.1.168). H. distanced himself, however, from his model and made something individual of his own poetry of attack. The traditional view is that Lycambes promised his daughter, Neobule, in marriage to Archilochus, but revoked the offer; for this the poet so savagely attacked them that they committed suicide (30–1); this may, however, be a misunderstanding of a literary fiction (so M. L. West, *Studies in Greek elegy and iambus* (Berlin and New York 1974) 25–8). At any rate the themes of his poetry were censured (Plut. *Moral*. 45B, Quint. *IO* 10.1.60) and Pindar reckoned his misfortunes were owed to his violence (*Pyth*. 2.54–6). H. shares the feeling and declines to imitate what appears faulty, the *res*.

agentia = *agitantia* 'harrying' (*OLD* 15).

26 ne: 1.13n. H. anticipates a belittling of his achievement and even a charge of inconsistency for reviling imitators without showing sufficient independence himself.

ideo: only here in H. (cf. 1.10n.), but not uncommon in Lucr., as might be expected. *breuioribus* 'scantier' or perhaps 'shorter-lived'.

27 timui: 5.2n. *mutare* 'change completely'; the same sense in a passage of literary history is found at *S*. 1.4.7 *mutatis tantum pedibus numerisque* (Préaux); H. concedes this point of dependence upon his model.

modos 'rhythms' with which supply *carminis* ἀπὸ κοινοῦ.

carminis artem: the formal aspect of the poetry.

28–9 Sappho and Alcaeus, seventh-century lyric poets from Lesbos, are H.'s role models; they too retained Archilochus' metres, yet in such a way as to continue poetic tradition whilst preserving their independence.

28 'Masterly Sappho regulates (12.16n.) her poetry with the metre (*OLD pes* 11b) of Archilochus.' H. defends himself on the ground that his relation to Archilochus is exactly the same as Sappho's and Alcaeus'; their sole area of dependence is the metre: *numeros, modos, pede*. There can be no question of any change in the metrical form, since that is the point at issue: *timui mutare | modos*. Fraenkel, however, took the verb to mean 'moderates' and insisted that *Archilochi musam* belong together, a more regular word order which none the less produces an unconvincing interpretation (341–6; against him see N–H on *C*. 1.35.6). To moderate is to change and changing the model in respect of his metre would destroy the coherence of H.'s argument, as Lejay noted. The gen. *Archilochi* is thus separated from the word it must depend on, but since the context focusses not upon metre in general, but specifically on the metre of Archilochus, ambiguity is out of the question (for similar dislocations see H–S 692).

H. has a view of Archilochus that was probably widespread, though it is now only found most fully stated in late metricians, e.g., Marius Victorinus. Archilochus was deemed the father of all lyric thanks to his metrical diversity, which inspired imitation, rivalry and the production of yet more verse patterns by his successors: *adeo fecundus uarietate carminum et singularis artificii in excogitandis nouis metris hic auctor est ut et ceteris uatibus imitationis suae in componendis metris obseruantiam parem studiosa aemulatione praestiterit. nam plerique sequentis aeui his informati metrorum figurationibus et quibusdam aliis auctore Archilocho uarias numerorum species et ipsi commenti posteris tradiderunt* (*GLK* VI 141, 143).

mascula refers to Sappho's success as a poet, a man's calling before her (cf. Lady Winchilsea, *The Introduction* 10–11 'Alas! a woman that attempts the pen | Such an intruder on the rights of men'); her 'masculine' interest in women may also be hinted at (*C*. 2.13.24–5 *Aeoliis fidibus querentem | Sappho puellis de popularibus*). In addition H., refining upon the view of lyric metres mentioned above, may have believed that Sappho, while in essence faithful to the verse patterns of Archilochus, added to them on occasion the 'heroic' (hence *mascula*) dactyls of Homer (cf. the discussion by the metrician Bassus in *GLK* VI 258 and by Terentianus 2539–50). He cannot of course be referring to her purely dactylic poetry, nor to those of her verses that were thought to be derivations of the pure dactyl (cf. Terentianus 2148–80).

29 Supply *Archilochi pede* with *temperat* ἀπὸ κοινοῦ.

ordine dispar 'different in arrangement' too (*dispositio*, οἰκονομία) of the different subject matter (25); cf. *AP* 40–1 *cui lecta potenter erit res, | nec facundia deseret hunc nec lucidus ordo*. Since Archilochus' organization of his poems could be faulted (e.g., by Longin. *Subl*. 33.5), Alcaeus did well to avoid imitating a defect in his artistry.

30–1 develop the notion of Archilochus' *res*.

31 socerum = Lycambes (25n.). For *oblinat* see *possim* 1.12n. *atris* 'spiteful' (*OLD* 11).

31 sponsae = Neobule (25n.), dat. of disadvantage; *famoso* 'defamatory', see L. on *S*. 2.1.68 *famosis ... uersibus*; *nectit* 'causes ... to be woven' (1.100n.).

32 hunc = Alcaeus, the lyrist specially favoured by H. because of the active part he played in civic life, cf. *C*. 1.32, 2.13.24–8. No one had

imitated him at Rome before H., hence *non ... ore*. (Sappho was more
noted for her love poetry, and H. knew his limitations.)

32-3 Latinus ... fidicen: cf. *Latio* 24, 3.12 and *C*. 4.3.23 *Romanae
fidicen lyrae*; the basic difference from his models is the use of the Latin
language; herein lies the core of H.'s originality, his greatest service to
his fellow citizens and the chief source of his pride (see *Ep*. 2.2.121
quoted in Introduction p. 19 n. 71).

33 uulgaui: cf. *C*. 4.9.3-4 *non ante uulgatas per artes|uerba loquor socianda
chordis*.

   immemorata: a coinage = ἀμνημόνευτος; cf. *C*. 3.1.2-3 *non prius |
audita. ferentem* 'bringing' (*OLD* 26c).

34 ingenuis marks H.'s ideal reader off from the 'servile' herd of
imitators; it goes with *manibus* ἀπὸ κοινοῦ. The whole line shows that
this reader 'gets to grips with' the text personally, without the services
of an anagnostes, who was a slave (so Obbar). The line forms a gliding
transition to H.'s preferred readership; cf. *S*. 1.10.81-7, where, as here,
he showed a marked preference for the leaders of society as well as
artistic kindred spirits.

35-49 Discussion is brought to a close with another aspect of the
independence of H.'s literary life, his refusal to stoop to courting favour
and his unwillingness to answer the charge of false modesty (41-9).

35 Scire uelis urbanely introduces an argumentative point (B. on
Ep. 2.1.35). Some readers, not necessarily different from the *imitatores*
19, but surely not those of 34, hypocritically run down (perhaps as
unoriginal) the poems they admire in private (cf. N–H on *C*. 2.20.4
inuidiaque maior). Their behaviour recalls that of the supposed *uir bonus*
at 16.40-5.

   opuscula 'poor little productions', the diminutive is self-
depreciatory.

36 premat 'disparages' (*OLD* 23), connected by adversative asyndeton to the preceding clause. *iniquus* is probably adverbial, though
inique was available; on the other hand, H. may wish to suggest that
such a person is constitutionally biased.

37-40 H. canvasses neither the herd nor the experts. The sentence is
articulated by the anaphora of *non ego* (cf. *C*. 2.20.5-7, quoted at Introduction pp. 6-7) and bound into a unit by the electoral metaphor.

37 uentosae: their fickleness makes courting the vulgar a waste of
time (cf. *C*. 1.1.7 *mobilium turba Quiritium*, 3.2.20 *arbitrio popularis aurae*).

suffragia: cf. *Ep*. 2.2.103 (quoted at 1.6n.). The poet becomes metaphorically a candidate for election to office, buying support (Introduction pp. 28–30).

38 impensis cenarum 'expenditure on meals'; for the gen. see *TLL* VII 1.551.60. Meals and clothing were typical presents given to secure votes, cf. Sall. *Iug*. 4.3, Cic. *Mur*. 77, *Off*. 2.58.

tritae, i.e. not new, suggests that securing the people's favour is hardly difficult; *munere uestis* = Catull. 69.3.

39 nobilium 'great', cf. *C*. 1.29.13 *nobilis Panaeti* (J. Ebert, *W.Jbb*. 7 (1981) 149–51). Some, however take it ironically, but this blurs the focus, which the anaphora and the shared metaphor direct upon only the common people and experts. The appositional phrase, which describes H. as one of the audience at recitations to which invitations were issued (cf. *Ep*. 2.2.67 *uocat hic auditum scripta*), explains why he has no time for the professional critics.

ultor 'avenger' in that he defends the poets he admires from the sort of attack described in 35–6. Some however take it to mean 'requiter', an unusual sense, again ironical, but one that accords with the common use of *ulcisci* (Shackleton Bailey 102). H. pays them back by reciting his own pieces (*S*. 1.4.73, quoted at 20.5n.).

40 ambire tribus keeps up the electoral metaphor (6.52n.), here applied to the professional teachers of literature, who also exercised some influence as critics (e.g., Valerius Cato, Caecilius Epirota; see *J.R.S*. 69 (1979) 147). Moreover, since they were often of servile background, the contrast between free and slave which informs the argument is underpinned. The *grammatici* delivered instruction and literary judgement from *pulpita* 'platforms'.

41 hinc illae lacrimae = Ter. *Andr*. 126, which became a proverbial expression (Cic. *Cael*. 61; Otto §904).

theatris 'auditoria', not theatres, cf. N–H on *C*. 2.1.10; there is still extant in Rome a small nymphaeum, misleadingly called the *auditorium Maecenatis* (Richardson 44–5).

42 nugis = *uersus et ludicra* (1.10n.); *pondus* 'claim to consideration' (*OLD* 6; B. on *AP* 320).

43 rides: H. is not believed, his self-depreciation is reckoned to be ironical. The subj. of *ait* is H.'s imaginary disputant (*inquit* is altogether commoner in this usage, K–S I 6).

Iouis = Augustus (*OLD* 5b). To anticipate the ruler's deification was a strategy of Hellenistic court poets (Gow on Theocr. 7.93), but H. coyly puts the words in another's mouth. For *Iouis auribus* cf. the anonymous bucolic in Pap. Vindob. Rainer 29801 = D. L. Page, *Greek literary papyri* (London 1942) 502.6 πῆι μελέων κλέος εὐρύ, τὸ καὶ Διός οὖατ' ἱαίνει 'where the wide fame of your songs, that delight even the ear of Zeus?'

44 fidis 'you are confident that' governs acc. (*te solum*) and infin.; it pointedly echoes 22. For the self-satisfaction of poets see Arist. *EN* 4.1.1120в14 'all men, e.g. parents and poets, prefer what they make themselves', Catull. 22.17 *tam gaudet in se tamque se ipse miratur* (of the poetaster Suffenus), Cic. *Tusc.* 5.63 *neminem cognoui poetam . . . qui sibi non optimus uideretur.*

manare ... mella 'to drip honey drops'; the acc. is a sort of internal obj., a syntactical Grecism = στάζω (K–S 1 278, Roby §1123). The 'honey of poetry' (cf. *examen* 23) is a traditional metaphor (W. Wimmel, *Kallimachos im Rom* (= *Hermes Einzelshriften* 16, Wiesbaden 1960) 271 n. 2, to which add Lucr. 1.935-50).

45 tibi: 2.30n. The nostrils, *naribus*, indicate mood, proverbially disdain (Otto §1198); H. appears to be the first to refer to the nose's expressive power with any regularity (cf. 5.23). The complementary infin. *uti* with *formido* is poetic syntax (K–S 1 673).

46 formido = *nolo* (cf. 16.60, 18.93nn.); there is some truth in the charge. *ungui* exposes the effeminate squabbling of the salon, for the fingernail is a woman's weapon (*C.* 1.16.17).

47 iste 'this of yours' justifies H. in declining to pursue the debate: he has not been allowed a say in the choice of terms.

locus: perhaps the *theatrum* (41), now seen as an amphitheatre where gladiators fight. Before a *recitatio* it seems to have been the custom for authors to discuss their works and anticipate criticism in a *praefatio* (cf. Quint. *IO* 8.3.31 for reference to such preliminaries by Seneca and Pomponius). Presumably debate was not invariably courteous. Rather than argue the point, H. retires from the field, to avoid further aggravation. Yet he has made it clear that Augustus is interested in his poetry.

diludia 'intermission' seems to derive from gladiatorial combat, but is not found elsewhere; cf. *Ep.* 2.2.97-8 for gladiatorial imagery used of the 'blows' of praise inflicted upon each other by Rome's poets. The collection has come full circle with a reminiscence of the opening image of the first epistle.

48–9   The sentence is composed upon the figure *gradatio*, whereby the thought moves up through increasingly important stages. The pivotal word, *ira*, ends one clause and line and begins another, a figure called *catena*.

48   genuit: 2.48n. *trepidum* 'excited' (*OLD* 3b), cf. Lucr. 3.834 *belli trepido . . . tumultu*. The dangers of *ira* glance back to 2.13, 15, 62–3 and 3.33; cf. *C*. 4.15.19–20 *non ira* [*eximet otium*], *quae procudit enses* | *et miseras inimicat urbes*. H.'s point is that it does not take much to set the ball rolling; unless stopped it will ruin personal relations (*inimicitias*) and international harmony (*bellum*).

Strictly considered this is the last epistle of the collection since the next poem abandons the epistolary fiction for direct address. It is appropriately dedicated to Maecenas, first and last on H.'s lips; the pattern conforms to that of the collection of odes, which was dedicated to Maecenas in the first poem of all, and in which the penultimate poem, 3.29, was also addressed to him. Here, as in VII, Maecenas' role is exemplary; earlier he was the ideal patron, here the ideal reader. There is a good analysis of the letter by W. S. Smith Jr in *T.A.P.A.* 114 (1984) 255–71, though his view that symptotic imagery informs the poem is hard to accept *in toto*.

Epistle XX

1–8   H. addresses the book of epistles, soon to be published, as if it were a slave boy who yearns for the pleasures of the city. H., as a *uates*, prophesies the fate of the boy/book.

1   Vortumnus, an Etruscan god, had a statue in one of Rome's best-known shopping streets, the *uicus Tuscus*, behind the temple of Castor (Richardson 363, 429); books too were on sale there. It is not clear which *Ianus* H. had in mind here (Richardson 206, cf. 1.53–4n.).

spectare 'have in view' (*OLD* 9) recalls the dangers of ardent gazing exposed in VI (4n.).

2   prostes 'expose yourself for sale' (like a modern-day rent-boy). The Sosii, also named at *AP* 345, were booksellers.

pumice mundus: abrasive pumice stone would be used by a boy to rub from the skin hair that might betray advancing years (cf. *C*. 4.10.2

insperata ... pluma); used on papyrus, it produced a smooth surface and edge (Fordyce on Catull. 22.8).

3 H. has not only locked but sealed his book case (*scrinium*; ancient pictures of cases suggest that they had a lock of some sort); modest poems would not press for publication and a modest slave would keep behind locked doors. Take *grata* with *clauis* ἀπὸ κοινοῦ.

4 paucis: cf. *S.* 1.10.74 *contentus paucis lectoribus.*

ostendi: pres. pass. infin., understand *te* as subject acc.; see *relinqui* 15.5n.

communia 'public places' (*OLD commune* 2). The book/boy wants what the poet/master, a devotee of Callimachean exclusivity, deplores, cf. Callim. *Epig.* 28.4 Pf. = *HE* 1044 σικχαίνω πάντα τὰ δημόσια, where literature and vagabond lovers are also compared.

5 non ita nutritus: H. preferred to avoid recitations (*S.* 1.4.73 *nec recito cuiquam nisi amicis, idque coactus*), but his book pines for wider notoriety.

fuge quo 'avoid (10.32n.) the place to which ... '; the verb cannot imply dismissal yet, but gives a warning. *descendere* 'to go down (to a place of business or other activity)' (*OLD* 4).

6 emisso 'published' of the book (*AP* 77 *emiserit*), 'let go' of the boy (cf. 18.71n.); dat. with *tibi*. Likewise the bailiff in XIV is not given a second chance.

7 uolui 'was I after' (*OLD* 16).

quid: 15.44n.; *laeserit* (fut. perf.) hints at criticism of the book (*OLD* 4) and sexual exploitation of the boy (*OLD* 3b).

et 'and yet' (*OLD* 14, *TLL* v 2.893.30). *scis* here governs a pres. infin. *cogi* which clearly refers to a future event; this seems a colloquial usage, common in Plautus (Sonnenschein on *Most.* 17 *quod te in pistrinum scis actutum tradier*).

8 in breue te cogi: the book would be rolled up tight so as to fit into a storage box (*OLD breue* 1e 'confined place', cf. Luc. 2.613 *se cogentis in artum*). Porphyrio, however, reckoned that the book would be read only piecemeal after dinner (whence *plenus*), not as a whole and in order. The application of the phrase to the slave is unclear (Fraenkel 358 n. 2 might have offered a translation); perhaps he is being 're-duced' in status or prosperity (Duff on Sen. *Dial.* 12.13.4 compares *in ordinem redigere*).

plenus 'sated'; the book's reader and the boy's lover require fresh stimulus.

9–18   The prophecy continues into the slave's old age.

9   Diviners commonly offer their prophecies with some reserve (*C.* 3.17.12–3 *aquae nisi fallit augur* | *annosa cornix*, Virg. *A.* 1.392 *ni frustra augurium uani docuere parentes*).

odio 'annoyance' (*OLD* 5); *peccantis* 'wrongdoer' implies sexual transgression (*OLD* 3b).

10   **Romae** attests H.'s pride in his success. For the subjunc. *deserat* see 16.23n.

aetas 'youth' (*OLD* 4a). The first buyer of the book/boy will dispose of him, and he will fall into less gentle hands.

11   **contrectatus:** cf. 19.34, *S.* 1.4.71–2 *nulla taberna meos habeat neque pila libellos,* | *quis manus insudet uulgi* (H. keeps his *Sermones* to himself and his friends), and again there is a sexual innuendo, 'fondled' (*OLD* 2). In this condition three possibilities await the book/slave.

12   **tineas** 'lice' will infest the boy and gnaw at the disregarded book if it manages to stay in Rome (esteemed books were stored in cedarwood to preserve them from mites). It will be *taciturnus* because no one reads it aloud.

inertes 'philistine', lacking a sense of *ars* (Cic. *Fin.* 2.115).

13   **fugies:** the book/slave may run away to seek a fresh audience, for preference in N. Africa (it would not do to head east, where Greek held sway).

uinctus: or the book may be 'bound up' in a parcel by the bookseller, the slave put in a 'chain gang' (perhaps as a punishment for vice). *mitteris* is fut.; Ilerda (mod. Lleida, Lerida) is in Spain. For real poetry, the lyric *Odes*, H. is pleased at the prospect of a cultivated provincial readership, cf. *C.* 2.20.19–20 *me peritus* | *discet Hiber Rhodanique potor*.

14   **monitor** = H. himself, who is like the exasperated driver in a fable (Aesop 197 Hausrath).

15   **male:** 3.31n.

16   **quis ... laboret:** 1.49–51n. For the quasi-caesura see 10.9n. As West observes (19), H. inverts the sense of the fable, by applying it not to the contentious driver but to the ass which refuses to be saved.

17–18   The theme of education is ironically resumed from the beginning of the collection. But H.'s epistles will not have the grand moral function of Homer, rather they will be used as a cheap text for the first reading lessons (*elementa*) of poor children (*S.* 1.10.74–5 *an tua ...* | *uilibus in ludis dictari carmina malis?*). This suits their unpoetic status.

17   manet 'is in store for' (*OLD* 4); *ut* introduces a consecutive clause explaining *hoc* (Bo 414); with *docentem* understand *te*.

   pueros elementa docentem < Aratus, *HE* 767 παισὶν βῆτα καὶ ἄλφα λέγων. (The borrowing may suggest that H. took Aratus' addressee, Diotimus, to be a poet down on his luck.)

18   extremis in uicis 'at the ends of streets', i.e. *in triuio*, where cheap lessons could be had (so Torrentius and S. F. Bonner, *A.J.P.* 93 (1972) 509–28).

   balba: second childhood will distort the slave's pronunciation so that it is like that of the children he teaches; but poetry should be a corrective of poor enunciation (*Ep*. 2.1.126). Reference to the slave's old age (*senectus*) closes the section.

19–28   The book/slave's departure is now taken for granted, and H. advises it on what it is to say about its author/master, if occasion arise. (It is assumed here that the image reverts to the book exposed to sale and does not continue that of the aged schoolmaster, but this is one of the most debated passages in the book.) The book is to utter a sort of *uita*, starting with parentage; this looks back to the notion that personal poetry reveals the life of the writer (cf. *S*. 2.1.30–4 on Lucilius' self-revelation). There is, however, no encouragement to recall H.'s chief claim to fame, his reputation as a poet. That has been dealt with in the previous letter. Here he presents himself as the successful citizen.

19   sol tepidus: i.e. in the evening, when many prefer to do their shopping, like H. himself in *S*. 1.6.111–15. If, however, the image of the schoolmaster is still dominant, the reference may be to the warmth of mid-morning; lessons began at chilly dawn. Numerous loungers (contrast *paucis* 4) eavesdrop on the lesson and the enlarged company prompts the slave to reminiscence (indeed, parents might attend the class, as did H.'s father, cf. *S*. 1.6.82). The teacher would thus be transformed from a humble *ludi magister* into a *grammaticus*, who traditionally gave fuller information on author and text (so Obbar). For *tibi* see 1.80n.

20–2   H.'s humble birth was no bar to his ambitions, which are plainly regarded as honourable.

20   libertino ... patre: abl. of origin; it recalls *S*. 1.6.6, 45–6 and 58 *non ... me claro natum patre* (Introduction p. 5).

   in tenui re: cf. *C*. 2.20.5–6 *ego pauperum | sanguis parentum*.

21   maiores pennas: contrast the feebleness of the unenterprising at 17.39–40; for the metaphor of wings cf. *Ep*. 2.2.50 *decisis pinnis* (Otto

§280). For the sense of the comparative see 10.43n.; for the fut. *loqueris* 4.15n.

22 Cf. *S.* 1.6.63–4 *placui tibi* [Maecenas], … | *non patre praeclaro, sed uita et pectore puro.* Self-made men emphasize merit, and belittle inherited privilege, cf. Cic. *Mur.* 17, Sall. *Iug.* 85.16–17 (Marius).

generi: for the dat. see 6.54n.; the extension of the usage to a thing (albeit one's *genus* is presumably a part of oneself) is poetic syntax, here metrically generated (*genere* would be hard to accommodate). *uirtutibus* echoes the approval of the enterprising at 17.41–2.

23 me primis Vrbis … placuisse: *sc. loqueris.* H. was proud of his social success throughout his life (17.35; *S.* 2.1.75–6 *me* | *cum magnis uixisse*). For the sentiment cf. Theognis 34 'he found favour with those in great power' and esp. Terence's prologue to *Adel.* 17–19 *quod illi maledictum uehemens esse existumant,* | *eam laudem hic ducit maxumam, quom illis placet* | *qui uobis uniuorsis et populo placent,* i.e. the *primores urbis.* Hadrian composed an epitaph on the first-century B.C. Greek poet Parthenius, in which it was recorded that he was honoured by leading men (*FGE* 2147).

belli … domique go with *placuisse.* H. had been *tribunus militum* (Introduction pp. 5–6) and may have been with Maecenas during the campaign against Sextus Pompeius and at the battle of Actium (N–H on *C.* 2.6.8): hence the locative, *belli.* He was not just a poet, as his intentional omission of his calling here makes plain, but had seen public service (cf. the epitaph of Aeschylus which refers to his having fought at Marathon, but says nothing of his tragedies: *uita* §11).

24 corporis exigui: an unusual descriptive gen., the abl. would be commoner (E. Löfstedt, *Syntactica*² (Lund 1956) 159); cf. *S.* 2.3.308–9 *ab imo* | *ad summum totus moduli bipedalis* and Augustus *apud* Suet. *uita Hor.* 58 Rostagni *statura deest.*

praecanum 'prematurely grey', rather than 'grey at the front'; a coinage = προπόλιον. *solibus aptum* 'suited to, i.e. fond of sunny days'.

25 irasci celerem = ὀξύχολον; the complementary infin. with an adjective (cf. *C.* 1.15.18 *celerem sequi*) serves as an equivalent for the compound epithet. H. confesses irritability at *S.* 2.3.323 *horrendam rabiem* and *C.* 3.9.23 *iracundior Hadria.*

tamen ut: cf. *sed ut* 16.6n. For the need to be forgiving see *S.* 1.3.141 *inque uicem illorum patiar delicta libenter* and *Ep.* 2.2.210 *ignoscis amicis?* (a question to ask oneself).

26 percontabitur: first here with a common noun (instead of a pronoun) as obj.; prose would have *de aeuo* (K–S 1 302). *aeuum* 'age' (*OLD* 8).

27 H. was born on 8 December 65 B.C., so he wrote this between that date in 21 and 20 B.C.; this is the first reference by a Roman poet to his birthday; cf. Ov. *Tr*. 4.10.5–6, Prudentius *praef*. 24.

28 dixit 'declared' (*OLD* 10c 'as a magistrate'); on 1 January 21 B.C. M. Lollius began his consulship alone because Augustus declined to serve, albeit elected; in due course Q. Aemilius Lepidus was elected his colleague (Lollius presided), after defeating L. Iunius Silanus in a by-election (Dio 54.6.1–3; E. Groag, *RE* XIII 2.1380.28–45; Syme, *RR* 371). The reading of the chief MSS *duxit* 'escorted as a newly elected colleague', though defended by V. M. Warrior, *R.M.* 133 (1990) 144–57, is a use otherwise unattested and inherently strange, according to Dr J. Briscoe (*per litteras*), who urges that at Livy 7.24.11 the paradosis *dixit* should not be altered, and that at 37.47.7 the transmitted *duxit* should be emended to *dixit* (see his n. *ad loc*., p. 365). The peculiarly Roman form of dating with which the poem and book end sounds a characteristic note of realism from the poet of contemporary society.

The scholiasts make it plain that this poem was censured in antiquity for not being a letter; it is clearly a fictive conversation, *sermo*, with the book. Their defence was that the beginnings and ends of works were more freely handled (Porphyrio cites Lucretius 1 and the end of Virgil's fourth *Georgic*).

The poem artfully discloses a final inconsistency of the poet's. All along he claims to want only the approval of a few and to compose with their opinion in view. Yet publication belies this attitude and no one can deny that he secretly wants the widest possible renown. To demonstrate this, H. throws the blame upon the book itself, in the person of a less than modest *uerna*, proud of his looks; the book/slave insists upon having its way and the artist, with many a shudder, grants its wish, but with warnings that recall those to the bailiff in XIV: there will be no looking back. That is to say, the artist must endure the treatment the public choose to mete out. He cannot complain of it, just because he has, however reluctantly and against his better judgement, courted it.

The epilogue is specially composed to hold this place in the collection (Introduction p. 49). Since the epistles are in theory unpoetic,

H. can adopt quite a different tone in speaking of (and to) them than he does when boasting of his achievement as a lyric poet in the last poems of the second and third books of *Odes* (a point neglected by S. J. Harrison, 'Deflating the *Odes*: Horace, *Epistles*, 1.20', *C.Q.* 38 (1988) 473–6). Nothing he says in this epilogue, moreover, makes any allusion to his earlier, genuinely poetic activities; it is a conclusion to this collection alone.

Further reading: J. Bramble, *Persius and the programmatic satire* (Cambridge 1974) 59–62.

Addenda

1.7   crebro: the adverbial form, only here in H., appears to be colloquial (*TLL* IV 1122.3–1123.56); poets prefer the adjectival form.

3.36   Virgil's heifer disturbs the peace of the herd by exciting rival bulls to battle; H.'s will mark the restoration of harmony in Tiberius' *cohors* (itself a sort of *grex*, cf. 9.13) after 'bullish' (34) young men are reconciled.

5.8, 26:   see 16.50n.

6.20   For(um) et: for the elision (here of a 'middle' syllable) see *loco* 7.57n.

10.4–5   quidquid negat … adnuimus pariter: H. elaborates a proverbial definition of friendship as enunciated e.g. by Sallust, *Cat.* 20.4 *idem uelle atque idem nolle, ea demum firma amicitia est* (Otto §83).

ABBREVIATIONS AND REFERENCES

(1)   H.'s works are abbreviated as *S*. (*Sermones*), *Epod*. (*Epodi*),
       C. (*Carmina*), *CS* (*Carmen Saeculare*), *Ep*. (*Epistulae*), *AP* (*Ars
       Poetica*).

(2)   References to *Ep*. I omit the book number; references within
       the same poem of *Ep*. I also omit the poem number.

(3)   Periodical abbreviations are generally as in *L'Année philologique*.
       The titles of Latin works generally follow *OLD*. Other abbrevi-
       ated references appear below, after a list of bibliographical
       studies.

Bibliographical studies

E. Thummer, *Anz. A.W.* 15 (1962) 129–50, 32 (1979) 21–66
F. Cupaiuolo, *B.S.L.* 2 (1972) 73–5
G. Draeger and M. Angermann, *Horaz-Bibliographie* (Berlin 1975)
W. Kissel, *A.N.R.W.* II 31.3.1515–20
O. A. W. Dilke, *ibid*. 1857–65 (covers *Epistulae* for 1950–80)

Akurgal	Akurgal, E. (1985) *Ancient civilizations and ruins of Turkey*. Istanbul
Axelson	Axelson, B. (1945) *Unpoetische Wörter*. Lund
B.	Brink, C. O. (1971) *Horace on poetry* II. *The Ars Poetica*. Cambridge
	(1982) *Horace on poetry* III. *Epistles Book* II. Cambridge
Bo	Bo, D. (1960) *Q. Horati Flacci opera* III, *Indices*. Turin
CAH	*The Cambridge ancient history*. Cambridge
CIL	*Corpus Inscriptionum Latinarum* (1863–). Berlin
Campbell	Campbell, A. Y. (1924) *Horace: a new interpretation*. London
FGE	Page, D. L. (1981) *Further Greek epigrams*. Cambridge

Fraenkel	Fraenkel, E. (1957) *Horace*. Oxford
G–H	Gärtner, H. and Heyke, W. (1964) *Bibliographie zur antiken Bildersprache*. Heidelberg
G–L	Gildersleeve, B. L. and Lodge, G. (1895) *Latin grammar*. London
GLK	Keil, H. (1855–80) *Grammatici Latini*. Leipzig
GP	Gow, A. S. F. and Page, D. L. (1968) *The Garland of Philip*. Cambridge
HE	Gow, A. S. F. and Page D. L. (1965) *Hellenistic epigrams*. Cambridge
H–S	Hofmann, J. B. and Szantyr, A. (1972) *Lateinische Syntax und Stilistik*. Munich
Hand	Hand, F. H. (1829–45) *Tursellinus siue de particulis latinis commentarii*. Leipzig
Heitland	Heitland, W. E. (1921) *Agricola*. Cambridge
Housman	Housman, A. E. (1972) *Collected classical papers*, edd. F. R. D. Goodyear and J. Diggle. Cambridge
Jachmann	Jachmann, G. (1981) *Ausgewählte Schriften*, ed. C. Gnilka = *Beiträge zur klassischen Philologie* Heft 128. Königstein/Ts.
K–S	Kühner, R. and Stegmann, C. (1962) *Ausführliche Grammatik der lateinischen Sprache*. Munich
L.	Lejay, P. (1911) *Oeuvres d'Horace: Satires*. Paris
L–S	Long, A. A. and Sedley, D. N. (1987) *The Hellenistic philosophers*. 2 vols. Cambridge
LS	Handford, S. A. (1947) *The Latin subjunctive*. London
LSJ	Liddell, H. G., Scott, R., Jones, H. S., McKenzie, R. (1968) *A Greek–English lexicon* (9th edn with Supplement). Oxford
Leo (1878)	Leo, F. (1878, repr. 1963) *De Senecae tragoediis obseruationes criticae*. Berlin
Leo (1912)	Leo, F. (1912, repr. 1966) *Plautinische Forschungen*.[2] Berlin
Löfstedt	Löfstedt, E. (1942) *Syntactica* I.[2] Lund
McGann	McGann, M. J. (1969) *Studies in Horace's first book of Epistles* (Collection Latomus 100). Brussels
McGlynn	McGlynn, P. (1963, 1967) *Lexicon Terentianum* I A-O, II P-V. London and Glasgow

Nägelsbach	von Nägelsbach, K. F. (1905) *Lateinische Stylistik.*[9] Nuremberg
Nilsson	Nilsson, N.–O. (1952) *Metrische Stildifferenzen in den Satiren des Horaz.* Uppsala
N–H	Nisbet, R. G. M. and Hubbard, M. (1972) *A commentary on Horace: Odes Book* I. Oxford
	Nisbet, R. G. M. and Hubbard, M. (1978) *A commentary on Horace: Odes Book* II. Oxford
NLS	Woodcock, E. C. (1959, repr. 1985) *A new Latin syntax.* London
OCD	Hammond, N. G. L. and Scullard, H. H. (1970). *The Oxford classical dictionary,* 2nd edn. Oxford
OLD	Glare, P. G. W. (1968–82). *Oxford Latin dictionary.* Oxford
Otto	Otto, A. (1890, repr. 1962) *Die Sprichwörter und sprichwörtlichen Redensarten der Römer.* Leipzig
PLF	Lobel, E. and Page, D. L. (1955) *Poetarum Lesbiorum Fragmenta.* Oxford
PMG	Page, D. L. (1962) *Poetae melici Graeci.* Oxford
Paget	Paget, R. F. (1973) *Central Italy: an archaeological guide.* London
RAC	*Reallexikon für Antike und Christentum* (1941–) Leipzig and Stuttgart
RE	*Real Encyclopädie der klassischen Altertumswissenschaft* (1893–1980) Leipzig
Richardson	Richardson, L. (1992) *A new topographical dictionary of ancient Rome.* Baltimore and London
Roby	Roby, H. J. (1889). *A grammar of the Latin language from Plautus to Suetonius. Part* II*: Syntax.* London
Ruckdeschel	Ruckdeschel, F. (1911) *Archaismen und Vulgarismen in der Sprache des Horaz,* Erlangen Dissertation
Salmon	Salmon, E. T. (1967) *Samnium and the Samnites.* Cambridge
Shackleton Bailey	Shackleton Bailey, D. R. (1985) *Profile of Horace.* London
Syme, *AA*	Syme, R. (1988) *The Augustan aristocracy.* Oxford
Syme, *RR*	Syme, R. (1939, 1952) *The Roman revolution.* Oxford

TLL	*Thesaurus linguae Latinae* (1900–). Munich
Treggiari	Treggiari, S. (1991) *Roman marriage.* Oxford
Waltz	Waltz, A. (1881) *Des variations de la langue et de la métrique d'Horace dans ses différents ouvrages.* Paris
West	West, D. (1967) *Reading Horace.* Edinburgh
Winbolt	Winbolt, S. E. (1903) *Latin hexameter verse.* London
Wölfflin	Wölfflin, E. (1933) *Ausgewählte Schriften.* Leipzig

< = 'derived from'
> = 'the source of'
)(= 'contrasts with'
≈ = 'similar to'

Editions and translations consulted

Some of the following editions have no commentary; a number of those with commentary are either combined with the *Sermones* or form part of complete editions. The latest edition is usually cited.

Bentley, R.	Amsterdam 1713 (edn 2; edn 1 Cambridge 1711)
Cuningham, A.	London 1721
Dacier, A.	Paris 1709 (edn 3)
Dilke, O. A. W.	London 1966 (edn 3)
Dillenburger, W.	Bonn 1867 (edn 5)
Doering, F. W.	Oxford 1838
Dübner, J. F.	Paris 1855
Fairclough, H. R.	Cambridge, Mass., and London 1929 (Loeb Classical Library)
Greenough, J. B.	Boston 1887
Kiessling, A.	Berlin 1889 (edn 1)
Kiessling A. and Heinze, R.	Berlin 1984 (edn 4)
Kirkland, J. H.	Chicago 1893
Klingner, F.	Leipzig 1959 (edn 3)
Krüger, G. T. A. and Krüger, G.	Leipzig 1900 (edn 14)
Krüger, G. and Hoppe, P.	Leipzig 1920
Lambinus, D.	Paris 1587 (edn 3)
Lejay, P.	Paris 1906 (edn 2)

Macleane, A. J.	London 1853
Macleod, C.	Rome 1986 (English translation with brief notes)
Morris, E. P.	New York 1909
Müller, L.	Vienna 1893
Munro, H. A. J.	London 1869
Obbar, S. and Schmid, T.	Leipzig 1841–7
Orelli, I. G., I. G. Baiter and W. Mewes	Berlin 1892 (edn 4)
Préaux, J.	Paris 1968
Ribbeck, O.	Berlin 1869
Rolfe, J. C.	Boston 1901, edn 2 1935
Rudd, N.	Harmondsworth 1979 (English translation)
Sabbadini, R.	Turin 1970
Schmid, T.	Halberstadt 1828–30
Schütz, H.	Berlin 1883
Shuckburgh, E. S.	Cambridge 1883
Villeneuve, F.	Paris 1935 (French translation, Budé series)
Wickham, E. C.	Oxford 1903
Wieland, C. M.	Frankfurt am Main 1986 (German translation, ed. M. Fuhrmann)
Wilkins, A. S.	London 1892

INDEXES

1 Latin words

absens 'distant' **11**.21

ac (introduces comparison) **16**.32

bene uiuere 'live happily' **6**.56, **11**.29, **15**.45

cado (of words) **18**.12

cum 'in . . . ' **16**.30; 'now that . . .' **15**.4

dicere 'sing of' **1**.1, **16**.26, **19**.7–8, 32; used periphrastically **4**.2

dissigno **5**.16

distare + dat. **7**.23, **18**.4

domi **6**.44

donec + subjunc. **16**.23, **18**.63, **20**.10

dum + pres. indic. **2**.2

dum + final subjunc. **2**.42

dum 'all the while' **2**.21, **7**.79, **18**.8, **19**.16

durare + partic. **1**.82

enim **18**.19

et 'and yet' **20**.7; 'even' **18**.38; 'or' **15**.33, **17**.30, **18**.38; epexegetic or explanatory **12**.8, **18**.54, 103; postponed **15**.35

fido **19**.22, 44

fidus **5**.24

formido 'refuse' **19**.46

furtiuus **3**.20

in **2**.39 (**11**.23), **18**.109

ineptus **17**.32

latus **7**.26

laudo 'decline politely' **11**.21

libenter **11**.24

metuo 'be unwilling' **16**.60; 'disdain' **18**.1

minor (verb) **8**.3

multum adverbial **3**.15, **10**.3

ne (elliptical use) **1**.13, **12**.25, **18**.58, **19**.26

-ne = nonne **16**.31; = *num* **10**.14, **19**.14

neque . . . nec introducing co-ordinated comparison **11**.11–16, **18**.39–40

neu (adds prohibition after positive command) **11**.23, **13**.16, **18**.110

numerus **2**.27

odi **7**.20, **14**.20, **18**.25, 89

omnis **5**.2

oportet **2**.49, **10**.12

pacto **6**.10

pauor **6**.10, **18**.99

planus **17**.59

pono = depono **1**.10, **10**.31, **16**.35

praesertim **18**.50

procul **7**.32

prodoceo **1**.55

proprius = suus **7**.51

pulcher **2**.3, **7**.3

-que 'or' **5**.27, **15**.9, **16**.70

-que et **6**.14, **7**.58, **14**.19

qui **6**.42, **16**.63

quia colloquial **8**.4–7

recte 'morally' **2**.41; 'in a desirable manner' **6**.29, **16**.16; 'justifiably' **12**.2

rus 'estate' **14**.5, **15**.17, **18**.60; *rure* (locative) **7**.1, **14**.10

sapere, sapienter **10**.44, **15**.45, **18**.27

sed **15**.13

si 'but if' **5**.6, **6**.68, **12**.7, **17**.11

simul = simulac **6**.11, **7**.90, **10**.8

tamen 'besides' **7**.23 (**14**.26); = δέ **12**.25

timeo 'disdain, refuse' **5**.2, **19**.27

tu (strengthens exhortations) **2**.63, **11**.22, **16**.53, **18**.37, 44

uita 'way of life' **7**.95

ultro 'readily' **12**.22

ut (parenthetic) **18**.67; (qualificatory) **16**.6, 12, **20**.25

utor **7**.57; 'spend' **12**.22; 'make friend of' **17**.2

283

2 General